Will T. Cohen
The Concept of "Sister Churches"

STUDIA OECUMENICA FRIBURGENSIA

(= Neue Serie der ÖKUMENISCHEN BEIHEFTE)
Herausgegeben vom
Institut für Ökumenische StudienFreiburg Schweiz

67

Will T. Cohen

The Concept of "Sister Churches" in Catholic-Orthodox Relations since Vatican II

WIPF & STOCK · Eugene, Oregon

THE CONCEPT OF "SISTER CHURCHES" IN
CATHOLIC-ORTHODOX RELATIONS SINCE VATICAN II

Copyright © 2017 Aschendorff Verlag GmbH & Co. KG, Münster. All rights reserved. Except for brief quotations in critical publications or reviews, no part of this book may be reproduced in any manner without prior written permission from the publisher. Write: Permissions, Wipf and Stock Publishers, 199 W. 8th Ave., Suite 3, Eugene, OR 97401.

Wipf & Stock
An Imprint of Wipf and Stock Publishers
199 W. 8th Ave., Suite 3
Eugene, OR 97401

www.wipfandstock.com

PAPERBACK ISBN: 978-1-4982-9970-1
HARDCOVER ISBN: 978-1-4982-9971-8

Manufactured in the U.S.A.   JULY 24, 2017

About the cover illustration:
The cover illustration shows the calling of the sons of Zebedee as represented on theBernward column (circa 1020), a Romanesque bronze column in HildesheimCathedral. The detail shows Jesus with his right hand outstretched to James andJohn. In his left hand, Jesus holds a book as a symbol of the Word of Life, which ishimself. The design of the book in the form of an ear is echoed by the folds of therobes of Jesus, emphasizing the unity of person and message. From the boat, thedisciple reaches out his hand towards Jesus. Does he grasp the written letters orreach for the living Word? On this choice depends the vitality of our theology andthe fertility of our commitment to the community of the Church.

For the letter kills, but the Spirit gives life ...
Now the Lord is the Spirit, and where the Spirit of the Lord is, there is freedom.
2 Cor 3:6 and 3:17

Contents

Preface by Metropolitan Kallistos Ware V

Preface by Cardinal Kurt Koch VII

Author's Preface XI

Summary XIV

Acknowledgments XV

Abbreviations XVI

Introduction 1

Chapter 1:
The Concept of "Sister Churches" Prior to Vatican II 5

I. The earliest shape of the concept 5
    1. John's Second Epistle – plurality and personality 5
    2. Revelation 2-3 – locality and temporality 6
    3. Second Corinthians 11:2 – a local church as bride 8
    4. First Clement and Ignatius of Antioch 9

II. The further sense of the concept: similar standing 11
    1. Churches as sisters in Basil the Great and Pope Innocent I 11
    2. Mother churches as sister churches 13

III. A new tension between "mother church" and "sister churches" 21
    1. Rome as *mater ecclesia* according to the western reformers 23
    2. The 12th century Byzantine understanding of patriarchal
       sister churches 28

IV. The imperial factor 37
    1. Sister churches in a single Christian empire 38
    2. Sister churches amidst imperial division 40
    3. Sister churches in a post-imperial context 45

Chapter 2:
Modern Development of the Use of "Sister Churches"
in Catholic-Orthodox Relations: 1958-1972 48

I. Background 49

II. First usages; terminological asymmetry between the two parties 53

III. Rome reciprocates in using the expression "sister churches" 61

Chapter 3:
Patterns and Ambiguities in 20th Century Usage 70

I. The question of the precise identities of the "sisters" 72
    1. The see of Rome and the see of Constantinople as sister churches 74
    2. The (Roman) Catholic Church and the (Eastern) Orthodox Church .. 81
       a) Letters and speeches up to 1980 pairing the Catholic Church
          and the Orthodox Church 82
       b) Texts from 1980 on pairing the Catholic Church
          and the Orthodox Church 89
    3. The Catholic Church and the Orthodox Churches 98
    4. The Catholic Churches and the Orthodox Churches 102
II. Summarizing Reflections 106

Chapter 4:
Catholic Theological Reflection on the Concept of Sister Churches 111

I. Six contributions in Catholic theological reflection on "sister churches" 112
    1. Emmanuel Lanne 112
       Lanne's commentary on Paul VI's *Anno ineunte* 113
       Lanne's understanding of the basis of the concept of sister churches . 114
       Canonized holiness as a qualification of sister churches 116
       Whether there can be sister churches on the regional level 117
       Implications of recognizing another church as a sister church 118
       Mutual recognition as sister churches and a re-reception of Vatican I 122
    2. Yves Congar 123
    3. Waclaw Hryniewicz 126
       An ecclesiology of sister churches excludes "soteriological exclusivism" 128
       "Sister churches" on the regional level 132
       Doctrine and ecumenism 134
       "Ecumenical Aporetics" 136
    4. Adriano Garuti 138
       Distinctions in usage 139
          The Catholic Church is *not* the sister of the Orthodox Church
          (usage 2) 141
          Catholic Church = Roman Catholic Church = universal church,
          which cannot be a sister church (usage 3) 143
          Orthodox and Catholic particular churches as sister churches
          (usage 4) 144
       Communion in faith and in government as prerequisites for
       sister churches status 145
       Patriarchal sister churches? 149

    5. The Congregation for the Doctrine of the Faith 151
        The CDF's *2000 Note on the Expression "Sister Churches"* 151
        The local church and the universal church 154
        Subsists in 157
    6. Hervé Legrand 162
        Legrand's critique of the idea of the priority of the universal church . 165
        Legrand's interpretation of *subsistit in* 169
II. Concluding Observations 173

Chapter 5:
Orthodox Theological Reflection on the Concept of Sister Churches.... 182

I.   Orthodox advocates of the idea of "sister churches"
    in Orthodox-Catholic relations 183
    1. John Meyendorff 183
    2. Metropolitan Maximos Aghiorgoussis of Ainou 190
    3. John Erickson 193
    4. Metropolitan Damaskinos Papandreou 199
II. Orthodox critics of "sister churches" in Orthodox-Catholic relations .. 205
    1. Letter to the Ecumenical Patriarch from the Sacred Community of
       Mount Athos 205
    2. John S. Romanides 210
    3. George Metallinos, and the Orthodox debate concerning
       non-Orthodox baptism 216
    4. Archbishop Dmitri Royster of Dallas 230
III. Concluding Observations 235

Chapter 6:
The Adequacy and Value of the Concept of Sister Churches
for Catholic and Orthodox Ecclesiology 241

I.   Comparison of Catholic and Orthodox advocates of "sister churches" . 241
II. Comparison of Catholic and Orthodox critics of "sister churches" 245
III. Proposals in response to critics of "sister churches" 251
A. Response to Catholic concerns 252
    1. Why the Orthodox Church may be called the sister of the
       Catholic Church 252
    2. What is valuable about the supra-diocesan usage 258
    3. How "sister churches" may apply to the two overarching Churches
       of East and West 263

    B. Response to Orthodox concerns 265
         The Branch Theory inverted 272
  IV. Concluding Observations 277

Chapter 7:
Conclusion 281

Bibliography 285
    1. Patristic, medieval and early modern works 285
    2. Modern works concerned wholly or in part with the subject of
       "sister churches" 287
    3. Official ecclestical texts, correspondence between hierarchs,
       and ecumenical documents 290
    4. Other works 292

Index of Names 299

Preface by Metropolitan Kallistos Ware

How are we to understand the phrase 'Sister Churches', used repeatedly since the 1960s in the Catholic-Orthodox dialogue? This present book, to the best of my knowledge, is the first occasion on which the full meaning of this concept has been explored in a thorough and systematic way. Dr. Will Cohen has made a fresh and constructive contribution to the growing *rapprochement* between Orthodoxy and Rome. His book is well documented and closely argued, critical yet eirenic. I found it definitely hopeful in spirit.

'The concept of Sister Churches,' says Dr. Cohen, 'is far from self-explanatory.' That is certainly true, and it shows how timely this book is. He rightly describes the expression "sister Churches' as 'a profoundly disruptive term', to be used with the 'greatest care'. He even calls the expression 'paradoxical' and 'apophatic'. It is not a technical term in common law. Its connotation varies widely, depending on the level at which it is being employed: whether the universal (the Orthodox Church as a whole, vis-à-vis the Roman Catholic Church as a whole), or the regional (sister Patriarchates), or the local (the level of the diocese). Indeed, Dr. Cohen distinguishes no less than five different ways in which the concept can be interpreted.

Not only is the precise meaning of 'Sister Churches' unclear; the very idea is controversial. Its use is rejected on the Roman Catholic side by, for example, the CDF (the Vatican Congregation for the Doctrine of the Faith) in its famous *Note* of 30 June 2000, and by specialists such as Adriano Garuti, at any rate if it is applied to the Roman Catholic and Orthodox Churches in their entirety. It is rejected even more emphatically by many Orthodox – on Mount Athos and elsewhere – who see it as contrary to their conviction that the Orthodox Church is the true Church of Christ, one and unique. At the same time the concept has many staunch defenders, alike among Catholics and Orthodox. In a fair and balanced way, Dr. Cohen states the arguments on either side. He himself views the notion of 'Sister Churches' in highly positive terms, but he does justice to the opposite viewpoint. He is strict and rigorous in his evaluation, yet never polemical.

As this book clearly indicates, the theme of 'Sister Churches' raises many complex issues. Dr. Cohen asks, among other things: How complete is the schism between Orthodoxy and Rome? How far do Catholics and Orthodox share a common faith? How far can theological 'pluralism' be carried, without impairing unity in the faith? Does the notion of 'Sister Churches' imply some kind of 'Branch Theory' of the Church? To what extent do Orthodox recognize the presence of divine grace in the Roman Catholic Church and the validity of Catholic sacraments? (Here there is a sharp difference of opinion among Orthodox theologians.) Does the universal Church have priority over the local Church, or should we think rather in terms of a 'perichoretic' relationship? What is the meaning of the statement by Vatican II that the Catholic Church 'subsists in' the Roman Catholic communion? Does this differ from saying that the Roman Catholic Church *is* the one true Catholic Church? On all these points Dr. Cohen has pertinent comments to make, but wisely he does not claim to provide final answers; for he recognizes that in these matters there is an ongoing debate – what he calls an 'unfinished conversation' – not only *between* our two Churches, the Catholic and the Orthodox, but also *within* each communion.

I have read this study with particular interest, because I am myself among those Orthodox who have reservations about the language of 'Sister Churches'. Personally I have always avoided using this phrase in my own writings. Dr. Cohen has made me think again about the whole subject, and although I cannot say that I have entirely changed my mind, his book has certainly challenged me in a way that I find disturbing yet positive.

Much of what Dr. Cohen has to say is directly relevant to the present discussions in the Joint International Commission for Theological Dialogue between the Roman Catholic Church and the Orthodox Church (to which I myself belong). I shall take his book with me to our next meeting. It should be compulsory reading for all the participants.

'Today unity is the *anankē*,' our necessary vocation, our appointed destiny, the Ecumenical Patriarch Athenagoras used to say. 'Reunion will be a miracle,' he added, 'but a *miracle in history*.'[1] Our task is to remove the human obstacles that hinder the working of this divine miracle. Undoubtedly the present book will help to diminish these human obstacles, and for that we should all be sincerely grateful.

Kallistos Ware
Metropolitan of Diokleia

---

1 See Olivier Clément, *Dialogues avec le patriarche Athénagoras* (Paris: Fayard, 1969), pp. 303, 307.

Preface by Cardinal Kurt Koch

"Sister Churches" – this expression is a sign of hope for the full *communio* of all the episcopal Churches in apostolic succession. In this sense, the assessment with which Will Cohen begins his study signals something very troubling – "This term ... has now fallen into disgrace" (p. 5). I hope, however, that Will Cohen's book will be able to give new validity to the reconciliatory force of the expression and reality of sister churches in the theology and in the life of the Church in East and West.

A remarkable development should be noted on the Catholic side: Based on the Second Vatican Council, in the last decades there has been a convergence of the expressions *particular churches* and *sister churches*. In the decree on ecumenism, *Unitatis Redintegratio*, the discussion of sister churches is introduced in the form of a mere description: "Among other matters of great importance, it is a pleasure for this Council to remind everyone that there flourish in the East many particular or local Churches, among which the Patriarchal Churches hold first place, and of these not a few pride themselves in tracing their origins back to the apostles themselves. Hence a matter of primary concern and care among the Easterns has been, and still is, to preserve the family ties of common faith and charity which ought to exist between local churches as sister Churches" (UR 14). This assertion applies exclusively to the relationship among the eastern Churches.

During the Council, meanwhile, a change in ecclesiological self-understanding takes place: The plural *churches* is not considered a principle of division, but as the expression of the true being of the Church. This holds, however, only if the plural is applied not on the level of the one, holy, catholic and apostolic Church, which we profess in the Creed, but at the level of the particular churches. In this regard, the Dogmatic Constitution on the Church *Lumen Gentium* describes the relationship between the bishops in the college of bishops and between them and the bishop of Rome as parallel to the relationship of the local churches with one another as particular churches *(ecclesiae particulares)* and with the local Church of Rome. The theology of *sister churches* is closely linked to the collegiality of the bishops: "The collegial union is apparent also in the mutual relations of the individual bishops with the particular churches and with the universal Church. [...] The individual bishops, however, are the visible principle and foundation of unity in their particular churches, fashioned after the model of the universal Church – in and from which churches comes into being the one and only Catholic Church" (LG 23).

In his encyclical *Ut unum sint*, Pope John Paul II appropriates for Catholic ecclesiology the identification of *particular churches* with *sister churches*. An entire chapter of the encyclical is entitled *Sister Churches*. Appealing to *Unitatis Redintegratio* 14, the Pope continues: "Following the Second Vatican Council, and in the light of earlier tradition, it has again become usual to refer to the particular or local churches gathered around their bishop as 'sister churches'." (no. 56). Sister churches are hence particular churches/local churches, which fully realize in themselves the Church of Christ and for this very reason are oriented essentially and necessarily toward *communio* with all other local churches. For a local church is a complete church, but not the whole Church. Accordingly, Pope John Paul II articulates the hope: "The traditional designation of 'sister churches' should ever accompany us along this path" (ibid.).

Thus, the expression *sister churches* is not an arbitrary option for the Catholic Church. By acknowledging the Orthodox Churches as true particular churches, she recognizes them as sister churches, as is stated in the declaration of the Congregation for the Doctrine of the Faith, *Dominus Iesus*, in the year 2000: "The Churches which, while not existing in perfect communion with the Catholic Church, remain united to her by means of the closest bonds, that is, by apostolic succession and a valid Eucharist, are true particular churches. Therefore, the Church of Christ is present and operative also in these churches, even though they lack full communion with the Catholic Church, since they do not accept the Catholic doctrine of the Primacy" (no. 17). The canon law of the Catholic Church employs an almost identical formulation when it defines the Catholic particular churches in CIC 369: "A diocese is a portion of the people of God which is entrusted to a bishop for him to shepherd with the cooperation of the presbyterium, so that, adhering to its pastor and gathered by him in the Holy Spirit through the gospel and the Eucharist, it constitutes a particular church in which the one, holy, catholic, and apostolic Church of Christ is truly present and operative."

Altogether, I am grateful to Will Cohen for his careful documentation and analysis of the highly variable reception history of the theology of *sister churches* and for his formulation of the most important theological questions that should be considered further in the Orthodox-Catholic dialogue. His book encourages us to clarify and deepen together the theology of *sister churches* as the *Note on the expression "Sister Churches"* of the Roman Congregation for the Doctrine of the Faith prompted in the year 2000. Thus, the theological term *sister churches* can continue to be a sign of hope on the path toward a shared being of the Church, which admittedly will achieve its aim in the restoration of the one and undivided Church in East and West, and in the resumption of full

Eucharistic communion as the Ecumenical Patriarch Athenagoras expressed it in 1968 with these words full of promise: "The hour of Christian courage has come. We love one another, we profess the same common faith, let us set out together on the path toward the glory of the shared holy altar" *(Tomos Agapis 227).*

Cardinal Kurt Koch
President of the Pontifical Council for Promoting Christian Unity

Author's Preface

In the several years since I completed research on the concept of "sister churches," provisional Orthodox episcopal assemblies have been formed in regions of the so-called diaspora and planning has been intensified for a Great and Holy Council of the Orthodox Church now scheduled for 2016. Serious and lively discussion of the nature and meaning of primacy in its relationship to conciliarity at the various levels of the church is robust among Orthodox theologians today. Meanwhile Pope Benedict XVI made the historic and ecclesiologically significant announcement of his retirement in February 2013. The need for further reflection on and integration of conciliarity at the regional level into an overall ecclesiology of the Catholic Church is expressed as follows by Benedict's successor, Pope Francis:

> The Second Vatican Council stated that, like the ancient patriarchal Churches, episcopal conferences are in a position "to contribute in many and fruitful ways to the concrete realization of the collegial spirit". Yet this desire has not been fully realized, since a juridical status of episcopal conferences which would see them as subjects of specific attributions, including genuine doctrinal authority, has not yet been sufficiently elaborated.[1]

In his recently released encyclical *Laudato Si,* Francis cites national episcopal conferences twenty-one times, quoting bishops from fifteen countries around the world as well as two larger regional bodies of bishops, the Latin American Episcopal Conference (CELAM) and the Federation of Asian Bishops' Conferences (FABC). And, significantly, the bishop quoted at most length in the encyclical's opening section is Patriarch Bartholomew.

All these developments point to the ongoing and renewed relevance of the concept of sister churches in Catholic and Orthodox ecclesiology and in the bilateral relations between the two traditions. Indeed the actual language of sister churches in Catholic-Orthodox ecumenical exchanges seems now to be re-emerging after a long absence in official Catholic parlance at least.[2] When

---

1   Evangelii Gaudium §32, http://w2.vatican.va/content/francesco/en/apost_exhortations/documents/papa-francesco_esortazione-ap_20131124_evangelii-gaudium.html

2   Official Orthodox statements that refer to the church of Rome as a sister church have been numerous and quite consistent (not from all but from many Sees, and even if always protested by Orthodox anti-ecumenists). For example, on being informed of the imminent retirement of Pope Benedict, Patriarch Bartholomew issued a statement that concluded with the words, "From the Phanar, we pray that the Lord will manifest

Pope Francis received in audience a delegation from the Ecumenical Patriarchate on June 28, 2014, he began by saying, "The Solemnity of the Holy Patrons of the Church of Rome, the Apostles Peter and Paul, once again gives me the joy of greeting a delegation from the sister Church of Constantinople."[3] So too at the end of Vespers on November 29, 2014, on the eve of his visit to the Phanar for the Feast of St. Andrew, Pope Francis remarked: "This evening my heart is full of gratitude to God who allows me to be here in prayer with Your Holiness and with this Sister Church after an eventful day during my Apostolic Visit."[4] In the days leading up to the meeting of Pope Francis and Ecumenical Patriarch Bartholomew in Jerusalem in late May 2014 (in commemoration of the 50th anniversary of the historic encounter there between Pope Paul VI and Patriarch Athenagoras), Cardinal Sean O'Malley of Boston and Metropolitan Methodios of the Greek Orthodox Archdiocese of Boston released a joint letter that also included this language of sister churches: "As Popes and Patriarchs have affirmed, we have come to see ourselves as 'sister churches' who are responsible together for affirming the faith of the Apostles."[5]

---

his worthy successor as the head of the sister Church of Rome, and that we may also continue with this successor on our common journey toward the unity of all unto the glory of God." (Press Release, Ecumenical Patriarchate, Feb. 14, 2013, printed in *SEIA Newsletter of the Eastern Churches and Ecumenism*, no. 209: February 28, 2013, p. 1). Toward the end of his congratulatory message following the election of Pope Francis, Bartholomew said, "Permit us also ... to convey our unfeigned wishes and fervent prayers that your papal tenure may prove to be a source of peace in our world of turmoil and division, a refuge and consolation for our Lord's poor and suffering brothers and sisters, as well as a continuation of our journey toward reconciliation and consolidation of the dialogue for the unity of our Sister Churches" (Website of the Ecumenical Patriarchate, March 14, 2013, printed in *SEIA Newsletter of the Eastern Churches and Ecumenism*, no. 210: March 31, 2013, p. 1.) When Patriarch John of Antioch was received by Pope Francis at the Vatican in late September or early October 2013, he issued a statement that began, "The Patriarch of Antioch, of the Greek Orthodox and all the East, Youhanna X Yazigi, joins and prays with the sister Church of Rome, for peace in Syria, in Lebanon, in the Mashreq and worldwide." (*Asia News*, Oct. 3, 2013, printed in *SEIA Newsletter of the Eastern Churches and Ecumenism*, no. 217: Oct. 31, 2013, p. 2.)

3 www.zenit.org/en/articles/pope-francis-address-to-ecumenical-patriarchate-delegation
4 http://en.radiovaticana.va/news/2014/11/29/pope_francis_ecumenical_prayer_with_patriarch_bartholomew/1112996
5 Joint Letter of May 21, 2014, printed in *SEIA Newsletter of the Eastern Churches and Ecumenism*, no. 224: May 31, 2014, p. 3.

The term seems bound to continue to resurface wherever Catholics and Orthodox reflect on their respective traditions in relation to one another. Careful study of the history of the language's use in modern times against the backdrop of the communion shared and damaged between the two traditions through the first and second millennia can sharpen our perception of ecclesiological pitfalls to which each communion has been prone – and illumine the narrow path of discernment along which each in faithfulness to its own authentic ecclesiology may yet find itself joined by the other in full freedom, mutual respect, and joy.

Will Cohen

Feast of Ss. Peter and Paul, June 29 2015
Scranton, Pennsylvania

Summary

Closely associated with Catholic-Orthodox *rapprochement* in the latter half of the 20th century was the emergence of the expression "sister churches" used in various ways across the confessional division. Patriarch Athenagoras first employed it in this context in a letter in 1962 to Cardinal Bea of the Vatican Secretariat for the Promotion of Christian Unity, and soon it had become standard currency in the bilateral dialogue. Yet today the expression is rarely invoked by Catholic or Orthodox officials in their ecclesial communications. As the Polish Catholic theologian Waclaw Hryniewicz was led to say in 2002, "This term ... has now fallen into disgrace."

This dissertation traces the rise and fall of the expression "sister churches" in modern Catholic-Orthodox relations and argues for its rehabilitation as a means by which both Catholic West and Orthodox East may avoid certain ecclesiological imbalances toward which each respectively tends in its separation from the other. Catholics who oppose saying that the Catholic Church and the Orthodox Church are sisters, or that the church of Rome is one among several patriarchal sister churches, generally fear that if either of those things were true, the unicity of the Church would be compromised and the Roman primacy rendered ineffective. Orthodox who oppose recognizing Rome as a sister church generally do so on the grounds of the assumption that the Latin West has been in heresy since the schism and without true sacraments. Both positions have significant weaknesses, historically and theologically. At the same time, they present a positive challenge. Proponents of the language of sister churches in Catholic-Orthodox relations have not always managed to make sufficiently clear (1) that conciliarity and primacy are complementary principles, and (2) that amidst the ongoing lack of full communion, the expression "sister churches" has a paradoxical character, reflecting an anomalous circumstance that cannot remain unresolved indefinitely. Building on the groundwork laid by theologians from both traditions, this study attempts to bring out each of these points more clearly in order to show the legitimacy of the expression "sister churches" for Orthodox and Catholic ecclesiology alike, and thus to show that, finally, they are not two ecclesiologies, but one.

This dissertation by Will T. Cohen was submitted to the Faculty of the School of Theology and Religious Studies of the Catholic University of America in 2010 and approved by Paul McPartlan, D.Phil., as Director, and by John Erickson (extern), M.Phil., John Galvin, Dr. Theol., and Joseph Komonchak, Ph.D., as Readers.

Acknowledgments

I am grateful for the support, encouragement and patience of the many people who contributed in various ways to my work on this dissertation. The idea to focus a dissertation on "sister churches" was first suggested to me by Fr. Joseph Komonchak on the basis of a section I had devoted to the topic in a doctoral seminar paper. I am grateful to him both for planting the seed and for his thoughtful critique as a reader later on. Fr. John Erickson's work in Orthodox ecclesiology has been an inspiration to me since my days as an MDiv student at St. Vladimir's Orthodox Theological Seminary, and his perceptive feedback as a reader of the dissertation has likewise been invaluable.

I am indebted in a particular way to my dissertation director, Msgr. Paul McPartlan. At every stage of the process, he offered extraordinarily steady and insightful guidance. Amidst the bewildering number and importance of all his various academic, ecclesiastical and ecumenical commitments, Msgr. McPartlan always gave my project the energy and time it required, and did so with the utmost grace, putting me in mind of those of whom C.S. Lewis has written, "They will usually seem to have a lot of time: you will wonder where it comes from." In a manner that equally defies explanation, Msgr. McPartlan manages repeatedly to make the kind of space for the ideas of others without which those ideas do not take their true shape, and for this gift, received in countless conversations with him about Christian unity and division, I am also very grateful.

Finally, I would like to thank Prof. Barbara Hallensleben for her keen interest in the subject of my study and for her dedicated efforts and wise editorial choices in seeing the manuscript through to publication in the *Studia Oecumenica Friburgensia* monograph series.

ABBREVIATIONS

AAS   *Acta Apostolicae Sedis:* www.vatican.va/archive/aas/index_ge.htm

ANF   Originally *Ante-Nicene Christian Library* (8 vols.). Ed. by Alexander Roberts and James Donaldson (Edinburgh: T & T Clark, 1867-85). Then published as *Ante-Nicene Fathers*. Ed. by Alexander Cleveland Coxe, American edition (Buffalo, NY: Christian Literature, 1885-97), unauthorized but for an additional vol. 9 as an original publication; Reprint, Peabody, MA: Hendrickson, 1994 with further vol. 10 containing a newly prepared *Annotated Index of Authors and Works of the Ante-Nicene, Nicene, and Post-Nicene Fathers, First and Second Series*.

Mansi   J.D. Mansi, *Sacrorum conciliorum nova et amplissima collectio*, 55 vols. (Florence etc., 1759-1962).

NPNF   *A Select Library of the Christian Church: Nicene and Post-Nicene Fathers*. In 2 series (14 vols. each). Ed. by P. Schaff (1st series) and by P. Schaff and H. Wace (2nd series) (Buffalo, NY: Christian Literature, 1887-94; Reprint, Grand Rapids, MI: Eerdmans, 1952-56; Reprint, Peabody, MA: Hendrickson, 1994-99).

PG   J.P. Migne, ed., *Patrologia Graeca*, 161 vols. (Paris, 1857-66).

PL   J.P. Migne, ed., *Patrologia Latina*, 217 vols. (Paris, 1844-55).

Introduction

Among the phenomena closely associated with *Catholic-Orthodox rapprochement* in the latter half of the 20th century was the emergence of the expression "sister churches" used in various ways across the confessional division between the two traditions. Ecumenical Patriarch Athenagoras (1948-1972) first employed it in this context in a letter in 1962 to Cardinal Bea of the Vatican Secretariat for the Promotion of Christian Unity, and within a few years, it had become standard currency first in the *Tomos Agapis* – the collection of exchanges in the "dialogue of love" between Constantinople and Rome – and then also in the international theological dialogue that was officially launched between the Orthodox Church and the Roman Catholic Church in 1980. It was invoked on numerous occasions by Popes Paul VI and John Paul II, the latter going as far as to speak of a "doctrine of sister churches" in his 1995 encyclical *Ut unum sint*.[1] Yet today the expression "sister churches" is scarcely to be seen or heard in the documents and speeches of Orthodox and Catholic officials engaged in the bilateral dialogue. As the Polish Catholic theologian Waclaw Hryniewicz was led to say already in 2002, "This term ... has now fallen into disgrace."[2]

This dissertation traces the rise and fall of the expression "sister churches" in modern Catholic-Orthodox relations and argues for its rehabilitation.

Chapter 1 demonstrates how the roots of the expression are embedded deeply in the Christian tradition by examining uses of the language of sister churches in scriptural, patristic and medieval sources. Although occurrences in those sources are relatively few they are sufficient to allow us to derive at least a basic definition of a sister church, and they also make it possible to see how the expression's acceptance or rejection historically might have depended in some degree on political factors. For example, while there was a single Christian empire encompassing East and West, Rome had no objection to

---

[1] John Paul II, *Ut Unum Sint*, 60. Available at www.vatican.va/holy_father/john_paul_ii/ encyclicals/documents/hf_jp-ii_enc_25051995_ut-unum-sint_en.html

[2] "The Cost of Unity: the Papal Primacy in Recent Orthodox Reflection," lecture given at the Faculty of Theology, Katholieke Universiteit, Leuven/Belgium, December 13, 2002, subsequently published in *The Journal of Eastern Christian Studies* 55:1-2 (2003), 1-27 and reprinted in W. Hryniewicz, *The Challenge of Our Hope: Christian Faith in Dialogue* (Washington, DC: The Council for Research in Values and Philosophy, 2007), 201. Quotations are from the reprinted text.

seeing itself as a sister church in relation to the major Eastern sees, albeit a privileged sister with certain prerogatives the others did not have. When there were two empires, an Eastern and a Western, Rome *did* object, strenuously, to being counted as a sister church of any other and insisted on being the mother of all. Then, once there was no longer any empire, Rome once again came to embrace the language of sister churches in its relations with the Orthodox East.

Chapter 2 offers a detailed look at the exchanges between Constantinople and Rome in that new, post-imperial atmosphere in which the Second Vatican Council took place and the expression "sister church" began to be used again not only by Orthodox officials to speak of the church of Rome (or the Roman Catholic Church as a whole), but also, by the late 1960s, by Catholic officials to speak of the church of Constantinople (or the Orthodox Church as a whole). This chapter provides considerably more raw data than analysis, but, in Chapter 3, some of the same data – as well as further data from subsequent decades – is organized and examined with a more specific intent. Instead of focusing simply on the burgeoning use of the language of sister churches by Orthodox and Catholics, the aim in Chapter 3 is to focus more closely on ambiguities surrounding its use, ambiguities relating not so much to what the expression intrinsically means, but to exactly which churches it is intended to apply to in any given instance. Concern over just this question was what led the Vatican Congregation for the Doctrine of the Faith (CDF) to issue its *Note on the Expression "Sister Churches"* in the year 2000.[3] The CDF's *Note* denied the legitimacy of applying the expression to the entire Catholic Church and the entire Orthodox Church (or any other), while it endorsed applying it to the relationship between particular Catholic churches (i.e., dioceses) and particular Orthodox ones. Examples of each of these two usages – as well as of several others – are grouped according to type in Chapter 3, in part simply in order to see which of the various possible ways of using the expression were most prevalent during the years between Vatican II and the release of the CDF's *Note*, and in part in order to begin to explore the ecclesiological ramifications of one usage versus another.

Chapter 4 surveys Catholic theological reflection on the concept of sister churches beginning with important studies on the topic by Emmanuel Lanne in the mid-1970s. The perspectives of Yves Congar, Waclaw Hryniewicz, Adriano Garuti, the CDF itself (given that its documents are rich in theological

---

3 Congregation for the Doctrine of the Faith, *Note on the Expression "Sister Churches"*, June 30, 2000: www.vatican.va/roman_curia/congregations/cfaith/documents/rc_con_cfaith_doc_20000630_chiese-sorelle_en.html.

reflection), and Hervé Legrand are also explored. Especially in Chapter 4's treatment of Garuti, the CDF, and Legrand, it becomes apparent that among Catholics the debate about "sister churches" continually intersects with the debate surrounding two other ecclesiological issues: the interpretation of "subsists in" in paragraph 8 of the Constitution on the Church, *Lumen Gentium*, promulgated at Vatican II, and the relationship between the local church and the universal church. Together, these *three* issues (the question of "sister churches" being the third, and all three having obvious relevance to Roman primacy) clearly form a very tightly interwoven nexus of ideas. Recent Catholic writing on "sister churches" confirms this with frequent references to the other two issues, while Catholic writing on the other two issues almost never refers to the "sister churches" debate, which has garnered less attention generally. But one of the conclusions of Chapter 4 is that the "sister churches" debate, if properly resolved, may be seen as holding the key to resolving the other two.

Orthodox authors, both those who approve the expression's use in Orthodox-Catholic relations and those who oppose it, are examined in Chapter 5. Advocates view its modern use by the Catholic Church in relations with the Orthodox as a welcome shift in Catholic ecclesiology, bringing it closer to Orthodox ecclesiology. Such is the perspective of John Meyendorff, Metropolitan Maximos Aghiorghoussis (Pittsburgh), John Erickson, and Metropolitan Damaskinos Papandreou (Switzerland). Orthodox critics, meanwhile, among whom are included John Romanides, representatives of the monastic communities on Mount Athos, and Metropolitan Dmitri Royster (Dallas) of the Orthodox Church in America, reject outright the expression's use in relations between Orthodox and Catholics. In consequence, they strongly objected to the language of sister churches that appeared in the Balamand Statement issued in 1993 by the Joint International Commission for Theological Dialogue between the Roman Catholic Church and the Orthodox Church, as well as to Balamand's recommendation not to (re)baptize converts from one church to the other. The longstanding debate within Orthodoxy over the status of non-Orthodox sacraments is shown in Chapter 5 to be closely related to the debate about "sister churches" vis-à-vis the Catholic Church.

Chapter 6 consists, first, of a comparison of Catholic and Orthodox advocates of the language of sister churches in the bilateral dialogue. Advocates turn out to hold in common a view of the schism as being what Congar called a "gradual estrangement", which never became total and which might yet be reversed. Catholic and Orthodox critics, meanwhile, whose positions Chapter 6 compares next, share a view of the schism as a cut-and-dried falling away of one party from the ecclesial reality maintained by the other; they only disagree, of course, about which party fell away from which. Also shown to be a common feature of Catholic and Orthodox critics is a propensity to see primacy and conciliarity as conflicting rather than complementary principles, with Catholic critics seeing the concept of sister churches as a threat to Roman primacy, and Orthodox critics seeing Roman primacy per se as incompatible with the authentic life of Orthodox sister churches.

In the last section of Chapter 6, I offer a pair of theological proposals that respond to the respective concerns of Catholic critics and Orthodox critics. First, I argue that the usage proscribed by Garuti and the CDF's *Note*, whereby the two churches as a whole are described as sisters, is not only ecclesiologically defensible but valuable, and that the usage endorsed by the *Note*, whereby particular Catholic and Orthodox churches are called sister churches, is in fact – while certainly defensible – of more limited value for Catholic-Orthodox relations. Here, following Legrand, I argue for the importance of sister churches on the regional level. I also argue for the importance of what I call the *secondness* of Constantinople both in the past and for any hope of reconciliation between the Orthodox and Catholic churches in the future. Finally in Chapter 6, I argue that in the ecclesiology of both churches there is an asymmetrical understanding of *how* the Church of Christ is present in each of the two, an asymmetry expressed in Catholic ecclesiology by the teaching that the Church of Christ subsists in the Catholic Church alone (but is nevertheless paradoxically present and operative elsewhere), and in Orthodox ecclesiology by the notion of the *ecclesia extra ecclesiam*. This asymmetry, I contend, should not be taken to mean that either the Orthodox Church or the Catholic Church – whichever of the two is regarded as the unique embodiment of the visibly one church – is self-sufficient. Rather, notwithstanding the asymmetry there is an *interdependence* that can and should be mutually acknowledged, an interdependence such that neither can claim it can do without the gifts of the other so long as it actually perceives the other to be the fruitful bearer of gifts of God to his Church. The two principles of asymmetry and interdependence, held paradoxically together in order to condition one another properly, give the expression "sister churches" in the context of the formal separation between Orthodox East and Catholic West a genuine theological value.

Chapter 1
The Concept Of "Sister Churches" Prior To Vatican II

I. The earliest shape of the concept

1. John's Second Epistle – plurality and personality

In writings that survive from antiquity and the early Middle Ages, the actual phrase "sister church" or "sister churches" is rarely found. It does not appear at all in the Bible. One closely related phrase, however, which appears in 2 John 13, is the phrase "your elect sister" (τῆς ἀδελφῆς σου τῆς ἐκλεκτῆς). In closing the letter, the author writes, "The children of your elect sister greet you."[1] It is generally agreed that the phrase "elect sister" refers here not to a particular woman by the name of ἐκλεκτῇ, but to the local church from which the author is writing.[2] In the opening verse of this brief epistle, the same word ἐκλεκτῇ is used: "The elder to the elect lady (ἐκλεκτῇ κυρίᾳ) and her children, whom I love in the truth, and not only I but also all who know the truth, because of the truth which abides in us and will be with us for ever" (2 Jn 1-2). Just as "your elect sister" in the closing verse refers to the community sending the letter, so "the elect lady" in this opening verse refers to the community receiving it; the two communities are thus sisters of one another.

Such is the position of Emmanuel Lanne, who, beginning in the 1970s, investigated the scriptural and patristic roots of the expression "sister churches".[3] We are still unable to ascribe detailed content to it, beyond noting that it entails the personification of a local community in distinction from and in relation to

---

1 Unless otherwise indicated, all scriptural quotations are from the Revised Standard Version (*The New Oxford Annotated Bible: Revised Standard Version*, ed. Herbert May and Bruce Metzger [New York: Oxford University Press, 1973]).
2 See Georg Strecker, *The Johannine Letters: A Commentary on 1, 2, and 3 John*, trans. Linda M. Maloney, ed. Harold Attridge (Minneapolis: Augsburg Fortress, 1996), 220-221; Judith Lieu, *The Second and Third Epistles of John: History and Background* (Edinburgh: T&T Clark, 1986), 65; D. Moody Smith, *First, Second, and Third John* (Louisville: John Knox Press, 1991), 139; inter alia.
3 E. Lanne, "Églises sœurs: implications ecclésiologiques du *Tomos Agapis*," *Istina* 20 (1975) 47-74, reprinted in E. Lanne, *Tradition et Communion des Églises: recueil d'études* (Leuven 1997), 501-535. Also in the same volume, "Églises Sœurs et Église Mère Dans le Vocabulaire de l'Église Ancienne," 625-636. (References to these articles are from *Tradition et Communion des Églises*; translations are mine).

another local community, but this in itself is an important, indeed a vital, point of departure. It means several things that it might be easy to overlook. Most obviously, it means that we are concerned with plurality on the level not just of the Christian individual but of the Christian community. A community that has the designation "elect sister" cannot but be one among two or more such communities; a single sibling is a contradiction in terms. In addition, each sister church is conceived of already in John's epistle as *a person*. The personification of a particular community, in addition to its being one of two or more, must also be recognized as inherent in the very meaning of "sister" when that phrase is used in an ecclesial sense.

These two features together, plurality (each community is one among others) and personality (each community is described in the figure of a person) comprise already a sufficient basis for discerning where else in the biblical and early patristic sources there are instances in which the concept of sister churches may be implicitly present.

2. Revelation 2-3 – locality and temporality

Lanne observes that the Book of Revelation, "without employing the term sisters for the Churches to which the letters of chapters 2 and 3 are addressed, marks a tendency to personify the local community under a feminine form, the ἐκκλησία, to whom is assigned an angel."[4] One of the ways this personification is indicated in these two chapters is by the use of the second person *singular* pronoun in each message to a local church. Since in modern English the singular and plural forms of the second person pronoun are the same, while in Elizabethan English they are distinguished, it will be convenient to quote from the King James translation of the relevant passages.

In the address to the church in Ephesus we read, "I know thy works (τὰ ἔργα σου), and thy labour and thy patience (τὸν κόπον καὶ τὴν ὑπομονήν σου)" (Rev 2:2).[5] In the message to the church in Smyrna the singular form of the second person pronoun is used everywhere it possibly can be, for example in verse 10, "Fear none of those things which thou shalt suffer". Where the singular form would render the meaning incoherent, the plural appears, but

---

4   Lanne, "Églises sœurs," 509.
5   Granted that it is, to be exact, to the *angel* of each church that John is commanded to write the words contained in each of the messages, it is nonetheless the community itself that is effectively addressed. This is stated explicitly in the refrain, "He that hath an ear, let him hear what the Spirit saith unto the churches (ταῖς ἐκκλησίαις)" (Rev 2:11, 29; 3:6, 13, 22).

only until it can give way again to the singular: "behold, the devil shall cast some of you into prison, that ye may be tried; and ye shall have tribulation ten days: be thou faithful unto death, and I will give thee a crown of life." The pattern of personification is especially strong in the message to the church in Laodicea to which is attributed even physical attributes of a person: "I counsel thee to buy of me gold tried in the fire, that thou mayest be rich; and white raiment, that thou mayest be clothed, and that the shame of thy nakedness do not appear; and anoint thine eyes with eye-salve, that thou mayest see."

Since each local church mentioned in Revelation 2-3 is presented not only as one among many, but also in personified form, this may be considered as having particular relevance to the concept of sister churches. What may be suggested from this set of texts that was not already noted based on 2 John may be summarized in two further points.

First, whereas in John's letter the distinct locality of each of the local churches was not mentioned,[6] here a particular location is given in connection with each of the seven churches – in every case, it is a city. Moreover, never is more than one "thou" addressed in one city. Theoretically, there might have been different messages conveyed to communities of different origins, compositions, or leadership *within a single location*, but this never occurs, neither here nor elsewhere in the NT. The relationship between ecclesial personality and geographical integrity appears already to be very strong in the scriptural witness.

A second point that bears noticing is that the conditions of the respective churches addressed by "the Spirit" in Revelation 2-3 vary widely. In what seems to be the worst case, that of the church in Sardis, the local community is spoken of in terms that suggest it is on the brink of ecclesial extinction.

> 'I know thy works, that thou hast a name that thou livest, and art dead. Be watchful, and strengthen the things which remain, that are ready to die: for I have not found thy works perfect before God. Remember therefore how thou hast received and heard, and hold fast, and repent ... Thou hast a few names even in Sardis which have not defiled their garments; and they shall walk with me in white: for they are worthy' (Rev 3:1c-4).

The community whose fidelity is most highly commended, on the other hand, namely the church in Philadelphia, is told to "hold that fast which thou hast,

---

[6] It should be noted, however, that at least one early manuscript has the words "the Church which is at Ephesus" interpolated before the phrase "your elect sister" in 2 John 13. Cf. Lanne, "Églises sœurs," 508, citing R. Schnackenburg, *Die Johannesbriefe* (Freiburg i.Br. 1953), 283.

that no man take thy crown" (Rev 3:11). Thus it can be seen that the church described as "dead" or "on the point of death" still has hope of being revivified by the grace of God, while even the steadiest and most vibrant church must still re-commit itself to God in order not to be excluded from the victory toward which it seems headed. From this a further feature of all churches and hence of sister churches may be inferred, namely that they exist in the realm of unfolding history, susceptible to both rehabilitation and misdirection. A church invulnerable to the possibility of error, of taking a wrong turn in any meaningful sense, would not be a sister church.

Finally, a word may be said about the nature of the potential rehabilitation of the church in or near a condition of spiritual death. As this is presented in the passage concerning the church in Sardis, it is evident that the makings of the rehabilitation, should it occur, will come from gifts and resources proper to that church itself. The church in Sardis is urged to "strengthen what remains," to "[r]emember what you received and heard," to "keep" what the very church in Sardis was originally given. Mention is made as well of the few righteous people who remain there. Although none of this is incompatible with receiving guidance or correction from other churches, it is noteworthy that in the Revelation passage, the focus is clearly on what is inherently promising about each church in its own integrity. What ensures a local church's ongoing *potential* for rehabilitation (which is not guaranteed) is the ongoing activity of the communication of the Spirit addressed to this church, however harsh the message may be. "Those whom I love, I reprove and chasten; so be zealous and repent" (Rev 3:19). Conversely, what underlies a local church's ongoing vulnerability to going astray is the inherent possibility of not "hearing" what the Spirit says to the churches.

To summarize the points made thus far: a sister church is (1) one of two or more; (2) figured as a person, i.e. addressed (potentially if not expressly) as "thou". More inferentially based on the Revelation passage in which the actual term "sister" does not appear but relations among local churches are described, it may also be suggested that a sister church is (3) rooted in a particular place, typically a city or town; (4) a church that exists in the realm of ongoing history. These four qualities of plurality, personality, locality, and temporality seem to be essential characteristics of local churches that might be described as "sister churches."

3. Second Corinthians 11:2 – a local church as bride

According to these criteria, another church that might potentially qualify as a sister church is that which is spoken of in 2 Corinthians 11:2. This is an unusual passage in that here a local church is figured as a bride.⁷ "For I am jealous over you with godly jealousy: for I have espoused you to one husband, that I may present you as a chaste virgin to Christ (ἡρμοσάμην γὰρ ὑμᾶς ἑνὶ ἀνδρὶ παρθένον ἁγνὴν παραστῆσαι τῷ Χριστῷ)." In this passage the local church is not, in fact, addressed precisely as "thou"; Paul instead uses the plural form of the second person pronoun to address the Corinthian Christians, primarily as individuals. Yet it is as a single corporate body – as a "pure bride" – that he says he has hoped to present them, as "to her one husband." In this sense, the church is indeed personified. It is also concretely located – in Corinth – and is spoken of, furthermore, as one among many: Paul says only a few verses later, "I robbed other churches by accepting support from them in order to serve you" (2 Cor 11:8). Finally, the temporal condition of the local church in Corinth is expressed by Paul's fear that its members "will be led astray from a sincere and pure devotion to Christ" (2 Cor 11:3); hence his plea, "Do bear with me!" (2 Cor 11:1b). The vulnerability of the community to pernicious influences, as well as its capability to recover its firmness of faith and purity of devotion, are both indicated. It should also be noted that Paul's appeal is not to his own authority *per se* but to the authority of the gospel which he has preached and they have accepted.⁸ Far from imposing something on them from outside, Paul's effort is to re-orient the Corinthians to what is proper to them as a Christian community, to the gifts – most centrally, that of the spirit (2 Cor 11:4) – that are already theirs.

4. First Clement and Ignatius of Antioch

According to Lanne, important texts from the sub-apostolic period offer further, if still indirect, witness to the concept of sister churches. Lanne notes about one of the earliest preserved Christian documents outside the New Testament, the late first-century text known as "Clement's First Letter" (96 or 97 AD), that it is a correspondence not between individuals but between churches, and that "Clement does not hesitate to consider the church of Rome and that of Corinth as two personal entities, of which the one can address the other with

---

7   More typically in the NT, when there is bridal imagery for the church, it is the singular, universal church that is at issue. Cf. Eph 5:32, Rev 19:7-9 and 21:2. In none of these cases is a "sister churches" motif present, since, in all of them, it is the universal church represented by the figure of the bride/spouse.
8   Cf. also Gal 1:8: "But even if we, or an angel from heaven, should preach to you a gospel contrary to that which we preached to you, let him be accursed."

fraternal admonitions".[9] Also evident in this letter is the theme of mutual vulnerability ("We are writing in this vein, dear friends, not only to admonish you but also to remind ourselves. For we are in the same arena and involved in the same struggle" [7.1]), as well as an obvious specificity of each community's location.

In the letters of Ignatius of Antioch, which do not invoke the phrase "sister churches," a peculiar expression is used by which the local church is personified. The expression is "the charity of the brothers"; in the letter to the Philadelphians this "charity," as the grammatical subject of a sentence, is what actually *greets* those to whom the letter is addressed. "The charity of the brothers who are at Troas greets you."[10]

Another respect in which the local church is personified in the writings of Ignatius is not mentioned by Lanne but is a well known feature of Ignatian ecclesiology. For Ignatius, the bishop is the person in whom the unity of the local church is embodied. In the letter to the Trallians, Ignatius writes of his impression that the character of the church at Tralles is

> above reproach and steady under strain. It is not just affected, but it comes naturally to you, as I gathered from Polybius, your bishop. By God's will and that of Jesus Christ, he came to me in Smyrna, and so heartily congratulated me on being a prisoner for Jesus Christ that in him I saw your whole congregation (ὥστε με τὸ πᾶν πλῆθος ὑμῶν ἐν αὐτῷ θεωρῆσαι). I welcomed, then, your godly good will, which reached me by him ...[11]

In the person of the bishop the whole congregation is epitomized and made present. The point perhaps bears emphasizing: for Ignatius, having a presiding bishop grants a church the character of being a corporate personality.

The relevant sub-apostolic texts considered here, while not substantially adding to the shape of the concept of sister churches, and while still only hinting at an adumbration of that concept in an indirect way, do offer reason to

---

9 Lanne, "Églises sœurs," 509.
10 I have translated Lanne's rendering ("Églises sœurs," 511) of the Greek: Ἀσπάζεται ὑμᾶς ἡ ἀγάπη τῶν ἀδελφῶν τῶν ἐν Τρωάδι (cf. PG 5, 705C). The English translation by Cyril Richardson in *Early Christian Fathers* (New York: Touchstone, 1996), 111, "The brothers in Troas send their love and greetings," is a smoother rendering which has the disadvantage, however, of obscuring the way in which the local church is personified in Ignatius' thought. More recent English translations retain the original syntax, awkward as it is. See for example *ANE*, vol. 1, 85: "The love of the brethren at Troas salutes you."
11 Richardson, *Early Christian Fathers*, 98.

think that its application might extend beyond the limits of the New Testament into the patristic era.

II. The further sense of the concept: similar standing

1. Churches as sisters in Basil the Great and Pope Innocent I

Up to this point, sister churches have been conceived in terms of their common attributes as churches. But as early as the fourth century the word "sister" was used to speak of relations between two or more churches jointly distinguished from other churches. In two early texts – written only a few decades apart, one in the East, the other in the West – the word "sister" refers only to certain local churches that had in common a comparable preeminence.

In a letter to the Neocaesareans in 375 AD, Basil the Great expressed disappointment that "the greatest Churches, which have related to one another as sisters from antiquity, are now in discord" (αἱ μέγισται τῶν Ἐκκλσιῶν καὶ ἐκ παλαιοῦ πρὸς ἀλλήλας ἀδελφῶν τάξιν ἐπέχουσαι).[12] He was referring to recent difficulties between his own church, in Caesarea, and the church in Neocaesarea. Lanne observes that it is remarkable that Basil would have spoken of these two as "sisters," for the latter city had come to have a considerable Christian presence only long after the church of Caesarea had been well established.[13] But the reputation of Gregory the Wonderworker, Neocaesarea's first bishop and a protégé of Origen, appears to have been a factor, as Lanne suggests, in Basil's readiness to consider Neocaesarea as a sister church of Caesarea, which itself owed much to the spiritual legacy of Origen.[14] Another possible factor was that the church of Neocaesarea had not directly been founded by the church of Caesarea.

---

12 Basil of Caesarea, Ep. 204, 7; PG 32, 756A, as quoted by Lanne, "Église sœur et Église mère," 635. English translation in *NPNF* vol. 8 (2nd ser.), 245.
13 Cf. Lanne, ibid. 635. Lanne also mentions that in a text of several years earlier, Gregory of Nazianzus had referred to Caesarea as the mother of almost all the other churches. For discussion of this text of Gregory, see below, pp. 17-19.
14 This view finds support in the remark of Basil earlier in the letter, "if it tend much towards intimacy to have the same teachers, there are to you and to me the same teachers of God's mysteries, and spiritual Fathers, who from the beginning were the founders of your Church. I mean the great Gregory, and all who succeeding in order to the throne of your episcopate, like stars rising one after another, have tracked the same course": Ep. 204, in *NPNF* vol. 8 (2nd ser.), 243.

In 415 AD, Pope Innocent I wrote to the priest Boniface discussing possibilities for reconciliation between Rome and Antioch. In this letter, Innocent spoke of the two sees as siblings: "The Church of Antioch, which the blessed apostle Peter rendered illustrious by his presence before coming to Rome, on the basis of which she is like the sister of the Church of Rome, has not tolerated being separated from her for very long."[15]

In Lanne's interpretation of these two passages emphasis is given to the idea that between sister churches there is an identity of faith. Of the churches of Caesarea and Neocaesarea mentioned in the first passage, Lanne says that "they are united as sisters in the preaching of the same faith; perhaps also, in the thought of Basil, by the heritage of Origen. But even so understood, this 'fraternity' comes down to the sharing of the same Christian faith."[16] While it is no doubt true that they did share the same Christian faith and that this was a matter of essential importance, there was also another matter at issue, which seems more directly relevant to Basil's use of the word "sisters". This is the matter of reputation and influence. For it is in the same breath as he speaks of the "greatest Churches" that Basil mentions their sibling relationship. To be sure, their "greatness" would not have been unrelated to the faith they shared, yet other churches also shared the same faith but were not included in the category of "the greatest Churches" that Basil specifically designates as sisters here.

Lanne's reading of the second text corresponds to his reading of the first. After noting that the appeal by Pope Innocent to a specifically Roman understanding of Petrine primacy would have been of little interest to eastern prelates, Lanne suggests that, in any case, "the motivation of the fraternity of the two Churches remains the same: the apostolic faith received by each one of them in the person of the apostle Peter."[17]

In Innocent's letter, in fact, there is nothing said about Peter's having bestowed one and the same *faith* on the church of Rome and the church of Antioch, though of course it was well understood that he had done so. Instead, there is specific mention of how his presence in each see had similarly rendered

---

15 Innocent I, Ep. 23, PL 20, 546A. "Ecclesia Antiochena, quam prius quam ad urbem perveniret Romam, beatus apostolus Petrus sua praesentia illustravit, velut germana ecclesiae Romanae, diu se ab eadem alienam esse non passa est." It may be noted that rather than use the word *soror* as he might have, Innocent I opted here instead to use *germana*, perhaps because its root meaning is "having the same father," Peter in this case. I am indebted to Fr. Joseph Komonchak for pointing out this distinction.
16 Lanne, "Église sœur et Église mère," 635.
17 Ibid. 636.

each of them *illustrious*. Again, the connection seems strong between the concept of sister churches and the idea of the similar standing of the particular churches to which it is applied, in this case a similar preeminence, not *unrelated* to their sharing the same faith but not deriving from that factor alone.

As Basil and Innocent used the term in the passages quoted above, a secondary meaning of the expression "sister churches" emerges. Here, sister churches are those that share a similar status not necessarily characteristic of all churches.

2. Mother churches as sister churches

Why any churches came to be seen as having a certain preeminence had to do with numerous factors, from the need to resolve ecclesiastical differences to the external mission of the church within an imperial context. As it happened, preeminent churches were almost always those of a metropolis, that is, they were "mother-city" churches. Sometimes they were referred to explicitly as "mother churches." At this point it becomes evident that in order to treat the concept of sister churches adequately some attention must be given to the concept of mother church. What follows is an excursus on the latter concept's development. Since it is a topic of potentially overwhelming complexity, our purpose in entering into it at all will be limited to demonstrating two basic points: 1) that in early Christian tradition, the one Church is figured frequently enough as the mother of individuals, but not as the mother of local churches;[18] and 2) that where the phrase *mater ecclesia* comes to be predicated of a local church in relation to another, it is not only the relationship of mother church to daughter church that is attested, but also the relationship between one mother church and another mother church, and, hence, something at least suggestive of an apparent relationship of *mother churches as sister churches*.

The biblical *locus classicus* with respect to the concept of the church as mother is Galatians 4:26 where Paul speaks of the "Jerusalem above" as "our

---

18 In Cyprian's *Ad Fortunatum*, written probably in 253 amidst persecution under Gallus, there is a passage that could possibly be seen as depicting the universal church as mother of local churches. This is where Cyprian writes, referring to the seven churches mentioned in Rev 2-3, "Cum septem liberis plane copulatur et mater origo et radix; quae Ecclesias septem postmodum peperit, ipsa prima et una super Petrum [With the seven children is associated, to be sure, also the Mother, the origin and root that subsequently begot seven churches, she herself having been first and alone founded upon Peter by the voice of the Lord]". PL 4, 668C. Quoted by J. Plumpe, *Mater Ecclesia: An Inquiry into the Concept of the Church as Mother in Early Christianity* (Washington, DC: The Catholic University of America Press, 1943), 97.

mother." In Revelation 21:2 this "Jerusalem above" is further described as "coming down out of heaven from God, prepared as a bride adorned for her husband". Here the Church is very clearly the universal, pre-existent, eschatological church, and there is no idea of *churches* deriving from it. When Paul in the Galatians passage speaks of "our mother," this is the mother not of our churches but of us all as Christians.

Joseph Plumpe has found significant evidence from the second century that the faith itself was spoken of as "mother".[19] Indeed Plumpe regards the concept of "mother faith" as an anticipation of the concept of "mother church." It is notable, then, that in the examples Plumpe adduces of the faith as mother, this faith is always the mother of individuals (not churches), as in Polycarp's *Letter to the Philippians*. "If you will but look into [Paul's letters] closely, you will be able to build up yourselves into the *faith* given to you; and this, followed by hope and preceded by love for God, for Christ, for our neighbor, 'is the *mother* of us all.'"[20] The same holds true in the *Acta Ss. Iustini et Sociorum* which date from roughly 165 AD. In this text, when one of the six companions of Justin, named Hierax, is asked by the prefect Junius Rusticus about the whereabouts of his parents, Hierax replies, "Our true father is Christ, and *faith* in Him is our *mother*".[21] In the mystical tradition of such theological inheritors of Origen as Methodius of Olympus, there is a remarkable sense in which the mother church is nothing other than the individuals who have been conceived and nurtured and perfected by the faith which they then, as mothers, engender in other individuals. These perfected individuals are said to *become* the Church.[22]

---

19 Plumpe, *Mater Ecclesia*, 18-20.
20 Plumpe, *Mater Ecclesia*, 18, citing Polycarp's *Letter to the Philippians* 3:2. The author observes in a footnote that in the *textus receptus* of Gal 4:26 the word πάντων is inserted before ἡμῶν (rendering the "Jerusalem above" not just "our mother" but "the mother of us all") and that in quotations of Gal 4:26 in the works of Irenaeus, Origen, Cyril of Jerusalem, Gelasius of Caesarea, Jerome, Augustine, Chrysostom, and Pseudo-Melito, one finds occurrences of πάντων ἡμῶν. From this fact, Plumpe concurs with all editors of Polycarp's letter that Polycarp is alluding here to Gal 4:26.
21 Plumpe, *Mater Ecclesia*, 19, citing the *Acta* 4.8 (Plumpe's emphases).
22 "And those who are still imperfect and only beginners are borne to the salvation of knowledge and formed as by mothers in travail, by those who are more perfect, until they are brought forth and regenerated unto the greatness and beauty of virtue; and when these by the progress of their growth in their turn have become the Church, they, too cooperate in the birth and nurture of other children, bringing to fruition in the womb of the soul, as in the womb of a mother, the unblemished will of the Logos" (Methodius, *Symposium*, 3.8.74f.: 37.9-15, quoted by Plumpe, *Mater Ecclesia*, 115).

Having looked at references to the universal *mater ecclesia* and to the πίστις μήτηρ (an equally universal reality) and having seen that in neither case do local churches figure as their offspring, we turn now to cases where maternity is itself predicated of a local church.

In the second epistle of John, there is an implicit notion of the maternity of a local church. The "elect lady" (κυρία) is addressed along with "her children" (τοῖς τέκνοις), in relation to whom she must obviously be regarded as mother. But this maternity is, like that of the church universal in Galatians 4 and Revelation 21, strictly a maternity vis-à-vis individuals, not other local churches.

The first indication, still not much more than a glimmer, of a different dynamic, in which *churches themselves* are spoken of as being related in a filial way to a mother church, appears in Irenaeus. Lanne has found that it is in the third Book of Irenaeus's *Against Heresies* that "one encounters for the first time the indication of the maternal character of the Church applied to a local church" – and here one should further specify, applied to a local church vis-à-vis other local *churches* (rather than only individuals). The church to which such a maternal character is ascribed is that of Jerusalem.[23]

In the passage in question, Irenaeus has just reflected on the moment in Acts 4:23-31 when Peter and John, having seen and been dismissed by the chief priests, "returned," as Irenaeus writes, "to the rest of their fellow-apostles and disciples of the Lord, that is, to the Church," and spoke of what had occurred and how they had acted in Christ's name. In Irenaeus' comments, which focus especially on verse 24 ("And when they heard it, they lifted their voices together to God"), one can discern the shape of the idea of the motherhood of a local church. Irenaeus writes:

> These [are the] voices of the Church from which every Church had its origin; these are the voices of the metropolis of the citizens of the new covenant; these are the voices of the disciples of the Lord, the truly perfect, who, after the assumption of the Lord, were perfected by the Spirit ... For at that time and place there was neither Valentinus, nor Marcion, nor the rest of these subverters [of the truth], and their adherents. Wherefore God, the maker of all things, heard them. For it is said, 'The place was shaken where they were assembled together; and they were all filled with the Holy Ghost, and they spake the word of God with boldness' to every one that was willing to believe.[24]

The idea that one local church is the mother of other local churches is suggested above all in the statement, "These are the voices of the Church from which

---

23 Lanne, "Église sœur et Église mère," 628.
24 *ANF*, vol. 1, 431.

every Church had its origin". It might be suggested that this could still be a reference to the universal, pre-existing Church and that the subsequent assertion, "these are the voices of the metropolis of the citizens of the new covenant," might perhaps be seen as speaking of an atemporal, non-geographical heavenly Jerusalem. But such an interpretation is undermined by the sentence several lines later in the passage where Irenaeus writes, "For *at that time and place* there was neither Valentinus, nor Marcion, nor the rest of these subverters [of the truth], and their adherents," as well as from Irenaeus' quotation from Acts saying that the "*place* was shaken where they were gathered together."²⁵ On at least one indispensable level, it is the earthly Jerusalem of which Irenaeus speaks here, the geographically rooted city in which Peter and John, together with the other apostles and disciples who heard their report, bore the evangelical witness described in Acts 4 at a particular time in history.

Moreover, the *maternity* of this church of the earthly city of Jerusalem is expressed not only by the general sense of the passage but by the use of the particular word "metropolis," a word singled out by Lanne for special notice. Etymologically, as Lanne points out, the word "metropolis" (μητρόπολις) has the significance of mother city, "in other words of a city which has founded or colonized other cities."²⁶

Irenaeus would have had no reason to conceive of this mother-city church, even though in one sense it was very much a local church, as a sister church of any other. The reason is plain. When the events recounted in Acts 4 took place, as yet there were no local churches other than that of Jerusalem. This was a unique instance in which the local church and the universal church entirely coincided.²⁷ Only in that instance could someone have said altogether literally, "one church, one city."

It is not surprising in light of the reflections above that all the earliest references to a local church as mother of other churches were to Jerusalem. The term was used in this way of Jerusalem in the First Council of Constantinople

---

25 Emphases added.
26 Lanne, "Églises sœurs," 513, n. 30. Plumpe, on whose work Lanne frequently relies, has observed (*Mater Ecclesia*, 2, n. 2) that "[t]he word μητρόπολις is long overdue for a special study."
27 Walter Kasper has made this point, saying that the Pentecost Church was in fact "universal and local in its single reality." W. Kasper, "Zur Theologie und Praxis des bischöflichen Amtes," in *Auf neue Art Kirche sein: Wirklichkeiten – Herausforderungen – Wandlungen*, Munich 1999, 44.

Chapter 1: The Concept of "Sister Churches" prior to Vatican II 17

(381 AD).[28] The idea is also suggested in the Greek and Syriac anaphoras of St. James and, in the mid-5th century, appears again in the "Ecclesiastical History" of Theodoret of Cyrus, where Theodoret is writing of the transmission of the *Acta* of the second ecumenical council (I Constantinople).[29] In its application to Jerusalem, the phrase also passed into the Latin world.[30]

Through the first three centuries and into the early fourth, there is no known reference to any local church as mother of other local churches, apart from the unique case of Jerusalem. It is nowhere attested in Cyprian's writings. As Plumpe observes, "When Cyprian speaks of the Church as *Mater* (or *Mater Ecclesia* or E.M.), he means – without exception, I believe – the universal Church, the *Ecclesia Catholica*, not the church at Carthage, Rome, or elsewhere."[31]

Late in the fourth century, in several letters of Gregory Nazianzen one does find the application of the term mother church to a local church other than Jerusalem. Writing from his own church to that of Caesarea in the same province, he refers to the latter church's maternity. The church of Caesarea was preparing for its episcopal election, and Gregory sought to recommend Basil for the office. In the first of two letters sent in the year 370, Gregory urged the Caesareans to exercise discernment in their upcoming election, whose importance he underscored by saying that just as the light of the body is the eye, so "the light of the Church is the Bishop." He went on:

> You must then take thought for the whole Church as the Body of Christ, but more especially for your own, which was from the beginning and is now the Mother of almost all the Churches, to which all the Commonwealth looks, like

---

28 PL 13, 1201C: "Hierosolymitanae autem ecclesiae, quae mater est omnium ecclesiarum, reverendissimum ac religiosissimum Cyrillum episcopum indicamus, qui et canonice ab episcopis provinciae olim fuit ordinatus, et plurima variis in locis contra Arianos certamina subiit."

29 Cf. B.-Charles Mercier, "La liturgie de saint Jacques, edition critique du texte grec avec traduction latine," *Patrologia Orientalis* 26 (Paris, 1948), pp. 206-207 at line 26 and pp. 218-219 at line 2; A. Raes, trans. and ed., *Anaphorae Syracae* (Rome: Pontificio Istituto Orientale, 1953), 152ff; and Theodoret, *Ecclesiastical History* V, 9, 17, as cited by Lanne, "Églises sœurs," 513. See also Maximos Aghiorgoussis, *In the Image of God* (Brookline, MA: Holy Cross Orthodox Press, 1999), 161.

30 Cf. Theodosius' *De Situ Terrae sanctae* (circa 550), ch. 7, CC, 175, p. 118, 1.5-8, as cited by Lanne, 513, n. 30.

31 Plumpe, *Mater Ecclesia*, 95. For Cyprian the universal Church is understood in a decidedly horizontal, i.e. "this-worldly" sense; it is remarkable that he never invokes Gal 4:26 when he speaks of the *mater ecclesia*. See Plumpe's comments in *Mater Ecclesia*, 104, n. 65.

a circle described round a centre, not only because of its orthodoxy proclaimed of old to all, but also because of the grace of unanimity so evidently bestowed upon it by God.[32]

The maternal character of the church of Caesarea is described in terms of its active authority, both in the present and over the years. It is because of its "orthodoxy" and its "grace of unanimity" that the Caesarean church is and has been recognized as the center of a circle. Unlike the case of Jerusalem, here there is no idea that this church actually *spawned* the others, but that it nourishes and guides them in their present life.

In another letter in which Gregory makes use of the phrase "mother church," the context is somewhat different. Here Gregory was writing to Basil to complain of a certain Bishop Anthimus of Tyana, a city which had just become the civil metropolis of a new Province (Cappadocia Secunda) created in the recent sub-division of the previously single Province of Cappadocia in 372 AD. Basil's city of Caesarea, which had been the metropolis of Cappadocia in its entirety until this sub-division, remained the metropolis of the rest of the region not included under Tyana's new sphere of influence. But Gregory of Nazianzus's church fell within Tyana's sphere, to his manifest regret.

In the pertinent passage, Gregory expresses to Basil his frustration that Bishop Anthimus in a recent meeting with Gregory treated him haughtily and "as though I ought only to look at him and his new Metropolis, as being the greater. Why, I said, do you draw your line to include our city, for we too deem our Church to be really a Mother of Churches, and that too from ancient times?"[33]

We may note the close parallelism indicated in this passage between the idea of a *metropolis* and the idea of a *mother church*. Not so clear are the reasons why Gregory thought of his own church as a mother church. Little is known about Nazianzus apart from the fact that it was a very small town. Centuries later, under Diogenes, it would become a metropolinate in its own right (by then the association between a mother-city and a metropolitan see had become more tenuous), but in Gregory's lifetime it had little stature. In any case Gregory makes no attempt to dispute the maternity of the "new" metropolis of Tyana; he only claims a qualitatively comparable maternity for his own church in spite of its peripheral role in the civic administration of Cappadocia.

---

32 Gregory Nazianzen, Ep. 41, in *NPNF* vol. 7 (2nd ser.), 450, quoted and discussed by Lanne, "Église sœur et Église mère," 631-632.

33 Gregory Nazianzen, Ep. 50, in *NPNF*, vol. 7 (2nd ser.), 454, quoted and discussed by Lanne, "Église sœur et Église mère," 632-633.

Whatever the exact basis for Gregory's use of the appellation, this passage presents two churches as "mother churches." It is the first time in all the sources we have seen where that is the case. With this juxtaposition of two local mother churches, it may be suggested that an ecclesiology of sister churches is implied, of the same kind that was seen in the texts of Basil and Innocent,[34] where the expression applies not to all churches by virtue of their sharing the same faith but only to some by virtue of similar status, especially a certain priority they claim to have with respect to other churches. The basis on which Gregory lodged his protest against another church's line of jurisdiction encroaching on the sphere of his own church was that *both* were mother churches, not just one. He did not expressly say they were sister churches of one another, but such a conclusion seems possible to infer from what he did say.

The results of our inquiry into early Christian usages of "mother church" may be summarized as follows: (1) Although the universal Church is described often enough as mother, hardly ever is it said to give birth to daughter *churches* that might then be construed as sister churches of one another.[35] (2) Early on, there is a notion of the faith as universal mother, but here as well it is not spoken of as the mother of churches, only of individuals. (3) In the earliest cases when maternity is predicated of a local church, it has reference not to other churches (i.e., daughter churches) but to individuals in their filial relationship to that local church. (4) When eventually a local church is called mother vis-à-vis other *churches,* the church so called is Jerusalem, a unique case, insofar as it was chronologically the first local church of all. (5) In the rare instances where other churches besides Jerusalem are called mother churches (e.g., Caesarea, or Neocaesarea), they stand, at least implicitly, in a mutual relationship of sister churches, not just in the basic sense that applies to all churches but in the more selective sense that Basil and Innocent both evoked when they described certain preeminent churches as sisters.

In all of this, it will not have gone unnoticed that the see of Rome has yet to be mentioned in connection with the idea of the maternity of the church. In his concluding chapter, aptly entitled "Rome's Silence," Plumpe observes, based on his research into the first three centuries, that the "practice of regarding and calling the Church *Mother* must have originated" somewhere in Asia Minor, and that "at Rome the concept and title were not in use at all during the entire period investigated"[36] (that is, during the first three centuries). The first pope

---

34 See above, pp. 11-13.
35 For a possible exception to this, see above, p. 13, n. 18.
36 Plumpe, *Mater Ecclesia*, 123, 126. Plumpe says, 128, citing H. Koch, *Cathedra Petri,*

to speak of the Church in any sense at all as mother was Damasus (366-384), and he did so not in dogmatic discourses (whether in his letters or synodal documents) but only in epigrammatic verses.[37] Moreover he applied *mater* not to Rome but to the universal church. While Plumpe regards the appeal to the motherhood of the Church in the early centuries as being essentially "one of affection, of sentiment and emotion" – qualities, Plumpe suggests, to which the Christian Romans of the time were rather little disposed in their theology – he still finds it surprising that the idea "did not lend itself to their [the Romans'] practical sense." After all,

> from the concept of the universal Church as Mother Church, to the concept of the church at Rome as *the* mother of the universal Church, was only one step. This must have been seen at Rome. But Rome did not take the step, at least not, it seems, till very late. Rome chose to assert her claim to the primacy on other grounds, historical and juridical, not on an emotional appeal imported from the East.[38]

By the late 6th century, Gregory the Great (590-604) had no hesitation in speaking of Rome as the "mother" church of Syracuse.[39] On a different occasion, appealing to the schismatic bishops of northern Italy to return to the catholic fold he used the phrase "mother church" as well, whether to signify the universal church or the church of Rome it is perhaps hard to say.[40] In either case he did not identify Rome as the mother of all other churches.[41] In this connection

---

86, that "the Church of Rome was first termed the universal Mother ("*Ecclesia Romana omnium Mater*") in a letter by the bishop Leontius of Arles, felicitating Pope Hilarus (461-468) on his accession to the see of Rome. At what later time Rome itself adopted such a title," Plumpe concludes, "I cannot say."

37 Such as those composed to the memory of the Roman presbyter Hippolytus, who became schismatic but at the end of his life was probably reconciled in exile. See Plumpe, *Mater Ecclesia*, 129.

38 Plumpe, *Mater Ecclesia*, 128.

39 Gregory the Great, Ep. III.12; PL 77, 614AB.

40 Addressing the schismatic bishops in northern Italy opposed to the 5th ecumenical council's condemnation of the Three Chapters, Gregory wrote, "Let, then, purity of faith bring your Charity back to your mother church who bare you; let no bent of your mind dissociate you from the unity of concord; let no persuasion deter you from seeking again the right way. For in the synod which dealt with the three chapters it is distinctly evident that nothing pertaining to faith was subverted, or in the least degree changed": Gregory the Great, Ep. II.51, in *NPNF*, 117.

41 A letter of Pope Innocent I (the same pope who called Antioch the "sister" of Rome by virtue of their common founder, Peter), to Decentius of Gubbio does make

his famous critique of the use of the title "Ecumenical Patriarch" by the patriarch of the Byzantine capital is pertinent. For Gregory, as he put it in his letter to the patriarch of Constantinople at the time, John the Faster (582-595), the problem with calling oneself "Ecumenical Patriarch" (and in doing so, John was merely carrying on a tradition already more than a century old) was that "if one Patriarch is called Universal, the name of Patriarch in the case of the rest is derogated."[42] Gregory may be seen as espousing an ecclesiology consistent with a notion of sister patriarchal churches. Yet his sense of the particular dignity of this whole *class* of preeminent churches, among which he includes Rome, does not keep him from being a strong proponent of Roman primacy as well. The two realities had not yet come to be seen as contradictory.

III. A new tension between "mother church" and "sister churches"

In exchanges between East and West in the 11th and 12th centuries, "sister churches" as an eastern conviction was pitted against Rome's self-assertion as "mother church." These exchanges occurred across a vast conceptual chasm that had opened up between the two traditions especially with regard to ecclesiology. The exchanges between popes (or their legates) and various eastern patriarchs in which eastern and western understandings of primacy and collegiality were argued back and forth, not very precisely, may be viewed as constituting at least a sincere effort to maintain contact, painful as this had become. It would be anachronistic to view them as any sort of full or adequate airing of contrasting dogmatic views well understood and defined by each party and

---

reference, without actually employing the word "mother," to Rome as the origin and the head of "all" other churches – though it is clear from the text that the "all" is in fact limited to the Latin world. (Cf. Innocent, Ep. 25, 1 [March 19, 416], Jaffé 311: PL 20, 551, as cited by Y. Congar, *Diversity and Communion* [Mystic, CT: Twenty-Third Publications, 1985], 30-31.) On how and when Rome's function of headship over "all" went from being understood and carried out only within the sphere of the West to being applied universally, see Brian Daley, "Structures of Charity: Bishops' Gatherings and the See of Rome in the Early Church," in Thomas J. Reese, ed., *Episcopal Conferences: Historical, Canonical and Theological Studies* (Washington, DC: Georgetown, 1989), 25-58.

42 Gregory the Great, Ep. V.43, in *NPNF*, vol. 12 (2nd ser.), 178. George Demacopoulos, "Gregory the Great and the Sixth-Century Dispute Over the Ecumenical Title," *Theological Studies* 70 (2009) 1-22, has shown that while Gregory started out defending the equal dignity of all patriarchs, he appealed later on to a specifically Roman Petrine privilege.

presented for the other's patient consideration. As one 20th century eastern Catholic has put it, speaking of the Orthodox who resisted the conception of the papacy put forward in the 11th and 12th centuries, "They were not in revolt against a mature doctrine of the primacy that had been decently presented to them in theory and in practice."[43] Also with regard to the primacy, the Church historian Pierre Battifol has remarked, "It is regrettable that so fundamental an issue was not settled by full discussion and by an ecumenical council during the centuries when there was still union."[44]

The difficulty now was that while the very point in dispute required conciliar consensus if it was to be resolved, it first had to be resolved in order for a council to be summoned. The point may be illustrated by considering the response of Pope Innocent III (1198-1206) to a proposal of Patriarch John X Camateros (1198-1206) that an ecumenical council be convened. Innocent III replied that a prerequisite for such a council's being assembled was that Constantinople should first admit the supremacy of the church of Rome.[45] Nothing came of the idea, for precisely the nature of Rome's primacy was what was in need of being worked out.

If, earlier in the Church's history, doctrines of comparable weight and universal relevance had always proved capable of being resolved, this had much to do with the fact that there had been just one polity, one *imperium* – encompassing, at least, Rome and Constantinople. It is no coincidence that the last of the seven councils (Nicaea II, 787 AD) regarded as ecumenical by East and West alike occurred only about a dozen years before this imperial unity was brought to an end by the crowning of Charlemagne (800 AD). Much has been written about how the establishment of the Carolingian empire was an affront

---

43 O. Kerame, "The Basis for Reunion of Christians: the Papacy Reconsidered," *Journal of Ecumenical Studies* 8:4 (Fall 1971) 803.

44 P. Battifol, *Cathedra Petri: etudes d'histoire ancienne d'eglise*, Unam Sanctam 4 (Paris: Cerf, 1938), 75-76, as quoted by Y. Congar, *After Nine Hundred Years* (New York: Fordham, 1955), 62.

45 Innocent III, Ep. I.354, PL 214, 328C: "... *monemus frat. tuam et exhor. in Domino, per apostolica tibi scripta mandantes quatenus omnimodam sollicitudinem et efficacem operam interponas ut Graecorum universitas redeat ad Ecclesiae unitatem et ad matrem filia revertatur* [... we advise and urge you, dear brother, in the Lord, and through these Apostolic letters, request that you employ every kind of skill and efficacious effort in order that all the Greeks may return to the unity of the Church and that the daughter may return to her mother]". See also S. Runciman, *The Eastern Schism: A Study of the Papacy and the Eastern Churches during the XI*th *and XII*th *Centuries* (Oxford: Clarendon, 1955), 143. See also below, p. 35, n. 78.

to the Byzantines, with some historians of the Church going so far as to suggest that it made the eventual schism inevitable.⁴⁶ However that may be, it is clear that a proper understanding of the ecclesiological differences between East and West in the 11th and 12th centuries cannot be gained without giving due attention to the tension between the two imperial systems operating by then.

1. Rome as *mater ecclesia* according to the western reformers

It has been shown that Rome arrived relatively late at the practice of using the term "mother church" at all, that Rome applied it to itself even later, and that around the end of the 6th century, Pope Gregory the Great characteristically spoke of Rome as the mother of Latin churches like that of Syracuse or those of northern Italy, churches within Rome's immediate jurisdiction, but did not speak of Rome as the mother of all churches in Christendom. By the 16th century, on the other hand, the designation of Rome as the *mater et magistra* of all churches everywhere had become customary: it appears a number of times in the acts of the council of Trent virtually in passing.⁴⁷

Standing in between were the 11th century western reforms. Two examples from that period may be offered that show the new way in which the term "mother church" was applied to Rome and the new emphasis given to it.

The year before Cardinal Humbert of Silva Candida, one of the papal legates charged with restoring relations between Rome and Byzantium at a politically delicate moment in history, anathematized the patriarch of Constantinople during his visit to the imperial capital in 1054, he exchanged polemical letters

---

46 "As regards Byzantium therefore, the coronation on Christmas day of the year 800 was a veritable betrayal; a present-day Catholic historian has gone so far as to write, 'The conferment of the Imperial title upon Charlemagne therefore marks on the part of the Pope, the intention of breaking with the Empire of the East." Y. Congar, *After Nine Hundred Years*, 22, with reference to J. de Pange, *Le Roi Chrétien* (Paris 1949), 167. Also cited in a footnote is Fustel de Coulanges, *Histoire des Institutions politiques*, 6, *Les transformations* (Paris 1892), 312: "The coronation of Charlemagne was, on the part of the Pope, a breach with Constantinople."

47 In Canon 3, for example, of the canons on baptism in Session 7, we read, "If anyone says that in the Roman church (which is the mother and mistress of all the churches) [(quae omnium ecclesiarum mater est et magistra)] there is not the true teaching on the sacrament of baptism: let him be anathema." Norman Tanner, ed., *Decrees of the Ecumenical Council*, Vol. II (London and Washington, DC: Sheed & Ward and Georgetown University Press, 1990), 685. The same phrase appears at several other points in the documents of Trent.

with Leo the Archbishop of Ochrida.[48] Among other concerns, Humbert raised the issue of the title "Ecumenical Patriarch." Humbert's grounds for objecting to it were different from those indicated in the letter of Gregory the Great to John the Faster some four centuries earlier.[49] Gregory's concern had been with the dignity and authority of all the patriarchs. Humbert, however, asserted that the title "Ecumenical Patriarch" was "a usurpation" of the right which belonged to the successors of Peter (who themselves had not even exercised it),[50] and in this letter Humbert spoke of Rome as the "head and mother" of other churches.[51] Here not just all other Latin churches, but all churches everywhere,

---

48 Leo of Ochrid's letter was sent to Bishop John of Trani, a high-ranking Greek prelate appointed by Constantinople to serve in southern Italy with its long tradition of Greek Christianity, but the letter was addressed not only to John but to "all the princes of the Frankish priests, the monks, the people, and the venerable pope himself" (Cf. Cornelius Will, *Acta et scripta, quae de controversiis ecclesiae graecae et latinae saeculo undecimo composita extant* [Leipzig and Marburg, 1861; repr., Frankfort: Minerva, 1963], 56). John had it delivered to the pope through the latter's secretary, namely Humbert, who was allowed access while the pope was under house arrest, a prisoner of the Normans. In Pope Leo IX's name, Humbert then composed the response, addressed to both Michael Cerularius (though Humbert used the title "bishop" instead of "patriarch" for him) and Leo of Ochrid. See Charles Frazee, "1054 Revisited," *Journal of Ecumenical Studies* 42:2 (Spring 2007) 266-267.

49 See above, p. 21.

50 "Qualis vero, et quam detestabilis atque lamentabilis est illa sacrilege usurpatio, qua te universalem patriarcham jactas ubique et scripto et verbo, cum omnis Dei amicus hujusmodi hactenus horruerit honorari vocabulo? Et quis post Christum convenientius posset insigniri hoc vocabulo, quam cui dicitur divina voce: *Tu es Petrus et super hanc petram aedificabo ecclesiam meam (Matth. 16)*, etc. Verumtamen quia ille non invenitur universalis apostolus dictus, quamvis princeps apostolorum sit constitutus, nullus successorum ejus tam prodigioso praenomine consensit appellaripenitus, licet magno Leoni praedecessori nostro et successoribus ipsius hoc sancta decreverit Chalcedonensis synodus" (Cornelius Will, *Acta et scripta*, 90).

51 PL 143, 776A: "Scripsisti siquidem nobis, quoniam si una Ecclesia Romana per nos haberet nomen tuum, omnes Ecclesiae in toto orbe terrarium haberent per te nomen nostrum. Quid hoc monstri est, frater charissime? Romana Ecclesia, caput et mater Ecclesiarum, membra et filias non habet? Et quomodo potest dici caput aut mater? Credimus enim propter quod et loquimur atque constanter profitemur: Romana Ecclesia adeo non est sola, vel sicut tu putas, una, ut in toto orbe terrarium quaecunque natio dissentit superbe ab ea, non sit jam dicenda vel habenda Ecclesia aliqua, sed omnino nulla; quin potius conciliabulum haereticorum, aut conventiculum schismaticorum, et synagoga Satanae." The corresponding text may be found in Will, *Acta*

including in the East, were understood as having a filial relationship to the church of Rome.

In an earlier letter in which Humbert had also had a hand, the prerogatives of Rome were likewise asserted in the strongest possible terms. Peter of Antioch (1028-1051), a moderate compared to some of his Byzantine contemporaries in his attitude toward Latin Christianity, had no reservations about keeping Pope Leo IX's name in the Antiochian diptychs even at a time when relations between Rome and Constantinople had broken down. Yet Peter thought the pope wrong to take a different approach from that of the four eastern patriarchs on the matter of azymes.[52] In discussing this issue in his correspondence with Patriarch Dominic of Grado, head of the Venetian Church (Peter deemed Dominic's title only honorary, since in his view the number of patriarchs was fixed at five), Peter seemed to suggest that in relations among the patriarchs, if there was not unanimity then the view of the majority, rather than simply that of the pope, should be decisive. Peter invoked the promise of Christ to be present whenever two or three were gathered in his name.[53]

A letter reached Peter soon after this – it was again Humbert who drafted it in Pope Leo IX's name – that sought to disabuse Peter of his notions of majority rule. In this letter, the church of Rome was referred to as the mother of the church of Constantinople, and the idea was also emphatically put forward that decisions of the Roman see were beyond appeal to any other tribunal.[54]

---

et scripta, 91-92. See also F. Dvornik, *Byzantium and the Roman Primacy* (New York: Fordham, 1966), 132.

52 The term "azymes" (derived from the Greek word ἄζυμος) refers to the unleavened wafers traditionally used in the eucharist by the western church, whereas in the East leavened bread is traditionally used. For an overview of the historical controversy, see J. Erickson, "Leavened and Unleavened: Some Theological Implications of the Schism of 1054," *St. Vladimir's Theological Quarterly* 14 (1970) 155-176.

53 "Καὶ ὃ ποιεῖν οἱ τῆς ἐκκλησίας τρόψιμοι παρελάβομεν, τοῦτο καὶ ὑμεῖς ποιεῖτε τοὺς τέσσαρσιν ἱεροῖς πατριάρχαις ἑπόμενοι, ὅτι τῶν πλειόνων ἡ ψῆφος χρατεῖ· εἰς δὲ, οὐδείς· ἀγαθοὶ δὲ οἱ δύο ὑπὲρ τὸν ἕτα." C. Will, 224. PG 120, 776B. Cf. Runciman, *The Eastern Schism*, 64.

54 Cf. Leo IX, Ep. 100, PL 143, 761A, where Rome is described as "*illius matris, quae jam cunctis paganorum crudelitatibus et diversorum tormentorum quaestionibus vexata et impugnata, ac, velut aurum, nimiis persecutorum flammis decocta, deliciosam filiam, videlicet Ecclesiam Constantinopolitanam edidit* [that mother, who, though already tormented and buffeted by all kinds of pagan cruelties and the questions of various tormentors, and purified like gold by the innumerable flames of her persecutors, gave birth to a beloved daughter, namely the Church of Constantinople]". See also in the

The reformers' determination to advance such claims was part of a movement to reshape western ecclesiological thought according to the needs then faced by the western church. Of this ecclesiological shift, an overview has been given by Congar:

> From the pen of Leo IX, often held by Humbert of Moyenmoutier, and from that of Gregory VII [Hildebrand], came an abundance of formulations of an ecclesiology of the Church understood as a single society under the authority of the pope. The pope is the universal bishop. The other churches exist because he calls bishops *"in partem sollicitudinis"* [to share his solicitude]. The canonists and theologians who contributed to this enterprise, transposed and attributed to the pope all the prerogatives of the Church; they tended to see the latter as a single diocese, of almost universal extent, and the pope as the source of every determination of its life ...[55].

One of the key factors that made this new self-understanding possible in the first place was the separation already well established by this time between East and West. The degree to which the western reformers were operating without much cognizance of the eastern tradition can be seen from a canonical shift they effected in the West's evaluation of the Ignatian council of 869-870. This council, convened amidst the dispute between Photius and Ignatios as rival claimants to the patriarchal throne in Constantinople, settled the matter by deposing Photius, with the approval of the legates of Pope Adrian II (867-872). Yet within a decade of its being held the council had been overturned by another synod, known as the Photian synod, with broad support in the East and with the express sanction of Adrian's successor, Pope John VIII (872-882).[56] However, the 11th century western reformers came to see in the earlier, Ignatian council a particular resource for carrying out their project: namely, a canon forbidding laymen to interfere in episcopal elections. This canon would be

---

same letter at 765B: "*Et sicut cardo immobilis permanens ducit et reducit ostium, sic Petrus et sui successores liberum de omni Ecclesia habent judicium, cum nemo debeat eorum dimovere statum, quia summa sedes a nemine judicatur* [And just as a stationary and permanent hinge opens and closes a door, so Peter and his successors enjoy unencumbered jurisdiction *(liberum judicium)* concerning all the Church, while no one should take away their standing, because the highest see is judged by no one]."

55 Y. Congar, "De la communion des églises à une ecclésiologie de l'Eglise universelle," in Y. Congar and B.D. Dupuy, eds., *L'Episcopat et l'Eglise Universelle*, Unam Sanctam 39 (Paris: Cerf, 1962), 238.

56 Cf. F. Dvornik, *The Photian Schism: History and Legend* (London: Cambridge University Press, 1948/1970), 309-317.

useful in the battle over investiture, and the reformers therefore went ahead with what amounted to a radical reinterpretation of the past two hundred years of tradition in the West with regard to the councils of 869-870 and of 879-880, respectively. About the former, they revived a short-lived idea – it had had currency only for ten years, and only in the West, from which the East during that decade was separated – that it was to be counted as the eighth ecumenical council. Reviving its status as such would, of course, have a negative impact on current relations with the Byzantine church in the 11th century. But those relations seemed no longer to be given much consideration, since by this time the two sides were estranged and in the West, as Dvornik has observed, the "existence of a Roman Emperor in Constantinople had all but faded from memory."[57] The conclusion drawn by Dvornik is that "the revival of the Eighth Council [i.e., of the idea that the Ignatian Council was the Eighth] by the Western Church would never have taken effect, had it not been for the severance of the Roman and the Byzantine Churches, as contact with the Greeks, so sensitive on this very point, would certainly have served as a powerful brake on the zeal of the canonists of the eleventh and twelfth centuries. This control gone, they found it only too easy to proceed unhindered."[58]

It was in these same circumstances of separation between East and West that the idea of Rome as mother of all the other churches gained prevalence. The same canonists were behind this development as well, and Dvornik's observation applies equally well here, for these canonists in promoting the idea of Rome as the mother of all churches certainly "proceeded unhindered" by what would have been a "powerful brake" exerted by the concerns and emphases of the eastern tradition. The formulation itself of Rome as the *mater ecclesiarum* seems first to have been set forth as early as the 9th century.[59] But the centrality it came to assume in the 11th and 12th centuries and the precise significance it then came to possess were profoundly shaped by the reality of the growing estrangement. Specifically, the separation between East and West made it easier

---

57 Dvornik, *Byzantium and the Roman Primacy*, 127.
58 Dvornik, *The Photian Schism*, 329.
59 According to Andrew Louth, *Greek East and Latin West: the Church AD 681-1071*, Church in History vol. 3 (Crestwood, NY: St. Vladimir's, 2007), 298, the basic assertion that "the Church of Rome was the mother of the Churches, *mater ecclesiarum*, their head, *caput*, and hinge, *cardo*," is able to be traced back to Nicholas I (858-867). Cf. Nicholas I, Ep. 75, PL 119, 905D: "Neque enim tam stolidus tamve poterit traditionis tramite devius inveniri, qui caeteris Ecclesiis privilegia servari et soli Romanae Ecclesiae adimi debere perhibeat, quae omnium Ecclesiarum magistra, mater et caput est."

for the reformers to disregard the meaningful distinction and maternity of any church other than the church of Rome.[60]

2. The 12th century Byzantine understanding of patriarchal sister churches

It was just this point of which certain Byzantine parties in their exchanges with the West sought to remind their interlocutors in the 12th century. They did so by means of the language of sister churches, used in the texts of two Byzantine hierarchs of that period. These were explicit occurrences such as are rarely to be found in the preceding or subsequent centuries, from apostolic times to the modern period. For this reason they have a particular importance for the study of the concept of sister churches. In 1136, the Greek theologian Nicetas, Archbishop of Nicomedia, engaging in a debate in Constantinople with Anselm of Havelberg, offered remarks on Roman primacy in which he invoked the expression "sister churches". Roughly sixty years later, Patriarch John X Camateros used the expression again, in a letter to Pope Innocent III. In modern discussions of the period these two uses of the expression are often treated as though they express one and the same ecclesiology.[61] But while they have certain features in common, there are differences between them of considerable importance.

The debate between Nicetas and Anselm was an official disputation organized by the imperial court and held, in its first phase, in the church of St. Irene in the Pisan quarter of Constantinople before relocating to Hagia Sophia because of the need for more space, given the large number of listeners it had attracted.[62] Anselm, a bishop and diplomat, had been sent to Constantinople by the German emperor Lothair III (1133-1137), who shared with the Byzantine imperial court

---

60 The sense that there was no church of similar standing to the church of Rome was also facilitated by the fact that, as Klaus Schatz has observed, "the two Churches in the West [besides Rome itself] with the strongest internal autonomy, the best-developed self-confidence, and the best-functioning episcopal-synodal structures (the Church of North Africa and that of the Visigoths of Spain) were eliminated by the Arab conquests ... This was also a precondition for the ultimate success of an exclusively 'Roman' influence throughout the West." K. Schatz, *Papal Primacy: From Its Origins to the Present*, trans. John Otto and Linda Maloney (Collegeville, MN: Michael Glazier, 1996), 72-73.

61 See below, Chapter 4, pp. 149-151; 153-154.

62 Cf. Walter Berschin, *Greek Letters and the Latin Middle Ages*, revised and expanded edition, trans. Jerold C. Frakes (Washington, DC: Catholic University, 1988), 220-221. See also H. Chadwick, *East and West: The Making of a Rift in the Church. From Apostolic Times to the Council of Florence* (Oxford and New York: Oxford, 2003), 228.

an interest in warding off the military aggressions of the Norman king Roger in Sicily; Nicetas belonged to a group of twelve official teachers in the Patriarchal Academy who chose him to represent them in the debate with Anselm – he was also spiritual director to Anna Comnena, daughter of the emperor.[63] The speeches of Nicetas from this debate have been preserved only in an account of it written up by Anselm fourteen years later, at Pope Eugenius III's request, and questions about their historical reliability have come increasingly to the fore in recent scholarship.[64] Henry Chadwick calls Anselm's *Dialogi* "a freely developed account of the conversations, based partly on memory, partly on notes by shorthand writers, but substantially adding new matter, evident from the attribution to Nicetas of statements derived wholly from Latin sources such as the *Liber Pontificalis* (e.g. Dial. 3.7, PL 188, 1218A)."[65] In fact, the particular statement noted by Chadwick and others[66] as being attributed to Nicetas but actually derived from the *Liber Pontificalis* is a statement that bears directly on the nature of the Roman primacy as Nicetas, allegedly, understood it. Moreover, this statement (to be examined shortly) is one that, in its comparatively robust conception of the Roman primacy, reflects one of the key differences between Nicetas and Patriarch John X Camateros in their respective ways of putting

---

63 See Chadwick, *East and West*, 228-29; see also Norman Russell, "Anselm of Havelberg and the Union of the Churches," *Sobornost* 1:2 (1979) 19-41, and 2:1 (1980) 29-41, especially at 23.
64 See, for example, Jay T. Lees, *Anselm of Havelberg: Deeds into Words in the Twelfth Century*, Studies in the History of Christian Thought, vol. 79 (Leiden / New York / Köln: Brill, 1998), 6, who observes that the *Dialogi* of Anselm "have too often been taken to represent Anselm's attempt to describe accurately an event from his own life. This they most certainly are not, and their literary nature needs evaluation." See also W.H. Principe, "Monastic, Episcopal, and Apologetic Theology of the Papacy, 1150-1250" in Christopher Ryan, ed., *The Religious Roles of the Papacy: Ideals and Realities, 1150-1300* (Toronto: Pontifical Institute of Medieval Studies, 1989), 132-133, who suggests there is reason to think "that Anselm balances his strongly papalist position by putting into Nicetas' mouth arguments not only of eastern theologians but also of westerners favouring a more conciliarist or synodalist view of the Church over a papal monarchial outlook." Lees (*Anselm of Havelberg*, 262-281) puts forward an interpretation consistent with this. Principe's analysis builds on that of Hermann-Joseph Sieben, "Die eine Kirche, der Papst und die Konzilien in den Dialogen des Anselm von Havelberg," *Theologie und Philosophie* 54 (1979) 219-251.
65 Chadwick, *East and West*, 229. On the correlation between the *Liber Pontificalis* and what Anselm has Nicetas say in the *Dialogi*, see below, p. 33, n. 75.
66 Cf. Russell, "Anselm of Havelberg," 31, n. 6 (in Part II of the article; *Sobornost* 2:1 [1980]).

forward the ecclesiological notion of "sister churches". The question naturally arises whether the difference really owes to any distinctive approach of Nicetas himself, or to Anselm's manner of recollecting and apparently reworking the speeches of his Byzantine partner in their debate.

Interestingly, the views ascribed to Nicetas have almost always been taken as typical of Byzantine ecclesiology of that era. Runciman considered the words Anselm attributed to Nicetas as a faithful expression of "the Byzantine case against the papal claims".[67] Dvornik similarly observed, "These words of Nicetas illustrate very well the position taken by the Byzantine Church."[68] It is not known when Anselm's *Dialogi* were first read by Orthodox theologians and scholars – perhaps not before the modern era – but where the remarks of Nicetas from Anselm's text are noted by recent Orthodox writers this is again done without suspicion. According to Kallistos Ware, "The Orthodox attitude to the Papacy is admirably expressed by a twelfth-century writer, Nicetas, Archbishop of Nicomedia."[69] To whatever extent the speeches ascribed to Nicetas might

---

[67] Runciman, *The Eastern Schism*, 115.

[68] Dvornik, *Byzantium*, 147. One finds a similar assessment in J.M. Hussey, *The Orthodox Church in the Byzantine Empire* (Oxford and New York: Oxford University Press, 1986), 180: "There is no independent account of the Greek side, but Anselm seems to represent the two points of view very fairly."

[69] Timothy Ware (Bishop Kallistos of Diokleia), *The Orthodox Church* (London: Penguin, 1963; repr. 1993), 49-50. Ware even adds (after quoting the passage from Nicetas quoted on pp. 39-40 below), "That was how an Orthodox felt in the twelfth century." See also M. Aghiorghoussis, "'Sister Churches': Ecclesiological Implications," in idem, *In the Image of God* (Brookline, MA: Holy Cross Orthodox Press, 1999), 162. Though focused on a topic other than Roman primacy, a recent ecumenical statement also treats the record of the debate between Anselm and Nicetas at face value and as bearing important testimony. "Anselm and Metropolitan Nicetas of Nicomedia held a series of public discussions about subjects dividing the Churches, including the Filioque, and concluded that the differences between the two traditions were not as great as they had thought (PL 188, 1206B-1210B)." ("The Filioque: a Church-Dividing Issue?" An Agreed Statement of the North American Orthodox-Catholic Theological Consultation, October, 2003, section II, para. 21. Text available in L. Veliko and J. Gros, eds., *Growing Consensus II: Church Dialogues in the United States, 1992-2004* [Washington, DC: USCCB, 2005], 377-401.) So too, in its *Note on the Expression "Sister Churches"* (June, 2000), the Congregation for the Doctrine of the Faith includes reference to Nicetas' alleged comments about Roman primacy and "sister churches" as though these were authentic expressions of a standard Byzantine perspective of the time, indeed indistinguishable from the perspective of John X Camateros later in the same century. See below, Chapter 4, pp. 149-151; 153-154. See,

owe their preserved form to revisions or even inventions of Anselm, in any case their reception, by Orthodox and non-Orthodox alike, as an authentic expression of Byantine thought, cannot be considered somehow merely a mistake. Rather, this reception is itself confirmation of the legitimate place of these speeches within the tradition of the Christian East. It is as properly belonging to this tradition that they are to be treated in the following analysis.

As would be expected, Nicetas' remarks about "sister churches" are closely associated with what he has to say about Roman primacy. How Nicetas understands these two realities as interrelated is indicated in several important ways when he says to Anselm,

> I neither deny nor reject the Primacy of the Roman Church whose dignity you have extolled, since it is read in our ancient histories that there were three patriarchal sister sees, Rome, Alexandria, and Antioch, among which Rome, the highest see in the empire, held the primacy. Thus Rome has been called the first see and it is to her that appeal must be made in doubtful ecclesiastical cases, and it is to her judgment that all matters that cannot be settled according to the normal rules must be submitted.[70]

Three points may be noted from this brief passage. First, for Nicetas, the relationship between the primacy of Rome and the idea of "sister churches" is conceived quite specifically in terms of a relationship between Roman primacy and *patriarchal* sister churches. Although this point may seem obvious, it involves a distinction that is not always observed, as has been seen even in the work of authors who write favorably of the idea of sister churches in the modern era.[71]

---

in addition, J. Spiteris, "Attitudes fondamentales de la théologie byzantine, en face du rôle religieux de la papauté au XIIème siècle," in *The Religious Roles of the Papacy*, op. cit., 171-192, especially at 173-174: "It is not possible to speak of the religious role of the papacy unless one first determines the ideological and theological criteria that inspired the two traditions [eastern and western] during this period and the basis on which they measured and judged this role. We have a typical example, revealing of these two mentalities, in the 'Dialogues' of Anselm, archbishop of Havelberg, with the Greek archbishop Nicetas of Nicomedia, which was held at Constantinople in 1136."

70 Anselm of Havelberg, *Dialogi*, III, vii. PL 188, 1217D-1218A. My translation of this portion of the text closely follows that of Dvornik (*Byzantium*, 145), who, however, unnecessarily renders *quod tres patriarchales sedes sorores fuerant* as "that there were three patriarchal sees closely linked in brotherhood"; I have opted instead for the more succinct and literal "that there were three patriarchal sister sees".

71 Something of this neglect has already been seen in the discussion of Lanne's interpretation of "sister churches" in Basil and Innocent, above, pp. 11-13. See also below, Chapter 4, pp. 117-118.

Nicetas may well have believed that all churches are sisters of one another insofar as they hold the faith in common, but this was not how he used the term. He used it instead – as both Basil and Innocent had done – to describe relations between or among major sees.

A second important point is that there is indication that Nicetas understood the Roman primacy within an imperial context. It was as "the highest see in the empire" that Rome held the primacy from ancient times. Rome's relationship to the *imperium* is a matter which will again arise in another portion of Nicetas' speech.[72]

Third, it should be observed that Nicetas not only recognized Rome's primacy of honor but understood this to involve concrete prerogatives not granted to any other sister church. These pertained especially to outstanding circumstances, those in which "matters ... cannot be settled according to the normal rules." Nicetas is forthright in saying that Rome is the Church to which "appeal must be made in doubtful ecclesiastical cases." Thus any notion of a merely honorary primacy that would have only an ambiguous function within the communion of churches or that would be contingent on whether other churches choose to recognize it is excluded.[73]

In the immediate continuation of the passage quoted above, further light is shed on how Nicetas understood Rome's primacy.

> But the Roman pontiff himself should be called neither the prince of the priesthood, nor the supreme priest, nor anything of that sort, but only the bishop of the first see. For in fact Boniface III, the bishop of Rome, who was Roman by nationality, and the son of John, obtained confirmation from the Emperor Phocas that the apostolic see of the blessed apostle Peter was head of

---

72 See below, p. 34.
73 Brian Daley, "Position and Patronage in the Early Church: the Original Meaning of 'Primacy of Honour'," *Journal of Theological Studies* (New Series) 44 (1993) 533, has convincingly shown that there was no "primacy of honor" without concrete privileges, and that "rank and power" were "inseparable from each other." The same point is made by the Orthodox theologian Vlassios Phidas, "Papal Primacy and Patriarchal Pentarchy in the Orthodox Tradition," in W. Kasper, ed., *The Petrine Ministry: Catholics and Orthodox in Dialogue* (Mahwah, NJ: Newman Press, 2006), 74: "It is evident that the honorary primacy is not a purely honorary privilege, as it is associated with an exceptional authority (*singularis auctoritas*), which consists in guaranteeing the unity of the Church in the true faith and in the canonical discipline." The remarks of Nicetas substantiate the viewpoint of Daley and Phidas and can only be coherently read in accordance with it.

all the Churches, since Constantinople at that time was saying that it was the first among all after the transfer of the empire.[74]

Nicetas held a view of the episcopacy in which members of the episcopal college are members not as individuals but as the heads of their churches. The head of the *entire* college, then, is not "the prince of the priesthood" but "the bishop of the first see". Such is the central point of Nicetas' remarks above. Just as worthy of notice, however, is the fact that in making this point, Nicetas affirms the ecclesial headship of Rome on the universal level against similar claims put forward by Constantinople. Once again it may be observed that Nicetas conceives of Rome's primacy in the context of the Byzantine empire, inasmuch as he says that Pope Boniface III "obtained confirmation from the Emperor Phocas that the apostolic see of the blessed apostle Peter was head of all the Churches". This imperial context in which Nicetas conceived of Rome as the first see no doubt made his conception distinct from the prevailing western conception.

The difference may be perceived in the passage of Nicetas most frequently cited in modern discussions of Roman primacy in the Byzantine perspective.

> But the Roman Church to which we do not deny the primacy among her sisters, and whom we recognize as holding the highest place in any general council, the first place of honor, that Church has separated herself from the rest by her pretensions. She has appropriated to herself the monarchy which is not contained in her office and which has divided the bishops and the churches of the East and the West since the partition of the Empire. When, as a result of these circumstances, she gathers a council of the Western bishops without

---

74   PL 188, 1217D-1218A. The last sentence of this quotation, "Nam et Bonifacius tertius, natione Romanus, urbis Romanae episcopus, ex Patre Joanne, obtinuit apud Phocam principem ut sedes apostolica beati Petri apostoli caput esset omnium Ecclesiarum, quia Constantinopolitana tunc temporis se primam omnium scribebat propter translatum imperium," is the one that Anselm took almost verbatim from the *Liber Ponificalis*, ed. L. Duchesne (Paris, 1886-1892), vol. 1, 316: "Bonifatius, natione Romanus, ex patre Iohanne Cataadioce, sedit mens. VIII dies XXII. Hic optinuit apud Focatem principem ut sedis apostolic beati Petri apostoli caput esset omnium ecclesiarum, quia ecclesia Constantinopolitana prima se omnium ecclesiarum scribebat." What must be kept in mind is the remarkable consistency of this statement with the rest of the comments of Nicetas and with viewpoints elsewhere expressed in the East in the 12th century, e.g. by Zonaras (see below, p. 46, n. 111). Indeed, what may be more surprising is not that Nicetas might have said this, but that it would be found in the *Liber Pontificalis* at all, given how the statement links Rome's primacy to Byzantine imperial confirmation.

making us (in the East) a part of it, it is fitting that her bishops should accept its decrees and observe them with the veneration that is due to them ... but although we are not in disagreement with the Roman Church in the matter of the Catholic faith, how can we be expected to accept these decisions which were taken without our advice and of which we know nothing, since we were not at that same time gathered in council? If the Roman Pontiff, seated upon his sublime throne of glory, wishes to fulminate against us and to launch his orders from the height of his sublime dignity, if he wishes to sit in judgment on our Churches with a total disregard of our advice and solely according to his own will, as he seems to wish, what brotherhood and what fatherhood can we see in such a course of action? Who could ever accept such a situation? In such circumstances we could not be called nor would we really be any longer sons of the Church but truly its slaves.[75]

Several of the same themes running through the passages quoted earlier make their appearance again here: the notion that in its proper form, Rome's primacy is embedded, as it were, within the structure of patriarchal sister churches; the acknowledgment that this primacy carries with it real prerogatives, among which, in this passage, is mentioned the right to preside at ecumenical councils. The concern with conciliarity permeates especially the latter segment of the passage, in which Nicetas draws an intentionally monstrous picture of a papacy so imperious and detached that there is no mutuality at all between Rome and the other major sees. Amidst the florid rhetoric of these descriptive lines, there are substantive points made, two of which have not been seen in the earlier portions of his speech. First, there is the idea that with "the partition of the empire" – an allusion to the crowning of Charlemagne in 800 AD[76] – an imperial element was introduced into the office of the bishop of Rome that from Nicetas' view does not belong to it. This, according to Nicetas, is what has "divided the bishops and the churches of the East and the West" ever since. Second, Nicetas asserts that "we" – evidently a reference to the entire eastern church – "are not in disagreement with the Roman church in the matter of the Catholic faith."

---

75 *Dialogi*, III, PL 188, 1219AD, as quoted by Dvornik, *Byzantium*, 145-146.
76 See the specific reference to Charlemagne by Nicetas, PL 188, 1231A. Spiteris, "Attitudes fondamentales de la théologie byzantine," op. cit., 178, comments about this that from Nicetas' point of view, "The churches were divided because the empire was divided; and the responsibility was entirely that of the pope, who had committed an act of betrayal in crowning Charlemagne."

Chapter 1: The Concept of "Sister Churches" prior to Vatican II 35

The next use of the expression "sister churches" by a Byzantine churchman in response to Roman claims occurred at the end of the 12th century. Pope Innocent III had raised the issue of Rome's status relative to the other patriarchal sees in a letter to Emperor Alexius in 1198. This letter by Innocent was written in response to imperial overtures to forge a military alliance between the Latins and Byzantines. Though generally favorable to the emperor's suggestion, the pope had replied that the church of Constantinople must first recognize the supremacy of the see of Rome; and here he spoke in terms of Rome as mother church and Constantinople as daughter church.[77] After the emperor sent a cautiously critical reply, a more elaborate response was sent from Patriarch John X Camateros. John was especially surprised at Rome's claim to be the mother of all the other churches, for it was his understanding that if any church was to be so considered, it should be the church of Jerusalem.[78]

---

77 Innocent III, Ep. I.354, PL 214, 327A: "Studeas etiam, imo sicut potes efficias ut Graecorum Ecclesia redeat ad sedis apostolicae unitatem et ad matrem filia revertatur [Strive then, however you can, to bring it about that the Church of the Greeks return to the unity of the Apostolic See and that the daughter be returned to her mother]." Cf. Runciman, *The Eastern Schism*, 142. See also above, p. 22, n. 45.

78 The patriarch's letter is quoted in Innocent III, Ep. II.208, PL 214, 757-758: "Et quomodo erit quod apud vos Romanorum Ecclesia mater, ut dixisti, communis aliarum Ecclesiarum, et secundum quas aliquas rationes et per quas unquam causas quaero addiscere dubitans. Quod autem mihi et plus extendit ambiguitatem dicam; et indulge mihi, sacerrime papa, si nunc primo hunc patriarchalem sacrum thronum me ascendentem, nondum de tali hac dubitatione diligentem solutionem addiscere accidit. Audiens enim quis in Psalmis David dicentem matutinis, *Sion dicet: Homo et homo natus est in ea* (Psal. LXXXVI, 5), secundum verum utique verbi et justitiae aequitatem Jerosolymitanam Ecclesiam matrem aliarum Ecclesiarum nominabit, praerogantem secundum fidem tam tempore quam et dignitate. In ea enim utique ut novissimus omnium Christus et natus est secundum carnem et conversatus, et docens atque praedicans nostram fuit salutem, novissime per crucem pro nobis mortem sustinens, lapidem in quo corpus hujus fuit sepultum, depositum ibi reliquit. Clare utique signum suae in terris conversationis ibi Christo discipuli occurrentes crediderunt, hunc filium Deo et Patri consubstantialem esse; quamvis perfectam humanam naturam indutus, sibi secundum substantiam homo tantum in superficie videbatur. Inde Christi mirabilium fons emanavit et inde, ut ex quodam principio, alii quidam exorti sunt divina fluentes fluvii et universum orbem irrigantes, rivos etiam Ecclesiae quae apud vos est replentes. Igitur nunquid ob haec et alia talia quis Jerosolymitanam Ecclesiam matrem omnium dicet Ecclesiarum? Aut non praeornatam praedicationem audisti Pauli? A Jerusalem clare debes incipi." (Cf. Runciman, *The Eastern Schism*, 143; Runciman's citation of Innocent III, Ep. II.211, PL 214, 768-769, seems incorrect.)

The tradition of attributing maternity to Jerusalem has already been noted.[79] Jerusalem's maternity, however, had tended to be understood diachronically, in the literal sense of Jerusalem's having been the ancestral church of all those that came afterwards; it did not generally imply something definite about Jerusalem's authority in the present.[80] Thus when Innocent, in his response to Camateros, explained that Rome's maternity did not have to do with her age but with her dignity,[81] his perspective conformed, in part, to a certain logic that could be found reflected in earlier tradition. Yet it also involved a new application of this logic that left unclear how the traditional roles of the Eastern patriarchates now fit in. Camateros' defensive response focused on that question especially:

> Where do you find in the holy Gospels that Christ said that the Church of the Romans is the head (κεφαλήν) and universal mother (μητέρα γενικήν) and the most catholic of all the churches at the four points of the compass; or by what ecumenical council was what you say about your church decided? ... It is not so, then, for these reasons that Rome is the mother of the other churches, but, as there are five great churches adorned with patriarchal dignity, that of Rome is the first among equal sisters ... So the church of the Romans has the first rank and is worthy of respect only (μόνῳ) on the basis of its dignity, being the first of the other churches which, as sisters (ἀδελφῶν) equal in honour (ὁμοτίμων) and having the same paternity (ὁμοπατρίων) are born of the same heavenly Father from whom, according to scripture, all fatherhood in heaven and on earth derives.[82]

Strictly speaking, Camateros does not deny the status of the church of Rome as the first see. Yet it is evident that compared to Nicetas, Camateros lays con-

---

79 See above, pp. 16-17.
80 The same ecumenical council at which, according to Theodoret's history (see above, p. 17), Jerusalem was called the "mother of all the churches," namely the synod of I Constantinople, accorded more authority in a concrete sense to the sees of both Rome and Constantinople than to Jerusalem. Cf. the famous canon 3 of Constantinople I: "Because it is new Rome, the bishop of Constantinople is to enjoy the privileges of honor after the bishop of Rome." *NPNF*, vol. 14 (2nd ser.), 178.
81 Innocent III, Ep. II.209, PL 214, 763CD: "cum Ecclesia Romana mater dicatur, non ratione temporis, sed ratione potius dignitatis". Runciman's citation in *The Eastern Schism*, 143 again seems incorrect when he refers to Innocent III, Ep. II.211.
82 For the full Greek text from which this excerpt is taken, see A. Papadakis and Alice Mary Talbot, "John X Camaterus Confronts Innocent III: An Unpublished Correspondence," in *Byzantinoslavica* 33 (1972) 36. With some adjustments, my translation follows that given by Congar, *Diversity and Communion*, 87.

siderably more emphasis on the equal dignity of the five major sees and considerably less on the singular primacy of Rome. Camateros does not enumerate, as Nicetas did, any concrete prerogatives of the church of Rome not granted to the other sister sees. By his use of the word "only" (μόνῳ), he implies a weak sense of these prerogatives. The overwhelming idea conveyed by Camateros is that of the *sameness* of the sister patriarchal sees. He refuses to affirm, as Nicetas had in some sense, that the church of Rome is the head of the other churches. The one-sidedness of Innocent's remarks seems to have elicited a comparably one-sided response.

IV. The imperial factor

The exchange between Innocent III and John Camateros is the last known attempt of the Roman and Byzantine churches to overcome their estrangement prior to the Fourth Crusade in 1204. Soon thereafter, when Patriarch John died, in 1206, a Latin named Morossini was appointed by Rome as patriarch of Constantinople against the will of the Greeks, who appointed a new one of their own.[83] Pope Innocent IV (1243-1254) seemed to have this moment in mind when, at the Council of Lyons in 1245, he looked back and decried the "schism of Romania, that is, of the Greek Church, which in our own time, only a few years ago, arrogantly and foolishly seceded itself from the bosom of its mother as though she were a step-mother."[84]

In his essential intuition, Pope Innocent IV seems to have been correct to draw a link between the Byzantine rejection of the Latin patriarch appointed by Rome in Constantinople and the Byzantine rejection more generally of the idea of Rome as its mother. The appointment of the Latin patriarch in the imperial capital must be seen in association with Rome's emergent self-understanding as mother of all the other churches – an emergent self-understanding whose principles were worked out without regard for the eastern tradition.

It may now be asked, however, whether Rome's growing insistence on being the mother of all churches, including the eastern churches, and its proportionate aversion to counting itself any longer as one of the patriarchal sister sees

---

83 See Chadwick, *East and West*, 235-37.
84 "Alium, quem pro schismate Romaniae, id est, Graecae ecclesiae, quae nostris temporibus et paucis evolutis annis a gremio matris suae, velut novercae, insolenter et insolerter decisa est et aversa." Matthew Paris, *Chronica Majora*, ed. Henry Richards Luard (London: Longman, 1872-1873), vol. 4, 434. The inference about Innocent's dating of the schism is made by Runciman, *The Eastern schism*, 160.

(which the Byzantines continued to regard it as being), actually represented an intrinsic rejection of the Pentarchy – the idea of the direction of the universal church by the patriarchs of the five principal sees – on the level of ecclesiological principle. The following pages suggest that it was, instead, the imperial system to which the eastern patriarchs belonged that Rome was rejecting.

1. Sister churches in a single Christian empire

The theory of the Pentarchy as this developed in the 6th century[85] met with little or no objection from Rome. This is largely because in its initial conception, as Dvornik observes, the theory "did not at all suppose absolute equality among the patriarchs," but was essentially "an expression of the universality of the Church," which "aimed at safeguarding the rights of the *Sacerdotium* which the *Imperium* should never infringe."[86] In Rome itself there were highly placed proponents of the theory of the Pentarchy as late as 870.[87]

The relationship that was most thorny during this period seems not to have been that between Rome and any of the eastern patriarchates in themselves, fraught with tensions though their interactions could be. On a more fundamental level, the truly ambiguous and volatile relationship was that between the pope's primacy in the Church and the ecclesiastical function of the Byzantine emperor. Nor did this ambiguity always sort itself out neatly along East-West lines during the first millennium. At times, western officials, and even popes themselves, could express rather "caesaropapist" ideas about the emperor's role. In a letter of Leo the Great (440-461) addressed to the Byzantine emperor (also named Leo), the pope invited imperial intervention into the affairs of the

---

85 The idea is expressed for the first time in the legislation of Justinian. Cf. Dvornik, *Byzantium*, 75-76. The five patriarchates of the Pentarchy were Jerusalem, Antioch, Alexandria, Constantinople, and Rome.

86 Dvornik, *Byzantium*, 103.

87 In the preface to his translation into Latin of the Acts of the Council of 869-870, the Librarian of the Roman Church, Anastasius, generally considered the most learned Roman ecclesiastic of the 9th century, expressed as follows the Roman conception of the Pentarchy: "Just as Christ has placed in His Body, that is to say, in His Church, a number of patriarchs equal to the number of the senses in the human body, the well being of the Church will not suffer as long as these sees are of the same will, just as the body will function properly as long as the five sense remain intact and healthy. And because, among them, the See of Rome has precedence, it can well be compared to the sense of sight which is certainly the first of the senses of the body, since it is the most vigilant and since it remains, more than any of the other senses, in communion with the body." Mansi, 16, 7, as translated and quoted by Dvornik, *Byzantium*, 104.

Church of Alexandria in order to oppose a faction there that the pope regarded as usurpers. Pope Leo urged the emperor "unhesitatingly to consider that the kingly power has been conferred on you not for the governance of the world alone but more especially for the guardianship of the Church".[88] Even into the 12th century one can find vestiges of this thinking in the West. A letter of Peter the Venerable, the last of the great abbots of Cluny, to the Byzantine emperor John II Comnenus around the year 1120, still speaks of the emperor as the one who "has been appointed to watch over all the Churches of the world."[89] Meanwhile among hierarchs in the East, where the emperor's administrative power in the Church had never been regarded as absolute in the first place,[90] assertions were sometimes made about Rome's authority that could sound rather "papalist". The following comment of the iconodule Patriarch Nicephorus, speaking of the just completed seventh ecumenical council, is an example:

> This Synod possesses the highest authority ... In fact it was held in the most legitimate and regular fashion conceivable, because according to the divine rules established from the beginning it was directed and presided over by that glorious portion of the Western Church, I mean by the Church of Ancient Rome. Without them [the Romans], no dogma discussed in the Church, even sanctioned in a preliminary fashion by the canons and ecclesiastical usages, can be considered to be approved, or abrogated; for they are the ones, in fact, who possess the principate of the priesthood and who owe the distinction to the leader of the Apostles.[91]

In speaking of II Nicaea (787) as possessing the "highest authority," Nicephorus did not mean that councils have more authority than popes, as would later be claimed by western conciliarism (and some modern Orthodox versions of the same). Rather, he meant to draw a contrast between two imperially convened councils – namely, this orthodox one, Nicaea II (787 AD), which had the support of Rome, and the recent iconoclast council, Hieria (753 AD), which had

---

88 Leo the Great, *Ep. 119*, NPNF, vol. 12 (2nd ser.), 100
89 Runciman, *The Eastern Schism*, 114, with reference to Peter's Ep. 39, PL 189, 260C: "Gratias omnipotenti Regi regum, cujus regnum regnum est omnium saeculorum, qui imperatoriam majestatem vestram super omnes Christiani nominis principes exaltavit, et ad tuendam toto orbe Ecclesiam suam, velut in medio Orientis, Occidentis, Aquilonis constituit."
90 See Deno John Geanakoplos, *Byzantine East and Latin West* (New York: Harper Torchbooks, 1966), especially the chapter "Church and State in the Byzantine Empire: A Reconsideration of the Problem of Caesaropapism," 55-83.
91 PG 100, 597A, 621D, as quoted by Dvornik, *Byzantium*, 96.

not. For Nicephorus, legitimate conciliarity and Roman primacy were mutually compatible and necessary. Indeed, Nicephoras was as much a promoter of the idea of the Pentarchy as he was of Roman primacy.[92] A similar pattern may be seen earlier with respect to Maximos the Confessor during the monothelite controversy.[93] Maximos, who, like Nicephorus later, faced circumstances in which the imperial power had set itself in opposition to what would emerge as the orthodox party in the Church, was led to write that the chair of the see of Rome had received "the power to issue commands to all the holy churches of God in the entire world".[94]

2. Sister churches amidst imperial division

How these appeals to Rome's authority made by champions of orthodoxy in the East, e.g., during the periods of imperially sanctioned monothelitism and iconoclasm, differed from the later appeals to Rome's authority made by the Gregorian reformers in the West was that in the latter case there was a greater sense of freedom in challenging not only individual emperors fallen into heresy, but the whole imperial structure. The response of eastern hierarchs and faithful, however strong their objections in a particular case, was invariably more conservative. If an emperor arose who turned out to be not a guardian of the church but a tyrant, there would certainly be suffering as a consequence, but the workings of providence were still to be trusted to bring down that emperor eventually, and to elevate a better one.

The persistence of the Byzantine belief in the enduring reality of a single Christian empire has been described in the following way by Meyendorff:

> Another essential element of the Byzantine world-view was an immoveable vision of the empire's traditional borders. At no time – not even in the fourteenth and fifteenth centuries – did the Byzantines abandon the idea that the empire included both East and West ... and that the "Old Rome" somehow remained its historical source and symbolic center in spite of the transfer of the

---

92 See Dvornik, *Byzantium*, 101-102.
93 For an extensive treatment of the controversy surrounding monothelitism and the theological contribution of Maximos, see Cyril Hovorun, *Will, Action and Freedom: Christological Controversies in the Seventh Century* (Leiden; Boston: Brill, 2008).
94 As quoted by Dvornik (*Byzantium,* 91), who cites the letter of Maximos to Rome, to the illustrious Peter (PG 91, 137-140, 144). Maximos at the same time placed great importance on the fact that "the supreme power which the bishop of Rome holds over the Church has been confirmed by the councils." (Cf. Dvornik, *Byzantium,* 98, n. 15 where the Latin text is given [Mansi, 10, 692]).

capital to Constantinople. There were theological polemics against the "Latins"; there was popular hatred of the "Franks," especially after the Crusades ... but the ideal vision of the universal empire remained ... As late as 1393, patriarch Anthony of Constantinople, in his oft-quoted letter to the grand-prince Basil I of Moscow urging him not to oppose the liturgical commemoration of the emperor in Russian churches, expresses the utterly unrealistic but firm conviction that the emperor is "emperor and *autokrator* of the Romans, that is of all Christians"; that "in every place and by every patriarch, metropolitan and bishop the name of the emperor is commemorated wherever there are Christians ..." and that "even the Latins, who have no communion whatsoever with our Church, give to him the same subordination, as they did in past times, when they were united with us." Characteristically, the patriarch maintains the existence of an imperial unity *in spite of the schism dividing the churches*.[95]

The same letter of patriarch Anthony to prince Basil I contains the statement, "It is impossible for Christians to have the Church, but not to have the Emperor."[96] Although some measure of reverence toward the Byzantine emperor may have lingered in the West as well, even into the 12th century, it was not to last much longer. Congar writes that already by the eleventh century, western canonical authorities were declaring "that there could be but one Emperor, as there was but one *Orbis*, and that Emperor must be Roman. The *Basileus* of Constantinople was therefore no longer the true Emperor, since he was in schism."[97] After the existence of the two empires of East and West had become a settled reality, then for Rome to acknowledge itself as a sister church of the Eastern sees would really have been tantamount to opting back into Byzantine imperial unity.[98]

---

95 Meyendorff, *Rome, Constantinople, Moscow*, 89 (original emphasis). The letter of Patriarch Anthony to Basil I is preserved in the patriarchal register published by F. Miklosich and I. Müller, *Acta patriarchatus Constantinopolitani* I (Vienna, 1862), 188-192. The relevant passages are translated in J.W. Barker, *Manuel II Palaeologus (1391-1425)* (New Brunswick, NJ: Rutgers University Press, 1969), 106-109.

96 The letter was written sometime between 1394 and 1397, and the statement in question was a direct rebuke to Basil I for having said, "we have the Church, but not the emperor". See Dimitri Obolensky, *The Byzantine Commonwealth* (New York: Praeger, 1971), 264.

97 Cf. Congar, *After Nine Hundred Years*, 22. Congar notes that in practice, the Byzantine *Basileus* did continue to be treated as Emperor.

98 Interestingly, this was not considered to be out of the question even as late as the latter decades of the 12th century, when, according to Runciman (*The Eastern Schism*, 120), Pope Alexander III was still uncertain that the existence of a western empire

Why Rome no longer believed in the Byzantine empire and in its own traditional place in it is a complex question. Any answer to it must take into account the failure of imperial policy, and of imperially sanctioned synods, to uphold orthodoxy through most of the iconoclast controversy of the 8th and 9th centuries.[99] As has been seen, this failure led some of the most ardent champions of orthodoxy in the East during that time to lay remarkable emphasis on Rome's authority themselves,[100] even as they also upheld the ideal of the pentarchy, demonstrating that in the first millennium, primacy and pentarchy were complementary rather than conflicting principles.

By the same token, and as has also been suggested, when Rome refused early in the second millennium to be counted any longer as one among several sister patriarchal sees, the patriarchal prerogatives of the eastern sees were not Rome's real target; the real target was the Byzantine imperium.

A consideration of resurfacing tensions between pope and emperor at the Council of Ferrara-Florence (1438-1445) aimed at reuniting the Greek and Latin churches – and of the pope's eventual acknowledgment there, however grudging, of a traditional fraternity between himself and Patriarch Joseph of Constantinople (1416-1439) – will further support this conclusion. The historian Deno Geanakoplos has written that at Florence, even "the ceremony for the signing of the document of religious union was held up over a severe argument between emperor and pope as to who first should sign his name to the forms. The argument hinged on [the] question of who had the authority to call the council into being in the first place."[101]

Tensions of the same sort had arisen over the seating arrangement in the cathedral at Ferrara where the Council convened before it was moved to Florence. Pope Eugenius IV wished to be in the middle, with Greeks to his right and Latins to his left. Emperor John Palaeologus objected, seeing it as his own prerogative to preside over ecumenical councils. The solution that was finally achieved indicates that the main consideration in the dispute concerned issues of polity. The papal throne was placed, as the Greeks wished, on the Latin side,

---

was a good idea in the first place and wondered "whether it might not be wiser to recognize [the Byzantine] Manuel as the sole legitimate Emperor."

99 For an overview of the controversy surrounding icons in Byzantium, see Ambrosios Giakalis, *Images of the Divine: The Theology of Icons at the Seventh Ecumenical Council* (Leiden; Boston: Brill, 2005).
100 See above, pp. 39-40.
101 Geanakoplos, *Byzantine East and Latin West*, 68.

but was elevated above all others including that of the emperor.[102] For the emperor of the West, another throne which corresponded to that of the Greek Basileus was set up on the Latin side – and left vacant due to the emperor's recent death. Meanwhile the seat of the patriarch of Constantinople, placed naturally among the Greeks, was at an ecclesiologically awkward elevation, neither quite here nor there, comparable to that of the highest ranking Roman cardinal. "Thus, contrary to traditional Byzantine theories, the Greeks at least symbolically were forced to recognize the supremacy of papal theocratic theory over both their emperor and patriarch."[103] Although "traditional Byzantine theories" may have suffered defeat in the matter of the seating arrangement, they did, in some sense, prevail at Ferrara-Florence in regard to another circumstance. When he arrived from Constantinople, Patriarch Joseph had refused to greet the pope by genuflecting and kissing his foot as was customary in the West. This refusal did not seem to reflect any anti-Latin sentiment on Joseph's part. The patriarch was an advocate of union with Rome according to the contemporary diary of Silvester Syropoulos, "who reports that the patriarch confided to intimates his hope that papal co-operation would permit him to cast aside the Greek church's servitude to the emperor and 'to recover the authority proper to me.' ... But the patriarch was disillusioned ... when he heard of Eugenius' demand that he kiss the pope's foot."[104] Geanakoplos observes that when the patriarch demanded to know what right the pope had to demand such subservience from him, "the Latin bishops replied that it was an ancient custom for all to kiss the pope's foot," including bishops and kings as well as the "emperor of the Germans."[105] The patriarch's response is unsurprising: "This is an innovation and I will not follow it."[106] He went on, "If the pope wants a brotherly embrace in accordance with ancient ecclesiastical custom, I will be happy to embrace him, but if he refuses, I will abandon everything and return to Constantinople."[107]

As it transpired, the patriarch was allowed to greet the pope without kissing his foot. But he was permitted this patriarchal dignity only so long as the encounter occurred in the pope's private quarters, "where few western eyes could

---

102 Geanokaplos, *Byzantine East and Latin West*, 97.
103 Ibid. 98.
104 Ibid. 95, with reference to Syropoulos, 93.
105 Ibid. 95.
106 Ibid. 95, quoting Syropoulos, 95.
107 Ibid. 95, quoting Syropoulos, 95.

witness the omission of this mark of subordination."[108] The political more than – as we would conceive it today – ecclesiological concern determining the manner and place in which the encounter between pope and patriarch was allowed to occur is significant. It shows that the reintroduction, into the new atmosphere of the West, of the older patriarchal dignities of the Byzantine world threatened to upset the order painstakingly established in the West by the 11th century reformers. This older reality of a patriarchal brotherhood, in which the bishop of Rome was included, had to be kept hidden. But that it was acknowledged at all is of no small significance. The West may have been strongly disinclined to remember the tradition of patriarchal sees ongoing in the East, but with strong enough prodding, it could still be made to do so.

If, in view of the above, it might be suggested that amnesia was the West's besetting temptation in the following centuries of estrangement, it might also be said that nostalgia was the East's. The ambivalence and frustration of Joseph is emblematic of how the East's ecclesiology remained in some sense unresolved, although certain core principles at the heart of it were properly in evidence in Joseph's responses at Ferrara. However worthy of preservation these principles may have been, in actuality, they were able to be lived out in only a very limited way. Well before the disappointment at Ferrara, the circumstances in which Joseph had found himself as patriarch of Constantinople were already profoundly unsatisfactory to him. As was noted above, Joseph felt that the Greek church was in servitude and his own proper authority suppressed or compromised by the position of the church vis-à-vis the Byzantine imperial power.[109] At the same time, such a sea change as had occurred in the West, with the utterly transformed arrangement there of relations between the papal and imperial powers, was too much for Joseph to absorb or accept when he discovered it upon arriving in Ferrara. He was unsatisfied to be in "servitude" to the emperor but unwilling, as well, to agree to give himself over to only another kind of subjection to a new kind of pope. No viable alternative availed him. In the end, Joseph's ecclesiological principles – although they did prevail in a technical sense in his encounter with the pope – still remained at a certain remove from visible history, from the actual public sphere, at least in the West at that time, and for a long time to come.

Yet by stopping Patriarch Joseph from returning – to what was for him a more familiar, but hardly more satisfactory, eastern world increasingly sealed off from the western world – Rome showed that it really did not, in the end,

---

108 Ibid. 95, with reference to Syropoulos, 96.
109 Ibid. 95, quoting Syropoulos, 93.

reject the traditional idea of the Pentarchy on the properly ecclesiological plane. It had only suppressed it in the circumstances, out of a fierce determination not to lose what gains it had made since the investiture controversy in securing the power of the *Sacerdotium* over the *Imperium*. Ultimately, therefore, the ecclesiology of sister churches was never fully renounced by Rome, notwithstanding its claim to be the mother of all the other churches.

3. Sister churches in a post-imperial context

Prior to Constantine, the concept of sister churches is discernible only indirectly and only in a sense applicable to all churches *qua* churches. With the rise of the Byzantine empire, there began to be hints of an emerging understanding of sister churches in a more special sense applicable only to some churches having priority over others. This latter understanding of sister churches was intrinsic to the theory of the pentarchy first put forward in the 6th century under Justinian. So long as the church of Rome together with the four eastern patriarchates that made up the pentarchy belonged together to the same imperial polity, then the idea of patriarchal sister churches, whereby Rome was the first among them, was generally accepted and even embraced by Rome, even if below the surface there may have been differences all along in how the pope and the eastern patriarchs construed the theory, particularly in terms of how Rome's primacy exactly fitted into it. It was only, in any case, after Rome made itself independent from the Byzantine empire – a development Rome undertook for defensible reasons, yet also with doubts of its own – that the idea of patriarchal sister churches (as put forward, for example, by Nicetas in his debate with Anselm) no longer was viewed favorably in Rome. In the East, the theory not only continued to find favor, but, as a bulwark against the *imperium* (as it always had been) took on importance in a new direction now that imperial functions were being performed with increasing assertiveness by the Roman church. It is at this time and for this reason that "sister churches" opposed itself to Rome as "mother of all churches," the latter designation seeming to bear an imperial more than a strictly ecclesiological meaning, as is illustrated by the establishment in Constantinople of a Latin Patriarchate after the 4th Crusade.[110]

As the estrangement gradually hardened and widened in the centuries that followed, patriarchal collegiality continued to be emphasized in the East – sometimes more in theory than in practice, as the Arab conquests had left all

---

110 Dvornik writes (*Byzantium and the Roman Primacy*, 155), "It was only after the conquest of Constantinople by the Latins that the Byzantines fully understood the development that had taken place in the idea of the Roman Primacy."

but Constantinople in decrepitude, and then in new ways with the conversion of Russia and the rise of Moscow as a patriarchal see. More than ever, it depended for its functioning on either the primacy of Constantinople[111] or on the unifying function of the emperor.[112]

Although very soon there was to be no more Byzantine empire, the idea of it was to live on in the consciousness of Orthodox Christianity as "Byzance-après-Byzance."[113] Only gradually has this faded, and still in modern times it has perhaps not faded altogether. And at the same time in the West, through the period of the "Syllabus of Errors"[114] and beyond, the imperial prerogatives of the church of Rome were firmly upheld even into the 20th century, though in practical reality they were less and less capable of having an impact on actual

---

111 As emphasized for example by Anna Comnena, who, contrary to the Byzantine canonist Zonaras, regarded Constantinople as Rome's successor, i.e. replacement. "The truth is that when power was transferred from Rome to our country and the Queen of Cities, not to mention the senate and the whole administration, the senior archbishopric was also transferred here. From the beginning the emperors have acknowledged the primacy of the Constantinopolitan bishop, and the Council of Chalcedon especially raised that bishop to the place of highest honour and subordinated to him all dioceses throughout the world." *The Alexiad of Anna Comnena*, I, xiii, trans. E.R.A. Sewter (London; New York: Penguin, 1969), 62. By contrast, Zonaras insisted that in describing Constantinople as second after Rome, the preposition "after" (μετα), must be interpreted in a hierarchical, not a chronological sense. See his remarks on canon 3 of I Constantinople, canon 28 of Chalcedon, and canon 36 of Trullo (*NPNF*, vol. 14 [2nd ser.], 178). A modern Orthodox scholar of canon law, Archbishop Peter L'Huiller, has observed about Chalcedon canon 28 that "neither the authors of the motion nor the fathers of Chalcedon who approved it had any intention of putting in doubt the primacy of Old Rome." Peter L'Huiller, *The Church of the Ancient Councils* (Crestwood, NY: St. Vladimir's Seminary, 1996), 272.
112 Here we may recall the remark quoted earlier of Patriarch Anthony, very shortly before the fall of the Byzantine empire. To Prince Basil I in Russia, he wrote expressing the conviction that without the emperor, there was no Christianity. See above, p. 41, n. 96.
113 See the classic study of that title by N. Iorga (Bucharest: Editions de l'Institut d'études Byzantines, 1935), available in English translation as *Byzantium after Byzantium*, trans. Laura Treptow (Portland, OR: Center for Romanian Studies, in Cooperation with the Romanian Institute of International Studies, 2000).
114 Issued by Pius IX in 1864 in response to many of the intellectual and political currents of modernism, the "Syllabus of Errors" continued to put forward as normative a vision in which the Catholic religion would be enforced by the State to the exclusion of other forms of worship (see no. 77).

events. This did not change the fact, however, that on the level of ecclesiastical consciousness, there persisted two imperial polities.

Only with the Second Vatican Council did this bifurcation on the level of the imperium really begin to be overcome.[115] It was then that the possibility opened up again for pope and patriarch – no longer yoked, in either case, to an imperial system – to regard themselves as brother bishops of sister churches. This was demonstrated by the revival of the actual use of the expression sister churches, not only by eastern hierarchs from whom it might have been expected, but, with unprecedented clarity and frequency, by popes. It was demonstrated as well by the dramatic gesture – the very antithesis of the choreography at Ferrara-Florence – of Pope Paul VI's falling down at the feet of the delegate of the Ecumenical Patriarchate, Metropolitan Meliton, during the latter's visit to the Sistine Chapel in Rome in 1975.[116] It is to this period in which the concept of sister churches was reintroduced into the relationship between Orthodox East and Catholic West that we now turn.

---

115 Often with reference to the "Decree on Religious Liberty" in its shift from the view that Catholicism should be the officially established religion of all nations, many commentators have spoken of Vatican II as marking the "end of the Constantinian era". See, among many other examples, John O'Malley, "The Style of Vatican II," *America* 188 (February 24, 2003) 12-15.

116 For an account of this dramatic incident, see E.J. Stormon, ed., *Towards the Healing of Schism: the Sees of Rome and Constantinople. Public statements and correspondence between the Holy See and the Ecumenical Patriarchate, 1958-1984* (Mahwah, NJ: Paulist Press, 1987), 293-295, no. 337.

Chapter 2
MODERN DEVELOPMENT OF THE USE OF "SISTER CHURCHES" IN CATHOLIC-ORTHODOX RELATIONS: 1958-1972

This chapter focuses on usage of the expression "sister churches" between Catholics and Orthodox from its emergence in the modern era to the stage when, as will be seen, it had become customary on both sides. Although the expression itself was used for the first time in 1962, the year 1958 serves as an appropriate starting point, both because the so-called "dialogue of love" between Constantinople and Rome, initiated in 1958 upon the election of Pope John XXIII, provided the context in which the expression was to come to the fore, and because closely related language which, in retrospect, may be seen as having had a certain affinity with "sister churches" was already being used in the late 1950s.

The rationale for choosing the year 1972 as the outer limit of the initial period of the expression's use is perhaps less easy to explain. We will see that already by the end of 1969, usage of the phrase by Catholic officials, which had lagged behind Orthodox usage, was now fully established. Also by 1969, all the various ways that the phrase *could* be used essentially *had* been, by representatives of both traditions. The year 1972 has been chosen nonetheless, in part because it was in that year that Athenagoras, who since mid-century had presided as Ecumenical Patriarch, died and was succeeded by Dimitrios I. In addition, the year 1972 saw the distribution of the first edition of the *Tomos Agapis* – the collection of letters, telegrams, and occasional addresses exchanged between Rome and Constantinople, which represents the primary source of material for this part of our study. Finally, for reasons not entirely clear, there is a relative paucity of substantive correspondence between the Vatican and the Phanar in the years 1970 (when only three brief communications were sent) and 1971 (when five were sent, some lengthy, yet still representing a small output altogether). For organizational convenience it seemed sensible, therefore, to include in the initial period the exchanges of those two subsequent years, even though 1969 itself might have functioned as a more proper point of demarcation. The division of the modern material at all into earlier and later periods is, in a sense, artificial – we will see in the next chapter that there was a great deal of continuity between the two periods – but it has the advantage of highlighting the fact that, for a time, use of the expression "sister churches" in Catholic-Orthodox relations was in a formative stage, whereas later on, it was a standard feature of the dialogue.

Yet even long after its sheer presence on the scene had become secure by the late 1960s and early 1970s, its actual meaning had not. Moreover, the difficulty of pinning this meaning down did not often seem to be much noticed by, or to give much pause to, those who employed it. Only rarely did they themselves allude to any ambiguity surrounding the term they were using. The reader, however, is likely to be struck by such an ambiguity on a number of occasions as examples of the expression's use are presented in this chapter. From time to time, interpretive difficulties will be noted in connection with the examples provided here, but for the most part, discussion and analysis of these difficulties will await the next chapter. The objective of the present chapter is limited primarily to showing the chronological development of the use of the term. In the process, the full range of the different *types* of usage will be effectively laid out, but without yet being given the systematic treatment that will follow in Chapter 3.

I. Background

In 1920, the Synod of the Ecumenical Patriarchate issued an encyclical "Unto the Churches of Christ Everywhere". The encyclical urged "that above all, love should be rekindled and strengthened among the [various separated] churches, so that they should no more consider one another as strangers and foreigners, but as relatives ".[1] Here an idea of family ecclesial relations cutting across confessional boundaries is expressed. However, where the specific phrase "sister churches" was used in the same document, it was still reserved for the relationship among Orthodox churches.[2]

By the late 1950s when Angelo Giuseppe Roncalli was elected Pope John XXIII, Protestant and Orthodox participants in a number of international ecumenical conferences had been actively seeking principled means for overcoming disunity among separated Christian communions,[3] while Catholic

---

1 Encyclical of the Ecumenical Patriarchate, 1920. The text in English is available in Michael Kinnamon and Brian E. Cope, eds., *The Ecumenical Movement: An Anthology of Key Texts and Voices* (Geneva and Grand Rapids, MI: WCC Publications and Eerdmans, 1997), 11-14.
2 Ibid. 12.
3 E.g., at Edinburgh (World Missionary Conference, 1910), Stockholm (Universal Christian Conference on Life and Work, 1925), Lausanne (First World Conference on Faith and Order, 1927), Oxford (Conference on Church, Community and State, 1937), Edinburgh again (Second World Conference on Faith and Order, 1937) and Amsterdam (First Assembly of the World Council of Churches, 1948).

theologians (Yves Congar being one of the most notable among them) had been busy behind the scenes working out the principles according to which the Catholic Church might participate in the movement. Roncalli himself had made many contacts with Orthodox Christians during his appointments as Apostolic Visitor to Bulgaria (1925-1935) and as Apostolic Delegate to Turkey and Greece (1935-1944), experiences which surely contributed to his decision shortly into his pontificate to announce "an Ecumenical Council for the universal Church" (1959)[4] – meant in part as an appeal to unity to communities separated from Rome – and to establish the Vatican Secretariat for Promoting Christian Unity (SPCU) (1960). The SPCU's founding purpose was that of enabling "those who bear the name of Christian but are separated from this Apostolic See ... to follow the work of the [upcoming] Council and to find more easily the path by which they may arrive at the Unity Jesus Christ sought from His Heavenly Father with fervent prayers."[5]

The initiative to forge closer relations especially between the Orthodox and Catholic Churches was coming not only from the Catholic side. Ecumenical Patriarch Athenagoras, already in 1958, with the illness and death of Pope Pius XII and the election of Roncalli as his successor, issued a series of press communiqués respectively expressing sympathy, sorrow and joy as well as solidarity in prayer with the "venerable Church of Rome."[6] Athenagoras, born Aristoklos Spyrou, had made a point of getting to know Catholics as he had continued his French language studies at the school of the Marian Brothers in Bitolj (in what today is Serbia) while serving there as an archdeacon early in the 20th century. As Archbishop of North and South America, he publicly embraced Archbishop (and later, Cardinal) Richard Cushing of Boston in what the caption of one newspaper photograph of the incident dubbed, "The first embrace between East and West." This encounter took place in 1947, a year before Athenagoras was elected Ecumenical Patriarch.[7]

---

4   AAS 51 (1959) 69.
5   *Superno Dei Nutu*, AAS 52 (1960) 436. English translation in Stormon, *Towards the Healing of Schism*, 31, n. 5.
6   "Press Communication of Patriarch Athenagoras on the death of Pope Pius XII," in Stormon, *Towards the Healing of Schism*, 27, no. 2.
7   Cf. Stormon, *Towards the Healing of Schism*, 5. The photograph and caption of the embrace between Athenagoras and Cushing are mentioned by Thomas Stransky in his introduction to the book. Stransky cites Aristide Panotis, *Les Pacificateurs: Jean XXIII – Athénagoras – Paul VI – Dimitrios* (Athens: Dragon, 1974), 58, as well as George Papaioannou, *From Mars Hill to Manhattan: The Greek Orthodox in America under Patriarch Athenagoras I* (Minneapolis: Light and Life, 1976).

With Roncalli's election roughly a decade later, promise for ongoing improvement in East-West relations in the Church increased further. Just two months into his pontificate, the new Pope issued a Christmas message on unity and peace in which he made particular mention of "the Orthodox Churches (as they are commonly called)."[8] Prior to this point, at least in the post-Tridentine period it had been customary in the Roman Catholic Church to refer to the Orthodox as "dissidents" or "schismatics" and not to dignify them with the designation of "churches."[9] Hence John XXIII's qualification of his use of the designation "Orthodox Churches," which, from the point of view of this study, was obviously a necessary designation representing an intermediate step before there could be any possibility of the use of "sister churches" on the Catholic side to refer to the Orthodox. Those which are not churches at all can hardly be sister churches.

Patriarch Athenagoras was quick to respond to the pope's communication with a New Year's message of January 1, 1959 in which he greeted with joy the

---

8   Stormon, *Towards the Healing of Schism*, 28, no. 4.
9   In the encyclical of Pope Pius XI, *Ecclesiam Dei (On St. Josaphat)*, promulgated November 12, 1923, Orthodox churches are not referred to as churches; instead, those among the Slavs, or Easterners, not in communion with Rome are addressed thus: "We invite most sincerely the Schismatics to join with Us in this unity of the Church" (n. 18). Elsewhere they are designated "Schismatic Easterners" (n. 19) and "Schismatic brethren" (n. 25). In a fairly typical text of the same year, "Les methodes d'apostolat oriental," published in *L'Union des Églises* 2 (1923) – a journal whose title did, admittedly, attribute some ecclesial status to the Orthodox – Fulbert Cayré wrote as follows of the method of setting up parallel Byzantine Catholic churches in the East: "Here are those who can most effectively work for the Union in the East, those who can directly address the dissidents to propose that they enter into the Roman communion, those who can obtain not just a few rare individual returns, perhaps scattered over several years, as one finds in centers where Latin missionaries are working, but who can bring about numerous returns, and even bring about the return of several important groups at the same time. It is in this way, and this way only, that one can foresee ... the end of the schism. The whole question of the union, therefore, boils down to the formation of an instructed, pious and zealous Eastern Catholic clergy" (p. 198; quoted by R. Roberson, *The Eastern Christian Churches*, 6th edition [Rome: Edizioni Orientalia Christiana, 1999], 195). Note that Cayré, like Pius XI, speaks nowhere of Orthodox *churches* – only of "groups". In another encyclical of Pius XI, *Rerum Orientalium*, promulgated on September 8, 1928, Orthodox are again referred to as "Schismatics" (see, e.g., n. 4). In the encyclical *Mystici Corporis* issued by Pope Pius XII on June 29, 1943, those outside the Catholic Church are not said to belong to churches.

sincere appeal for peace coming "from such a Christian centre as that of ancient Rome."[10] So far, the focus in the messages of both pope and patriarch was at least as much on peace among nations as on Christian unity. The latter seemed too delicate a topic at this point to be addressed on its own, outside the context of a number of safer references to world peace and human solidarity in general. When Athenagoras in his New Year's message did take up the question of "the renewed appeal for the unity of the Churches which Your Holiness recently made," it was with a mixture of caution and hope. He was careful to point out that "every appeal for unity must be accompanied by those indispensable definite deeds and endeavors which would prove that intentions are meant to be fulfilled." He concluded his message with the hope and prayer that "the most holy Church of Rome ... will turn in a brotherly spirit towards the East. This is what we desire and look for from the new Pope of Rome, John XXIII, who is personally so well known, loved, and respected in our parts."[11] The attribution (in hope) of a "brotherly spirit," not merely to the person of the pope but to the very "Church of Rome," still does not bring us into the orbit of the term "sister churches" directly, but does convey the idea of a sibling relationship between the churches in question.

Following the Pope's announcement later that month of his intention to convoke an ecumenical council, Athenagoras soon arranged for his personal representative, His Eminence Iakovos, the newly elected Archbishop of North and South America, to travel to Rome to meet with John XXIII.[12] Not since 1547 had a delegate of the Ecumenical Patriarch visited the Bishop of Rome. A reciprocal visit by the papal delegate to Turkey was paid to Athenagoras at the Phanar in April. Two years later, and with preparations for Vatican II well under way on the Catholic side, the Orthodox churches convened their first pan-Orthodox conference, in Rhodes (1961), where they were unable to reach agreement on whether to accept Rome's invitation to the various patriarchates to send delegated observers to the council. The Ecumenical Patriarchate would not send official observers of its own until the third session, in 1964. But in the meantime, contacts between Constantinople and Rome grew both in frequency and in depth.

---

10 Stormon, *Towards the Healing of Schism*, 30, no. 5.
11 Ibid.
12 The unpublicized meeting occurred on March 17, 1959. Official records of the meeting have yet to be made available. See Stormon, *Towards the Healing of Schism*, 9.

II. First usages; terminological asymmetry between the two parties

In late February of 1962, Cardinal Augustin Bea, the president of the Secretariat for Promoting Christian Unity, wrote to Patriarch Athenagoras to thank him for the hospitality shown to Monsignor Jan Willebrands, who earlier that month had visited the Ecumenical Patriarchate in his official capacity as the SPCU's secretary. In reference to what he had been told of Monsignor Willebrands' discussions with the Ecumenical Patriarch, the Metropolitans of the Holy Synod, and the members of the Commission for Ecumenical Affairs, Cardinal Bea observed, "I take pleasure in seeing in all this evidence of the constructive work in which we are now together engaged in the quest for unity. A beginning has now been made, and I hope that other contacts and discussions will follow the course which Your Holiness has so wisely set."[13]

In his letter of reply of April 12, 1962, Patriarch Athenagoras used for the first time the phrase "sister churches" to describe relations between the Catholic and Orthodox churches. "What you have to say in general terms about your desire for the *rapprochement* of the sister Churches and the restoration of unity in the Church moved us deeply, as it was bound to do, given the fact that we have repeatedly manifested our own readiness to do all in our power to contribute to this restoration."[14]

It would be several years before use of the phrase "sister churches" would be reciprocated by those in Rome with whom Patriarch Athenagoras was in contact. One can, however, find closely related *language* used by Cardinal Bea as early as 1962, in his letter to the Patriarch on July 24 of that year. This letter concerned the fact that it was to each of the autocephalous Orthodox churches, some of which had themselves approached the Vatican independently of the others, that the SPCU had chosen to send individual invitations to attend the upcoming council as observers, rather than sending all the invitations through Constantinople. Without discounting the delicacy of this decision, Cardinal Bea explained the circumstances and observed that it was "therefore with calm confidence that we have decided to send official invitations to the venerable Churches of the East, which, in spite of nine centuries of separation remain in the highest degree our brothers."[15]

Originally in French, this statement referring to the churches of the East as our "brothers" (frères) would certainly seem to be very close to saying that, with

---

13 Stormon, *Towards the Healing of Schism*, 34, no. 9.
14 Ibid. 35, no. 10.
15 Ibid. 40-41, no. 19.

respect to Rome, they are "sister churches," but it was not exactly the same. The latter expression, being more compact (and involving agreement in gender between modifier and noun) had something about it of a label, an almost formal term. In any case, Rome did not yet employ it. In another letter from Cardinal Bea to the Ecumenical Patriarch, written in early October after Rome had received word that the Orthodox churches were not going to send official observer-delegates,[16] the Cardinal stated that "we understand the difficulties of the situation for the Orthodox Churches, and we shall continue to do all in our power to maintain fraternal relations with them."[17]

Up until late 1965 there persisted an asymmetry in the language that was used, by the Ecumenical Patriarchate and by the Church of Rome respectively, to express the relationship between their churches. Constantinople continued from time to time to invoke the language of sister churches explicitly. Rome consistently used the somewhat more restrained language of fraternal relations between the churches. If this was for Rome a sort of intermediate step, going beyond what had previously been its hesitancy to apply the word "church" outside its own communion, but remaining still shy of what would subsequently be its affirmation of Orthodox and Catholic churches together as sister churches, perhaps it was a step enabled by and reflective of the traditional Catholic view of the validity of Orthodox orders – and in particular, of the Orthodox episcopate. Catholics and Orthodox in the 1960s might not all have been so sure that their churches were sisters of one another, but they were sure – especially the Catholics were – that their bishops were "brothers". It is conceivable that "brother bishop" language was therefore what under-girded the endorsement by Rome of the kind of "brother church" language they used at this intermediate stage before they eventually adopted the language of "sister churches" itself that was common currency on the Orthodox side from 1962.

In any case, the data of the ensuing three years, 1963-1965, demonstrates no significant change in the pattern described above as asymmetrical, with the Orthodox invoking the language of sister churches from time to time, and the Catholics going only as far as to speak in terms of fraternal relations. The next relevant text, beyond those reviewed thus far, was a statement issued by Patriarch Athenagoras at a meeting of the Holy Synod of the Ecumenical Patriar-

---

16   This decision on the part of the Orthodox was subsequently reversed, initially by the Patriarchate of Moscow the very next day (October 11), and subsequently by many of the other Orthodox Churches.

17   *Letter of Cardinal Bea to Patriarch Athenagoras* of October 10, 1962. Stormon, *Towards the Healing of Schism*, 42, no. 21.

chate on June 4, 1963, the day after the death of Pope John XXIII. "For in the person of the late venerable leader of our sister Church of Rome," the Patriarch remarked, "we discerned an inspired laborer well able to meet the challenge of present circumstances, and to train his gaze on those points of teaching of the Lord and of apostolic tradition which are common to both the Orthodox and Roman Catholic Churches."[18] For the second time in as many years, the patriarch used here a form of the expression "sister churches," with one sister being the church of Rome.

On September 9, 1963, Metropolitan Maximos sent a letter to the new Pope Paul VI congratulating him on behalf of Patriarch Athenagoras on his election as the successor of John XXIII. Metropolitan Maximos was the President of the Commission for Ecumenical Affairs in the Synod of the Ecumenical Patriarchate and had been chairman of the first Pan-Orthodox Conference in Rhodes (September 24 – October 2, 1961). After touching on the fruitful ecumenical efforts of Paul VI's predecessor and suggesting that Paul's election was itself indicative of Rome's desire to extend those efforts, Maximos concluded his letter by conveying the patriarch's best wishes to the pope "for a long and fruitful service in the holy sister Church of Rome, for the furtherance of the spirit of unity in the Christian world, and for the glory of the name of Our Lord Jesus Christ."[19]

Later that month, Paul VI wrote a letter in his own hand to Athenagoras, the first letter of a pope to a patriarch since 1584.[20]

> Let us entrust the past to the mercy of God, and listen to the advice of the Apostle: 'forgetting what is behind us, I am stretched forth towards that which is ahead, that I may seek to seize it even as I am seized by him.' We have been seized by him through the gift of the good news of salvation, by the gift of the same Baptism, and of the same priesthood, in which the same Eucharist is celebrated – the one sacrifice of the one Lord of the Church.[21]

The importance of this passage for our topic, in spite of its containing no direct reference to sister churches (or even to fraternal relations among churches), lies in the fact that it articulates a particular understanding of what is held in common by those whom the Pope merely identifies by the pronoun "we." Although he did not clarify to whom this pronoun exactly referred, it is obvious from the context that it referred to himself and the Patriarch, and not only as individuals,

---

18 Stormon, *Towards the Healing of Schism*, 45, no. 26.
19 Ibid. 52, no. 32.
20 See ibid. 10.
21 Ibid. 52, no. 33, with reference to Philippians 3:12-13.

but as heads of churches. This, then, was the first of a number of texts in which Paul VI would affirm a common baptism, priesthood, and eucharist between the Catholic and Orthodox churches. In more general terms, the same was done in the letter of reply sent by Athenagoras to Paul VI on November 22, 1963. In that letter Athenagoras spoke of the "grace we share together in the sacraments."[22] We will see that in several of the texts where Catholic and Orthodox churches were identified as sister churches, reference would be made to this sacramental foundation common to them both.

Four more times in the ensuing year and a half, the expression "sister church" or "sister churches" would be invoked explicitly by the Ecumenical Patriarch or by one of his delegates, while in the same time period, the Pope and members of the Roman Curia would speak slightly more cautiously of "fraternal relations" between churches. Athenagoras sent Paul VI a short Easter telegram on March 27, 1964, just a couple of months after the historic meeting of the two leaders in Jerusalem. The telegram ran as follows:

> We address a warm and brotherly greeting to Your beloved and esteemed Holiness on the occasion of the light-bearing feast of the Resurrection ... being celebrated next Sunday by the sister Church of the West, and we pray the Lord to grant rich grace to yourself and to the same sister Church, and to increase our charity, to the praise of his glory.[23]

To be noted is the choice of the phrase "the sister Church of the West." As will be discussed in Chapter 3, it is a phrase susceptible to more than one interpretation.

On May 19, 1964, Patriarch Athenagoras wrote to Pope Paul VI in appreciation of a recent visit from several papal representatives and of the letter they conveyed from the pope expressing Easter good wishes. "We thank you wholeheartedly for these wishes," the patriarch wrote, "and we beseech Christ our God, who through his death on the Cross entered into his glory, to take special care of you, so that you may enjoy good health for many years to come and cast lustre on the see of ancient Rome. May he enable you and the sister Church with all its members, over which you preside, to shine forth with a share in that inexpressible light of the Resurrection, and with glad hearts experience the joy arising from it."[24]

---

22 Ibid. 54, no. 35.
23 Ibid. 71, no. 58.
24 Ibid. 74-75, no. 65.

In another telegram from Athenagoras to Paul VI, on June 27, 1964, thanking the pope for his decision to restore the relic of St. Andrew to the church of his martyrdom at Patras, in Greece, Athenagoras wrote, "The whole Orthodox world rejoices. We thank you personally in a brotherly spirit, and ask the Lord, by the intercession of his Apostles Peter and Andrew, to bless our sister Churches aspiring towards unity."[25] Here as elsewhere, the precise identities of the sister churches intended are not made clear.

In February of 1965, a patriarchal delegation led by Metropolitan Meliton of Heliopolis and Theira (later, of Chalcedon) visited Rome. The visit was paid in order to convey in person the decision of the Third Pan-Orthodox Conference of Rhodes (which had taken place in November of 1964) to allow Orthodox churches individually to embark upon a dialogue with the Roman Catholic Church, a decision to which in principle there had been agreement at the Second Pan-Orthodox Conference of the previous year. In his address to the pope on this occasion, Metropolitan Meliton said,

> Our Orthodox East, aspiring towards the restoration of the ancient unity, beauty, and glory of the Church, has never ceased praying for total union, and has collaborated with other Christians for the development of the ecumenical spirit of reconciliation. In recent times it has turned towards its sister, your Roman Catholic Church, and in the First Pan-Orthodox Conference it unanimously confirmed its desire for this dialogue, and went on to lay down a programme for the furtherance of this sacred cause, noting that its successful outcome is to be striven for in stages and on a solid basis.[26]

In this text the sisters are "our Orthodox East" on the one hand and "your Roman Catholic Church" on the other. They are not any pair of local churches but the two entire communions.

The handful of texts just considered were all written or issued by Orthodox officials. From the Catholic side during the same period, a number of letters and speeches, beyond the few already cited, contained language of fraternal ecclesial relations – this rather than the explicit language of "sister churches" which was not to appear in any Catholic text prior to late 1965.

In a letter to Patriarch Athenagoras of December 20, 1963, Cardinal Bea mentioned his hope for "a growth and deepening of brotherly exchanges between our Churches."[27] A few months later, in another letter to the Ecumenical Patriarch, Cardinal Bea described discussions during a recent visit of papal

---

25   Ibid. 76, no. 67.
26   Ibid. 86, no. 87.
27   Ibid. 56, no. 39.

delegates to Constantinople as "very fruitful and full of hope for the development of brotherly relations between our two Churches."[28]

Pope Paul VI, in his allocution to Patriarch Athenagoras delivered on the Mount of Olives during the historic meeting there between the two figures, spoke of the difficulties on the path to union which undoubtedly confront "both sides," and noted that while doctrinal and disciplinary differences would need to be examined in due course, what could and must already go forward was "this brotherly love which is ever finding new ways of manifesting itself".[29] Interestingly, in a joint communiqué of the Pope and the Patriarch issued after their Jerusalem meeting, the language chosen was the more cautious language preferred by Rome (and used, often enough, too, by representatives of Constantinople, but in conjunction with the expression "sister churches"). "This meeting cannot be considered as anything other than a brotherly gesture, inspired by the charity of Christ, who left his disciples the supreme commandment to love one another, to pardon offences seventy times seven, and to be united among themselves."[30]

The two texts just quoted both show an apparent preference for describing an *act* or a *sentiment* as brotherly, rather than identifying a church or even a person as *brother*. This would seem to be another aspect of the more tentative approach on the part of Catholic officials during this stage of the bilateral relationship. As mentioned earlier, traditional Catholic ecclesiology was more prepared to recognize Orthodox bishops as brother bishops (of Catholic ones) than Orthodox churches as sister or sibling churches (of Catholic ones). But even with regard to episcopal fraternity, a certain hesitation on the Catholic side is evident, for a unique set of issues presented itself where the Pope was concerned. This is reflected in some of the early letters between Athenagoras and Paul VI, particularly in their greetings and signings off.

Historically, formalities of reciprocal address between hierarchs have not been without ecclesiological significance. Two brief examples may be offered that bear upon our subject. (1) In his book *The Eastern Schism*, Steven Runciman recounts the proposal made by the Patriarch Michael Cerularius in 1053 to insert the Pope's name again in the diptychs throughout the empire if his own name could be inserted again at Rome.[31] While the idea was never realized,

---

28 Ibid. 74, no. 64.
29 Ibid. 63, no. 49. The allocution of Pope Paul VI is dated January 6, 1964.
30 Ibid. 64, no. 50.
31 The absence of either hierarch's name in the diptychs of the other church dated back to 1025 when a proposal of Patriarch Eustathius that "the Church of Constantinople

it might have been pursued, according to Runciman, if certain sensitivities had been more carefully attended to. "But, most regrettably, Cerularius addressed the Pope as 'Brother,' not as 'Father,' the title with which in the past Patriarchs had usually recognized the Pope's seniority".[32] However much this was an insult – clearly it was not the principal factor in the worsening of relations between the sees – Runciman is surely correct that the question of protocol was significant. (2) A related set of observations appears in Nicholas Afanasiev's book *The Church of the Holy Spirit*, where the author critically describes certain ecclesiological tendencies in Tsarist Russia. "It became unacceptable for the bishops to address the patriarch as brother – for he is not a brother to the bishops but a common father ... The patriarch sought to gain for himself the position of a super-bishop or of a bishop's bishop."[33] In both examples, the expected manner of addressing a particular bishop is closely connected to the perceived place of that bishop's particular *church* in the overall communion of churches.

It is therefore appropriate for us to give some attention to the ecclesiological overtones in the formal terms of address with which Athenagoras and Paul VI opened and closed the letters they exchanged – letters that dealt so centrally, indeed, with relations between their churches. Although this data cannot do more than point toward conclusions that would need more solid support on other grounds, it should not be left out of consideration.

From the start of the correspondence between Rome and Constantinople, the Ecumenical Patriarchate adhered to a simple principle by which bishops of whatever rank are always understood as brothers of one another. In the late 1950s and early 1960s, Rome sometimes followed the same principle, but less scrupulously. When Cardinal Bea asked the patriarch "to accept the expression of my *fraternal* and respectful charity in the Lord,"[34] this was actually several months before he himself received episcopal consecration. Meanwhile Monsignor Willebrands, then a priest, thanked the patriarch for "the *paternal* charity

---

shall be called and considered universal in her own sphere, as that of Rome is in the world" was rejected by Pope John XIX. See S. Runciman, *The Eastern Schism*, 35-37.
32 Runciman, *The Eastern Schism*, 43.
33 Nicholas Afanasiev, *The Church of the Holy Spirit*, translated by Vitaly Permiakov (Notre Dame, Indiana: University of Notre Dame Press, 2007), 220. Afanasiev notes that strong as such patriarchal aspirations were in Russia, "just as in Byzantium, this attempt was unsuccessful, for historical circumstances did not support it."
34 Stormon, *Towards the Healing of Schism*, 32, no. 6 (emphasis added). Cardinal Bea was appointed as bishop in April 1962; the text quoted here is dated 6 December, 1961.

and trust which Your Holiness extended to me" during a visit made in early 1962.³⁵ Athenagoras, for his part, greeted Cardinal Bea as "our beloved *brother in Christ God*"³⁶ – this in a letter dated exactly a week after Cardinal Bea's episcopal consecration – while in his closing remarks to Monsignor Willebrands, he used the locution, "With *fatherly* affection ..."³⁷. Insofar as the pope was not directly concerned, the difference of approach between the Catholic and Orthodox correspondents was only very subtly different, if at all.

But over the question of how the pope himself was to be addressed there seems to have been a wider divergence. In a telegram from Metropolitan Maximos to Cardinal Bea, asking him to convey Easter wishes to the pope on behalf of the patriarch, the basic approach of Constantinople was set forth. "I beg Your beloved Eminence kindly to convey to His Holiness Pope John of Rome, the brotherly greetings, cordial salutations, and Easter wishes of the Ecumenical Patriarch Athenagoras. These are sent also to Your Eminence."³⁸ Again in a letter to Cardinal Bea shortly after the election of Paul VI, Athenagoras himself spoke of the Roman bishop as "the new Pope of Rome, our beloved brother in Christ Paul VI."³⁹ In the first letter directly from Paul VI to Athenagoras, on the other hand, the pope refrained from characterizing his relationship to the patriarch one way or the other – in either fraternal or paternal terms. But Athenagoras in his first direct correspondence to the pope did not hesitate to mention again his "fraternal message of congratulation," sent "with brotherly feeling," and he signed the letter, "Your venerable and most esteemed Holiness's dear brother in Christ ..."⁴⁰. The relative reticence of Paul VI persisted; characteristic was his way of closing his letter to Athenagoras of January 16, 1964: "In the charity of this same Christ we send you once more an expression of our esteem and affection."⁴¹ This may be compared with the typically more forthright closing words of Athenagoras in his letter to the pope on February 10, 1964, "... embracing Your Holiness with a holy kiss we remain with brotherly love and special respect. Your venerable Holiness's dear Brother in Christ"⁴². The patriarch, indeed, seemed to press the theme of mutuality and fraternity even further

---

35 Stormon, *Towards the Healing of Schism*, 34, no. 8 (emphasis added).
36 Ibid. 35, no. 10 (emphasis added).
37 Ibid. 36, no. 11 (emphasis added).
38 April 21, 1962. Ibid. 37, no. 13.
39 August 22, 1963. Ibid. 50, no. 31.
40 November 22, 1963. Ibid. 53-54, no. 35.
41 Ibid. 66, no. 55.
42 Ibid. 67, no. 56.

when he made a remark in the body of the same letter thanking Paul VI "for the fraternal contents of your missive."[43] It is hard to avoid the impression here that the patriarch thought he might succeed in saying for the pope what the pope as yet had been hesitant to spell out on his own.

Whether or not such nudgings contributed to the shift, an end did come to the reticence of Paul VI on the matter of his fraternal relations with Athenagoras. How he resolved the question is instructive. In a letter of April 18, 1964, he greeted the patriarch by calling him, for the first time, "Beloved Brother in Christ," yet he then proceeded immediately, as though to ensure that too much would not be made of the association, to include in this same "brotherhood" with himself and the patriarch another bishop of lesser rank. "This letter will be brought to you by our dear brother, His Grace Archbishop Joseph Marie Martin, Archbishop of Rouen, who together with our sons Monsignor Willebrands and the Very Reverend Father Duprey, is coming to Istanbul".[44]

From this point forward, Paul VI would refer to Athenagoras as brother (and to himself as Athenagoras' brother), just as Athenagoras had been referring to him as such. From these conventions alone, not very much can be inferred about how Rome's ecclesiological position may or may not have been undergoing a redefinition. But in the context of broader developments, Rome's terminological shift on the plane of episcopal relations does invite comparison with Rome's terminological shift soon to follow on the plane of *ecclesial relations* between the Holy See and the Ecumenical Patriarchate.

III. Rome reciprocates in using the expression "sister churches"

Not long after Paul VI referred to Athenagoras as his "brother in Christ," a Vatican official applied for the first time the term "sister church" to the See of Constantinople. The immediate background was a suggestion made in 1965 by representatives of the Ecumenical Patriarchate, Metropolitan Meliton of Heliopolis and Theira and Metropolitan Chrysostom of Myra, during their visit to Rome, that a joint commission be established to study the mutual anathemas of 1054. Vatican officials were favorable to the suggestion and a commission appointed to carry out this task was promptly established, having as its president on the Catholic side Bishop Jan Willebrands, secretary of the SPCU. On the occasion of the joint commission's inception on November 22, 1965, an address was given by Bishop Willebrands – whose instrumentality as a pro-

---

43 Ibid. 67, no. 56 (emphasis added).
44 Ibid. 72, no. 61.

moter and interpreter of the expression "sister churches" in Catholic usage will be seen at several points. This address opened as follows, according to notes taken at the time: "The Church of ancient Rome has taken note of the feelings and desires of its sister Church of new Rome with regard to the tragic happenings of 1054, particularly the mutual excommunications which at that time created a state of conflict and enmity between the two Churches."[45]

It appears that this marked the first time in history that a Vatican official referred to the church of Constantinople as the sister church of the church of Rome.[46] Unfortunately there is no official transcript of the address given by Bishop Willebrands in which this historically significant statement was reportedly made. (It seems to be the only text in the whole *Tomos Agapis* that is qualified as being "a summary based on notes taken during the speech".[47]) Within roughly a year and a half of the date of this address of Bishop Willebrands, the same language of sister churches was, in any case, applied by the Pope himself to the Catholic and Orthodox churches.

In the meantime, the common declaration of Paul VI and Athenagoras that was issued when the anathemas were formally lifted on December 7, 1965, opted for language of "the fraternal relations thus inaugurated between the Roman Catholic Church and the Orthodox Church of Constantinople."[48] The same occurred in Paul VI's papal Brief *Ambulate in dilectione* issued on that same occasion and containing broad statements that encouraged "further progress along the road of brotherly love" and that affirmed "this public testimony of Christian brotherhood."[49]

The Ecumenical Patriarchate seemed equally comfortable using the language of fraternal relations, too, as it had long done. In his simultaneously released Patriarchal "Tome," Athenagoras together with his Synod made reference to an outpouring in recent times of a "mutual care both of the Old and the New Rome for the cultivation of brotherly relations with one another."[50] The difference, though, over the following months, was that from the Orthodox side, this

---

45 Ibid. 121, no. 123.
46 It may be recalled that as early as the 5th century, Pope Innocent I had spoken of one of the other ancient patriarchates as Rome's sister; but then it was the Church of Antioch to which he referred, on the basis of their shared petrine foundation. See above, Chapter 1, pp. 11-13.
47 Stormon, *Towards the Healing of Schism*, 121.
48 Ibid. 126, no. 127.
49 Ibid. 128, no. 128.
50 Ibid. 130, no. 129.

language of fraternal relations alternated with the explicit language of sister churches. For example, Athenagoras wrote later the same month, in his 1965 Christmas letter to Pope Paul VI, "May [God] bless and lead to further results this new period, ushered in under happy omens, in the mutual relations of the two sister Churches."[51]

When the pope next wrote to the patriarch, offering his 1966 Easter greetings, he spoke only of his hope that mutual contacts established during the recently concluded council "should go on developing into an ever stronger brotherhood between our Churches."[52] By contrast, in an address to the pope the following year, on May 23, 1967, Archbishop Eugenios of Crete (which fell within the jurisdiction of Constantinople) spoke of a "new period of charity, in which the two sister Churches make their way through the world, setting equal store by unity and coexistence"[53]. The terminological asymmetry would not continue much longer. The pope in a message of July 13, 1967, expressing his intention to visit the Phanar, said that the visit would be meant to "give added firmness to the commonly felt hope for Christian brotherhood between the Churches and for peace in the world."[54] When the visit took place, the patriarch invoked the concept of sister churches in his address;[55] the pope in his own address did not – at least, not in the speech that he delivered himself. However, on the same day, in a text of the pope that was read out in Latin by Bishop Willebrands in the Latin Cathedral of the Holy Spirit and was then personally handed to the patriarch by the pope, the expression "sister Churches" not only appeared, but was elaborated upon in considerable depth.

This text, the Papal Brief *Anno ineunte*, dated July 25, 1967, was to assume a significant place in the history of relations between the Catholic and Orthodox churches, not least for its direct treatment of the concept of sister churches. The well known passage is worth quoting in full.

> God has granted us to receive in faith what the Apostles saw, understood, and proclaimed to us. By Baptism "we are one in Christ Jesus" (Gal 3:28). In virtue of the apostolic succession, we are united more closely by the priesthood and the Eucharist. By participating in the gifts of God to his Church we are brought

---

51 Ibid. 134, no. 132.
52 Ibid. 136, no. 133.
53 Ibid. 149-150, no. 156.
54 Ibid. 156, no. 171.
55 Athenagoras welcomed the Pope "as you come to bring the kiss of ancient Rome to her younger sister." Address of welcome, July 25, 1967 (Stormon, *Towards the Healing of Schism*, 159, no. 173).

into communion with the Father through the Son in the Holy Spirit. Having become sons in the Son in very fact (cf. 1 Jn 3:1-2), we have become mysteriously but really brothers among ourselves. In each local Church this mystery of divine love is enacted, and surely this is the ground of the traditional and very beautiful expression "sister Churches," which local Churches were fond of applying to one another (cf. Decree, *Unitatis Redintegratio*, 14).

For centuries we lived this life of "sister Churches," and together held the Ecumenical Councils which guarded the deposit of faith against all corruption. And now, after a long period of division and mutual misunderstanding, the Lord is enabling us to discover ourselves as "sister Churches" once more, in spite of the obstacles which were once raised between us. In the light of Christ we see how urgent is the need of surmounting these obstacles in order to succeed in bringing to its fullness and perfection the already very rich communion which exists between us.

On both sides we profess "the fundamental dogmas of the Christian faith on the Trinity, on the Word of God who took flesh of the Virgin Mary," as these "were defined in the Ecumenical Councils held in the East" (cf. *U.R.*, 14), and we have true sacraments and a hierarchical priesthood in common. In view of these facts it behooves us in the first place to work together in a fraternal spirit in the service of our faith, to find the appropriate ways which will lead us further on as we try to develop and make real in the life of our Churches the communion which, although imperfect, exists already.[56]

According to this text, it is the mystery of love enacted in each local church – a mystery which the pope particularly associates with participation in the gifts of God in the eucharist – that is "the ground of the traditional and very beautiful expression 'sister Churches.'"[57] The text at this point refers to the Decree on Ecumenism *Unitatis Redintegratio* promulgated at Vatican II on November 21, 1964. In that document, rather less is said on the subject than is said here by Paul VI. The relevant paragraph goes only as far as to observe that "among the Orientals," there has always been and still is great concern and care for "the

---

56 Stormon, *Towards the Healing of Schism*, 162-163, no. 176.
57 It should of course be noticed that the basis of the existing unity between the sister churches is not *limited* to the eucharist, according to the Brief *Anno ineunte*. If it is the eucharist that anchors everything else, this sacrament of unity is nonetheless connected with all the other realities mentioned in the Brief as being held in common by the Catholic and Orthodox churches: baptism, apostolic succession, priesthood, along with a shared history of ecumenical councils by which the deposit of faith was guarded and an ongoing profession of the same fundamental dogmas of faith proclaimed by those councils.

preservation in a communion of faith and charity of those family ties which ought to exist between local Churches, as between sisters."[58] The pope now goes a great step farther in asserting that the expression's application is not restricted to the Orthodox churches among themselves but extends across the existing division between Catholic and Orthodox churches.

An important commentary on *Anno ineunte* is offered in the letter of Bishop Willebrands to Patriarch Athenagoras of August 8, 1967, sent only a couple of weeks after the visit of the pope and his delegation to Constantinople where the brief had been issued. "I wish also to tell Your Holiness how utterly thankful I am," Bishop Willebrands wrote to the patriarch,

> for all that you have done for the unity of the Church, and more especially for [i.e., toward] the reconstitution in full and perfect unity of our two Churches – these Churches which His Holiness the Pope, in the message which I had the joy of reading in his name in the Church of the Holy Spirit, was pleased to call sister Churches, because of the communion which exists between us in the Lord. Was it not in fact this communion in the Lord that we celebrated, and which, as it was shown forth in the heads of the two Churches, filled the hearts of Christian people with joy and gratitude?[59]

This careful reflection on *Anno ineunte* from so close an associate of the pope – so close that it was he who was entrusted with the reading of the document on the occasion of its delivery – goes a significant distance in clearing up a certain ambiguity in Paul VI's application of the expression "sister churches." The same ambiguity surrounds the expression where it appears in many other texts of both Catholic and Orthodox authorship in the latter decades of the 20th century. In these texts, it is often unclear whether just two churches, or many churches, are to be understood as the sister churches being discussed. But according to what Willebrands says here, the churches that the Pope "was pleased to call sister Churches" were "our two Churches": precisely *our two*, rather than (what might otherwise have been meant) *many* local churches on either side. There still remains of course a further question: *which* two churches are being designated as sisters. That more than one answer to this question, too, is possible will be shown in Chapter 3.

Finally, this commentary of Bishop Willebrands is of great value insofar as it confirms that for Paul VI, "sister churches" was not merely a hypothetical

---

58 UR 14. Quotations from the documents of Vatican II are taken from A. Flannery, ed., *Vatican II: The Conciliar and Post Conciliar Documents*. New Revised Edition. (Northport, NY: Costello, 1992).
59 Stormon, *Towards the Healing of Schism*, 164, no. 178.

relationship toward which the two parties needed to continue to work. It was a reality rooted in a communion that already existed securely – though in an imperfect form, which therefore required of both parties that they continue working to perfect it.

With the Brief *Anno ineunte,* both in itself and as it was interpreted just two weeks later by Bishop Willebrands, we find that the concept of sister churches, from the Catholic side, was taking a more definite shape and was being endorsed with a more firm commitment than had been the case previously. This is further confirmed by the retrospective comments made some years later by Metropolitan Damaskinos of Tranoupolis and Father Pierre Duprey in their joint press conference of January 25, 1972, at the presentation of the *Tomos Agapis.* In their survey of high points in the bilateral relationship since the early 1960s, they prominently included the day in 1967 when "the Pope presented to the Patriarch Athenagoras the Brief *Anno Ineunte.*" "This text," they observed, "explains why the Catholic and Orthodox Churches are 'sister Churches.'"[60]

When the less explicit language appeared again, as it continued to do in both Catholic and Orthodox texts after August of 1967, this did not imply any reneging on the recognition of one another as sister churches. An address of Paul VI to Athenagoras in St. Peter's Basilica during the patriarch's visit to Rome in October 1967 omitted explicit mention of "sister churches," instead of which there was mention of actions being taken to remove "certain obstacles to the full development in the daily life of the Church of the sense of brotherhood that has been recovered step by step between the Orthodox and the Catholic Churches."[61] When the pope went on to list the common attributes or gifts by which the respective churches were already drawn together – "by a same obedience to the Gospel of Christ, by the same sacraments, and above all by the same Baptism and the same priesthood which offers the same Eucharist – the unique sacrifice of Christ – by a same episcopacy received from the Apostles"[62] – these were the very realities he had spoken of in *Anno ineunte* as being the basis for the identification of the Catholic and Orthodox churches as "sister churches" in spite of their imperfect communion.

Athenagoras, in his address in reply to the pope, also limited himself to references to fraternal feeling, and made no mention of sister churches either. Interestingly, here he gave indication, however, of seeing even in this language

---

60 Ibid. 246, no. 295.
61 Ibid. 175, no. 190.
62 Ibid. 176-177, no. 190.

of ecclesial fraternity a reflection of deeper truths of a dogmatic nature, rooted in the identity of the episcopacy.

> We greet each one of you [the pope together with other Catholic bishops in attendance] with brotherly feelings, and through you we extend our greeting to the whole venerable Roman Catholic hierarchy throughout the world. As we find ourselves in your midst, we have a strong feeling of brotherhood. This is not due to chance or to the sentimental impulse of the moment, but is based on truth in the Holy Spirit. Both you and we, Bishops of the holy Roman Catholic Church and our holy Orthodox Church, are bearers of the Holy Spirit as it were in earthen vessels: we hold the priceless pearl of the apostolic succession, which has been handed on to us without interruption by the imposition of hands.[63]

Two days later, in the common declaration by Pope Paul VI and Patriarch Athenagoras at the end of the patriarch's visit to Rome, the explicit phrase "sister churches" was included again, confirming that its absence in other recent texts had not signified any retraction or denial.

> While recognizing that in the journey towards the unity of all Christians there is still a long way to go, and that between the Roman Catholic and Orthodox Churches there still exist points to be clarified and obstacles to be overcome before arriving at the unity in the profession of faith which is necessary for reestablishment of full communion, they [Pope Paul VI and Patriarch Athenagoras] rejoice at the fact that their meeting has played a part in helping their Churches to make a further discovery of themselves as sister Churches.[64]

The following year, Bishop Willebrands, having just returned to Rome from a visit to Constantinople, included in a letter to the patriarch another explicit affirmation. "The Holy Father made a point of telling me this morning that he was very inclined to the view that a working group should study the theological reasons which either hinder or allow a practical expression in worship and sacramental participation of the profound communion, which, although not yet complete, exists here and now between the two sister churches."[65] Without having displaced all other ways of describing the same relationship, the expression "sister churches" had become customary by the end of 1969. In a pair of telegrams exchanged in October of that year, it was used both times: first by the patriarch, who (with respect to a Roman Synod of Bishops at which the pope was to preside) expressed prayerful thoughts and wishes "for the good of the

---

63   Ibid. 179, no. 193.
64   Common declaration of October 28, 1967. Ibid. 181, no. 195.
65   January 19, 1969. Ibid. 207, no. 245.

Roman Catholic Church, our beloved sister,"[66] and then by the pope, who prayed that "this Synod [in Rome] may be a new step towards the restoration to full communion of the two sister Churches."[67] An address given the following month by Athenagoras welcoming Cardinal Willebrands to the Phanar, unexceptional in one sense in that it described the Cardinal's visit as "a new sign and testimony of the brotherhood of our two Churches",[68] in another sense deserves particular notice. It singled out a specific feature of the relationship between the Catholic and Orthodox churches that Athenagoras felt had changed. Toward the end of his address, the patriarch observed, "Neither of us is calling the other to himself any more"[69]. The patriarch offered here an important interpretation of history. A new stage in Catholic-Orthodox relations, characterized increasingly as "fraternal" (and sometimes as a relationship of "sister churches") was succeeding an earlier stage marked by efforts to proselytize members of the other ecclesial tradition as though they were outside the Church of God.

I have tried to show that the increase in usage of the expression "sister churches" by officials in Rome was gradual but significant and that by the end of 1969, the term had gained currency for them as it had had currency already for some time in Constantinople, in spite of the fact that statements from both sees continued also to employ other terminology to express something of the same idea. The argument that a shift had indeed taken place by this point in time is supported by remarks made by Cardinal Willebrands in an address in reply to that of Patriarch Athenagoras cited above. Willebrands recalled with fondness his first visit to the Ecumenical Patriarchate, and went on: "Since then there has been a great increase in these exchanges of view, these visits made and returned, these courses of action agreed on together, which have led us, under the guidance of the Holy Spirit – a guidance which was sought with faith and followed with docility – to recognize one another as sister Churches, and to proclaim the fact officially. When we did these things, was it not the awareness

---

66 October 13, 1969. Ibid. 218, no. 267.
67 October 17, 1969. Ibid. 219, no. 269.
68 November 30, 1969. Ibid. 222, no. 274.
69 Ibid. 223, no. 274. The whole paragraph in which these words appear is as follows: "Blessed be God in that already both in the West and the East we are living through the great season of a return to the ancient unity. Neither of us is calling the other to himself any more, but like Peter and Andrew we betake ourselves, and take each other, too, to Jesus, our one common Lord, who brings about unity. We wish to remain with Jesus, to remain together, united, and to remain the whole day, the day that belongs to the last things and has no ending."

of the mystery of the Church, of its unity and catholicity, which was being deepened within us?"[70]

From Willebrand's perspective, recognition of one another as sister churches now had the status of an official fact. It was something that had been done. Roughly two and a half years later, there was to be a transition in the Ecumenical Patriarchate from Athenagoras, who died in July, 1972, to Dimitrios I. With respect to Catholic-Orthodox relations, the new patriarch inherited (as the successors to Paul VI would also do in 1978), a way of speaking and thinking about each other that had established itself firmly by 1969 and remained just as firmly in place into the early 1970s. At this stage of the dialogue, recognition of one another as "sister churches" was mutual, a *fact* affirmed by the highest representatives of the Ecumenical Patriarch as well as by those of the Holy See. It remains now to investigate more carefully the meaning of this fact. Toward this end, it is necessary to attempt to clarify precisely who the "sisters" are when the expression "sister churches" has been used in the modern period.

---

[70] Stormon, *Towards the Healing of Schism*, 225, no. 275.

Chapter 3
PATTERNS AND AMBIGUITIES IN 20TH CENTURY USAGE

The preceding chapter traced occurrences of the expression "sister churches" from its first modern use in Catholic-Orthodox relations in 1962 up to the death of Patriarch Athenagoras in 1972. The focus was on the Sees of Constantinople and Rome during those crucial years in which the expression came to be employed by both Patriarch Athenagoras and, eventually, Pope Paul VI and their respective representatives. The purpose was to give the most careful account possible of the development of the term, especially as long as this development seemed to be most conspicuously in a formative stage.

After 1972, the expression continued for several decades to be used much as it had been (by the Orthodox in the preceding decade, and by Catholics in the preceding five or six years). This continuity of usage is significant because it transcended the lifetime of any single patriarch or pope. Once the two leaders who had been most instrumental in introducing the expression into the vocabulary and ecumenical mentality of their respective churches had died, the expression endured in the very fabric of the dialogue.

But at the same time, its meaning had never exactly been settled or self-evident to everyone concerned. It was not always used in the same way. In particular, many texts in which the expression appeared left open the question of the specific identities of the churches referred to as sisters. Was the expression always being used to describe the relationship between the two local churches of Rome and Constantinople? Or did it sometimes refer to relations between the two overarching bodies of the Catholic Church and the Orthodox Church? Were there occasions, additionally, when it may have been intended to speak of many local churches on either side of the confessional division; or perhaps of many churches on one side and a single church on the other? These questions remained largely in the background in Chapter 2, but will now be taken up in a more direct and systematic way in this chapter.

This will involve looking again but through a different lens at some of the material from the period 1958-1972 which was presented in the last chapter, as well as drawing in material from the subsequent period, 1972-2000. The reader should not expect a mere chronological continuation of the story from where it left off at the end of Chapter 2; rather, what follows is an analysis of the material from Chapter 2 that now brings in the data also from 1972-2000, which does not break new ground but reiterates the same distinct patterns of usage. It is according to these several patterns that the material in this chapter will be organized into sections. (Within each section, chronological order will still be followed as much as possible.)

The year 2000 forms the outer limit of the time frame for a very definite reason. On June 30 of that year, the Vatican Congregation for the Doctrine of the Faith (CDF) issued its *Note on the Expression "Sister Churches"*. With the publication of that document, what had by then become a very regular use of the expression by participants on both sides of the dialogue was suddenly thrown into question. The *Note* functioned certainly to give pause to everyone officially involved in the effort to heal the Catholic-Orthodox division. It did not, in fact, prohibit use of the term "sister churches" across the division but sought to circumscribe its application significantly. A number of interested observers, Catholic as well as Orthodox, interpreted it as one more signal of a broader retrenchment perceived to be taking place in Catholic ecclesiology after an initially more liberal phase of post-Vatican II ecumenism. In Orthodox ecclesiology, too, there certainly had been an analogous, indeed a more forceful, backlash against any use of the expression except to describe relations among Orthodox churches themselves, and much of this backlash had come well before the CDF's *Note* was issued. The difference was that Orthodox misgivings about the legitimacy of the expression for Catholic-Orthodox relations did not come, for the most part, from official organs of the church;[1] therefore those Orthodox participants in the dialogue who saw fit to go on using the expression as they had done previously were free to do so regardless of criticisms of the expression that were leveled (for example, by the monastic communities on Mount Athos). The criticisms leveled by the CDF were of a different order and could not be disregarded by Catholic participants.[2] Since it was only after the CDF's *Note*, then, that the expression's place in the official theological dialogue was dramatically restricted, this chapter aims to look at usage up to the point of that document's publication in 2000.

One further preliminary note with regard to the methodology of this chapter: given that the subject of the study as a whole is the concept of "sister

---

1 From some autocephalous Orthodox churches, notably the Church of Greece, condemnation of the expression was issued on an official level, as will be discussed in Chapter 5, but this official condemnation still fell far short of ever achieving critical mass within the Orthodox communion as a whole.

2 In Chapter 4, the CDF's *Note* will be analyzed and assessed (see especially pp. 151-154 in Chapter 4, below), together with Catholic theological writings either supporting or critiquing it.

churches" in Catholic-Orthodox relations of roughly the past half century, the texts of most direct interest will naturally be those in which the expression "sister churches" explicitly appears. But once again – as in Chapter 2 – other texts will need to be considered insofar as they are able to shed light on the meaning of the expression even though they do not invoke it themselves. Particular attention will be given in this chapter to passages containing language that reflects one or another conception of the "two sides" in Catholic-Orthodox relations. Passages will be compared which offer varying perspectives on the ecclesial identities of the dialogue partners. The concern at this point is not so much to discern what it may mean for churches to be sisters, but to discern which churches are being talked about in any given instance. However, a clarification of the latter issue will be of considerable help in illuminating the former.

I. The question of the precise identities of the "sisters"

When the phrase "the sister churches" occurs in the *Tomos Agapis* – or even simply "our churches," or "between the churches" – there are five basic possibilities as to what may be meant by the author or the speaker with respect to the identities of the churches in question.

Of these five, one does not pertain directly to Catholic-Orthodox relations. This is the type of usage according to which the churches under discussion belong to a single, undivided communion. In the *Tomos Agapis* there are no occurrences of this type of usage with respect to Catholic churches, only to Orthodox ones. An example is the statement of Patriarch Dimitrios I on December 14, 1975 saying that as a prerequisite for "the dialogue with Rome," there was a need for "reaching an agreed statement on the part of all the sister Orthodox Churches."[3] Again on November 30, 1978, Patriarch Dimitrios I said that the Ecumenical Patriarchate "shall always maintain agreement and cooperation with our sister Orthodox Churches"[4]. In these examples, the concept of sister churches is applied in such a way that it does not cross confessional boundaries. It seems that it is also applied, implicitly, to patriarchal or autocephalous

---

3 Stormon, *Towards the Healing of Schism*, 291, no. 335.
4 Ibid. 346, no. 389. From the previous decade, see also the remark in the address of Metropolitan Meliton (November 22, 1965), "It is in this spirit that the Church of Constantinople understands its duty of service in the present situation towards its sister Orthodox Churches in various places" (Stormon, *Towards the Healing of Schism*, 120, no. 122).

churches and not only to all dioceses.⁵ In the texts pertaining to bilateral Catholic-Orthodox relations, the intra-confessional type of usage is found infrequently and will not receive extensive treatment here.

It is with the other four possibilities, which all involve a trans-confessional pairing or grouping of churches, that the present chapter is concerned. In all of them there is necessarily the presence of an *axis* – owing to the Catholic-Orthodox division – on either side of which is posited either a singular ecclesial subject, or a plural. The four possible pairings when we read of "our Churches," "the sister Churches," "our two Churches," etc., are as follows: (1) Rome and Constantinople; (2) the Catholic Church and the Orthodox Church; (3) the Catholic Church and the Orthodox churches; (4) the Catholic churches and the Orthodox churches. Discussion of each of the four will be offered in the pages that follow, with examples drawn, as has been mentioned, from the period 1958-1972 as well as the period 1972-2000. By far the most frequent types of

---

5   It is well known that Vatican II's Decree on Ecumenism included a statement on the concern of the Eastern churches for "the preservation in a communion of faith and charity of those family ties which ought to exist between local Churches, as between sisters" *(Unitatis Redintegratio,* para. 14), and there has been some debate as to whether that passage meant to refer to dioceses or to larger ecclesial units. See Chapter 4 below, pp. 117-118. In general, what defines a "local church" is a complicated question. Catholic ecclesiology uses the term to refer either to a diocese *or* to a larger jurisdictional unit, while the term "particular church," in Catholic parlance, is typically – though not always – reserved for the diocese alone. In Orthodox usage, "local church" can also have a range of meanings, probably most often, depending on the context, designating an archdiocese (i.e., metropolitanate) or patriarchate or autocephalous church, but also potentially referring to a diocese. What makes all of this especially confusing is that in certain texts of the Joint International Commission, notably the Ravenna Statement (2007), the "local" level is distinguished from the "regional" level (as well as the "universal" level) in ecclesiology. In this chapter I employ the term "local church" with an extended range of meanings which includes what the Ravenna Statement would describe as the regional level. This is an imperfect strategy, but one based on the observation that it is actually very rare – especially in the *Tomos Agapis* – that the "Church of Constantinople," for example, is really being thought of as a mere diocese and not as a more encompassing administrative unit, and yet it is rather frequently represented as a "local church" in contrast with the Orthodox Church as a whole. The criterion, then, for applying the designation "local" to any church is that it must be one of two or more and must be able to be precisely *located* at least at its source (if not in all of its offshoots), geographically. A regional grouping of churches, then, can still be considered under the category of a "local church" according to this criterion, but the universal church cannot.

occurrences are (1) and (2). As a consequence, these two will demand lengthier treatment than (3) and (4).

1. The see of Rome and the see of Constantinople as sister churches

On the level of official statements and exchanges, the thawing of Catholic-Orthodox relations in the late 1950s and early 1960s was primarily expressed by the leaders of the two sees of Rome and Constantinople. Given that this is so, it is not surprising that as these leaders and their representatives came to employ the expression "sister churches," they often applied it to these two sees themselves. In a number of texts, it is clear that this was their intention.

Through his intermediary Metropolitan Maximos, Patriarch Athenagoras congratulated Paul VI on his papal election in a letter (previously quoted) of September 9, 1963, and wished him "a long and fruitful service in the holy sister Church of Rome".[6] In a letter of February 23, 1965 to Patriarch Athenagoras, Cardinal Bea wrote, "The visit to Rome of their Eminences the Metropolitans Meliton of Heliopolis and Theira and Chrysostom of Myra has marked a new stage in the strengthening of fraternal relations between the Ecumenical Patriarchate and the Roman Church."[7] In a letter of reply on March 8, 1965, the patriarch was most likely referring again just to Rome and Constantinople when he wrote of "the new road that is being opened up in the mutual relations of our two Churches."[8] In a previously cited text of the same year, occasioned by the inception of a joint commission to study the anathemas of 1054, Bishop Willebrands spoke of the "Church of ancient Rome" and "its sister Church of new Rome".[9]

The minutes of this Joint Commission's proceedings contain report of "a unanimous agreement on the nature of the events in which the Churches of Rome and Constantinople were involved, and on the possibility of a common statement on their part regretting these events and removing them from the memory and the midst of the Church"[10]. On the occasion of the actual lifting of the anathemas on December 7, 1965, Paul VI in his Brief *Ambulate in dilectione* alluded to the strife in 1054 "between the Churches of Rome and Constantinople,"[11] and Athenagoras in his "Tome," delivered on the same occasion,

---

6 Stormon, *Towards the Healing of Schism*, 52, no. 32. See above, Chapter 2, p. 55.
7 Ibid. 89, no. 89.
8 Ibid. 89, no. 90.
9 Ibid. 121, no. 123. See above, Chapter 2, p. 62.
10 Ibid. 124, no. 124.
11 Ibid. 129, no. 128.

asserted that as a result of that strife "an obligation became incumbent on the Churches of Rome and Constantinople to imitate the divine goodness and love for humankind by jointly putting these matters right and restoring peace."[12] In a meeting with the pope later on the same day of the ceremony of December 7, Metropolitan Meliton exclaimed, "See now how the two apostolic sees of the Old and the New Rome have, by counsels known only to the Lord, bound up the past and are now freeing the present and opening up the future!"[13]

During the historic visit of the pope to the Phanar on July 25, 1967, Athenagoras, in his welcome address, spoke of the churches of Constantinople and Rome as sisters: "Thanks be to God, the author of marvelous things, who has today deemed us worthy ... to receive with boundless love and the highest regard Your very beloved and most revered Holiness, as you come to bring the kiss of ancient Rome to her younger sister."[14]

When the *Tomos Agapis* was presented to Paul VI on January 24, 1972, Metropolitan Meliton explained in his address to the pope that the title of the publication expressed "a love found again in Christ between the sees of Rome and Constantinople."[15] The dedication by Athenagoras in Paul VI's copy of the *Tomos* noted "the origin and growth of charity between the Churches of Rome and Constantinople".[16] The address by Paul VI in the Lateran Basilica on the same date included a recollection of "our immortal predecessor, St. Leo the Great, who by means of his letter to Flavian authoritatively upheld the Christological definition of the famous Council of Chalcedon, which made Rome and Constantinople brothers in the same definitive and felicitous faith"[17]. An address by Cardinal Willebrands at the Phanar "for the sixth anniversary of the lifting of the anathemas, and for the presentation of the *Tomos Agapis* to Patriarch Athenagoras," may profitably be quoted at length.

> The *Tomos Agapis*, which I have the honor to present to Your Holiness today on behalf of the Holy Father, and which includes some two hundred and eighty-four documents exchanged between the Church of Rome and the Ecumenical Patriarchate between the years 1958 and 1970, gives some idea of the

---

12 Ibid. 130, no. 129.
13 Ibid. 132, no. 130.
14 Ibid. 158-159, no. 173.
15 Ibid. 238, no. 290
16 Ibid. 239, no. 291.
17 Ibid. 242-243, no. 294, with reference to Leo the Great's *Ep.* 28 (also called the "Tome of St. Leo"), PL 54, 755-782; available in English translation in P. Schaff, *NPNF*, 2nd ser., vol. 14, 254-258.

distance covered. The idea of this publication was born here, in the course of the meetings in which we take our bearings and see what are the next possible stages for our journey forward – a journey which is cautious, because it must be certain – towards the restoration of full communion. This book is meant to be such a stage. It would be a good thing if our theologians could make a joint study of the implications of these texts and elucidate the theology of the Church and the idea of relations between the two Churches which inspire them. These theologians would have to make explicit this theology, which springs not only from the speeches and letters exchanged between the pastors of these two Churches, but also from the deeds which they have accomplished and which are often rich in symbolism. This volume is meant to be an occasion for discovering further, both on the speculative and on the practical level, the dimensions, the presuppositions and the implications of this theology. The theologians must evaluate its consequences upon the relations between our Churches and upon the growth of the almost total communion which already exists between them.[18]

Where they appear, the numerous occurrences of such phrases as "between our Churches," "between the two Churches," "of these two Churches," etc., are conditioned by the framework of the whole passage indicated in the first sentence where the focus is placed squarely on the correspondence "between the Church of Rome and the Ecumenical Patriarchate." At the same time, it may be said that there is a certain ambiguity as to whether all such phrases in the passage are best interpreted as referring only to those two sees and not also to the broader communions they represent.

After the death of Athenagoras in 1972, there continued to be many instances in which the churches spoken of in various connections were again identifiable as the specific churches of Rome and Constantinople. On the Feast of St. Andrew, which was to become an occasion of an annual visit to Constantinople by officials from Rome (as the feast of Saints Peter and Paul would be an annual occasion for a reciprocal visit to Rome from representatives of Constantinople), Cardinal Willebrands said in his address of November 30, 1973 that he thanked God for enabling him "to bring Your Holiness and the Church of Constantinople the greetings of His Holiness Pope Paul VI and the Church of Rome, and to assure you that he is praying that by the grace of God the two sister Churches may be fully reconciled, and that perfect communion may be reestablished between them."[19]

---

18 Stormon, *Towards the Healing of Schism*, 236-237, no. 289.
19 Ibid. 257-258, no. 310.

The address given by Patriarch Dimitrios I on the same day not only referred, in the opening paragraph, specifically to "the love, honor, and the sense of brotherhood towards the holy Church of Rome that has always existed in this holy Church of Constantinople,"[20] thus making very clear what two churches he had in mind at the start of his speech; it also spoke directly to the fact that in the dialogue of charity between Rome and Constantinople, then underway for more than a decade, many references to "churches" were open to interpretation and misinterpretation. "When we speak about 'our Churches' we have no thought of abandoning the concept of the Church according to which it is One, Holy, Catholic and Apostolic; what we have in mind is the local Churches, each having its own jurisdiction, and this being held in respect."[21] Here it is reasonable to assume that by "local" the Patriarch had in mind regional churches as well as local dioceses. But several other remarks in this same address, in which the dignity of the local church is continually affirmed, seem actually to call into question the legitimacy of any primacy beyond the level of the diocese; these remarks will be quoted and discussed in section II.4 below ("The Catholic churches and the Orthodox churches as sisters"). For now it should be observed that Patriarch Dimitrios seemed in the statement cited above to set down for the Orthodox – and perhaps also for Catholics – a principle with which it might be expected that all future references to "our churches" would conform: such references must apply strictly to local churches, not to anything else. But as the years went on, both on the Catholic side and on the Orthodox side – indeed, even within the subsequent letters and speeches of Patriarch Dimitrios himself – this principle was not consistently adhered to. As there had been, so there would continue to be occurrences of phrases such as "our churches" which could *not* be said to apply to local churches as these are commonly understood. In the next section (I.2, below) we will consider examples in which "sister churches" is predicated of supra-local ecclesial entities.

Of the many further examples that might be cited in which either the expression itself, or closely related language, was predicated of the two local churches of Rome and Constantinople, only a few outstanding instances need be mentioned. On June 29, 1977 (the feast of Ss. Peter and Paul), Pope Paul VI wrote in a letter to Patriarch Dimitrios I that the bonds of brotherhood "between the Old and the New Rome are from now on such that whatever touches the life of one of the two sister Churches enters also into the experience of the other,

---

20 Ibid. 259, no. 311.
21 Ibid. 259-260, no. 311.

through communion in the same Spirit."²² Upon the death of Pope Paul VI, Patriarch Dimitrios I sent a telegram expressing condolences and a shared participation "in the grief of our sister Church of Rome."²³ On December 2, 1979, Pope John Paul II in an address in Rome before the recitation of the Sunday midday Angelus expressed his "joy at the visit I was enabled to make to the Sister Church of Constantinople and to Patriarch Dimitrios I on the solemnity of St. Andrew the Apostle, who is the patron saint of that Church."²⁴

In a message of Dimitrios I to John Paul II sent on June 17, 1980 in anticipation of the feast of Saints Peter and Paul, the Patriarch wrote: "Blessed be God the Father of our Lord Jesus Christ who has granted our two sister Churches to commemorate and honor together the holy Apostles who are their patron saints"²⁵. On the eve of the feast, Metropolitan Meliton, visiting Rome for the occasion that year, saw fit in his address before the pope to glorify the Trinity, "since this year again the Churches of Rome and Constantinople are privileged to commemorate together as sister Churches the leading Apostles Peter and Paul"²⁶. On November 24, 1980, in a letter to Patriarch Dimitrios I written less than a week before the feast of St. Andrew, Pope John Paul II observed that it is "with a joy and hope renewed every year that we celebrate the feasts of the two brothers, the holy Apostles Peter and Andrew. I am convinced, in fact, that this union in prayer will help our sister Churches to hasten the day when full communion is reestablished between them."²⁷

Once the international theological dialogue was under way in 1980, the subject of discussion in the letters between Constantinople and Rome came to focus much more than previously on the general encounter between the Orthodox and Catholic churches in their totalities (the pairing to be discussed in subsection 2, below), but there were also ongoing references to the relationship of the two sees themselves as sister churches. In a letter to Dimitrios I on November 23, 1988, Pope John Paul II spoke of "the bonds of charity which unite our sister Churches of Rome and Constantinople".²⁸ Addressing Vatican

---

22 Ibid. 311, no. 356.
23 Ibid. 338, no. 383.
24 Ibid. 373, no. 409.
25 Ibid. 396, no. 416.
26 Ibid. 397, no. 417.
27 Ibid. 403, no. 422.
28 The letter is available in French at www.vatican.va/holy_father/john_paul_ii/letters/1988/ documents/hf_jp-ii_let_19881123_dimitrios-i_fr.html. Last accessed 4-18-08. English translation is mine.

officials visiting the Ecumenical Patriarchate on the occasion of the feast of St. Andrew in 1989, Dimitrios I said, "We, the Church of Constantinople, are happy to have among us, once again this year, and according to the beautiful established tradition, an official delegation from our sister Church of Rome"[29]. The message sent by Pope John Paul II on the same occasion referred to "the bonds of charity that unite our sister Churches of Rome and Constantinople."[30] Later in this address, the pope exhorted both Catholics and Orthodox to promote "a view of the other inspired by truth and charity and purged of the polemical attitudes of the past. We have solemnly recognized each other," he went on, "as sister Churches in almost total communion".[31]

On the Feast of St. Andrew in 1992, Patriarch Bartholomew (enthroned the previous year), said in his address to the visiting delegation from Rome, "These visits between the sister Churches of Rome and Constantinople established by those inspired leaders, Pope Paul VI and Patriarch Athenagoras I of Constantinople, are already an institution and bond in the life of our Churches." In his letter of November 26, 1995 to Ecumenical Patriarch Bartholomew, Pope John Paul II again invoked the expression, this time following words about his hope for a restoration of full unity, after which he concluded, "I pray specially for these intentions on this blessed day of the feast of the Apostle Andrew, solemnly celebrated by the Sister Church of Constantinople."[32]

An abundance of examples has been provided in which the churches relating to one another have been unmistakably identifiable as the church of Rome and the church of Constantinople. In many cases, they are described explicitly as "sister churches." Three comments may be made about this type of usage.

---

29 "Visit of Vatican Delegation to the Ecumenical Patriarchate for the Feast of St. Andrew, November 30, 1988," in *Information Service* 69 (1989/I) 13.
30 "Visit of Vatican Delegation ... November 30, 1988," 15.
31 Ibid. 16. John Paul II cites, here, the "Letter of Pope Paul VI dated February 8, 1971, *Tomos Agapis*, n. 283". It is to be noted that the letter of Paul VI to which John Paul II alludes did not actually contain the expression "sister churches," though perspectives relevant to it may be seen in Paul VI's remark "that between our Church and the venerable Orthodox Churches there already exists a communion which is almost complete – though still short of perfection – deriving from our common participation in the mystery of Christ and his Church" (Stormon, *Towards the Healing of Schism*, 232, no. 285).
32 Available in French at www.vatican.va/holy_father/john_paul_ii/letters/1995/documents/hf_jp-ii_let_19951126_patriarca-costantinopoli_fr.html. Last accessed 5-2-08. English translation is mine.

First, insofar as it concerns what for the time being we may call local churches, it is generally consistent with ancient usage. If there were anything novel or surprising about it, it would only be that it is applied to churches that are not in eucharistic communion with one another. On the other hand, even in this respect the usage may not be as groundbreaking as it might seem, since from earlier centuries there is some precedent for applying the language of sister churches to those whose communion with each other has become impaired. This was apparently the case when Pope Innocent I spoke of Antioch and Rome as sisters at a time (415AD) when leaders of the largest faction of the see of Antioch had yet to affirm the teachings of Nicaea that Rome was at pains to uphold.[33] Even more clearly, it was the case when Nicetas of Nicodemia (on behalf of the see of Constantinople) spoke of Rome as a sister Church in the mid-12th century and when Patriarch John Camateros did the same a few decades later.[34]

Second, we may note a certain affinity of another kind between the ecclesial use of "sister" by Innocent I in the early fifth century and the modern use of the expression in many of the passages we have just cited. It will be recalled that for Innocent, the basis on which Antioch and Rome could be considered as sister churches was their common Petrine foundation. This at least was the factor he mentioned explicitly. Something not unrelated seems to lie behind the modern use of the expression sister churches on those particular occasions when its application to Rome and Constantinople coincided with either of their patronal feast days. There is a difference: the apostle Peter was not the founder of *both* Rome and Constantinople (as he was of both Rome and Antioch). But the appeal to apostolic tradition is robust nonetheless. The affirmation of Rome, the "see of Peter," and Constantinople, the "see of Andrew," as "sister churches" clearly rests in large part on the status of Peter and Andrew as apostles; it is perhaps reinforced by a further appeal to the fact that the two were biological brothers.

Finally, a third general comment may be offered with regard to the type of usage whereby "sister churches" applies specifically to Rome and Constantinople. It may well be asked whether either the see of Constantinople or, what may be even more difficult to establish, the see of Rome is ever really an ecclesiastical reality that encompasses no more than "itself" in the sense of being a local diocese. Throughout most of their histories each of them has represented more than that. Therefore even when the expression "sister churches" is un-

---

33 See above, Chapter 1, pp. 11-13.
34 See above, Chapter 1, pp. 28-37.

doubtedly meant to apply "only" to the Church of Rome and "only" to the Church of Constantinople, one is still left with a less than clear-cut idea of just what the "Church of Rome" is, and likewise just what the Church of Constantinople is. This issue will be further explored in section I.3 below.

2. The (Roman) Catholic Church and the (Eastern) Orthodox Church

The application of the expression "sister churches" to Rome and Constantinople, however open it may be to interpretation, is still the most straightforward application and has raised the fewest questions of an ecclesiological nature. There is another type of usage, however, which is more or less as frequently attested in the *Tomos Agapis,* and in which the paired churches cannot be conceived as local churches – at least not as these are commonly understood. This is that type of usage in which the paired churches are "the Catholic Church" and "the Orthodox Church."

To be included in this same category are closely related variants such as the pairing "the Roman Catholic Church" and "the Eastern Orthodox Church," or "the Catholic Church of the West" and "the Orthodox Church of the East"; or even simply "the Church of the West" and "the Church of the East". Although these different ways of naming the two sides are sometimes of such significance as to require comment in themselves, it is appropriate to group them together insofar as they share the common feature of referring to just two ecclesial entities, each of which comprises an entire communion.

Unlike the previous section, which treated Rome and Constantinople as sisters, this section will itself be divided into two subsections, a fact which requires brief explanation. Whereas the pairing of Rome and Constantinople is found primarily in correspondence between just those two sees, the pairing of the Catholic Church and the Orthodox Church is found in two important sources: first, in the same correspondence between Rome and Constantinople; second, in many of the texts of the broader Catholic-Orthodox theological dialogue. That dialogue, in its most decisive and encompassing form, effectively began in 1980. Certainly, its anticipation and preparation informed a number of the statements made by officials of Rome and Constantinople in their correspondence with one another prior to 1980. Just as certainly, visits and exchanges of letters strictly between Constantinople and Rome continued thereafter just as much as before, and some of these will be noted, but the introduction in the early 1980s of the formal international dialogue, in which all of the fourteen autocephalous Orthodox churches throughout the world were represented, marked a new phase in modern Catholic-Orthodox relations. The second subsection, accordingly, will look at many of the common declarations of the international dialogue commission (as well as some related texts of the North American Orthodox-Catholic dialogue commission) where the Catholic Church as a whole and the Orthodox Church as a whole are paired, and, at times, described explicitly as sister churches.

In a significant number of instances in both subsections, examples will be included in which the plural form "churches" is susceptible, in principle, to more than one interpretation: it could mean just two churches (and then still leave open whether the two are Rome and Constantinople or are the whole Catholic Church and the whole Orthodox Church), or it could mean many churches on either side. Wherever such ambiguous examples are included here in this section I.2, the rationale for doing so – rather than including them in section I.1 (Rome and Constantinople) or I.4 (many churches on both sides) will be given in each particular case.

a) Letters and speeches up to 1980 pairing the Catholic Church and the Orthodox Church

In his welcome address to Cardinal Bea visiting the Phanar in April, 1965, Patriarch Athenagoras said of "our most holy brother Pope Paul VI" that he wished to "send him our cordial brotherly salutation and our warm thanks for the mission on which you come." He continued, "You are here to manifest to our Orthodox Church, in a more concrete form and within the context of sacred historical responsibilities, the positive response of the venerable Roman Catholic Church to the recent official communication, through our Patriarchal delegation, of the decisions of the Third Pan-Orthodox Conference."[35] He was referring to a resolution agreed upon by the Orthodox, at Rhodes, "to carry out the dialogue of charity without delay, and to make a careful preparation for the theological dialogue."[36]

There is no mention of "sister churches" in this text. Two churches, nevertheless, are named in the passage: they are "our Orthodox Church" and "the venerable Roman Catholic Church." Several lines later, the same pairing appears with only slight modification. "His Holiness," Athenagoras went on, referring to the pope, who had sent Cardinal Bea as his representative, "in coming forward with this positive response in the name of the venerable Roman Catholic Church, could not have communicated it to us, and through our lowly self to our entire Orthodox Church of the East, by means of a more suitable person

---

35 Stormon, *Towards the Healing of Schism*, 95, no. 94.
36 Ibid.

than Your Eminence."³⁷ Again the two churches named are "the venerable Roman Catholic Church" and "our entire Orthodox Church of the East." The latter is understood as being represented in some sense by Athenagoras.

On his visit to Rome, taken, as he put it, "[o]n the instructions of His Holiness the Ecumenical Patriarch Athenagoras I and of his Holy Synod," Metropolitan Meliton stated that the purpose of his coming was "so that we may convey to the venerable Roman Catholic Church, over which you gloriously preside, the joyful tidings of love and peace on the part of our holy Eastern Orthodox Church."³⁸ Later in this address, the language of sister churches was used explicitly. "Our Orthodox East, aspiring towards the restoration of the ancient unity, beauty, and glory of the Church, has never ceased praying for total union, and has collaborated with other Christians for the development of the ecumenical spirit of reconciliation. In recent times it has turned toward its sister, your Roman Catholic Church, and in the First Pan-Orthodox Conference it unanimously confirmed its desire for this dialogue"³⁹. The sisters in this passage are "our Orthodox East" and "your Roman Catholic Church."⁴⁰ Still later in the address when Meliton said that he looks forward to the beginning of a fruitful dialogue "between our churches," this cannot mean only Rome and Constantinople. It must refer rather to the Roman Catholic Church as a whole and to the communion of Orthodox churches as a whole. This is confirmed in a carefully worded sentence in which Meliton said,

> We propose then, by a unanimous decision of the Third Pan-Orthodox Conference in Rhodes, and by the mandate of His Holiness the Ecumenical Patriarchate, who in accordance with our ordinances, gives effect to this decision, to enter with your permission into communication with your authorized Secretariat, and through it to give your venerable Roman Catholic Church all the information which will bring it up to date with the decisions reached by the assembly of the Orthodox Churches.⁴¹

The two named parties are "your venerable Roman Catholic Church" and "the assembly of the Orthodox Churches." Thus it seems unlikely that in the prayer that follows shortly thereafter, in which Meliton envisioned his mission to Rome as "the blessed beginning of a regular well planned fostering of brotherly relations between our two Churches in a sincere dialogue of charity," the "two

---

37 Ibid. 95, no. 94.
38 Ibid. 85, no. 87.
39 Ibid. 86, no. 87
40 Cf. above, Chapter 2, p. 57.
41 Stormon, *Towards the Healing of Schism*, 86, no. 87.

Churches" are anything less encompassing than, once again, "your venerable Roman Catholic Church" and "the assembly of the Orthodox Churches." Supporting this view is the exhortation that comes soon afterward envisioning the day when "those of the West and those of the East" will be able to eat and drink of the same bread and chalice "to the glory of Christ and his One, Holy, Catholic and Apostolic Church."[42] Similarly, in his reply to Metropolitan Meliton, Pope Paul VI, also looking forward to such a day, stated, "In the future people will be able to say: here centuries of history reached their term; here a new stage in the relations between the Catholic West and the Orthodox East began."[43]

The correlation between "Catholic" and "West" on the one hand, and between "Orthodox" and "East" on the other, customary for many centuries and easily passed over without much notice, warrants a moment's reflection. The correlation is so strong that in the milieu of the *Tomos Agapis*, whether one speaks of Catholic-Orthodox relations or of East-West relations, there is equally little doubt as to what is meant. Of course those who belong to the ecclesiastical tradition that is of the "East" may well belong to a diocese in France or the United States, and those of the "West" to a diocese in Russia or Syria. Today, and indeed already for many decades and even for centuries in some parts of the world, the "Western" church is also in the East and vice versa. Yet in their bilateral relations, only the "Church of the West" is *called* "Western" and only the "Church of the East" is called "Eastern."

It is true that the circumstance of the "Eastern Catholic churches" complicates what is being said here, but not beyond measure. The existence of the Eastern Catholic churches has not sufficed to put a stop to that way of speaking that persists in conceiving of the division as precisely an *East-West* schism. It could even be argued, perhaps, that if it were a question of holding onto only one or the other of the two words in the phrase "Catholic West" in order to distinguish the communion thus signified, the more important word to hold onto, at least in the context of Catholic-Orthodox relations (i.e., of East-West relations), would be not the word "Catholic" but the word "West" – and not the word "Orthodox" but the word "East"! After all, the Catholic Church considers itself orthodox and the Orthodox Church considers itself catholic (and is even officially so designated). In doing so, moreover, neither side necessarily denies the catholicity or orthodoxy of the other. But it is with much more hesitation and ambivalence that the Catholic Church identifies itself as "Eastern" or the Orthodox Church as "Western," for here a more direct challenge to the eccle-

---

42 Ibid. 87, no. 87.
43 Ibid. 87, no. 88.

siality of the other side *is* involved. Some sense of how important this regional, or super-regional (hemispherical?), dimension of the identity of each of the two sides has remained into the late 20th century can be gleaned from considering the further set of examples below. Although these are still examples of the general type that pairs the two communions in their totalities, and a good number of them do use the designations "Orthodox" and "Catholic" much as one would expect, it is striking how many of the examples below (as also some of the ones already given just above) describe the two sides involved in the dialogue in terms of *East and West* – often without any explicit designation "Orthodox" or "Catholic" at all, yet always with the implicit understanding that the East means the Orthodox Church and the West the Catholic Church.

Metropolitan Athenagoras of Thyateira said in an address of December 28, 1963 on an official visit to Pope Paul VI that the latter's predecessor Pope John XXIII had "summoned the Second Vatican Council for the renewal of the Western Church."[44] In his Easter telegram of March 27, 1964, Patriarch Athenagoras offered his "warm and brotherly greeting," as was seen previously, "on the occasion of the light-bearing feast of the Resurrection, which is being celebrated next Sunday by the sister Church of the West"[45]. The same patriarch in his declaration of December 7, 1966 on the first anniversary of the lifting of the anathemas, after suggesting that "[m]odern man and his world cannot support any further the luxury of Christian division," observed: "In this matter the greatest share of responsibility is borne by our two ancient Christian Churches, the Roman Catholic Church of the West and the Orthodox Church of the East: both must advance courageously through practical measures towards unity."[46]

In the papal brief *Anno ineunte,* Paul VI looked forward to the day "when full communion will be reestablished between the Church of the West and that of the East."[47] This formulation appeared amidst introductory remarks early in the text; subsequently there was the allusion previously discussed[48] to Vatican II's *Decree on Ecumenism* when Paul VI mentioned "the traditional and very beautiful expression 'sister Churches,' which local Churches were fond of applying to one another." This may have seemed to urge an understanding of "sister churches" applicable to numerous local churches rather than the two

---

44 Ibid. 59, no. 44.
45 Ibid. 71, no. 58. Cf. above, Chapter 2, p. 56.
46 Ibid. 140-141, no. 142.
47 Ibid. 162, no. 176.
48 See above, Chapter 2, p. 64.

entire communions, yet the ensuing passage of *Anno ineunte* took a rather different turn. The relevant paragraphs have been quoted in full above.[49] The first began, "For centuries we lived this life of 'sister Churches,' and together held the Ecumenical Councils ...". The next began, "On both side ..." and the paragraph after that (not included in our earlier quotation of the passage), "Next we must on either side ...". The focus was again very much on *two*, but not really or exactly on just Rome and Constantinople considered as local churches. It is fairer to say that the pairing the pope had in mind here was what he had spoken of earlier in the brief as "the Church of the West and that of the East."

In their common declaration of October 28, 1967, Pope Paul VI and Patriarch Athenagoras discussed and gave their joint blessing to various sorts of "fruitful contacts between the Roman Catholic Church and the Orthodox Church".[50] In two communications of Patriarch Athenagoras from earlier that month, the same pairing occurs: first, in a letter to Paul VI of October, 6, 1967, in which the patriarch expressed the desire "to strengthen those fraternal relations between the holy Roman Catholic Church and our holy Orthodox Church which through the Lord's bounteous blessing have been freshly restored and are growing day by day",[51] and second, in his address of October 26, 1967 in St. Peter's Basilica, when he expressed his "firm hope that the whole Catholic Church and the whole Orthodox Church, by a common agreement of all their members, and with a sense of responsibility, will make the forward journey towards union with each other."[52]

Again in his telegram of October 13, 1969, Patriarch Athenagoras prayed that a Roman Synod then taking place would meet with success "for the good of the Roman Catholic Church, our beloved sister."[53] Four days later and directly in response to this telegram, Paul VI replied expressing his hope "that this Synod may be a new step towards the restoration to full communion of the two sister Churches."[54] There is no reason to believe that in making this statement he did not have in mind, too, the Roman Catholic Church as one of the sisters, and the Orthodox Church as the other.

---

49 See above Chapter 2, p. 63-64.
50 Stormon, *Towards the Healing of Schism*, 182, no. 195.
51 Ibid. 169, no. 186.
52 Ibid. 172-173, no. 189.
53 Ibid. 218, no. 267.
54 Ibid. 219, no. 269. Cf. above, Chapter 2, p. 68.

In an address of December 14, 1975, given in the Sistine Chapel following the public reading of a letter sent to him from Patriarch Dimitrios I, Pope Paul VI made reference to "the Eastern and Western Churches".[55] Only a few lines earlier in the Pope's address, he had explicitly paired "the Catholic Church and the Orthodox Church" – each in the singular – and he did the same again a few lines later.

By the end of 1975, members had been appointed to an Orthodox preparatory commission whose official title is deserving of notice: "Inter-Orthodox Theological Commission for the Preparation by the Orthodox Church of the Theological Dialogue with the Catholic Church."[56] Although a multiplicity of churches is, to be sure, indicated by the word "Inter-Orthodox," we still find here another typical pairing of "the Orthodox Church" with "the Catholic Church" with regard to the dialogue.[57] In an address of June 27, 1977, Metropolitan Meliton described a common aspiration "towards the restoration of complete communion between East and West, which was broken for a while for reasons known only to the Lord."[58] Here as elsewhere, "East" and "West" each had a fully ecclesial meaning.

Cardinal Willebrands used the expression "sister churches" twice during a 1977 visit to the Patriarchal Cathedral for the feast of St. Andrew. In both cases, it is not certain that he was referring to the Catholic Church and the Orthodox Church, but it is likely. First, just after noting that "[w]e Catholics and Orthodox believe … that the Church is the great sacrament of salvation", he stated that it was this "fundamental reality on which the relations between our two Churches – relations between sister Churches – are based."[59] Later on, Willebrands turned his attention to "the dialogue, so full of hope, that is now opening up," and related its concerns and its purpose to the eucharist, that mystery in which "multiplicity and variety that are visible on the surface are taken up in unity. It is there," he concluded, "in this light, that we shall discover and recognize one another as true brothers; that we shall recognize and discover that our Churches are truly sister Churches. In view of this, we consider

---

55 Stormon, *Towards the Healing of Schism*, 282, no. 332.
56 Ibid. 296, no. 340.
57 By contrast, the Catholic commission called itself the "Catholic Preparatory Commission for the Theological Dialogue with the Orthodox Churches." (Stormon, *Towards the Healing of Schism*, 296, no. 339.) This title will thus betreated under section II.3 below ("The Catholic Church and the Orthodox Churches").
58 Stormon, *Towards the Healing of Schism*, 308, no. 354.
59 Ibid. 313, no. 357.

the work being done in both our Churches by the Technical Commissions responsible for preparing the Theological Dialogue as most important."[60] The expression "both our Churches" reveals that here as in the earlier passage, it is a question of two rather than of many, and if we also bear in mind that the preparatory commissions represented the entire Catholic and Orthodox communions rather than just the sees of Rome and Constantinople, it is reasonable to conclude that these two communions each as a whole must have been the "sister churches" of which the Cardinal was speaking.

In an address of November 30, 1978 given to a delegation sent to Constantinople by John Paul II, Patriarch Dimitrios I referred to the present pope's two predecessors as "[t]wo outstanding figures of the Western Church," as a result of whose deaths, he went on to observe, "[w]e sorrowed with the sorrow of our sister Church".

For the first time since Paul VI had done so twelve years earlier, a pope (John Paul II) visited the Phanar in 1979. On that occasion, Patriarch Dimitrios I said in his welcoming address that the pope's visit, "full of Christian charity and simplicity as it is, has a significance far in excess of a meeting between two bishops of particular sees: we look on it as a meeting of the Western and Eastern Churches."[61] He went on to explain how the meeting was more than "simply a local matter." "The meeting does take place locally, but ... in terms of ecclesiastical definition it is linked geographically with the entire East and the entire West"[62]. In his address in reply, Pope John Paul II spoke of "those first Councils celebrated together by the East and the West," councils whose place-names (Nicaea, Constantinople, Ephesus, Chalcedon) are "known to all Christians" and are "particularly familiar to those who pray, study, and work in different ways for full unity between our sister Churches."[63] In the next paragraph he observed that "for a millennium these two sister Churches" – and we may note well the number, two – "were able to grow together and give detailed and developed expression to their great vital traditions."[64] The following day, the Pope reiterated the same idea in nearly identical terms: "For nearly a whole millennium, the two sister Churches grew side by side, as two great vital and complementary traditions of the same Church of Christ, keeping not only peaceful and fruitful relations, but also concern for the indispensable communion in

---

60 Ibid. 313, no. 357.
61 Ibid. 357, no. 400.
62 Ibid.
63 Ibid. 359, no. 401.
64 Ibid.

faith, prayer and charity, which they did not at any cost want to imperil, despite their different kinds of sensibility."[65] In this remark, the unicity of the Church is affirmed even as an historic Catholic-Orthodox duality is also fully recognized by the application of the expression "sister churches" to the two overarching ecclesial entities.

b) Texts from 1980 on pairing the Catholic Church and the Orthodox Church
Our focus now shifts from the letters and addresses exchanged between the Sees of Rome and Constantinople – though these will still be included from time to time – to documents of the Catholic-Orthodox theological dialogue, especially on the international level, that began to appear in 1980 (with some attention given as well to texts of the U.S. Orthodox-Catholic Consultation).[66] It is notable that such a shift in focus is possible with hardly any disruption in terms of the overall themes and patterns described thus far. This shows that ecumenical and ecclesiological perspectives specific to Rome and Constantinople were shared more broadly throughout the Catholic and Orthodox worlds. This is not to say, of course, that these perspectives were not also challenged and even hotly disputed, especially in some Orthodox circles (also, at a later stage, among Catholics).[67] But it means that there were Orthodox and Catholic theologians and bishops from all over the world and of significant influence who were inclined to conceive of the "two sides" engaged in dialogue and to apply the expression "sister churches" in much the same ways as Patriarch Athenagoras and Pope Paul VI had done (and Patriarch Dimitrios I and Pope John Paul II did after them). In particular, these theologians and bishops were quite willing to speak in terms of relations between the Catholic Church *as a whole* and the Orthodox Church *as a whole;* they were willing to speak of "East-West" relations in an ecclesial sense bearing this same meaning; and they were willing to identify, at times, these two entire communions as "sister churches" of one another.

The official name of the international Catholic-Orthodox dialogue commission – in existence from late 1979 to the present day – is itself a reflection of this way of thinking: it is the "Joint International Commission for Theological Dialogue between the Roman Catholic Church and the Orthodox Church." Comprised of thirty Orthodox and thirty Catholic representatives, this Joint

---

65 Ibid. 361, no. 402.
66 The name of this commission, which in 1994 was still the "U.S. Orthodox-Catholic Consultation," subsequently changed to be the "North American Orthodox-Catholic Consultation". What caused the name change was that the Canadian Catholic Bishops' Conference became an official co-sponsor on the Catholic side.
67 Such objections will be the focus of the subsequent two chapters of this study.

International Commission issued its first official document at the end of its inaugural plenary session (which had started at Patmos and continued at Rhodes) on June 1, 1980. The document was entitled, "Plan to Set Underway the Theological Dialogue between the Roman Catholic Church and the Orthodox Church."[68] Its opening sentence, under the subheading "Purpose of the Dialogue", was as follows: "The purpose of the dialogue between the Roman Catholic Church and the Orthodox Church is the re-establishment of full communion between these two churches."[69] Of utmost importance for our topic is that both in the title of the document and in its opening statement of purpose, two single churches are named. Moreover they are not local churches, at least not in any conventional sense, but are the two entire communions formally separated from one another.

At several junctures in the document, there is reference to the "dialogue between" (or the "elements which unite," or the "theological problems which exist between") the "Orthodox and Roman Catholic Churches". The plural form, so often susceptible to varying interpretations – it could mean just two and it could mean many on either side – in this document is closely followed in a number of instances by the clarifying phrase "the two churches".[70] Other clues in the document include another reference to "the Roman Catholic Church" and "the Orthodox Church" as a pair of singular entities.[71] In addition, the East/West binary appears three times, with no doubt that "East" refers in every one of the three instances to the Orthodox tradition, and "West" to the Catholic tradition.

---

68 Available in J. Borelli and J. Erickson, eds., *The Quest for Unity: Orthodox and Catholics in Dialogue. Documents of the Joint International Commission and Official Dialogues in the United States 1965-1995* (Crestwood, NY and Washington, DC: St. Vladimir's Seminary Press and United States Catholic Conference, 1996). All references to the "Plan to Set Underway the Theological Dialogue between the Roman Catholic Church and the Orthodox Church" (henceforth, the "Plan") and other statements of the Joint International Commission, as well as statements of the U.S. Orthodox-Catholic Consultation, are taken from this source, but citations will be according to each document's internal section numbers, with the relevant pages in Erickson and Borelli being given only once for each document at the outset. The "Plan" is found in Erickson and Borelli, 47-52.

69 "Plan," §I.

70 Cf. "Plan," §I; §II,1; §II,2; §II,3, para. 2; and §II,5.

71 "Plan," §II,3, para. 2.

In an address of June 28, 1980, Pope John Paul II reflected on the significance of the Joint International Commission's first plenary meeting the previous month.

> The Theological Dialogue which was officially opened on the Isle of Patmos is an important event: in Catholic-Orthodox relations it is the greatest thing that has happened not merely this year but for centuries past. We are entering into a new phase of our relations, since the Theological Dialogue is an essential element in a wider exchange between our Churches. In this Dialogue *both the Catholic and Orthodox Churches are involved as a whole*. As a result we have found the general framework, and within it the effective means, by which we can pin-point in their real context – beyond the range of preliminary prejudices and reservations – the various kinds of difficulties which still stand in the way of full communion.[72]

Commenting again several months later on the dialogue "that the Joint Commission between the Catholic and Orthodox Churches initiated this year," John Paul II wrote in a letter to Patriarch Dimitrios I that "old differences that led the Eastern and Western Churches to cease celebrating the Eucharist together are going to be tackled in a new and constructive way."[73] While this formulation is among the ambiguous ones as to whether what was meant were the *many* Eastern and Western churches, or simply the two, there was no such ambiguity in what was said by Cardinal Willebrands, visiting the Phanar on November 30, 1980 for the feast of St. Andrew, when he spoke of the theological dialogue "between the Catholic Church and the entire Orthodox Church."[74] In the same text and with apparently the same meaning – though here again, we are faced with a certain linguistic ambiguity – he referred to "the Churches of the East and the West," following this with an observation that never before in history had "the pursuit of unity between East and West been so free and sincere as in these times"[75].

---

72 Stormon, *Towards the Healing of Schism*, 400, no. 418 (emphasis added).
73 Ibid. 404, no. 422.
74 Ibid. 405, no. 423. To be noted, nevertheless, is the subtle asymmetry implied by the fact that Cardinal Willebrands did not see a need to refer to "the entire Catholic Church." More will be said on this under section I.3 when we discuss the pairing "the Catholic Church" and "the Orthodox Churches."
75 Stormon, *Towards the Healing of Schism*, 407, no. 423. Thematically, though not quite chronologically fitting here, are two other comments by Cardinal Willebrands: the first was on the sixteenth centenary of the Council of I Constantinople, which he described as "an occasion for both East and West to meditate at length on the one and

The first properly theological Agreed Statement (beyond the 1980 "Plan") produced by the Joint International Commission was the document entitled "The Mystery of the Church and of the Eucharist in the Light of the Mystery of the Holy Trinity," issued in Munich on July 6, 1982, at the end of the Commission's second plenary meeting.[76] In at least one passage in this text, the East-West binary is invoked in a manner that deserves notice, since it bears an ecclesial rather than simply a geographical significance. "Without wishing to resolve yet the difficulties which have arisen between the East and the West concerning the relationship between the Son and the Spirit, we can already say together that ...".[77] By "East" and "West" are obviously meant here the two respective churches, yet once again.

In another passage in the document, in which there is discussion of catholicity in both time and space, the language of sister churches appears explicitly, yet with considerable ambiguity of meaning.

> Today, mutual recognition between this [i.e., each] local church and the other churches is also of capital importance. Each should recognize in the others, through local particularities, the identity of the mystery of the Church. It is a question of mutual recognition of catholicity as communion in the wholeness of the mystery. This recognition is achieved first of all at the regional level. Communion in the same patriarchate or in some other form of regional unity is first of all a manifestation of the life of the Spirit in the same culture or in the same historical conditions. It equally implies unity of witness and calls for the exercise of fraternal correction in humility. This communion within the same region should extend itself further in the communion between sister churches.[78]

The U.S. Orthodox-Catholic Theological Consultation, which had been in existence since 1965 and already by this time produced nine agreed statements of its own, in its generally positive response to the 1982 Munich text on the "Mystery of the Church" observed in reference to the passage just quoted that "the appeal to the term 'sister churches' is unclear."[79] How the U.S. Consultation framed the

---

undivided Trinity" (Stormon, 434, no. 447). The second was at the Phanar for the feast of St. Andrew, on November 30, 1983, when he remarked upon "the quest for full unity between the Churches, for full unity between the Churches of the East and the West" (Stormon, 465, no. 474).

76 Borelli and Erickson, *The Quest for Unity*, 53-64.
77 "Mystery of the Church," §I,6.
78 Ibid. §III,3 (b).
79 Para. 7 in "A Response to the Joint International Commission for Theological Dialogue between the Orthodox Church and the Roman Catholic Church Regarding the

question it felt the Joint International Commission's use of the expression "sister churches" left unanswered is interesting. "Does it refer to patriarchates or jurisdictions in full communion or to the special relationship between the Orthodox Church and the Roman Catholic Church?"[80] Of these two alternatives, the first, "patriarchates or jurisdictions in full communion," is the one type of usage (intra-confessional) that is not contested at all. The second is the type presently under examination, pairing the two whole communions as sisters, and it is significant that this type may well have been used in the initial Agreed Statement produced by the Joint International Commission.

In the second session of its fourth plenary meeting, at Bari, Italy on June 10, 1987, the Joint International Commission issued its second Agreed Statement, "Faith, Sacraments, and the Unity of the Church."[81] This document contains no usages of the expression "sister churches," but its pairing of "East" and "West" in an ecclesial sense is striking in a number of passages. For example, there is the observation that "our two traditions, eastern and western, thus experience a certain diversity in the formulation of the content of the faith being celebrated."[82] In the next paragraph, it is stated that "[t]he Eastern Church in its baptismal rite uses the Niceo-Constantinopolitan Creed. Faithful to its own tradition, the Western Church conveys to the catechumen the text called 'the Apostles' Creed.'"[83] Another passage contains the assertion, "During the centuries of the undivided Church, diversity in the theological expression of a doctrine did not endanger sacramental communion. After the schism occurred, East and West continued to develop, but they did this separately from each other."[84] Yet another states, "The history of the baptismal rites in East and West ... shows clearly that the three sacraments of initiation form a unity. That unity is strongly affirmed by the Orthodox Church. For its part, the Catholic Church also preserves it."[85] It should also be noted that at numerous points in the Bari document, occurrences of the phrase "both churches," or "the two churches," are unmistakably references to the Catholic Church and the Orthodox Church.[86]

Document: 'The Mystery of the Church and of the Eucharist in the Light of the Mystery of the Holy Trinity,'" in Borelli and Erickson, *The Quest for Unity*, 65-68. Henceforth to be cited as "Response to the Munich Statement."

80 "Response to the Munich Statement," para. 7.
81 Borelli and Erickson, *The Quest for Unity*, 93-104.
82 "Faith, Sacraments, and the Unity of the Church," para. 19.
83 Ibid. para. 20.
84 Ibid. para. 26.
85 Ibid. para. 38.
86 Cf. ibid. paras. 4, 14, 46, 49, 50, 52.

That this is so in a document expressly concerned with the theme of the unity of the Church makes it perhaps especially worthy of attention.

At the end of the sixth plenary meeting of the Joint International Commission, in Freising, Germany, on June 15, 1990, a Communiqué was issued[87] in which it was observed, "The term 'Uniatism' indicates here the effort which aims to bring about the unity of the Church by separating from the Orthodox Church communities or Orthodox faithful without taking into account that, according to ecclesiology, the Orthodox Church is a sister-Church which itself offers the means of grace and salvation."[88]

On the one hand, a clear conception of the Church as one and indivisible is indicated by the phrase "the unity of the Church," which in this passage is certainly a reference to the one, holy, catholic and apostolic Church as professed in the Creed; and, on the other hand, a readiness to speak of the Orthodox Church in its entirety as a "sister church" – of, there can be no doubt, the Catholic Church – is equally in evidence. Thus the unicity of the Church of God and a Catholic-Orthodox ecclesial duality are simultaneously affirmed once again.

The Balamand Statement, "Uniatism, Method of Union of the Past, and the Present Search for Full Communion," was issued at the end of the seventh plenary meeting of the Joint International Commission on June 23, 1993.[89] It almost immediately proved to be a lightning rod in the controversy over the concept of sister churches, which it employed. Reactions to Balamand will be considered in subsequent chapters, but an important feature of this text is to be noted at this point, namely its frequent pairing of the Orthodox Church and the Catholic Church in their entireties. This is indeed the predominant pattern in the Balamand Statement.[90]

To begin with, the document refers on several occasions to "the church of the West and the church of the East" (or vice versa) and to the need to reestablish communion between them.[91] It also speaks of "the Catholic Church" in tandem with "the Orthodox Church," each in the singular.[92]

---

87 The text of the 1990 Freising Communiqué is available in the Vatican publication *Information Service* 73 (1990/II), 52-53.
88 Freising Communiqué (June 15, 1990), §6.b.
89 Borelli and Erickson, *The Quest for Unity*, 175-183.
90 It is not the only pattern; exceptions to it will be examined below, in sections I.3 and I.4.
91 Cf. "Uniatism, Method of Union of the Past," para. 7, para. 8, para. 9.
92 Ibid. para. 10.

Later in the document the phrase "sister churches" appears; it is set in opposition to the type of proselytism that would seek to bring members of the other church over to one's own. "Because of the way in which Catholics and Orthodox once again consider each other in their relationship to the mystery of the Church and discover each other once again as sister churches, this form of 'missionary apostolate' described above, and which has been called 'uniatism,' can no longer be accepted"[93]. Whether the sister churches in this passage are understood as many local Catholic and Orthodox churches or as the two Catholic and Orthodox communions as a whole is not immediately clear. The next paragraph, however, perhaps offers a clue where it states that "[o]n each side it is recognized that what Christ has entrusted to his Church ... cannot be considered the exclusive property of one of our churches."[94] It would seem that what must be meant here is not *any* "one of our [many] churches" but *either* "one of our [two] churches".

Another passage in the Balamand text cites the encyclical of John Paul II, *Slavorum Apostoli*, in which the expression "sister churches" was used. "According to the words of Pope John Paul II, the ecumenical endeavor of the sister churches of East and West, grounded in dialogue and prayer, is the search for perfect and total communion"[95]. The rest of the passage in which these words appeared in *Slavorum Apostoli* indicates that the pope himself had in mind just two churches, not many, when he used the phrase "the sister churches of East and West." The following sentence from the encyclical leaves no doubt of this: "Cyril and Methodius, in their personality and their work, are figures that awaken in all Christians a great 'longing for union' and for unity between the two sister Churches of East and West."[96] The Balamand Statement (like the Bari document in this respect, and unlike the Valamo document) also frequently makes use of those types of phrases that imply the pairing of two overarching ecclesial entities – such phrases as "between the churches,"[97] "between our churches,"[98] "on the part of both churches,"[99] "in the two churches,"[100] "between

---

93 Ibid. para. 12.
94 Ibid. para. 13.
95 Ibid. para. 14.
96 *Slavorum Apostoli* (June 2, 1985), no. 27. The encyclical is available at www.vatican.va/holy_father/john_paul_ii/encyclicals/documents/hf_jp-ii_enc_19850602_slavorum-apostoli_en.html
97 "Uniatism, Method of Union of the Past," para. 19, para. 21.
98 Ibid. para. 20.
99 Ibid. para. 24.
100 Ibid. para. 25.

the two churches,"[101] "of the other church,"[102] and "of the two churches."[103] As to which two churches are meant there is little doubt, as seen for example in paragraph 24 when it is urged that religious liberty be respected with regard to those "who wish to be in communion either with the Orthodox Church or with the Catholic Church."

Finally, in the response (October 15, 1994) of the U.S. Orthodox-Catholic Consultation to the Balamand Statement,[104] the same pattern is discernible, as when the assertion is made that "the history of relations between our two churches often has been a tragic one,"[105] or when the phrases "either of our churches"[106] and "only one of our churches"[107] appear. Also deserving of notice is a sentence that reads, "To be sure, there may be cases in which conscience leads an Orthodox or a Catholic Christian to enter the other church."[108] These several passages that speak of relations between two churches, where the two in question are definitely the Catholic Church and the Orthodox Church, provide the context for interpreting the document's following observations regarding the concept of sister churches.

> We also note the [Balamand] Document's use of the concept of 'sister churches' (cf. §14). The use of the venerable term in modern Orthodox-Catholic dialogue has helped to place relations between our churches on a new footing. We hope that, when the International Commission resumes work on ecclesiology, it will be able more fully to explore its precise significance and manifold implications. The concept of sister churches includes the notion of mutual respect for each other's pastoral ministry. As the Balamand Document states, 'bishops and priests have the duty before God to respect the authority which the Holy Spirit has given to the bishops and priests of the other church and for that reason to avoid interfering in the spiritual life of the faithful of that church' (§29).[109]

---

101 Ibid. para. 29, para. 30.
102 Ibid.
103 Ibid. para. 30.
104 "A Response of the Orthodox-Roman Catholic Consultation in the United States to the Joint International Commission for Theological Dialogue between the Orthodox Church and the Roman Catholic Church regarding the Balamand Document (Dated June 23, 1993): 'Uniatism, Method of Union of the Past, and the Present Search for Full Communion," in Borelli and Erickson, *The Quest for Unity*, 184-190. Henceforth to be cited as "Response to the Balamand Statement."
105 "Response to the Balamand Statement," para. 6.
106 Ibid. para. 14.
107 Ibid. para. 15.
108 Ibid.
109 Ibid. para. 12.

From the phrases "between our churches," "each other's" ministry, and, within the quoted sentence from Balamand, "of the other church," we are again led to the conclusion that the designation "sister churches" is here being applied to the relationship of the Catholic Church and the Orthodox Church each in its entirety.

This conclusion is strengthened by what is expressed by two co-chairmen of the U.S. Consultation, each of whom contributed a brief foreword to the volume edited by Borelli and Erickson and entitled *Quest for Unity* (1996) in which appear most of the documents analyzed here. Archbishop Rembert Weakland, the Catholic co-chairman, wrote of the "centuries of estrangement between the Eastern Church and the Western Church"; he also wrote of "restoring relations between East and West".[110] In the other foreword, Bishop Maximos of Pittsburgh had this to say of the U.S. Consultation: "We have responded to the work of the Joint International Commission for the dialogue between our two sister churches, the 'two lungs' of the one Church of Christ. These two have to synchronize anew their breathing, so that the Church of Christ may begin breathing properly again."[111] We have now surveyed dozens of instances in which the two entire communions of the Catholic Church and the Orthodox Church are paired, and are spoken of in some cases as sister churches. Three overall comments may be offered with regard to this type of usage.

First, it should be observed that the application of the expression "sister churches" to the (Roman) Catholic Church and the (Eastern) Orthodox Church represents something of a new way of applying the concept. Neither the Catholic Church nor the Orthodox Church is normally identified as a local church, certainly not in the way that such sees as Antioch, Rome, or Constantinople typically have been and still may be.

Second, the sheer abundance of occurrences of this type of usage should be regarded as an important issue for reflection. If the usage is not overtly in line with ancient usage, what were the factors that impelled so many participants in the Catholic-Orthodox dialogue – both in the theological dialogue and in the "dialogue of charity" – to invoke it as often as they did? The fact that the usage was so overwhelmingly favored by officials of both churches, who simply assumed it to be applicable and natural, cannot be lightly dismissed.

Third, it may be recalled from Chapter 1 that a relationship of sister churches never excluded (as Francis Dvornik showed in his analysis of the

---

110 Borelli and Erickson, *The Quest for Unity*, 1.
111 Ibid. 3.

Pentarchic idea[112]) real differences between or among the sisters in terms of their status, function or authority. If numerous participants in the Catholic-Orthodox dialogue in the latter decades of the twentieth century were inclined to describe the Roman Catholic Church and the Orthodox Church as sister churches, this does not necessarily mean that they were implying a simple parity between them.

3. The Catholic Church and the Orthodox Churches

In an address on November 22, 1965, Metropolitan Meliton drew a deliberate distinction between the Orthodox *Church* and the Orthodox *churches*.

> We encounter each other on the road where love is being restored between the Roman Catholic Church and the Orthodox Church, a road which was opened up by Pope Paul VI and Patriarch Athenagoras I through their holy meeting in Jerusalem, and then widened by exchanges and declarations of good quality, and by significant acts on both sides. This has been so on the one hand between the Roman Catholic Church and the Church of Constantinople and also the other local Autocephalous Orthodox Churches, and on the other hand between the Roman Catholic Church and the Orthodox body as a whole.[113]

In the last sentence where Metropolitan Meliton set forth two ways of formulating the Catholic-Orthodox relationship, his ecclesial conception remained constant with regard to the Catholic side. The shift occurred only on the Orthodox side. In both formulations, it was the "Roman Catholic Church," whereas he shifted from a vision of *all* the local Autocephalous Orthodox churches to a vision of the Orthodox Church as a single entity.[114] The fact that he did not adjust the terms with which he characterized the Catholic dialogue partner, but did adjust his characterization of the Orthodox partner(s), points up a difference of emphasis between the two ecclesiological traditions. This difference, which has complex roots and can be interpreted in a number of ways, underlies a way of speaking, occasionally attested in modern Catholic-Orthodox relations, whereby the Catholic Church in the singular is set beside a multiplicity of Orthodox churches.

In an address by Paul VI at the conclusion of a visit of Patriarch Athenagoras to Rome on October 28, 1967, the pope asked that through God's

---

112 Cf. above, Chapter 1, p. 38.
113 Stormon, *Towards the Healing of Shcism*, 119, no. 122.
114 It may be noted that with regard to the Orthodox, the distinction was not between the whole church and the particular chuches, but between the whole and the regional ecclesial groupings, e.g. patriarchates.

guidance, "the Roman Catholic Church and the Orthodox Churches" might take further steps toward full communion.[115] The common declaration of pope and patriarch issued the same day spoke again of hope "for the restoration of full communion between the Roman Catholic Church and the Orthodox Churches".[116]

Pope Paul VI wrote in his Easter letter of March 26, 1975 to Patriarch Dimitrios I that the "Catholic Church will study with great interest any proposals that may be submitted to it, especially those that come from the Orthodox Churches."[117] It is also to be noted that the title given, later in 1975, to the Catholic preparatory commission, formed to help lay the groundwork for the start of the international Catholic-Orthodox dialogue, was such that the Orthodox side was conceived as a plurality of churches: "Catholic Preparatory Commission for the Theological Dialogue with the Orthodox Churches."[118] Another formulation which sometimes occurs and which is closely related to this way of conceiving of the two sides of the dialogue should be mentioned here. In a letter of October 18, 1965 to Patriarch Athenagoras, Cardinal Bea wrote of "the relations between the Roman Catholic Church and the Patriarchate of Constantinople."[119] On either side of the Catholic-Orthodox axis, reference is made to a single church, but in fact, there is a notable discrepancy between the two *kinds* of churches named: the Patriarchate of Constantinople is well understood to be one among other Orthodox patriarchates, whereas certainly the Roman Catholic Church is *not* typically understood to be one among other Catholic churches. The same discrepancy presents itself in several other texts in the *Tomos Agapis*,[120] one of which may be especially noted for its containing a form of the expression "sister churches." This was a telegram of August 7, 1978, sent

---

115 Stormon, *Towards the Healing of Schism*, 180, no. 194.
116 Ibid. 181, no. 195.
117 Ibid. 274, no. 326.
118 Ibid. 296, no. 339.
119 *Ibid.* 116, no. 119.
120 Paul VI and Athenagoras in their common declaration of December 7, 1965 spoke of "the fraternal relations thus inaugurated between the Roman Catholic Church and the Orthodox Church of Constantinople" (Stormon, *Towards the Healing of Schism*, 126, no. 127), and in another common declaration, of October 28, 1967, they spoke of the readiness of the "Roman Catholic Church and the Ecumenical Patriarchate" to address pastoral problems. (ibid. 182, no. 195) In his address of November 30, 1974 in the Patriarchal Cathedral, Father Pierre Duprey described an "atmosphere of brotherly love between the holy Roman Catholic Church and that of Constantinople, and more generally of the whole Orthodox Church" (ibid. 270, no. 322).

by Patriarch Dimitrios I upon the death of Pope Paul VI, in which the patriarch exclaimed that the "Ecumenical Patriarchate as sister Church shares with its whole soul in the grief of the holy Roman Catholic Church and the entire Roman Catholic world."[121] In this formulation, a particular Orthodox church which is one of a number of Orthodox churches of the East is said to be the sister church of a Roman Catholic Church which, on its side of the confessional division, is the one and only Catholic Church of the West.

On November 28, 1979, in a speech given at the airport in Rome prior to his departure for Turkey, Pope John Paul II spoke of his desire "to show, as a theological dialogue draws near, the importance which the Catholic Church attaches to its relationship with the venerable Orthodox Churches."[122] He expressed himself similarly once he had arrived at the Phanar when he described "the deep feeling of the Catholic Church for the Eastern Orthodox Churches, and its sense of brotherly solidarity with them."[123] It should be noted that this pattern – in which a single Catholic Church is said to relate fraternally with multiple Orthodox churches – was not the only one according to which John Paul II conceived of the two sides of the dialogue. In the very same speech he spoke of the Orthodox Church and the Catholic Church as "these two sister Churches,"[124] and again in a speech the following day, he referred to the "Orthodox Church" in the singular as well as the "Orthodox Churches" in the plural.[125]

In a speech given only a few days later, after his return to Rome, Pope John Paul II quoted a passage in Vatican II's *Decree on Ecumenism* in which multiple churches in the East are discussed in relation to a single church in the West. "I am happy to recall what the Council Fathers recognized when they noted that 'from their very origins the Churches of the East have had a treasury from which the Church of the West has drawn many elements of its liturgy, spiritual tradition, and its body of law' (*Unitatis Redintegratio*, 14)."[126] Another address of Pope John Paul II, on December 10, 1979, referred both to the Orthodox Church in the singular and to the Orthodox churches in the plural: "Therefore, together with the Theological Dialogue, certainly so necessary, which is to begin in the near future between the Catholic Church and the Orthodox Church as a whole (that is to say, with all the Orthodox autocephalous Churches), we

---

121 Stormon, *Towards the Healing of Schism*, 327, no. 373.
122 Ibid. 356, no. 399.
123 Ibid. 359, no. 401.
124 Ibid.
125 Ibid. 360-361, no. 402.
126 Ibid. 374, no. 409.

continue to need the dialogue of brotherly love and *rapprochement*."[127] In language close to that of Metropolitan Meliton more than a dozen years earlier,[128] we find John Paul II, too, struggling to arrive at the best way of identifying the Orthodox communion, whether as church or as churches, and, meanwhile – also like Metropolitan Meliton – not struggling with the same question with regard to the Catholic communion.

In the properly theological dialogue between Catholics and Orthodox, there are few passages – only three altogether – in which many churches are posited on one confessional side, and a single church on the other. One of the three comes at the beginning of the Balamand Statement and conforms to the pattern seen thus far: "At the request of the Orthodox Churches, the normal progression of the theological dialogue with the Catholic Church has been set aside so that immediate attention might be given to the question which is called 'uniatism.'"[129] Remarkably, however, the other two examples, also in the Balamand Statement, reverse this pattern. In its discussion of the tensions between Orthodox and Eastern Catholics, the text speaks of "the difficulties which these Oriental Catholic Churches present to the Orthodox Church."[130] It mentions in a similar way "the relations between the Orthodox Church and the Oriental Catholic Churches."[131] Quite unusually, we are given a picture of one Orthodox Church and many Catholic churches. In spite of its rarity, this curiously inverted picture may be of value in opening up important ecclesiological perspectives otherwise obscured. For one thing, it seems to invite us to recognize that within the Catholic tradition, too, a reality of ecclesial pluralism may indeed be operative – and on more than just the level of dioceses.

In general, however, what must be concluded from the more well-attested pattern of relating a single Catholic Church to multiple Orthodox churches is that this reflects a greater emphasis in the Eastern tradition on a level of author-

---

127 Stormon, *Towards the Healing of Schism*, 377, no. 410.
128 See above, pp. 94-95.
129 "Uniatism, Method of Union of the Past," para. 1. Possibly, there is one other occurrence of this type, in an agreed statement of the U.S. Orthodox-Catholic Theological Consultation, "Apostolicity as God's Gift in the Life of the Church" (1986), where, in paragraph 12, differences of emphasis are discussed between "the Eastern Churches" and "the Roman Church." But this example would be more clearly of the type we are examining if, instead of "the Roman Church," the text had said "the Roman Catholic Church." In any case, beyond the opening sentence of Balamand, there are no other examples of this type in the texts of the international Catholic-Orthodox dialogue.
130 "Uniatism, Method of Union of the Past," para. 17.
131 Ibid. para. 23.

ity neither strictly local nor universal, but regional. For it is not that the one Roman Catholic Church is being set alongside many local Orthodox dioceses, but rather alongside various Orthodox autocephalous churches. A question that arises, then, when the expression sister churches is applied to the (Roman) Catholic Church vis-à-vis one or more of the particular Eastern Orthodox churches, is the extent to which the Roman Catholic Church itself may be regarded, in some sense, as a regionally specific church: the church of the West.

4. The Catholic Churches and the Orthodox Churches

Rarest of all the ways of presenting the Catholic-Orthodox axis is to speak of many churches on both sides. Only a very few cases appear in which such a meaning can be established solidly.

In his address of November 30, 1973,[132] Patriarch Dimitrios I sought to clear up certain ambiguities of ecclesiological language. "When we speak about 'our Churches' we have no thought of abandoning that concept of the Church according to which it is One, Holy, Catholic and Apostolic; what we have in mind is the local Churches, each having its own jurisdiction"[133]. Viewing this observation in light of the speech as a whole, it would seem that any sort of ecclesial pluralism except that which exists strictly on the level of the local diocese was seen by Dimitrios I as incompatible with the principle of the unity of the Church. This stance, which is dubious from the perspective of traditional Orthodox ecclesiology, was again reflected in Dimitrios I's remark in the next paragraph, where he said in a scarcely veiled criticism of claims of papal primacy, "[w]e are all ... purely and simply fellow bishops."[134] All of this may also be perceived as being generally in harmony with a most unusual formulation which appears twice near the end of the Patriarch's address: this is where he invoked not only the customary term "Pan-Orthodox," but also, in tandem with it, the almost unheard-of term "Pan-Catholic."[135] In the relevant passage, he first expressed the wish to establish certain ground-rules according to which "hence-

---

132 See above, pp. 77-78.
133 Stormon, *Towards the Healing of Schism*, 259, no. 311.
134 Ibid. no. 311.
135 Besides these two occurrences in this single address of Patriarch Dimitrios I, the term does not appear in the *Tomos Agapis* (though Dimitrios I says something similar in an address of November 30, 1978 when he comments on preparations "for the Theological Dialogue, both from the Pan-Orthodox side and the equally representative Roman Catholic one" (Stormon, *Towards the Healing of Schism*, 345, no. 389).) By contrast, the term "Pan-Orthodox" is ubiquitous.

forth all our Pan-Catholic and Pan-Orthodox meetings, dialogues, and deliberations, will be held",[136] and then went on a few lines later to assert that "from now on all our joint enterprises and deliberations directed towards unity, even though they may be worked out, in accordance with the decisions of the third Pan-Orthodox Conference, on a basis simply involving two parties [viz., Rome and Constantinople], will have no definitive result, except as decided on a Pan-Catholic and Pan-Orthodox level."[137]

The linguistic move made here by Dimitrios I to ascribe ecclesial multiplicity to the Catholic dialogue partner (just as it is ascribed to the Orthodox partner) actually undermines what is often held by Orthodox ecclesiologists about the Roman Catholic Church – namely that it is, in essence, the Patriarchate of the West.[138] According to this traditional Orthodox understanding, the Roman Catholic Church is one of several preeminent churches. The term "Pan-Orthodox" serves to refer to the *rest* of the preeminent churches. This term "Pan-Orthodox," in the context of international inter-Orthodox and ecumenical issues, is virtually never used with respect to local churches (in the strict sense of local dioceses). It is a way of speaking about patriarchates and autocephalous churches – i.e., of large regional or national ecclesial units. Dimitrios I was implicitly speaking about these when he mentioned "the third Pan-Orthodox Conference," for this was a conference of the heads of *regional* churches, not of the bishops of local dioceses. But no comparable plurality of larger administrative ecclesial units exists in the Catholic West as it does in the Orthodox East. (It is also very doubtful that Dimitrios I had in mind any idea of the Eastern Catholic patriarchates.) Thus the "many-ness" ascribed to the Catholic dialogue partner could not really have a parallel meaning to the "many-ness" that is involved when there are references to the "Orthodox churches" in discussions of global Orthodoxy.

---

136 Stormon, *Towards the Healing of Schism*, 261, no. 311.

137 Ibid.

138 The remarks of Bishop Hilarion Alfeyev are in this regard typical of a longstanding Orthodox view: "In the Byzantine epoch there were four Eastern Patriarchates: of Constantinople, of Alexandria, of Antioch, and of Jerusalem. The Patriarchate of Rome was considered as 'first among equal' in the diptychs up until 1054, when the ecclesiastical relations between East and West were interrupted. Thus, in the West, there was only one Patriarchate of Rome, while in the East there were four Patriarchates. The Patriarchate of the West together with the four Eastern Patriarchates constituted the so-called 'pentarchy'." (Bp. Hilarion, "Pope's Title 'Patriarch of the West' Removed," posted in the online publication *OrthodoxyToday.org* on March 9, 2006, accessible at www.orthodoxeurope.org/ (accessed May 15, 2008).

It is appropriate in this connection to point out once again that whereas at least a handful of times in the *Tomos Agapis*, one can find mention of the "sister Orthodox churches," there is no parallel instance of any intra-Catholic usage of the expression.[139] The absence of a reference to the "sister Catholic churches" in texts spanning some four decades of "the dialogue of charity" as well as the theological dialogue is a fact of no small significance. It suggests that the pre-eminence characteristic of the major sees of the East was characteristic of no church in the West apart from Rome itself.

In light of this, and of what has been said in a related way about the questionable suitability of the term "Pan-Catholic" – at least, its lack of parallelism to the customary and fitting term "Pan-Orthodox," which has properly applied to regional churches – it will perhaps now be more readily possible to make sense of the very few further instances in which there are posited many churches on both sides of the Catholic-Orthodox axis.

A passage in the Valamo document offers an incontrovertible instance in which plurality is ascribed to both the Orthodox and the Catholic sides of the dialogue. "This hierarchy or *taxis* soon found its canonical expression, formulated by the councils, especially in the canons received by all the churches of the East and West."[140] The councils subsequently mentioned include those running from Nicaea (325) to the Council of St. Sophia (879-880), an historical period at the beginning of which, at least, the organization of the Church into a system of metropolitanates and patriarchates was only in its formative stages. Thus in this case, "all the churches of the East and West" must have meant, or been meant to include, not only preeminent churches but local churches of all sizes and degrees of influence. It therefore does not necessarily entail any recognition of a plurality of *regional* Catholic churches in the contemporary situation.

Two passages in the Balamand Statement discuss Orthodox churches in the plural in relation to Catholic churches in the plural. One of them explicitly invokes the expression "sister churches". This passage comes just after the point has been made that "what Christ has entrusted to his Church ... cannot be considered the exclusive property of one of our Churches" and that therefore "any rebaptism must be avoided"[141]: "It is in this perspective that the Catholic Churches and the Orthodox Churches recognize each other as sister churches, responsible together for maintaining the Church of God"[142].

---

139 See above, Chapter 3, p. 72.
140 Sacrament of Order," para. 52.
141 "Uniatism, Method of Union of the Past," para. 13. See above, p. 95.
142 Ibid. para. 14.

It is difficult to say what *sort* of "Catholic Churches" are meant here. One answer would simply be to say that they are local Catholic churches (in the strict sense of local dioceses), and that, in consequence, the passage also means to speak of local Orthodox churches (in that same sense). This interpretation is certainly plausible. At the same time, it should be noted that in a subsequent paragraph, in successive sentences, mention is made of "Oriental Catholic Churches" and of "Orthodox Churches" – both in the plural. This suggests that the many sister churches in question are actually such churches as the Ukrainian Catholic Church, the Ruthenian Catholic Church, etc., alongside the Ukrainian Orthodox Church, the Romanian Orthodox Church, etc.

The second relevant passage would seem to lend further weight to this possible interpretation. It comes in the context of a discussion of the means by which "to put an end to everything that can foment division, contempt and hatred between the churches."[143] The next sentence reads: "For this the authorities of the Catholic Church will assist the Oriental Catholic Churches and their communities so that they themselves may prepare for full communion between Catholic and Orthodox Churches."[144] Clearly, many Catholic churches and many Orthodox churches are indicated (as opposed to just two), but it seems that administratively speaking, the "Oriental Catholic Churches" mentioned in the passage are themselves larger ecclesial entities than local dioceses.

With respect to the relatively few examples we have now seen in which the Catholic-Orthodox encounter is described in terms of many churches on both sides, two concluding observations may be made. First, it is significant that both in the *Tomos Agapis* and in the broader Catholic-Orthodox theological dialogue, this is the *least attested* of all the four types of usage of the expression sister churches across the confessional division (and the least attested, more generally of the Catholic and Orthodox participants in the dialogue.) Second, in the one instance in which it is certain that many Catholic churches and many Orthodox churches have been described as sister churches of each other, it has been shown that most likely, the sister Catholic churches were Eastern Catholic counterparts to autocephalous Orthodox churches. In other words, they were administratively self-governing Catholic churches on the regional level. If so, these churches might also be considered sisters of the church of Rome, not just as all local churches are sisters of all others but as only certain preeminent churches are sisters of each other.

---

143 Ibid. para. 21.
144 Ibid.

II. Summarizing Reflections

We have now seen that the expression "sister churches" has been predicated of (1) the church of Rome and the church of Constantinople, (2) the Catholic Church and the Orthodox Church, (3) the Catholic Church and (one or more of) the Orthodox churches, and (4) Catholic churches and Orthodox churches. What conclusions and comparisons may be drawn regarding these various usages?

Earlier it was mentioned that usage (2) is without any obvious precedent in antiquity or the middle ages. By contrast it is possible to find witness in those periods to usage (1), both actual explicit witness as in the 12th century Byzantine texts in which Rome and Constantinople (along with other Eastern sees) were called sister churches, and implicit witness as when Gregory the Great emphasized the dignity of all the patriarchates or when Roman officials endorsed the idea of the Pentarchy. Such examples could equally be said to offer historical precedence for usage (3), if, that is, what was meant by "the church of Rome" in those examples may be understood as the same as what has been meant by "the Catholic Church" in usage 3 in the 20th century.

This raises an important question that may be formulated in terms of an ambiguity associated first of all with usage (1). It is the question of just what is meant by "the church of Rome," and just what is meant by "the church of Constantinople" when they are called sister churches or are otherwise described in relation to one another. In a great many of the texts we have reviewed in 20th century Catholic-Orthodox relations, it seems that the church identified as "the church of Rome," or the Roman church, led by the pope, is none other than what is elsewhere called "the Catholic Church". In other words, at least where the Catholic ecclesial subject is concerned, usages (1) and (2) are not as different as they may initially appear. As suggested above, this would imply an affinity as well between (1) and (3).

On the other hand, the designation "the church of Rome" in usage (1) is possible to interpret in another way, in the sense of a strictly local church, in which case its affinity would be not with usages (2) or (3), but with usage (4). For if the designation "the church of Rome" is understood to connote a local Catholic Church, then by definition it would be one of many such Catholic churches.

But this requires calling attention, in turn, to the ambiguity inherent in usage (4). Reference to ecclesial plurality on the Catholic side could be intended on the level of particular Catholic churches or on the level of regional groupings of particular Catholic churches. If, in usage (4), the designation "Catholic churches" signifies strictly particular Catholic churches, and if it is in *that* sense that "the church of Rome" in usage (1) is to be interpreted – always only as a particular church, and "the church of Constantinople" therefore also only as a particular church and nothing more – then there is most certainly no kinship at all between (1) and (2), or, for that matter, between (1) and (3). And in that case the ecclesiological basis for usage (2), as well as for usage (3), would be that much more difficult to establish.

As will be seen in Chapter 4, Catholic critics of the use of the expression "sister churches" in 20th century Catholic-Orthodox relations are opposed, precisely, to usages (2) and (3), and approve of usages (1) and (4). That is, they approve of (1) and (4) on the condition that usage (1) is interpreted in such a way that "the church of Rome" is understood as one of the many Catholic churches, *and* that these many Catholic churches (of usage 4) are understood as particular churches, not as larger ecclesial entities, i.e. not as Catholic patriarchates or national churches.

How all of this may be evaluated ecclesiologically will be considered to some extent in Chapter 4 and further addressed in Chapter 6. What must be pointed out at this juncture is simply the remarkable discontinuity between the actual 20th century usage of the expression "sister churches" by Catholic and Orthodox officials and the understanding that Catholic critics have articulated of how the expression may properly be used. For as has been seen, usage (4) in actual 20th century ecclesiastical life – already, the usage least attested of all – seems almost never to have been concerned with particular churches on both sides of the division, but with preeminent local churches (i.e., regional ecclesial bodies) on both sides. Specifically, the rare times that *many Catholic churches* have been spoken of in the context of the bilateral dialogue, it has almost certainly been with reference to Eastern Catholic churches such as the Ukrainian Catholic Church, the Romanian Catholic Church, etc.[145]

It is difficult to establish a single instance in the texts pertaining to 20th century Catholic-Orthodox relations when "the church of Rome" could be understood as signifying merely Rome as a diocese and nothing more. Mean-

---

145 The one exception was the passage in which Ecumenical Patriarch Dimitrios I invoked the peculiar term "pan-Catholic" to suggest an ecclesial plurality on the Catholic side supposedly parallel to that which on the Orthodox side is typically expressed by the term "pan-Orthodox," which he also used, but without noting that this term itself, whenever it occurs in the bilateral dialogue, connotes churches on the regional level such as patriarchates and autocephalous churches which on the Catholic side do not exist, except, again, among the Eastern Catholic churches.

while, the instances when the designation "the church of Rome" in 20th century Catholic-Orthodox relations has been used interchangeably with the designation "the Catholic Church" are too many to count. The conclusion to be drawn on the basis of the raw data, at least, is that usages (1), (2), and (3) all accord with one another much more, in terms of how they conceive of the Catholic ecclesial subject, than any of them accords with usage (4). In the 20th century, Rome is often described as a sister church; the Catholic Church is often described as a sister church; but the Catholic *churches* – whichever they might be – are rarely so described.

With regard to the Orthodox ecclesial subject in each of the four usages, the matter is somewhat different. The difference has to do with the longstanding structural dissimilarity between Orthodox East and Catholic West, namely the existence in the East of several major sees and in the West of only one (a difference which clearly accounts for why usage (3) is asymmetrical in the way that it is). For many Catholics it is customary to move rather fluidly back and forth between speaking of the Roman Church and the Roman Catholic Church (or simply the Catholic Church); terminologically, at least, the particular is allowed to stand for the whole. Such is much more rarely the case with regard to Constantinople and the Orthodox Church. When someone speaks of the church of Constantinople, it is almost never simply assumed that he or she is speaking of the entire Orthodox communion.

Orthodox ecclesiology itself seems to be divided as to whether, and in what circumstances, "the church of Constantinople" *can be* said to represent the entire "Orthodox Church". There are remarks in the *Tomos Agapis* that presuppose the idea of a presiding function of the Ecumenical Patriarch vis-à-vis the entire Orthodox communion. Archbishop Eugenios of Crete observed during a visit to Rome on May 23, 1967, "This new period of charity, in which the two sister Churches make their way through the world, setting equal store by unity and coexistence, was opened up by the most blessed Pope John XXIII of unforgettable memory, and also by Your Holiness and your beloved brother, our venerable Ecumenical Patriarch Athenagoras, who presides over the Eastern Church."[146] The same perspective is reflected in the observation of Cardinal Willebrands, quoted earlier, in which Pope Paul VI and Ecumenical Patriarch Athenagoras were spoken of as "the heads of the two Churches".[147] Also to be recalled is the vision of sister Orthodox and Catholic churches put forward by

---

146 Stormon, *Towards the Healing of Schism*, 150, no. 156. Eugenios describes the church of Crete as "part and member" of the church of New Rome.
147 See above, Chapter 2, p. 65.

John Meyendorff: "In relations with the West, Constantinople acted as the real head of the entire East. This was particularly evident during the Council of St. Sophia (879-880), which was a bilateral settlement between the two practically equal centers of Rome and Constantinople, headed by pope John VIII and patriarch Photius."[148]

Between Catholic Pope and Orthodox Ecumenical Patriarch, the manner of presiding may differ, but insofar as it can be described as a sister of the Catholic Church, it would seem that the Orthodox Church as a whole must have its proper head, with certain prerogatives that belong to no other Orthodox patriarch or bishop. On this hinges the issue of whether the Orthodox communion may be spoken of meaningfully as a *single* church in the absence of the emperor as the effective locus of visible unity. The shocking comment made several years ago by Walter Kasper, "We are increasingly conscious of the fact that an Orthodox Church does not really exist,"[149] was no mere crude provocation by an outsider to Orthodoxy. One need only recall the 14th century comment of Patriarch Anthony, "For Christians there is no church without emperor,"[150] to realize that visible ecclesial headship remains a vital question for Orthodox ecclesiology in a post-imperial context.

In sum, two understandings would render usage (2) an ecclesiological impossibility. One would be if the Orthodox Church is understood to be nothing more than so many local churches. The other would be if the Catholic Church is understood to be nothing less than the universal church. Indeed, in that case

---

148 Meyendorff, John. *Rome, Constantinople, Moscow*, 20-21. Meyendorff makes the further observation that the "authority and actual power of the 'ecumenical patriarch' during the entire medieval period and until the fall of Constantinople (1453) always remained inseparable from that of the emperor." Cf. also J. Zizioulas, "Roman Primacy: An Orthodox Perspective," in J. Puglisi, ed., *Petrine Ministry and the Unity of the Church* (Collegeville, MN: Michael Glazier, 1999), 115-125 at 122.

149 A citation of this comment is found at www.orthodoxengland.org.uk/cardinal.htm. In subsequent years, Cardinal Kasper has not hesitated to designate the Orthodox Church in the singular. E.g., speaking of the Mother of God, "thanks to her intercession before God's throne, she will gather together perfectly the Catholic Church and the Orthodox Church in the one and only Church of Christ." *Homily at the Mass in Honor of Our Lady of Kazan*, St. Peter's Basilica, August 26, 2004. Available at www.vatican.va/roman_curia/pontifical_councils/chrstuni/card-kasper-docs/rc_pc_chrstuni_doc_20040826_homily-kazan_en.html. It should perhaps also be noted that in the same homily, Cardinal Kasper spoke of "unity between the Catholic Church and the Russian Orthodox Church."

150 Cf. above, Chapter 1, p. 41.

the Catholic Church could be the sister church neither of the Orthodox Church as a whole (usage 2) nor of any one of the several major Orthodox sees (usage 3). A necessary corollary of such an understanding seems to be that the designation "the church of Rome," whenever it is described as the sister of Constantinople (usage 2) or of any other Eastern see, must be understood neither as the whole Catholic Church of the West, nor (what is almost the same thing) as the patriarchal see of Rome, but always strictly as the Roman diocese.

Chapter 4
CATHOLIC THEOLOGICAL REFLECTION ON THE CONCEPT OF SISTER CHURCHES

Between 20th century occurrences of the expression sister churches and commentary on those occurrences, a distinction cannot always easily be drawn. Sometimes when Catholic and Orthodox churches in the modern era have been described as sisters, specific reasons have been given as to why the designation is appropriate. Such was the case especially in the 1967 papal brief *Anno ineunte* in which Paul VI surrounded his momentous use of the expression with a richly theological discussion of its meaning.[1] Still, it remains generally true that the phenomenon of the expression's earliest modern use and increasing proliferation in the 1960s and early 1970s came before there was an abundance of reflection on what the expression signified. The words seemed to be proclaimed first and given deliberate thought and consideration afterwards.

The present chapter examines the interpretive battle over the meaning and legitimacy of the expression "sister churches" that has taken place over the past three and a half decades among Catholic theologians. The Vatican Congregation for the Doctrine of the Faith weighed in with its *Note on the Expression "Sister Churches"* in the year 2000, and this text bears special importance in the Catholic debate, but discussion of the expression began some decades before that and has continued in the years since. Five Catholic theologians who have written in depth on the subject of sister churches in the latter half of the 20th century or the first years of the 21st are Emmanuel Lanne, Yves Congar, Waclaw Hryniewicz, Adriano Garuti, and Hervé Legrand. The work of each of these five will be explored in the pages to follow, as will the CDF's *Note*, to be considered in its own right as a sixth theological contribution to the Catholic discussion.[2]

Attention will be given to several basic questions. It will be important in each case to see which categories of usage outlined in Chapter 3 are endorsed and which are not, whether explicitly or implicitly. Of no less interest will be the theological foundations that are thought to underlie the expression. The matter of what *qualifies* a church as a sister church is of obvious significance in any effort to apprehend the meaning of the concept for Catholics; but in addi-

---

1 See above, Chapter 2, pp. 63-66.
2 In a more tangential way (since they did not directly address the topic of sister churches), other authors' contributions will also be taken into consideration, notably those of Paul McPartlan and Francis Sullivan.

tion to looking at qualifications, we will look at what consequences or implications are said to flow from recognizing another church as a sister church. Also to be noted will be the significance given, if any, to regional structures of authority in reflection on the concept of sister churches.

It will be seen that several of these questions intersect with two ongoing controversies in Catholic ecclesiology, one having to do with the relationship between the local church and the universal church,[3] the other with the significance of the phrase *"subsistit in"* in the Dogmatic Constitution on the Church, *Lumen Gentium*, promulgated at Vatican II.[4] Some discussion of these two questions will be necessary in order to give a full account of the Catholic debate over how the expression "sister churches" is properly to be understood.

I. Six contributions in Catholic theological reflection on "sister churches"

1. Emmanuel Lanne

In April of 1974, an unofficial symposium was held in Vienna at which some thirty Orthodox and Catholic theologians from around the world were in attendance. One of the Vienna symposium's five topics (all pertaining in some way to issues of ecclesiology and communion between East and West in light of new developments of the past decade) concerned the ecclesiological implications of the expression "sister churches" in the *Tomos Agapis* – the volume, then recently published, of official correspondence between Rome and Constantinople since 1958.

An Orthodox and a Catholic theologian each delivered a paper on the issue. In spite of their independent authorship, their respective essays bore the same title: "Églises-sœurs: implications ecclésiologiques du *Tomos Agapis*". The paper so titled that was presented by the Orthodox theologian, John Meyendorff, will be considered in Chapter 5, to be concerned with Orthodox reflection on the concept of sister churches. The present chapter, focusing on Catholic theological perspectives, will begin with an overview and analysis of the companion essay presented at the Vienna symposium by the French Benedictine theologian, Emmanuel Lanne.[5]

---

3   See below, pp. 154-157; 165-169.
4   The phrase "subsists in" was used in *Lumen Gentium* 8 to indicate how the one Church of Christ professed in the Nicene Creed relates to the Catholic Church as a visible, canonical communion. See below, pp. 157-162; 169-173.
5   E. Lanne, "Églises-sœurs: implications ecclésiologiques du *Tomos Agapis*," *Istina* 20

Lanne was one of nine appointees to the Catholic Preparatory Commission for the Theological Dialogue with the Orthodox Churches in December 1975; he was then among the twenty-nine Catholic representatives appointed in 1980 to the Joint International Commission for Theological Dialogue between the Roman Catholic Church and the Orthodox Church. Lanne was the first Catholic writer to offer sustained reflection on the concept of sister churches in its modern use in Catholic-Orthodox relations. Already in 1974 he spoke at the Vienna symposium of a "theology of sister Churches."[6]

Lanne's contribution will be considered from two angles: first, what constitutes the basis of the concept of sister churches from the Catholic point of view; second, what are the ramifications of the Catholic recognition of another church as a sister church? As a preliminary step, it is important to consider which usages of the expression Lanne regards as legitimate. This may be gauged by examining his comments on Paul VI's *Anno ineunte*.

Lanne's commentary on Paul VI's 'Anno ineunte'

Referring to the Brief as a whole, Lanne writes, "In a solemn document, Pope Paul VI intended to signify what from now on should be the characteristic note in relations between the Catholic Church and the Orthodox Church. To do this he used the expression 'sister Churches,' whose content he explicated."[7] Lanne begins with an extensive discussion of the Brief's opening sentence, which reads as follows:

> At the beginning of the 'Year of Faith,' which is being celebrated in honor of the nineteenth centenary of the martyrdom of the holy Apostles Peter and Paul, we Paul, Bishop of Rome and head of the Catholic Church, convinced that it is our duty to undertake any action that may serve the universal and holy Church of Christ, meet once more our beloved brother Athenagoras, Orthodox Archbishop of Constantinople and Ecumenical Patriarch.[8]

According to Lanne, the dual titles used here by the Pope to refer to himself as "Bishop of Rome and head of the Catholic Church" correspond to the dual titles he used to refer to Patriarch Athenagoras as "Orthodox Archbishop of Constantinople and Ecumenical Patriarch." Lanne suggests that Pope Paul VI was

---

(1975) 47-74. Reprinted in expanded form in E. Lanne, *Tradition et Communion des Églises: Recueil d'Études* (Leuven: Leuven University Press, 1997), 501-535. All citations are to the reprinted text.

6   Cf. Lanne, "Églises-sœurs," 506.
7   Lanne, "Églises-sœurs," 501. Translations here and below are mine.
8   Stormon, *Towards the Healing of Schism*, 162, no. 176.

effectively correlating his own position as chief pastor of the Catholic Church to the position of Athenagoras as chief pastor of the Orthodox Church, thus drawing a certain correspondence between the two churches themselves. Lanne is convinced, then, that in this text "the Pope establishes a distinction between the Catholic Church of which he says he is the head and 'the universal and holy Church of Christ' in the service of which he says he is persuaded of his duty to undertake everything he can do."[9]

To support this interpretation, Lanne cites an earlier text of Paul VI, written less than two weeks prior to the publication of *Anno ineunte,* in which the pope had referred to himself by the same pair of titles, "bishop of Rome and head of the Catholic Church," and had also spoken of his hopes for the "reestablishment of perfect communion between the Orthodox Church and the Catholic Church."[10] A further support, not mentioned by Lanne but in line with his argument, is found in the second paragraph of *Anno ineunte*. There Paul VI expresses his hopes for "the day when full communion will be reestablished between the Church of the West and that of the East," and proceeds to speak of "the Church" in the singular, as an overarching entity whose ability "to bear more effective witness" to the gospel will be enhanced precisely by the reestablishment of full communion between the two churches of East and West. Here again Paul VI appears to identify the Catholic Church more closely with the church of the West than with the universal Church.

Lanne clearly endorses applying the language of sister churches on the level of the two whole communions. He does not actually say, however, how this usage might be seen as consistent with earlier, pre-20th century usage, in which the expression was applied to local churches. Paul VI did not spell this out himself, so it is perhaps not surprising that Lanne did not either.

Lanne's understanding of the basis of the concept of sister churches

Continuing his analysis of *Anno ineunte,* and referring to "sister churches" at the local or particular level, Lanne takes up the issue of what constitutes the

---

9   Lanne, "Églises sœurs," 503.
10 Ibid. 503, n. 6. The text of Paul VI is his Message of July 13, 1967 to Patriarch Athenagoras communicating his intention to visit the Ecumenical Patriarchate. Stormon's English translation is more ambiguous than the French original as Lanne reproduces it. The Stormon translation of the relevant phrase is "restoration of perfect communion between the Orthodox and the Catholic Churches" (Stormon, *Towards the Healing of Schism,* 156, no. 171), whereas Lanne gives us the French as "rétablissement d'une parfaite communion entre l'Église orthodoxe et l'Église catholique".

theological basis of the designation, again from the perspective of Paul VI. Lanne writes that it is in its second paragraph that the document

> turns to establishing the theological foundation of the designation 'sister Churches', which will be explicit in the rest of the Brief. This foundation is the fraternity of the children of the Father in Jesus Christ. Given by salvation in Jesus Christ, it is closely associated with charity and peace. The message of John to the Churches of Asia (I Jn 1,3), which connects in an intimate and necessary way the communion between John and the faithful to communion with the Father and with his Son Jesus Christ, is going to ground the theology of sister Churches.[11]

In the Brief itself, it is not until the third paragraph that the pope speaks of "the ground of the traditional and very beautiful expression 'sister Churches'", and when he does so, he mentions several factors: (1) the apostolic faith; (2) baptism; (3) apostolic succession; and (4) eucharist.[12] For Paul VI the concept of sister churches is grounded concretely in these ecclesial gifts received and held in common by the sister churches.

Lanne's idea that the foundation of the designation sister churches "is the fraternity of the children of the Father in Jesus Christ," while true and important as far as it goes, could be misleading if not situated in the full context provided in the Brief's third paragraph in which the grounds for the language of sister churches are explicitly described. In this paragraph, the "mystery of divine love" is clearly the eucharist, which is mentioned together with the priesthood and apostolic succession as "gifts of God" shared by Catholics and Orthodox.

In fact, Lanne himself at times cites these very ecclesial gifts of God as the basis of fraternal communion and thus as the basis of the designation sister churches: "it is a communion which has its foundation in the gifts of God to his Church, faith, baptism, priesthood and eucharist."[13] In a similar way, Lanne draws from his analysis of UR the conclusion that "by the priesthood and the

---

11 Lanne, "Églises sœurs," 504.
12 "God has granted us to receive in faith what the Apostles saw, understood, and prolaimed to us. By Baptism 'we are one in Christ Jesus' (Gal 3:28). In virtue of the apostolic succession, we are united more closely by the priesthood and the Eucharist. By participating in the gifts of God to his Church we are brought into communion with the Father through the Son in the Holy Spirit ... In each local Church this mystery of divine love is enacted, and surely this is the ground of the traditional and very beautiful expression 'sister Churches'" (Stormon, *Towards the Healing of Schism*, 162, no. 176).
13 Lanne, "Églises sœurs," 505.

eucharist, there is a very close *(étroite)* relationship between Catholics and Orthodox".[14] He further elaborates: "this relation is that of a communion with God which creates *a Christian fraternity of a different quality* from that which exists with Christians whose [ordained] ministry and eucharist are questionable in the eyes of the Catholic Church."[15] Finally, this "Christian fraternity of a different quality" is what grounds the expression sister churches in the most proper sense.

> Without entering at all into the problem posed for the Catholic Church by the sacraments of other Christians, one will be entitled to infer that in what concerns the Orthodox Churches and in general the Churches of the East – Chalcedonian and non-Chalcedonian – the Catholic Church recognizes having in their regard a fraternity which permits it to be said according to a true designation that they are sister Churches. Sister Churches because they celebrate the same eucharist as we do, founded on the same priesthood of apostolic origin.[16]

For Lanne, then, while the fundamental fraternity shared among all baptized Christians clearly underlies the communion ecclesiology of sister *churches*, it is not the sole or sufficient basis for recognizing a church as a sister church. A Christian fraternity "of a different quality," rooted in the priesthood (of apostolic origin) and the eucharist, is required as well. Elsewhere Lanne describes this as "sacramental fraternity". He writes: "Sacramental fraternity and apostolicity (of origin, of succession and of doctrine) are thus two capital motifs which authorize Catholics to consider the Orthodox churches as sister churches of theirs, because there cannot be but a single and unique Church of Jesus Christ."[17]

Canonized holiness as a qualification of sister churches

Beyond shared faith and sacraments, Lanne discusses a further factor, which he regards as more prominent in the East, by which Christians recognize one another as members of sister churches.

---

14 Ibid. 526.
15 Ibid. (emphasis added).
16 Ibid.
17 Ibid. 527. It is notable that here Lanne holds that when faced with a multiplicity of churches, insofar as they possess the aforementioned ecclesial gifts in common, there is an *obligation* to call them sisters *because there is only one Church*. When he applies the term sister churches to the relationship between the two entire communions, it seems that he is using the same reasoning.

In order for one to be able to speak of Churches and a fortiori of sister Churches, according to the point of view of Orthodox tradition, it is not sufficient that there be 'validity' of apostolic succession and of the sacraments, as conceived by western scholasticism. It is also necessary that the quality of the Church be corroborated by the continuity of the experience of the saints, of those who, in the community, live most clearly [by] the grace of Christ, are men of the Spirit and witness by their existence to the anticipated presence of the coming kingdom.[18]

Recognition of a church as a sister church involves the exercise of a type of discernment not reducible to strictly rational logic. In 20th century Catholic-Orthodox relations, it seems that mutual reevaluation coincided with an *experience* of one another's ecclesial reality, a vital component of this experience being, in the case of Catholics, the perception of an unbroken, still flowing stream of saintliness in the Orthodox communion. As Lanne suggests: "The continuity of holiness – and of canonized holiness – as much in the East as in the West is one of the most important criteria of the ecclesial reality of the two segments of Christianity and of the possibility for each community to rediscover the other as sister Church."[19]

Whether there can be sister churches on the regional level

Lanne gives little weight to the concept of sister churches as applied to regional churches. His remarks on this point come in the context of his reflections on UR 16, with its statement that distinct ecclesiastical laws and customs followed by the Eastern churches were sanctioned by ancient synods and ecumenical councils. Lanne suggests that it is significant that the Decree at this point did *not* "develop a certain theology of sister Churches" – namely, one associated with regional structures – that he says it *might* have developed. Based on this *argumentum ex silentio* in regard to UR 16, Lanne concludes:

> Whatever be the prestige of the grand Sees of the East, that which makes Churches sister Churches is not the decisions of even Ecumenical councils, primitive usages or recognized privileges, but the fraternity in the faith and the sacraments, in apostolicity and in the life of the gospel – in a word, in that which one readily calls Christian 'sanctity' which incorporates us in the one holy One, Jesus Christ, and makes of us children of the father.[20]

---

18 Lanne, "Églises-sœurs," 529.
19 Ibid. That it was indeed a "rediscovery" may be seen from the remarks made by John Romanides describing Roman Catholic publications of an earlier era that denied the existence of Orthodox saints beyond the patristic age. See below, Chapter 5, p. 212.
20 Cf. Lanne, "Églises-sœurs," 527-528.

UR 16, to which the passage above is making reference, in fact did not invoke the expression "sister churches" at all, and the conclusion that Lanne draws from it seems tenuous. This is so especially given that in UR 14, where the term "sister churches" *is* directly invoked – the only place in the Decree where it is – we do find reference to "Patriarchal Churches."

Rather than conclude as Lanne does that "that which makes Churches sister Churches" is not a function of "Ecumenical councils, primitive usages or recognized privileges," it would be more appropriate simply to draw a distinction between two types of usage. On the one hand, there is the sense in which all local churches are sister churches of one another, because of their having the same sacraments and faith. On the other hand, there is another sense in which churches preeminent in their regions are sisters of other churches preeminent in *their* regions. It should not be necessary, in order to affirm the great importance of the first type of usage, to deny the significance of the second type.

Lanne's de-emphasis on the role of concrete regional structures in an ecclesiology of sister churches is seen also in a distinction Lanne draws elsewhere when he speaks of "the categories of the Church both in the proper sense and in the analogical sense," with the "analogical" referring to groupings of local (diocesan) churches.[21] Such groupings cannot be designated as churches in the proper sense, Lanne wishes to say, with the implication that patriarchates and/or autocephalous churches (or even metropolitanates, presumably) are not to be designated as sister churches in the proper sense, either. Only particular churches are.

Lanne's intent here seems to be to advance an ecclesiology of communion, but his neglect of the regional level of the Church's life favors a two-tiered ecclesiology of the type which, as will be seen later in this chapter, the CDF's 2000 *Note* would promote. In such an ecclesiology, what is certain is that there is the particular church, and the universal church – without anything in between about which there can be much certainty at all.[22]

Implications of recognizing another church as a sister church

Turning now to Lanne's views about the implications of recognizing a church as a sister church, two themes will be paramount. First, Lanne holds that the

---

21 Lanne, "Églises-sœurs," 523.
22 Lanne is not always consistent in his approach to the issue of sister churches on the regional level. At times he indicates an implicit endorsement of that usage, e.g. in the passage quoted below, p. 120, in which he speaks of "the recognition of the Orthodox Church of Greece as sister Church of the Catholic Church."

concept of sister churches implies an ecclesiology directly opposed to the practice of uniatism as a method of union. Second, Lanne suggests that the rediscovery, by the Catholic West and the Orthodox East, that they are sister churches, leads to the conclusion that the two traditions are called to rethink, together, what is the precise nature of the authority of the Roman see.

In his 1975 article "Églises unies ou Églises sœurs: un choix ineluctable,"[23] Lanne again took as his starting point the Brief *Anno ineunte*. But his focus now was on the implications rather than the foundations of the concept of sister churches. "Pope Paul VI himself, in particular in the Brief *Anno Ineunte* ... drew the consequences of a theology of sister Churches. Among these consequences, one of the most important in view of the progressive re-establishment of full canonical and sacramental communion, is the disappearance of the proselytism of one Church in regard to the other."[24]

By proselytism, Lanne in this context has in mind any attempt to bring members of the other church over to one's own church. While both traditions have a long history of accepting as converts individual members from the other tradition, the effort to bring over entire communities of the other tradition has been, historically, an approach more characteristic of the Catholic Church, one that has gone under the name of "uniatism".[25]

Lanne's reflections on the topic of uniatism preceded by almost two decades the recommendations made by the Joint International Commission for Theological Dialogue between the Roman Catholic Church and the Orthodox Church in its 1993 Balamand Statement.[26] In that document, uniatism is rejected as a

---

23 E. Lanne, "Églises unies ou Églises sœurs: un choix ineluctable," *Irénikon* 48:3 (1975) 322-342. This article appeared in English translation the following year as "United Churches or Sister Churches: A Choice to be Faced," *One in Christ* 12 (1976) 106-123. The original article is reprinted in *Tradition et Communion des Églises*, op. cit., 485-500. Citations in this case are to the English text.

24 Lanne, "Églises-sœurs," 487. This idea was touched on indirectly by Patriarch Athenagoras in 1969 when he said, "Neither of us is calling the other to himself any more". See above, Chapter 2, p. 68, n. 69.

25 See Robert Taft, "The Problem of 'Uniatism' and the 'Healing of Memories': Anamnesis, not Amnesia," paper delivered on the occasion of the 21st Kelly Lecture, University of St. Michael's College, Toronto, Canada (Dec. 1, 2000), then published in *Logos: a Journal of Eastern Christian Studies* 41-42 (2000-2001) 155-196.

26 "Uniatism, Method of Union of the Past, and the Present Search for Full Communion." Lanne was still a member of the Joint International Commission at the time this document was produced. Certain aspects of the document have been discussed in Chapter 3 above, pp. 94-96.

method of union to be employed in the present or in the future, much as Lanne rejected it as a method of union in 1975. Also in that document, what is presented as the antithesis of uniatism is an ecclesiology of sister churches[27] – again, just as Lanne in 1975 presented uniatism and "sister churches" as ecclesiological opposites.

A notable feature of Lanne's discussion of this contradiction is that he saw it as actually inscribed in the corpus of official texts of Vatican II. Referring to the pair of decrees both promulgated on November 21, 1964, *Orientalium Ecclesiarum* (on the eastern Catholic Churches) and *Unitatis Redintegratio* (on ecumenism), Lanne asserted that "the two texts remained basically irreconcilable. One dealt with the united Churches [i.e., Eastern Catholic churches] and proposed them as a model for eastern Christians coming 'to Catholic unity' (OE 25); the other treated the Orthodox Churches as sister Churches (UR 14)."[28] Lanne attributes the contradiction to "the complexity of the situations created over the centuries, and [to] the errors of a past which cannot be done away with by the stroke of a pen."[29]

According to Lanne, the teaching of Vatican II that the Church of God is built up through the celebration of the eucharistic mystery in Orthodox churches[30] – a teaching he regards as foundational for the recognition of the Orthodox churches as sister churches – should have certain practical consequences which, he says, the Catholic Church since Vatican II has not always followed in its relations with the Orthodox. He describes at length the circumstances of the new appointment by Rome, in July of 1975, of an apostolic exarch in Athens for the small Byzantine Greek Catholic community in existence there since 1920. The Orthodox archbishop of Athens at the time reacted strongly against this development. Lanne explains the problem in terms of the clash between an ecclesiology of uniatism and one of sister churches:

> The existence of the apostolic exarchate of the Greek rite in Athens, appointed by Rome, is the negation of the recognition of the Orthodox Church of Greece as sister Church of the Catholic Church. How does one justify, in effect, the presence of a Church concurrent on the same soil as the Greek Orthodox, even while one recognizes this Orthodox Church to be truly the Church of God in

---

27 "Uniatism, Method of Union of the Past, and the Present Search for Full Communion," n. 14 and 15.
28 Lanne, "United Churches or Sister Churches," 115.
29 Ibid. 116.
30 UR 15.

its sacramental life and in all its historical, spiritual, liturgical, canonical and theological patrimony (cf. UR14-17)?[31]

The older ecclesiology closely associated with uniatism is in evidence, according to Lanne, in *Lumen Gentium*'s chapter three, as well as in the *Nota Praevia* pertaining to that chapter. Lanne sees these texts, insofar as they expound a "hierarchical pyramid-ecclesiology,"[32] as having "in principle compromised ... the ecclesial reality of the Orthodox Churches".[33] These are texts in which the teaching of Vatican I on the relationship of the pope to the college of bishops and to the universal church is reiterated in such a way that leaves very much in question the authentic episcopal status of Orthodox bishops.[34] Appended to the *Nota Praevia*, however, and aimed at neutralizing or softening its sting, was a "Nota Bene," which made reference to "the power exercised *de facto* among separated Eastern Christians, about which there are divergent opinions." Lanne says of this: "the *Nota Bene* itself was a discreet invitation addressed to theologians to continue to work along new lines, the Commission which worked out the Constitution not having succeeded in putting forward satisfactory solutions. It implicitly recognized that though the delimitations proposed by the hierarchical communion in this text corresponded to the internal logic of Roman Catholic ecclesiology they did not take into account the ecclesial facts of eastern Christianity."[35]

---

31 Lanne, "Églises-sœurs," 499.
32 Lanne, "United Churches or Sister Churches," 122.
33 Ibid. 117. The *Nota Praevia*, or preliminary note of explanation, appended to *Lumen Gentium* as part of the "Notificationes" given by the Secretary General of the Council to the bishops on November 16, 1964 (five days before *Lumen Gentium*'s approval by the assembled bishops by a vote of 2,151 to 5), was intended as an official interpretation offered by "higher authority," that is, by the pope, of the doctrine of collegiality that was set forth in chapter III of the draft for the constitution.
34 "The college or body of bishops has for all that no authority unless united with the Roman Pontiff, Peter's successor, as its head, whose primatial authority, let it be added, over all, whether pastors or faithful, remains in its integrity. For the Roman Pontiff, by reason of his office as Vicar of Christ, namely, and as pastor of the entire Church, has full, supreme and universal power over the whole Church, a power which he can always exercise unhindered" (LG, n. 22). The *Nota Praevia* makes the same point throughout and in further detail. In these texts it is difficult or impossible to find evidence or even allowance for the fact that, as Lanne puts it, "[t]he Churches of the East and of the West have never had communion with Rome in the same way." (Lanne, "United Churches or Sister Churches," 123).
35 Lanne, "United Churches or Sister Churches," 118.

Lanne presents as stark and irreconcilable alternatives (1) "the old concept of 'the return of the Orientals to Roman unity,'" and (2) the "new paths" opened by the writings and actions of Paul VI and the Decree on Ecumenism which are based on "an ecclesiology of sister churches."[36]

Mutual recognition as sister churches and a re-reception of Vatican I

For Lanne, the Catholic recognition of the Orthodox Church as a sister church has particular bearing on the dogmatic decisions of Vatican I. The latter, according to Lanne, "must be recognized for what they are: definitions which were taken without the participation of the sister Church of the East".[37] This does not mean that there must be an erasing by the West of its own history, but rather a reinterpretation. Lanne elaborates:

> In fact, since its origins, the Christian East always recognized an authority of the Roman See without peer. But over time this authority assumed in the West forms which the East ignored and which are alien to its own ecclesiological evolution. It is this that the Decree on Ecumenism of Vatican II recognized in its Paragraph 14 and which Pope Paul VI implicitly sanctioned by his authority with the Brief *Anno Ineunte* and by the two subsequent documents of which mention has been made.[38] The ecclesiology of the fraternity of sister Churches thus requires, as Paul VI recognized, a new perspective on the relations between Rome and the Churches of the Orthodox East, a rediscovery which implies that we rethink together, and not without Orthodoxy, what is the nature of the particular authority which the East recognizes in the See of Peter.[39]

A connection can be seen between this conclusion and the point made by Lanne in his interpretation of the opening sentence of *Anno ineunte*. There, according to Lanne, Paul VI intended to make a distinction between the Catholic Church of the West and the entire Church of God, thereby allowing the possibility for the Catholic Church of the West and the Orthodox Church of the East to regard themselves as sister churches within the one and only Church of God. Within this universal church the bishop of Rome, while traditionally

---

36 Lanne, "Églises-sœurs," 499-500.
37 Ibid. 534. Here Lanne suggests the need for "long fraternal explanations" to enable a "reciprocal comprehension" between the two traditions, and argues that such mutual comprehension would be progressive and would follow, rather than precede, the restoration of "full canonical communion".
38 Address of Paul VI to Athenagoras on the latter's visit to Rome, October 26, 1967 (Stormon, *Towards the Healing of Schism*, 174, no. 190) and the Joint Declaration two days later (ibid. 181, no. 195).
39 Lanne, "Églises-sœurs," 533.

recognized by the churches of the East as well as those of the West as having a unique role, would not have the same prerogatives in East and West, respectively.

2. Yves Congar

It would be difficult to overstate the influence of the French Dominican priest Yves Congar on conciliar and post-conciliar Catholic ecclesiology and ecumenism. The texts in which Congar gave attention directly to the expression sister churches are relatively few and of limited length, but theologically concentrated. In his article, "Évaluation ecclésiologique des Églises non-catholiques," published in 1977,[40] Congar devoted several pages to the topic under the subheading "A category ancient and new: 'Sister Churches'." Much of this material was then included in a slightly expanded reflection on the same subject in Congar's book, *Diversity and Communion,* in the ninth chapter, concerned with the relationship of the Orthodox Church and the Roman Catholic Church.[41] Here again under a subheading of "Sister churches," Congar offered his reflections on the term's meaning.

Like Lanne, Congar views the expression "sister churches" as a properly theological one. Noting that "the dialogue in charity" began in 1965 with the lifting of the mutual anathemas of 1054, Congar writes: "However, from that time on it has been ballasted with a theology of extreme importance, that of sister churches."[42] Also in line with Lanne's reflections on the topic, Congar describes *Anno ineunte* as "by far the most profound and important text" in which the phrase sister churches occurs, and Congar specifically mentions Lanne as having "made a thorough commentary on it".[43] In summarizing Lanne's analysis of *Anno ineunte,* Congar refers to Lanne's discussion of "the communion and brotherhood of the churches of the first three centuries and their agreement with what the decree *Unitatis Redintegratio* says of the Eastern church."[44] Congar goes on:

---

40 "Évaluation ecclésiologique des Églises non-catholiques," in Gerard Békés and Vilmos Vajta, eds., *Unitatis Redintegratio 1964-1974: the Impact of the Decree on Ecumenism,* Volume 71 in the series *Studia Anselmiana,* ed. P. Giustiano Farnedi (Rome: Pontificio Ateneo S. Anselmo, 1977), 63-97.
41 Congar, *Diversity and Communion,* 85-92.
42 Ibid. 86. Congar calls it an "admirable term".
43 Ibid. 88-89, with reference to Lanne, "Églises-sœurs. Implications ecclésiologiques du Tomos Agapis," *Istina* 20 (1975) 47-74.
44 Congar, *Diversity and Communion,* 89.

> This character of sister churches is based on the reality of a common quality as children of the same Father, in Jesus Christ, which makes the relationship fraternal; however, this quality is made specific at the sacramental level of the church not only by common baptism – which the Roman church shares with the Protestant communions – but also by a common priesthood, the apostolic succession, and the eucharist. These are realities which ensure that there is truly a church, indeed a true church.[45]

Clearly, according to what Congar says here, being a true church is a necessary qualification for being a sister church. The concept is rooted in the fraternity of all baptized Christians but has its proper application only where the ecclesial gifts of priesthood, apostolic succession and eucharist have continued to be preserved intact in each church.

Congar shares with Lanne a willingness to envision as sister churches the entire Catholic Church and the entire Orthodox Church. This can be seen at several points, as when Congar describes how the Eastern and Western contingents at the council of Ferrara-Florence viewed one another at the time:

> In Florence, both sides were aware that only the participation of the two parties made the council ecumenical. According to the vocabulary used at the Council of Florence, it was a question of restoring *unio* or *unitas* between two churches, the schismatic situation between which had not affected their profound substantial community. There was not a church on the one side and a group which was not the church on the other. The church was split in two.[46]

With regard to these two churches, elsewhere Congar stresses that *"[i]t is the same church"* that is encountered in both.[47] In keeping with this understanding, Congar notes that he himself "more than once [has] wished that the church would begin again to breathe through its two lungs, an image which His Holiness John Paul II has also used several times."[48] These two lungs represent, for Congar, the one church in *"two different traditions,"*[49] or, as in the following passage, the one church in *two churches*:

> The substance of faith and sacramental reality which is common to the Orthodox Church and the Roman Catholic Church does not come from the Roman church, as is the case with the Protestant communions of the Reformation. *Unitatis redintegratio* links it with apostolicity. So it is that the churches are

---

45 Ibid.
46 Ibid.
47 Ibid. (emphasis in original).
48 Ibid.
49 Ibid. 90.

Chapter 4: Catholic Theological Reflection on "Sister Churches" 125

sisters, not daughters. Paul VI went so far as to speak of a "universal and holy church of Christ" embracing the two sister churches.[50]

Congar does not raise any objection to this manner of speaking of dual churches within the unity of the one, holy, catholic and apostolic church of Christ.

The element of apostolicity mentioned in the passage above is emphasized by Congar in an especially significant way. Not only are apostolicity of faith and of unbroken episcopal succession implied, but also independent apostolicity of origin. The idea of Rome as mother of other churches, and not sister, can be squared with the concrete historical facts of the Reformation and Anglican communions, but not with those of the Orthodox communion.[51] "It was in fact a basic criticism of the Byzantines," Congar recalls, "that the Roman church put herself in the position of *mater et magistra*, mother and mistress, and then went on to treat the other churches, particularly those of the East, not as sisters but as daughters and infants."[52] Congar cites the pertinent 12th century texts of Nicetas of Nicomedia and John X Camateros that we examined in Chapter 1.[53] He also commends the designation by Patriarch Athenagoras of the church of Constantinople as Rome's "younger sister, *neotera adelphe*",[54] and asks poignantly: "Has Rome revised, adjusted, sharpened up the conception of what she is to the other churches, particularly to the Eastern churches? How can she, why should she, continue to be mother, mistress and head?"[55]

A further similarity between Lanne's and Congar's perspectives may be noted. As was seen above, one of the specific ramifications of the Catholic

---

50 Ibid. 90.
51 Congar observes that although the "character and title of sister churches" seemed to have been extended to the Anglican communion by Paul VI in a well-known reference he made in 1970 to the Anglican church as "ever-beloved sister" of the Catholic Church, in fact "[t]he expression does not have the same content here as it does in the case of the churches of the East. There is no apostolicity here independent of that of Rome" (Congar, *Diversity and Communion*, 91-92, with reference to Paul VI's homily of October 25, 1970 commemorating the canonization of the forty martyrs from England and Wales.) Available at www.vatican.va/holy_father/paul_vi/homilies/1970/index.htm (accessed October 25, 2009).
52 Congar, *Diversity and Communion*, 90.
53 See above, Chapter 1, pp. 28-37.
54 See above, Chapter 2, p. 63, n. 55.
55 Congar, *Diversity and Communion*, 91. It may be noted that "head" need not mean "mother". There is, from the Byzantine point of view, a viable conception of Rome's ecclesial *headship* (but not motherhood) vis-à-vis the Eastern sees, as was discussed in Chapter 1, p. 41. See also below, pp. 149-150; 153-154.

recognition of the Orthodox Church as a sister church is, in Lanne's view, that the decisions of Vatican I made apart from the Eastern sister church will need to be re-interpreted with the participation of both churches as a condition for their unity. Congar touches on this point when he writes:

> Replying on 30 November 1969 to Patriarch Athenagoras, Cardinal Willebrands spoke of the ministry of Peter, coryphaeus of the college of apostles, being transmitted to his successors, and he said: "This service of authority for unity must be looked at again in the light of the gospel and the authentic apostolic tradition, in a dialogue of love and truth between our churches, as being all churches and ecclesial communities of Christianity." This new study is taking place. It presupposes patient and profound historical and ecclesiological rethinking.[56]

Willebrands was speaking of all Christian churches and ecclesial communities, but it is significant that Congar includes the quotation in the section of his own book concerned with relations specifically between Catholics and Orthodox, where he has gone to considerable lengths to show that they are sister churches not just in potential but at present, and also that they are so by virtue of their independent apostolicity. One may reasonably conclude that it is Congar's view that special weight should be given to the conclusions at which these Catholic and Orthodox sister churches would arrive together on the subject of the proper exercise of papal authority.

We have seen that in Congar's usage, the expression "sister churches" often refers to the two overarching communions, Catholic and Orthodox, each as a whole. He also implicitly indicates an understanding of the expression as applicable on the regional level when he states that in the East the idea is common "that it would be impossible to hold an ecumenical council without the patriarchate of Rome."[57] Congar does not seem to use the expression to describe particular (diocesan) Orthodox and Catholic churches.

3. Waclaw Hryniewicz

The Polish Catholic theologian Waclaw Hryniewicz began writing on the theme of sister churches as early as 1987.[58] Like Lanne, he had been appointed a member of the Joint International Commission for Theological Dialogue between

---

56 Congar, *Diversity and Communion*, 91.
57 Ibid. 89.
58 Cf. W. Hryniewicz, "Der Dialog der Schwesterkirchen: Nach dem wiederholten Treffen der Katholisch-Orthodoxen Kommission in Bari," *Ostkirchliche Studien* 36 (1987) 311-326.

the Roman Catholic Church and the Orthodox Church from its inception in 1980. Hryniewicz has continued to explore the significance of the concept of sister churches and related issues in articles published through the 1990s and into the present century.[59]

The contribution of Hryniewicz to the Catholic discussion of the topic is significant in three ways. (1) Hryniewicz further develops the contrast between "sister churches" and uniatism. (2) He suggests, here in contrast to Lanne, that the concept of sister churches implies an integral place for regional structures of authority in the overall communion of local churches. (3) In his remarks concerning what he calls "ecumenical aporetics," Hryniewicz points toward something that must be taken into account in any interpretation of the language of sister churches across the confessional division between Orthodox East and Catholic West, namely the paradoxical quality of this language. This third contribution, which is the least direct, is perhaps the most important.

As to how Hryniewicz employs the term, he does not seem to apply it to particular Catholic and Orthodox churches. He does apply it to regional churches such as patriarchates, as will be seen. On a number of occasions he also describes as sister churches the entire Catholic Church and the entire Orthodox Church – for example: "Only in the second half of the 20th century did there emerge an ecumenism that could finally bring the rapprochement of the Catholic Church and the Orthodox Church. At last there came the time for a real dialogue between the two 'sister Churches'."[60] In another passage, discussing Catholic ecclesial expansion in traditionally Orthodox regions, he writes: "This devalues the RCC's attitude to the Orthodox Church as her 'sister Church' declared by Vatican II."[61] In these and other places, Hryniewicz' view

---

59 His recent articles on the topic include "Reconciliation and Ecclesiology of Sister Churches," *Eastern Churches Journal* 2:3 (1995) 55-72; "The 'Union' of Brest and the Ecclesiology of Sister Churches," *Eastern Churches Journal* 4:1 (1997) 107-124; "Ecumenism and the Kenotic Dimension of Ecclesiology," *Internationale Kirchliche Zeitschrift* 91 (2001) 22-43; and "Between Trust and Mistrust: Ecumenical Relations and Theological Dialogue between the Catholic Church and the Orthodox Church," in *The Challenge of Our Hope: Christian Faith in Dialogue* (Washington, DC: Council for Research in Values and Philosophy, 2007), 167-184. All of these articles are included in *The Challenge of Our Hope*; citations are from this volume.

60 Hryniewicz, "Between Trust and Mistrust," 168.

61 Ibid. 174. Hryniewicz is imprecise here about what Vatican II "declared." Only once did the council invoke the expression "sister churches" (UR 14), and there it was to refer only to relations of Orthodox churches among themselves. An ecclesiology of sister churches may be inferred – as was seen in Lanne's analysis – from this and

of the two churches within the one and unique Church of God finds expression.⁶² Hryniewicz does not defend this usage; he simply employs it. In general, Hryniewicz says little about the basis of the concept of sister churches, even at the level of particular churches. His reflections focus on what should be the consequences when churches recognize one another as sister churches.

An ecclesiology of sister churches excludes "soteriological exclusivism"

Hryniewicz writes in reference to the international Catholic-Orthodox dialogue: "With the progress of years the dialogue with the Orthodox has become an experience of the inevitable choice between [an] ecclesiology of Sister Churches and [an] ecclesiology of conversion."⁶³ In a number of his articles, Hryniewicz offers a textured account of how the "ecclesiology of conversion" was prevalent in the Catholic Church's relations with the Orthodox over many centuries. He observes that at the root of this ecclesiology was the belief, widely held in the Catholic Church until Vatican II, that it is impossible to be saved outside the visible unity of the Catholic Church. As an example of this belief, Hryniewicz provides a quotation from the Council of Florence:

> The unity of the Church's body is of such great importance that church sacraments can help in being saved only those people who remain in this unity, and only they can obtain the eternal reward through fasts, charity and other pious deeds and practices of Christian life. No one who remains outside the Catholic Church, in disunity with it, can be saved, no matter how great his [or her] charity might be, and even if he [or she] might have spilt [his or her] blood for Christ.⁶⁴

---

other conciliar documents, but it was not until Pope Paul VI's Brief *Anno ineunte*, two years after the close of the council, that the Catholic magisterium applied the expression across the division between Catholic and Orthodox churches.

62 An important image (or pair of images) is offered in this connection when Hryniewicz quotes the 19th century Polish historian Jan Długosz, who more than half a century before Yves Congar spoke of the "two lungs" of the Church. Hryniewicz writes that Długosz "described the disastrous consequences of the conquest of the imperial city [Constantinople] by Turks in the following words: 'Of the two eyes of Christendom one has been torn out, of its two hands one has been cut off.'" (Hryniewicz, "The Florentine Union: Reception and Rejection," in *The Challenge of Our Hope*, 208-209, with reference to Joannis Dlugossii, *Historiae polonicae* V, lib. XII, in: *Opera omnia* XIV, Cracoviae 1878, 145).

63 "Between Trust and Mistrust,"168.

64 *Decree of the Council of Florence for the Jacobites* (1438-1445), DS 1351, as quoted by Hryniewicz, "Universal Salvation: Questions on Soteriological Universalism," in *The*

Such claims to "soteriological exclusivism," Hryniewicz contends, were what eventually led to the phenomenon of uniatism which attempted to bring those understood to be outside the Church Catholic back into its fold. "The constitution *Magnus Dominus* (1595)," he writes, "which proclaimed the Union of Brest ... says that Ruthenian Bishops came to the conclusion that they themselves and the flock entrusted to their responsibility 'had not been members of Christ's body which is the Church, because they lacked any link with the visible head of his Church, the supreme Roman Pontiff'."[65]

Here the concerns of Lanne may be recalled regarding the third chapter of *Lumen Gentium* and the *Nota Praevia* where, he argues, doubt is cast on the episcopal – and therefore, by extension, the ecclesial – status of those not in communion with the bishop of Rome,[66] this in contrast with the outlook of *Unitatis Redintegratio* especially in its affirmative statement in para. 15 that in the celebration of the eucharist in Orthodox churches "the Church of God is built up."[67] At issue is a universalist ecclesiology, on the one hand, with ecclesiality being grounded in canonical communion with the pope, and a eucharistic ecclesiology, on the other, with ecclesiality grounded in the catholicity of the local church in communion with other local churches. The latter ecclesiology was foreign to the thought of the Roman officials who promulgated the constitution *Magnus Dominus*, which went on to observe of the Ruthenian bishops and their flocks, "They firmly decided to return to the Roman Church, their Mother and the Mother of all the faithful, to come back to the Roman Pontiff, the Vicar of Christ on earth, the common Father and Shepherd of the whole Christian people."[68] Hryniewicz points out that in the Union of Brest, the

---

Challenge of Our Hope, 53. Interestingly, there are also grounds for seeing in the Council of Florence an ecclesiology that has much more affinity with the concept of sister churches. See the relevant comments of Congar above, pp. 159-60.

65 "*Non esse membra corporis Christi, quod est Ecclesia, qui visibili ipsius Ecclesiae capiti Summo Romano Pontifici non cohaererent*" (*Documenta Unionis Berestensis eiusque auctorum* [1590-1600], ed. A.G. Welykyj, Romae [1970, No. 145], 218, as quoted by Hryniewicz, "Ecumenical Lessons from the Past," 227. For a more complex account of the Union of Brest, see Taft, "The Problem of 'Uniatism' and the 'Healing of Memories'," op. cit. (see above, p. 119, n. 25); Boris Gudziak, *Crisis and Reform: The Kyivan Metropolitanate, the Patriarchate of Constantinople, and the Genesis of the Union of Brest* (Cambridge, MA: Harvard University Press, 1998).

66 See above, pp. 121-122.

67 See above, p. 121.

68 "*...firmiter decreverunt redire ad suam et omnium fidelium Matrem Romanam Ecclesiam, reverti ad Romanum Pontificem Christi in terries Vicarium, et totius populi*

bishops and other clergy and faithful of the metropolitan Church of Kiev were received into the Church of Rome "not as a Metropolitan Sister Church, but simply as individuals, coming back to the Church from 'outside' and asking *individually* for reunion."[69]

The denial of the ecclesiality of the Kievan Christians amounted to a repudiation on two levels. First of all, they were not deemed members of local diocesan churches. But this also meant that such churches did not together comprise a regional church, a "Metropolitan Sister Church," as Hryniewicz puts it. The text of *Magnus Dominus,* in addition to speaking of Rome as the mother of all the faithful, also speaks, at another point, of Rome as "the Head, the Mother and the Teacher of all Churches *(Caput, Mater et Magistra Omnium Ecclesiarum)*."[70] We may reflect that the Council of Trent had done the same some decades earlier; Trent, however, had been a council convened in the more clearly circumscribed western context of the counter-reformation, whereas the document *Magnus Dominus* explicitly involved relations between West and East, yet with no adjustment of terms or conceptual framework. In the Latin world, the idea of Rome as the mother of all the other – Latin – churches was neither an abstraction nor an innovation. It did not require the dissolution of any existing organic relations of ecclesial maternity and filiation among these other – Latin – churches. But with regard to the East, the idea of Rome as the mother of all the other churches could only be realized at the expense of such organic relations. As Hryniewicz succinctly expresses it, "The union of Ruthenians with Rome resulted in breaking the union with their mother Church of Constantinople."[71] Hryniewicz again points to the link between uniatism and

---

christiani communem Patrem et Pastorem" (*Documenta Unionis Berestensis,* no. 145, 218-219, as quoted by Hryniewicz, "Ecumenical Lessons from the Past," 227).

69 Hryniewicz, "Ecumenical Lessons from the Past," 227.

70 *Documenta Unionis Berestensis,* 221, as quoted by Hryniewicz, "Ecumenical Lessons from the Past," 227.

71 Hryniewicz, "Outliving the Schism," in *The Challenge of Our Hope,* 253. The fact that the union occurred so soon after Trent indicates a new tendency in Rome to see not just Western Protestants but also now Eastern Christians as "dissidents" outside the Church, who needed to be saved by being brought back within the unity of the Church, a unity whose source and principle medieval and early modern Catholicism held to be strictly papal. On this point, cf. Emmanuel Lanne, "The Connection between the Post-Tridentine Concept of Primacy and the Emerging Uniate Churches," *Wort und Wahrheit,* Supplementary Issue Number 4 (December 1978), 99-108; reprinted in *Selection of the Papers and Minutes of the Four Vienna Consultations between Theologians of the Oriental Orthodox Churches and the Roman Catholic*

soteriological exclusivism when he writes that "[t]he 'uniate' movement ... tended to ignore Orthodoxy as a spiritual locus of salvation, grace, and truth; thus breaking away from the old tradition of Sister Churches."[72] By his reference to "the old tradition of Sister Churches," Hryniewicz seems to be alluding to the fact that Rome at one time did not deny the ecclesial reality of the Eastern churches. It must be said, of course, that when Rome eventually did deny it, this was in the context of a new situation: a schism of unprecedented duration. We might note that in the first millennium there had been divisions but of much shorter length; Rome had persisted throughout those early centuries in affirming the Church in the East as "a spiritual locus of salvation, grace, and truth," due to the relationship of full communion that either was presently enjoyed between Rome and the Eastern sees or was always expected to be restored again soon (e.g., with the deposing of an iconoclast Byzantine emperor, etc.). Midway through the second millennium, the expectation had changed.

Hryniewicz' overall treatment of the unfolding history in which uniatism arose leaves out this matter of receding expectations. An Eastern Catholic (Melkite) Patriarch, Maximos IV Saigh, whose significant influence at Vatican II is widely acknowledged, has touched on it in the following words.

> It would be possible to maintain that the relations between Rome and the various eastern churches were not definitively broken till the day when Rome became impatient of waiting for a general reunion of the churches or lost hope in its possibility, and accepted into its unity some groups of separated eastern Christians ... Thus, paradoxically, the partial union of some groups of eastern Christians with the Roman See put an end to attempts at world-wide reunion between east and west.[73]

The attempt to convert the other comes into play when the attempt to reconcile with the other is no longer seen as having the possibility of success.

Hryniewicz says of the 1729 decree issued by the *Sacra Congregatio de Propaganda Fide* banning *communicatio in sacris* with the Orthodox that it was "a logical consequence of an ecclesiology of conversion and soteriological

---

Church: *1971, 1973, 1976 and 1978 in one volume* (Vienna: Ecumenical Foundation Pro Oriente, 1988), 242.

72 Hryniewicz, "The Florentine Union: Reception and Rejection," in *The Challenge of Our Hope*, 207.

73 From a speech made by the Patriarch at Düsseldorf in 1960, "The Catholic East and Christian Unity: our Vocation as Unionists," excerpts of which appeared in E.J. Barbara Fry, "Patriarch Maximos IV and the Vocation of the Catholic Eastern Churches," *The Eastern Churches Quarterly* 15:1-2 (1963) 81.

exclusivism"[74]. He sees the same ecclesiology reflected in the words of Pope Urban VIII (1623-1644), speaking to the Ruthenians: "Through you ... I hope to convert the East *(Per vos, mei Rutheni, Orientem convertendum spero).*"[75] Moreover, Hryniewicz discerns continuing evidence of an "ecclesiology of absorption and annexation"[76] today in the establishment of new ecclesiastical structures parallel to those already in existence in areas under the jurisdiction of the other church.

> [W]as it necessary to create an ecclesiastical Catholic province in Russia? ... The choice is inevitable between the ecclesiology of 'sister Churches' and the slippery ground of confessionalism. Once a competitive logic is introduced, it would destroy the logic of 'sister Churches'. Without respecting 'canonical territory' one risks only an endless quarrel in the Church.[77]

"Sister churches" on the regional level

Hryniewicz at times touches on the need for regional structures of authority in the Church. In his essay on Orthodox responses to *Ut unum sint* (1995), in which Pope John Paul II invited non-Catholics and Catholics to reflect together on how papal primacy might be exercised differently today without compromising its essential mission, Hryniewicz approvingly describes the ecclesiological positions of the Orthodox Metropolitan John Zizioulas:

> ... the primacy should always be exercised in a synodal way, either on [a] local or regional level or on [the] universal one. The Bishop of Rome as

---

74 Hryniewicz, "The Florentine Union," 220. The 1729 decree is found in Mansi, 46, 99-104.
75 *Acta S.C. de Propaganda Fide,* vol. I, Rome 1953, 10, n. 12, as quoted by Hryniewicz, "The Florentine Union," 219.
76 Hryniewicz, "Ecumenical Lessons from the Past," 238.
77 Hryniewicz, "Between Trust and Mistrust," 178. In mentioning the creation of an ecclesiastical Catholic province in Russia, Hryniewicz was referring to the fact that on February 11, 2002, the Vatican announced the decision of Pope John Paul II to elevate the existing administrative structures of the Roman Catholic Church in the territory of Russia to the status of dioceses, such that the territory would henceforth be construed by the Vatican as a Roman Catholic province headed by a Roman Catholic metropolitan. For a response to this development, see the comments of February 12, 2002 of Patriarch Alexis II of the Moscow Patriarchate at www.mospat.ru/archive/ne202122.htm. Historically, there were no episcopal or diocesan structures of the Roman Catholic Church in Russia until 1769 (see Dennis J. Dunn, *The Catholic Church and Russia* [Aldershot, Hants, England and Burlington, VT: Ashgate, 2004], 33).

prótos would exercise his universal primacy not as a primacy of jurisdiction, but in a truly synodal way, cooperating with the existing patriarchates and heads of autonomous Churches. So understood, the universal primacy would be carried out in communion with others, and not directly and in isolation. The Bishop of Rome would be the first among all other heads of the Churches.[78]

Hryniewicz indicates a connection between this vision of primacy and the concept of sister churches when he writes at another point:

> Perhaps in the future the Roman Catholic Church will find enough courage to begin a structural reform which requires a new logic of thinking. This logic demands respect for the autonomy of local and regional Churches. It urges giving up the claim of the immediate jurisdiction over those Churches and understands the primacy as a real diakonía for the unity of the Sister Churches.[79]

The same ecclesiological vision in which the universal church is understood as a communion of *regional* churches – and not merely of local, diocesan churches – is expressed by Hryniewicz elsewhere in the following way:

> It is possible to imagine the structure of the Church once more united in the form of the very concrete collegiality of the existing patriarchates (Rome, Constantinople, Alexandria, Antioch, Jerusalem, Moscow, Romania, Serbia, Bulgaria) as well as those which should be created – for example, Canterbury, Africa, South America, India and others ... Autonomy has to be given to the local and regional churches and direct jurisdiction over these churches rejected, a jurisdiction which still dominates today. Doing so would show the way in which primacy is understood as a service for unity.[80]

The "collegiality" of which Hryniewicz speaks in this passage clearly applies not merely to relations among all diocesan bishops (and their local churches) everywhere, but to a number of more particular fraternal relationships among the heads of regionally important churches. In this perspective, the pope is the first among those who are themselves first, not only as bishops of local dioceses, but as metropolitans or patriarchs.

---

78 Hryniewicz, "The Cost of Unity: the Papal Primacy in Recent Orthodox Reflection," in *The Challenge of Our Hope*, 197.
79 Ibid. 198.
80 Hryniewicz, *Nasza Pascha z Chrystusem*, Lublin 1987. Translated and quoted by Maciej Bielawski, "Thinking about Church with Hope: the Example of Wacław Hryniewicz," in *The Challenge of Our Hope*, 283.

Doctrine and ecumenism

Before considering Hryniewicz' treatment of "ecumenical aporetics," it must be noted that an anti-doctrinal strain in his writings sometimes clouds the substance of his analysis.

> In fact, we are all, till now, prisoners of our own errors, alienated from one another in spirit. I would be inclined to say even more: we are above all prisoners of our doctrines, denominational differences and divergences. It means that there exists a sort of ecclesiological captivity of doctrine.[81]

A passage such as this comes close to drawing a parallel between "errors" and "doctrines," and thus gives the unfortunate impression that the main hindrance to the unity of the Church is an excess of doctrinal fidelity. Such statements do not well serve the ends of ecumenism, whose association with indifferentism is already strong enough in the minds of many.

Hrienewicz' general neglect of the theological underpinnings of the concept of sister churches permits him to make certain statements that seem to be at odds with standard Catholic positions. "The dialogue between the Roman Catholic Church and the Evangelical Lutheran Churches has contributed during the last years significantly to broadening the very understanding of the expression 'Sister Churches', used so far only in relation to the Orthodox Church. In mutual relationship between Catholics and Lutherans this expression has become almost a self-explanatory concept."[82] Hryniewicz offers no further comment at this point. Yet if anything has emerged throughout our investigations of its use and interpretation, it is that the concept of sister churches is far from self-explanatory. Moreover, the application of the concept between the Catholic and Lutheran communions, whatever the practice may have been informally, is nowhere endorsed in official statements or documents of the Catholic Church. To say, as Hryniewicz does in the same essay, that the "risen Christ and the Holy Spirit remain on both sides of each division in the Church,"[83] runs the risk of minimizing the significance of division and of overlooking what are at times – on just one side of a schism, and not both – distortions in the faith and life of the Church so serious that the very identity of the Church can no longer be affirmed where those distortions predominate. An ecclesiology of sister churches will have been rendered meaningless if, in the last analysis, it comes to be indistinguishable from a belief that schism and

---

[81] Hryniewicz, "Ecumenism and Kenotic Dimensions of Ecclesiology," 18.
[82] Ibid. 143.
[83] Ibid.

heresy do not actually exist, or that, somehow, all sides of all divisions are in schism and heresy equally.

When Hryniewicz presents a more strictly theological articulation of his views on the subject, the result is questionable.

> The lack of visible communion remains only a historical event; it does not destroy the ontological unity of the Church. An ideal and all-embracing unity has never been achieved in the history of Christianity but ontological unity can persist even amidst splits and divisions. Its divine core has never been broken and this remains a bright and shining reality even amidst an imperfect communion of the Churches. In other words, the one and unique Church of Christ subsists in single denominational Churches.[84]

What is actually said in *Lumen Gentium* n. 8 is that the Church of Christ subsists in the Catholic Church.[85] Whether its subsistence in other churches was meant to be absolutely excluded has been a subject of debate, but it should be noted that the position taken by Hryniewicz has an increasingly uncertain place within the mainstream of Catholic ecclesiology, if it remains within it at all.[86] Hryniewicz goes on to say of what he calls the "denominational Churches,"

---

84 Hryniewicz, "Mystery of Unity Amidst Division," 113-114.
85 Hryniewicz himself makes no explicit reference to LG 8 in his article, though the allusion is evident.
86 Recent Catholic magisterial interpretation of LG 8 has argued that, from the very nature of the concept, there can be only one subsistence, namely in the Catholic Church (see below, pp. 157-162). The contrary position of Hryniewicz may have been more common at one time among Catholic ecclesiologists. See, for example, Michael Fahey, *Orthodox and Catholic Sister Churches: East is West and West is East* (Milwaukee: Marquette University Press, 1996), 41: "It is one thing to speak glowingly about sister churches and to proclaim that the Church of Christ subsists not only in the church of Rome but in the other churches as well, but quite another thing to adapt our practices to coincide with that those [sic] affirmations." Hervé Legrand, in holding that the Church of Christ should be understood as subsisting also in the Orthodox Church, although more restrained than Hryniewicz, offers what might be considered an essentially similar view (see below, pp. 169-173). For another recent perspective along the same lines, see Joseph Famerée, "Local Churches, Universal Church and Other Churches in *Lumen Gentium,*" *Ecclesiology* 4:1 (2007) 67: "the assertion that the sole Church of Christ subsists in the Roman Catholic Church does not exclude the possibility that the one Church of Christ may also subsist in another Christian Church in which all the constituent elements of ecclesiality could be found." Neither Fahey nor Famerée engages directly with the texts of the CDF of recent years on "subsists in" that will be considered later in this chapter.

presumably including the Catholic Church: "None of those ... should claim to be exclusively identical with the Church of Christ." While it is widely agreed that in LG 8, the conciliar fathers were intent on avoiding an exclusive identification between the Catholic Church and the Church of Christ, it is clear that they sought language that would also avoid implying any kind of parity between the Catholic Church and others. Instead, by the language of "subsists in" they introduced a paradoxical idea of the mystery of the one Church outside the visible unity of the Church.[87] Hryniewicz in some instances conveys too little appreciation of this element of paradox in post-conciliar Catholic ecclesiology especially in regard to the ecclesial status of other churches. In other instances, however, Hryniewicz himself illuminates the paradoxical quality of the ecumenical endeavor in an important way, as shall now be considered.

"Ecumenical aporetics"

Hryniewicz calls attention to an idea that has such a capacity to illuminate the expression "sister churches" in its 20th century use by Catholics and Orthodox that it must be mentioned here – in spite of the fact that Hryniewicz does not directly relate it to "sister churches" himself, touches on the idea only briefly, and, in what he does say about it, even pursues a certain line of thought that becomes somewhat tangled. All these limitations notwithstanding, Hryniewicz contributes something distinctive and valuable in his discussion of what he calls "ecumenical aporetics".

Although Hryniewicz has a section with this heading in one of his articles, the precise meaning of the phrase is not fully explained, and must be inferred. As Hryniewicz does say, the word *aporía* derives, in its Christian context, from the passage in St. Paul's Second Letter to the Corinthians when the apostle exclaims that "we are perplexed, but not driven to despair" (ἀπορούμενοι ἀλλ' οὐκ ἐξαπορούμενοι, 2 Cor 4:8). Hryniewicz observes, "*Aporía* means an apparently insurmountable difficulty or contradiction."[88] He elaborates: "To put it more descriptively: we do not know what to do, the situation seems to be desperate, we worry, there is no solution to our difficulties, but nevertheless we do not give up."[89] Hryniewicz further notes that the apostle meant to "show an essential element of Christian existence as such, a dialectical coexistence of

---

87 Cf. the Council's explicit teaching in LG 8 that there are elements of the Church outside the visible bounds of the Catholic Church.
88 Hryniewicz, "Ecumenism and Kenotic Dimensions of Ecclesiology," 145.
89 Ibid.

helplessness and courage to hold on, which could be applied to ecumenism as well."⁹⁰

Just how *aporía* – signifying a certain helplessness in the face of an impasse or contradiction – is applicable to ecumenism is something that Hryniewicz sets out to illustrate by way of a comparison, on one level interesting, and on another not entirely fitting. He compares the present-day desire for unity amidst Christian division with the ancient desire for baptism in circumstances that did not allow for it to be performed.

> Early Christianity knew the so-called 'baptism of desire'. The belief in its existence originated in a very difficult period of history when a reception of the baptism was physically impossible. For martyrs the death suffered for Christ was considered to be a 'baptism of blood'. The others who could not receive the baptism 'through water and the Spirit' (Jo 3:5), strongly desired to do so. Christians believed that those were baptized by the baptism of the very desire.
>
> The concept of the baptism of desire may offer a certain ecumenical analogy. The strong wish for unity can be fulfilled in a situation, when churches are not yet able and ready to overcome the divisions and to acknowledge themselves mutually as churches, although they share the basic truths of the Christian faith. I believe this desire for unity is a kind of inner personal anticipation of the reconciled diversity. It achieves in the heart of a Christian something that our churches, for various reasons, are not able yet to achieve. He or she becomes then a human being inwardly free from impoverishing division and separation. Remaining loyal to his or her Church they recover a living consciousness of belonging together in Christ and to be members of His 'one holy catholic and apostolic Church'. They rediscover their deep spiritual fellowship with other Christians.⁹¹

One can perhaps think of examples when the tension Hryniewicz describes has existed between an individual ecumenist and his or her not so ecumenically-minded church. But there are potential problems with this approach. When the interior desire of the individual is opposed to the official teaching of his church, we are perilously close once again to Hryniewicz' earlier notion that churches as institutions are prisoners of their doctrines. A wedge is driven between charity (located in the hearts of individuals) and truth (on which the official churches are stuck).

More particularly, any notion that the institutional churches lack an ecumenical spirit that their members possess as individuals certainly breaks down

---

90 Ibid.
91 Hryniewicz, "Conclusion," in *The Challenge of Our Hope*, 266.

when it comes to the expression "sister churches" in the context of Catholic-Orthodox relations. For here, the official churches themselves have given expression to their longing for unity. They have done this even while divided. Herein lies what might be called a true ecumenical *aporía*.

Although, as has been said, Hryniewicz does not interpret the specific issue of sister churches in these terms himself, his notion of aporetics has an important application in this context. Churches that have long identified themselves by their division from one another now identify themselves *with* one another across that division, prior to and in anticipation of bridging it. As used by Catholics and Orthodox in the 20th century, the term "sister churches" has a significance it did not bear in previous epochs: namely, the significance of surprised discovery, which can only be understood against the background of the centuries-old schism. Because, until recently, each tradition had perceived the schism as an irreversible fact of history, taking the step of calling one another sister churches really has meant that each institution has put itself at odds with *itself*. The expression implies a self-critique by each tradition of its own standard account of the division, and it makes the ongoing circumstance of the division appear, suddenly, nonsensical. In both of these ways, the expression "sister churches" is a profoundly disruptive term. It confronts each church with – compared to what it had thought it knew – contradictory new information about the other and thus about itself, driving the two churches alike into the predicament of having to say, as Hryniewicz aptly puts it, "We do not know what to do."[92]

4. Adriano Garuti

For more than a quarter century (1975-2002), Adriano Garuti was an official in the Congregation for the Doctrine of the Faith (CDF) in the Vatican. In 1996 he published a study entitled "'Chiese sorelle': Realtà e interrogative," later published in English translation as an appendix to his book on Roman primacy

---

92 In the *Book of Acts*, it is written of those who are told by Peter that the one they put to death was, after all, none other than the Christ, whom God has vindicated, that "when they heard this they were cut to the heart, and said to Peter and the rest of the apostles, 'Brethren, what shall we do?'" Something remarkably similar must be understood to have been present in the response of those 20th century Catholic and Orthodox Christians who were startled by the realization that their historical condemnations of one another's churches had been a mistake. In this light, the expression's use in the context of the schism should never be unaccompanied by a sense of repentance and urgency.

and ecumenism.⁹³ Between Garuti's 1996 article and the CDF's *Note on the Expression "Sister Churches"* issued in 2000 (the topic of the next section) there are strong affinities, as will be noted.

Distinctions in usage

Garuti is concerned to distinguish what he considers legitimate from illegitimate uses of "sister churches" in the context of relations between Catholics and Orthodox. In reference to the bilateral dialogue, he observes:

> It is necessary ... to draw attention to a certain confusion in assigning the title of 'sister'. On the regional level it is generally attributed to the local Church understood 'above all as an ensemble of different dioceses' which 'took the form of autocephalous patriarchates with their own canonical structure, preserving among themselves communion in faith, sacramental life and brotherly relations.' At the same time, it is extended to the relations between the Catholic Church and Orthodox Church in their totality and between the ecumenical patriarchate and the other Orthodox Churches.⁹⁴

Among various types of usage, Garuti first mentions here that which applies on the regional level, when the term is predicated of a local church "understood above all as an ensemble of different dioceses". The example is given of two or more patriarchates maintaining fraternal relations of sacramental communion and agreement in faith; the past tense is used here ("took the form"), suggesting a more historical perspective. Garuti next identifies the usage whereby the entire Catholic Church and the entire Orthodox Church are said to be sister churches. Then, presenting what one would expect to be a third type of usage, he notes that the expression has been applied to relations between the ecumenical patriarchate and other Orthodox churches. This again must refer exclusively to the regional level of patriarchates or national autocephalous churches. It seems to have reference to the present more than the past, and refers to intra-Orthodox relations only. Still, its resemblance to the first type of usage is so close that it must be seen as merely another description of it.

---

93 The original article appeared in *Antonianum* 71, no. 4 (1996) 631-86. It was then reprinted as "Sister Churches: Reality and Questions," in *The Primacy of the Bishop of Rome and Ecumenical Dialogue*, trans. ed. by Michael Miller (San Francisco: Ignatius, 2004), 261-327.

94 Garuti, "Sister Churches," 280-281, with reference to Russian Orthodox–Roman Catholic Conversations (Odessa, March 13-17, 1980), Joint Communiqué *(Information Service* 44, 1980, 113b).

Hence the passage cited above presents two alternatives: usage on the level of regional churches, and usage on the level of the entire Orthodox Church and the entire Catholic Church. In the official response of the U.S. Orthodox-Catholic Consultation to The Munich Document of the Joint International Commission, mention was made of both of them. Garuti writes in view of this document (and quoting from it): "It has now been admitted in the context of ecumenical dialogue that 'the appeal to the term "sister Churches" is unclear. Does it refer to patriarchates or jurisdictions in full communion or to the special relationship between the Orthodox Church and the Roman Catholic Church?'"[95]

While noting these two types of usage from the 1980s and the uncertainties concerning them, Garuti also notes a third type of usage, and the precision it gained in the 1990s. This is when the expression is applied to churches on the strictly diocesan level. Garuti refers to this third type of usage in his treatment of a joint declaration of the Catholic Church and the Assyrian church of the East.[96] He observes that by 1994, "No longer are the Catholic Church and the Assyrian Church as such termed 'sisters', but rather their respective particular Churches." He quotes from the joint declaration: "'Living by this faith and these sacraments, it follows as a consequence that the particular Catholic churches and the particular Assyrian Churches can recognize each other as sister Churches'."[97] Finally, a further type of usage to which Garuti calls attention, and which

---

95 Garuti, "Sister Churches," 281, with reference to "Response to the Munich Statement," op. cit. (see above, Chapter 3, p. 92-93, n. 79. Garuti himself cites the document as published in *Diakonia* 18 (1983) 176.

96 Signed by Pope John Paul II and the Assyrian Patriarch Mar Dinkha IV on November 11, 1994, the "Common Christological Declaration between the Catholic Church and the Assyrian Church of the East" was published in *L'Osservatore Romano*, Weekly English Edition (November 16, 1994), 1. While the Assyrian Church of the East is not within the communion of Eastern Orthodox churches (nor of Oriental Orthodox churches), its status from the perspective of the Catholic Church sheds light on how the Catholic Church generally understands the concept of sister churches in its relations with the Orthodox, too.

97 IS, no. 88 [1995], 3, as quoted by Garuti, "Sister Churches," 279. In official documents issued or endorsed by the Catholic Church, this usage had not always been carefully distinguished up to this point from the usage involving the two entire communions. As one editorial observed, "[I]t is not said that the two Churches, Catholic and Assyrian, are the sister Churches, but that the particular Churches which form these two Churches can recognize each other as sister Churches. There is here a subtle nuance which merits being noted, because it is the first time, to our knowledge, that

will be discussed in due course, is that by which one or another Orthodox patriarchate is spoken of as the sister church of the Roman Catholic Church.[98]

Altogether, then, Garuti identifies four possible pairs (or sets) of ecclesial subjects of which the expression sister churches may be predicated. These may now be re-ordered slightly so as to indicate their correspondence – which is not always exact – with the categories set out in Chapter 3: (1) regional churches, i.e. metropolitan provinces or patriarchates, "among themselves," that is to say, in full communion with one another; this corresponds to the usage mentioned first in Chapter 3 and *not included among the four categories* pertaining directly to Catholic-Orthodox relations; (2) the Catholic Church and the Orthodox Church; this corresponds to usage 2 in Chapter 3; (3) the Roman Catholic Church and any one or more of the Orthodox patriarchates; this corresponds to usage 3 in Chapter 3; and (4) any one or more of the many Catholic churches on the diocesan level and any one or more of the many Orthodox churches on the diocesan level; this corresponds, in theory, with usage 4 in Chapter 3, but only if usage 4 is interpreted, *contra* the evidence adduced in Chapter 3, such that the "many churches" on both sides are dioceses, rather than larger ecclesial units.[99] Notice ought to be taken of the fact that usage 1 from Chapter 3 (Rome and Constantinople) is missing from Garuti's pairings; we will return to this.

Among those Garuti does include, it shall now be seen which of them he considers legitimate applications and which not.

The Catholic Church is not *the sister of the Orthodox Church (usage 2)*

Garuti argues that one must utterly reject any idea "that two Churches exist, the Catholic Church and the Orthodox Church, which constitute two parts of the one Church that existed in the first millennium" and that these two Churches "exist as two universal sisters, each in possession of her own primate," since this would mean, according to Garuti, that the "Church of Christ no longer exists as one in history, but is *in fieri* [in the state of becoming] through the convergence or reunification of the two sister Churches, which is hoped for and promoted by dialogue: at least in the second millennium, she exists only as an ideal and not in a real and historical manner."[100]

---

in a declaration of this kind this distinction has been formulated so carefully." *Irénikon* 67 (1994) 450, as quoted by Garuti, 279, n. 104.
98 Cf. Garuti, "Sister Churches," 324, and see below, pp. 143-144.
99 See above, Chapter 3, pp. 107-110.
100 Garuti, "Sister Churches," 326.

In Garuti's characterization of this usage, a number of elements are indicated, not all of which are necessarily intrinsic to it. To describe the Catholic Church and the Orthodox Church as sister churches does presuppose "that two churches exist," certainly; it also presupposes that they "constitute two parts of the one Church," as Garuti also says; further, it presupposes, or requires, that "each [be] in possession of her own primate". But along with or in consequence of all this, it need not be that they "exist as two universal sisters". If it did, then, certainly, Garuti's objection of ecclesial duality, violating the oneness of the Church, would apply. But it may be asked whether what Garuti rejects is not an exaggerated picture of the likeness of two parallel churches. Between Old Rome as the first see of Christendom and New Rome as the second there always was, after all, a proper *taxis*. Even at its most robust, the primacy of Constantinople within the Byzantine Empire did not presume to encroach upon the unique primacy of Rome at the level of the universal church.[101]

Lanne and Congar were both inclined to identify the Catholic Church with that of the West and the Orthodox Church with that of the East. In doing so, they identified neither church (rather than both) as universal. This seems to be among the most crucial points of difference between their approach and Garuti's.

It may be asked whether Congar's famous image of the "two lungs," to describe how the Catholic Church and the Orthodox Church relate to one another in the one body of the Church, does not perhaps reinforce, however, the very sense of parallelism which leads Garuti to reject as dualistic any formulation suggesting that the Orthodox and Catholic Churches in their totalities are sister churches. Two points may be made in this regard. First, as just mentioned, Congar did not posit a duality on the universal level. Rather, he spoke of the universal church as "embracing the two sister churches."[102] Second, it should be recognized that the image of the "two lungs" may not actually be sufficient, by itself, to account for the nature of the relationship between Old and New Rome, since the image suggests an undifferentiated equality between them, rather than a *taxis*.

---

101 There is no indication that the church of Constantinople sought to be regarded as the arbiter of otherwise irresolvable disputes in the West (as Rome was the church to which those in the East would appeal who could not resolve their differences), nor that the patriarch of Constantinople ever entertained the idea that his prerogative to preside at ecumenical councils was equal to that of the pope.

102 Cf. above, p. 125.

Catholic Church = Roman Catholic Church = universal Church, which cannot be a sister church (usage 3)

Another usage that is objectionable from Garuti's perspective is that by which the Ecumenical Patriarchate (or any other Orthodox patriarchate) is said to be the sister of the Catholic Church. Garuti asserts, for example, that "the expression used by Patriarch Dimitrios I on the occasion of the death of Paul VI is incorrect: 'The Ecumenical Patriarchate as sister Church shares with its whole soul in the grief of the holy Roman Catholic Church and the entire Roman Catholic world'."[103] The reason Garuti sees this as incorrect is that, as he puts it, "it is theologically unacceptable to say that the individual particular Churches, or groups of particular Churches, are sisters of the Catholic Church in her totality (universal Church), composed of all the Churches, each of which is, in her proper place, the very same Catholic Church."[104]

Contained in Garuti's remark here – if one includes in it the quoted words of Dimitrios – are three ecclesial terms predicated of the same ecclesial subject. The three terms are "Roman Catholic Church" (Dimitrios' favored term for it), "Catholic Church" and "universal Church". Garuti employs the three interchangeably. His doing so is what makes inevitable his rejection of the idea that the Roman Catholic Church could possibly have a sister church. But the drawback of his approach becomes evident if one considers the difference between saying, on the one hand, that the Orthodox churches belong to the universal church, and saying on the other hand that they belong to the Roman Catholic Church. The incoherence of the latter idea seems to have led both Congar and Lanne to avoid identifying the "Catholic Church in her totality" (if what is meant by this is the Roman Catholic Church) with the universal church.[105]

---

103 Garuti, "Sister Churches," 324, n. 301. Garuti cites Stormon, *Towards the Healing of Schism*, 327, no. 373-374. The exact quotation is from no. 373, whereas no. 374 contains language that is similar but not exactly the same.
104 Garuti, "Sister Churches," 324.
105 Garuti's position would also seem to require saying that the universal church that was Greek as well as Roman in the first millennium was rendered exclusively Roman in the second millennium by the schism. This difficulty has been pointed out in similar terms by Francis Sullivan, "*Quaestio Disputata*: A Response to Karl Becker, S.J., on the Meaning of *Subsistit in*," *Theological Studies* 67 (2006) 404: "It seems to me that identifying the Church of Christ exclusively with the Catholic Church during the second millennium would mean claiming that in 1054 the Church of Christ simply ceased to exist in the East."

Orthodox and Catholic particular churches as sister churches (usage 4)

As to a usage Garuti considers acceptable, he admits that the expression "could be utilized to refer to one particular Catholic Church, including the Church of Rome, and to one particular Orthodox Church."[106] It is obvious that in saying "one" particular Catholic Church, and "one" particular Orthodox church, Garuti means *any one* of the many particular churches on either side, indeed all of them, including even Rome; hence this statement's inclusion under category 4 (many churches on both sides). But in addition to its relevance to usage 4, this statement also offers insight into Garuti's perspective on the lone usage from Chapter 3 that is not represented in his list at all, namely Chapter 3's usage 1, pairing the church of Rome and the church of Constantinople. Attention was called at the end of Chapter 3 to the inherent ambiguity of that usage insofar as it invariably leaves open the question: "the church of Rome" on what level (and to a lesser extent also the question: "the church of Constantinople" on what level)? Garuti indicates here his own view: the way in which the church of Rome may be acceptably called the sister church of another church is strictly as one diocese to another. Thus he links Chapter 3's usages 1 (Rome and Constantinople) and 4 (many churches on both sides) – while defining 4 specifically as many *particular* churches on both sides. That is, Rome and Constantinople *as dioceses* can be, like any other Catholic and Orthodox dioceses, described as sister churches of one another.

Yet even this usage that Garuti endorses is one that seems to hold a precarious place in his ecclesiological approach. On the face of it, Garuti is consistent with the official Catholic position that Orthodox particular churches are true churches.[107] His affirmation of them as true churches, however, combined with his affirmation of the Roman Catholic Church as the universal church, creates a difficulty. If, as was said at Vatican II, the universal church exists in and is formed out of the particular churches,[108] and if the Orthodox churches are true particular churches, then the question arises: how can the (Roman) Catholic Church, to which the Orthodox churches do not belong, be simply identified as the universal church? It seems that one of the two affirmations will end up needing to yield to the other: either the true ecclesiality of the particular Orthodox churches will eventually need to be called into question in order to uphold the claim of universality for the Catholic Church, or the claim

---

106 Garuti, "Sister Churches," 327.
107 Cf. *Communionis notio*, 17 and *Dominus Iesus* 17.
108 Cf. *Lumen Gentium* 23.

to universality will need to be significantly qualified (as per Lanne, Congar) in order to go on affirming the particular Orthodox churches as true particular churches.

As will now be shown, Garuti moves discernibly in the direction of the first option in the remainder of his analysis: that is, in the direction of calling into question the true ecclesiality of the particular Orthodox churches.

Communion in faith and in government as prerequisites for sister churches status

Whereas Lanne and Congar, following such popes as Paul VI and John Paul II, unequivocally affirm Orthodox particular churches as true churches, Garuti raises questions in this regard. He opens the subject of the ecclesial status of Orthodox churches in the following way:

> In the final analysis, the reality of 'sister Churches' might be founded on the ecclesial status of the Orthodox Churches, in virtue of the faith that they have in common with the Catholic Church, regardless of their not yet complete communion with each other. It concerns two presuppositions that are considered as having been already achieved. They nevertheless raise a number of questions and therefore require a few clarifications so as to ascertain whether and in what sense we can continue to speak of 'sister Churches'.[109]

The two presuppositions to which Garuti alludes, and which he says raise questions and require clarifications, are indicated somewhat farther on when he writes: "The question arises, however, of the effective *community of faith* and of the impact of the incomplete canonical communion with the Successor of Peter."[110] Garuti devotes the next fourteen pages of his study to a discussion of these two issues – first, whether there is sufficient community of faith between Orthodox and Catholics to justify the ecclesial status of the Orthodox churches as true churches, and second, whether their ecclesial status as such is not also put in question by the fact that they remain severed from the bonds of *government* centered in the office of the papacy.

Garuti acknowledges, initially, that at least since Vatican II the Catholic Church has often affirmed that there is no substantial difference between the Catholic and Orthodox churches in terms of the apostolic faith.

> An *identity of faith* between the Catholic Church and the Orthodox Churches is generally affirmed, on the magisterial level as well as on the theological level. Indeed, it is explicitly emphasized that it is precisely by reason of the same faith

---

109 Garuti, "Sister Churches," 293.
110 Ibid. 295.

and the same apostolic heritage, and possession of the same ministry and Eucharist that the Orthodox Churches are true particular Churches, and that hence they can and must be considered sister Churches, even though there still remain points to be clarified and obstacles to be overcome before arriving at unity in the profession of faith, a necessary condition for the reestablishment of full communion.[111]

Garuti wishes to suggest, however, that these "points to be clarified" and "obstacles to be overcome" are not necessarily so minimal as is sometimes assumed on the Catholic side. In fact, from Garuti's perspective the unity in faith with the Orthodox that he admits is widely understood among Catholics as having been "already achieved" is far from self-evident. To make his point, he invites consideration of statements of a different kind made by the Catholic magisterium. These, he argues, show "that unity in faith does not yet exist".

> Equally explicit, however, are the affirmations about the "doctrinal disagreements to be resolved", "true and genuine disagreements in matters of faith" which "hinder full communion between Christians". From this arises the necessity of dialogue in view of [the need for] an adherence by all to the integral content of the faith, without compromise, and "in acceptance of the whole and entire truth", in order to attain the unity willed by God. It is recognized, therefore, that unity in faith does not yet exist; despite the progress made in dialogue, unity is still a goal to be achieved.[112]

Unfortunately, Garuti has taken the magisterial statements he quotes in support of his view out of context. Of the three quotations he includes about doctrinal differences – all are from Pope John Paul II's encyclical *Ut unum sint* – none pertains to relations with the Orthodox in particular; all refer to Catholic ecumenical relations generally. Where the subject of Catholic-Orthodox relations is addressed in the encyclical (nos. 50-61), the phrases that Garuti quotes cannot be found. Yet Garuti himself is definitely addressing the question of the unity or divergence of faith between just Catholics and Orthodox. It is significant that the sole document he cites as evidence for a lack of unity in faith between Catholics and Orthodox never actually proposes that this type of unity is lacking between *them*.

Perhaps there is a certain irony, then, in the fact that Garuti turns next to the Orthodox for support of his position. "With greater realism," he writes, "the Orthodox believe that there is no unity of faith with the Catholic Church, and

---

111 Ibid. (original emphasis).
112 Garuti, "Sister Churches," 296, with reference to *Ut unum sint*, Introduction and nos. 39 and 36.

they judge some doctrines and dogmas to be *Roman heresies*."[113] While this statement does represent the attitude of some Orthodox, obviously many other Orthodox would disagree. Garuti himself goes on to quote an Orthodox theologian with a far more positive evaluation of the Catholic Church. "Today," writes Nicholas Lossky of the Orthodox Church in France, "the Catholic Church and the Orthodox Church no longer treat each other as 'schismatic' and 'heretical'; they call each other 'sister Churches', thus they recognize each other fully as Churches."[114] Strangely, Garuti criticizes this Orthodox perspective as too optimistic. This is because it does not square with the belief about the Catholic Church that Garuti has identified as *the* Orthodox position: that there is no unity of faith and that some Catholic doctrines are heresies.[115]

After calling into question the degree to which the Orthodox and Catholic churches hold the same faith in common, Garuti proceeds to the second issue he regards as casting doubt on the ecclesial status of the Orthodox: the issue of visible administrative unity. "Contrary to what is sometimes said, communion between Churches, and hence the fullness of their ecclesial status, is not realized simply by a mutual recognition of their common faith, priesthood, and sacraments; also necessary are the bonds of 'ecclesial government, and communion', that is to say, a presupposed acceptance of the 'visible structure' of the Church."[116]

Here and at other points, Garuti raises the question of the "full" ecclesial status of the Orthodox.[117] The language of fullness as regards ecclesiality was used by the CDF in its Letter, *Communionis notio*, of May 28, 1992.[118] In that

---

113 Garuti, "Sister Churches," 298.
114 N. Lossky, "La présence orthodoxe dans la 'diaspora' et ses implications ecclésiologiques, de même que celles des Eglises orientales catholiques", *Irénikon* 65 (1992) 355. Quoted by Garuti, "Sister Churches," 299, n. 183 (translation mine).
115 Garuti ("Sister Churches," 298-299, n. 182) mentions that Orthodoxy's holding such a view (as he says it does) has even led some Catholics to suggest about the Orthodox "that they have passed on from schism to heresy," an idea that he admits "might seem an exaggeration," though he presents further support for it.
116 Garuti, "Sister Churches," 300.
117 Cf. Garuti, "Sister Churches," 310, where he writes that "it is only this reestablishment [of full unity in faith and communion] that will allow us to recognize the full ecclesial status of the Orthodox Churches and thus rediscover them fully as 'sisters'."
118 *Communionis notio* (full English title, "Letter to the Bishops of the Catholic Church on Certain Aspects of the Church Understood as Communion"), n. 13: " ... for each particular Church to be fully Church, that is, the particular presence of the universal Church with all its essential elements, and hence constituted *after the model of [in the image of] the universal Church*, there must be present in it, as a proper element,

document, the statement was made about the Orthodox that their existence as particular Churches is "wounded" insofar as they lack communion with the bishop of Rome as the head of the college of bishops.[119] For this reason each particular Orthodox church is less than "fully" church.[120]

Garuti admits that "[o]n the basis of *Communionis notio* one could conclude that they [the Orthodox churches] are true particular Churches," but he continues to lay more emphasis on why they are less than full churches than on why they are true churches. He says that they possess "certain elements of sanctification and of truth – especially apostolic succession and valid Eucharist".[121] But in explaining what follows from this, he does not make clear how or why Orthodox churches, possessing these "elements of sanctification and of truth," actually differ from ecclesial communities born of the Protestant Reformation, which themselves, though lacking apostolic succession and valid Eucharist, nevertheless possess certain other elements of sanctification and truth. Garuti writes of the Orthodox churches that they

> do have meaning and importance in the mystery of salvation and are instruments at the service of the Spirit of Christ, and hence they too participate in the proper mission of the Church of Christ, with which they have partial relationship. Nevertheless, these means "draw their salvific value from the fullness ... of the Catholic Church, Christ's one and only Church, which He has constituted the depositary of that fullness."[122]

The pattern that emerges in Garuti's work can be summarized simply as follows: whereas in much official Catholic teaching since Vatican II, and particularly in much official Catholic use of the expression "sister churches" since the late 1960s, the proximity between Catholic and Orthodox churches is emphasized and a certain distance between Orthodox churches and Protestant ecclesial communities is implicitly or explicitly recognized, Garuti reverses the trend; that is, he emphasizes instead the distance between Orthodox churches and the Catholic Church and, in the process, somewhat blurs the distinction between Orthodox and Protestant communities with regard to the Catholic Church.

---

the supreme authority of the Church: the episcopal college '*together with their head, the Supreme Pontiff, and never apart from him*'" (original emphasis).
119 Cf. *Communionis notio*, n. 17.
120 Cf. *ibid.* n. 13.
121 Garuti, "Sister Churches," 304.
122 Ibid., with reference to U. Betti, "Chiesa di Cristo e Chiesa cattolica. A proposito di un'espressione della 'Lumen gentium'," *Antonianum* 61 (1986) 726-755.

One sees this again where Garuti concludes this section of his analysis by qualifying the sense in which the Orthodox churches can be recognized as sister churches from the Catholic point of view:

> We may conclude, therefore, that although the Orthodox Churches possess elements of ecclesial status, the Church of Christ does not subsist in them: they are Churches, but in an imperfect and analogous manner with respect to the Church, from which they derive their existence and salvific efficacy. Consequently, equally imperfect and analogous is their condition as 'sisters'.[123]

In Garuti's presentation, there is a degree of erosion in the very significance of the designation "churches" when applied to the Orthodox. It should be noted that in the passage above, his unwillingness to affirm unequivocally even Orthodox particular churches as sister churches (of Catholic particular churches) is very closely connected to his way of interpreting the fact that, as he puts it, "the Church of Christ does not subsist in them." Altogether, Garuti offers what may be described as a minimalist interpretation of the meaning of "true churches" as applied to Orthodox particular churches.

Patriarchal sister churches?

In his analysis of the 12th-century Byzantine uses of the expression "sister churches" discussed in Chapter 1, Garuti gives further indication of his perspective on the concept of sister churches on the regional level, involving patriarchates. We have already seen his negative stance on any usage that would pair the Roman Catholic Church with an Eastern see (usage 3). Now some additional sense may be gained of what informs this stance.

It was mentioned in Chapter 1 that in a debate with Anselm of Havelberg in 1136, Archbishop Nicetas of Nicomedia invoked the expression "sister churches" as part of his critique of a form of Roman primacy he could not accept. Sixty years later, Patriarch John X Camateros, in correspondence with Pope Innocent III, and also in response to Roman claims he considered exaggerated, invoked the expression again. Although both Nicetas and Camateros relied on an idea of patriarchal sister churches, it was seen in Chapter 1 that the positions of Camateros were significantly more extreme: Camateros described Rome's primacy as "only" (μόνω) a primacy of honor and did not speak of any concrete prerogatives at all associated with it. Nicetas, by contrast, was specific in affirming Rome's role as the church to which appeal is to be made in circumstances when disputes cannot be resolved by the usual means, and Nicetas

---

123 Garuti, "Sister Churches," 305.

upheld an idea of Rome as the head of the other churches. Altogether, Nicetas was more careful to preserve a meaningful taxis in which the mutual relations of the sister patriarchal churches did not undermine Rome's position as the first among them with powers the others did not have. Nicetas attributed the estrangement between pope and eastern patriarchs to Rome's having appropriated to herself, as he saw it, an imperial character since the "partition of the empire," but he did not question Rome's right to exercise a unique authority within the universal church.

In his own treatment of the views of Nicetas and Camateros, Garuti often presents them as indistinguishable. Both, according to Garuti, used the expression "sister churches" in a spirit that was "decidedly anti-Roman and opposed to the primacy of the Bishop of Rome."[124] He admits that Nicetas "acknowledged a certain primacy of Rome" which included the right of appeal, but Nicetas is still cast as an opponent of the primacy of the Bishop of Rome insofar as he rejected the particular form of Roman primacy ascendant in the 12th century. Garuti describes this 12th-century understanding of the primacy without critical analysis or comment of his own:

> One of the most common formulae used to convey the growing awareness of the primacy of the Church of Rome and of her Bishop was *'Ecclesia Romana mater et caput omnium ecclesiarum'*, with its consequent claim that all Churches 'receive their being, their origin, and their continuity from the Roman Church' and for this reason 'should follow their mother if they want to live at all'. Against this the Eastern Christians propose the category of 'sister Churches,' 'born of the same father and hence worthy of the same honor'.[125]

It was, certainly, contrary to the understanding of the Eastern bishops, including Nicetas, that their own apostolic churches "receive[d] their origin" from the Roman Church. Yet in the speech of Nicetas there *was* recognition of the church of Rome as the head of the other churches. In Garuti's portrayal of the Byzantine view, what is set forth instead is a generic idea of the pentarchy wherein "the five patriarchs stand at the head of the entire Church."[126]

Contrary to Garuti's characterization, Nicetas had an understanding of the Church which integrated primacy with conciliarity. Garuti's polarization of these two realities reflects the later, more polemical encounter between John X Camateros and Innocent III, and he uncritically describes the view of the latter:

---

124 Ibid. 263.
125 Ibid., citing only J. Spiteris, *La Critica Bizantina* (Rome, 1979), 21. The source of the latter quote in this passage is not Nicetas but John X Camateros.
126 Garuti, "Sister Churches," 263.

"Faced with the problem of the return of the Greek Church into the bosom of the Roman Church, Innocent III emphasizes the need for the Greeks to return to the one sheepfold of Christ, to the one true ark of salvation, to the one pastor, to the one foundation, to the one mother, that is, the Roman Church."[127]

Garuti's uncritical presentation of 12th century Roman centralism, and his criticism of Byzantine responses to it, indicate that he takes a negative view of sister churches at the patriarchal level, not just historically, but in contemporary Catholic-Orthodox relations.[128]

5. The Congregation for the Doctrine of the Faith

Four years after Garuti published his article on the topic, the Congregation for the Doctrine of the Faith, with which he continued to be associated, issued its *Note on the Expression "Sister Churches"* (June, 2000). In what follows, the *Note* and its affinities with Garuti's article will first be discussed; then there will be consideration of two controversial issues, one of which presents itself in the *Note* explicitly, if only briefly – namely, the idea that in the relationship between the universal church and the local church, it is the universal church that has priority. The other issue to be considered is one that has arisen already at several points in this study: the interpretation of "subsists in" as used in *Lumen Gentium* 8. Although this issue does not receive direct attention in the *Note*, it can be seen as related to that document's rejection of the practice of designating the Catholic Church and the Orthodox Church as sister churches.

The CDF's 2000 Note on the Expression "Sister Churches"

Like Garuti, the *Note* denies the legitimacy of what we have been calling usage 2 (the Catholic Church and the Orthodox Church), and for the same reasons: "one should avoid, as a source of misunderstanding and theological confusion, the use of formulations such as 'our two Churches,' which, if applied to the Catholic Church and the totality of Orthodox Churches (or a single Orthodox Church), imply a plurality not merely on the level of particular Churches, but also on the level of the one, holy, Catholic and apostolic Church confessed in

---

127 Ibid. 264, with apparent reference to Innocent III, *Ep.* I.354, PL 214, 327A. Unwittingly it would seem, Garuti speaks of precisely two churches – the Greek and the Roman – when he describes the problem said to have been faced by Innocent III. This seems to contradict Garuti's otherwise strongly maintained notion that one must avoid any notion that "two churches exist". See above, p. 141-142.

128 See also below, p. 154, n. 136, which references a 1990 book by Garuti questioning the historical and ecclesiological basis of the designation of Rome as a patriarchate.

the Creed, whose real existence is thus obscured."[129] It is notable that in the CDF's injunction here, the only two levels of church structure that are mentioned are the diocesan level and the universal level. There is no regional plurality mentioned. Also in line with Garuti's perspective, the CDF's *Note* prohibits what we have been calling usage 3 – that is, applying the expression "sister churches" to the Catholic Church in relation to an Orthodox particular church or grouping of particular churches: "one cannot properly say that the Catholic Church is the sister of a particular Church or group of Churches. This is not merely a question of terminology, but above all of respecting a basic truth of the Catholic faith: that of the unicity of the Church of Jesus Christ."[130] In how it articulates both prohibitions, the *Note* suggests a total identification of the Church of Christ with the Catholic Church, as was seen in Garuti's presentation.

As to usages that the CDF endorses, there are two. The first is the usage mentioned initially in Chapter 3 as not pertaining to Catholic-Orthodox relations directly. The CDF's endorsement of it warrants being mentioned here insofar as it indicates a recognition in principle of ecclesiality on the regional level. "In fact, in the proper sense, *sister Churches* are exclusively particular Churches (or groupings of particular Churches; for example, the Patriarchates or Metropolitan provinces) among themselves."[131] Important for our purposes is what is said in the parentheses, where the CDF admits that two or more patriarchates of the same communion may properly be called sister churches.

In a subsequent statement, the *Note* asserts that the expression may be legitimately applied to any and all churches at the diocesan level so long as they are indeed churches (i.e., true churches), whether Catholic or not. "One may also speak of *sister Churches*, in a proper sense, in reference to particular Catholic and non-catholic Churches; thus the particular Church of Rome can also be called the *sister* of all other particular Churches."[132] In this endorsement of what we have been calling usage 4 (many churches on both sides), there is again the conspicuous mention of the church of Rome – as Garuti also mentioned it – and in exactly the same manner, such that a very narrow limit is set on *how* the church of Rome might be construed as a sister church of any other: strictly as one diocese to another diocese.

---

129 *Note*, n. 11.
130 Ibid.
131 *Note*, n. 10.
132 *Note*, n. 11.

Of course in the multitude of examples presented in Chapters 2 and 3 when Rome and Constantinople were called sister churches (usage 1), it is doubtful that these two churches were ever so described in their respective identities as mere dioceses. The overtones of that usage 1 seemed rather to suggest a much closer link with usages 2 (Catholic Church and Orthodox Church) and 3 (Catholic Church and one or more of the Orthodox patriarchates), in other words, an identification of "the church of Rome" with "the Catholic Church" as a whole – understood not as the universal church but as the church of the West. But the *Note*, again following the approach of Garuti, considers it dubious that Rome was ever a patriarchate that could legitimately have been understood as a sister church of the Eastern patriarchal sees even prior to the schism. As the following passage indicates, the *Note* views Roman primacy and patriarchal pentarchy as having been ecclesiological antagonists all along.

> In Christian literature, the expression [sister churches] begins to be used in the East when, from the fifth century, the idea of the Pentarchy gained ground, according to which there are five Patriarchs at the head of the Church, with the Church of Rome having the first place among these patriarchal sister Churches. In this connection, however, it needs to be noted that no Roman Pontiff ever recognized this equalization of the sees or accepted that only a primacy of honour be accorded to the See of Rome. It should be noted too that this patriarchal structure typical of the East never developed in the West.[133]

Speaking as it does of "patriarchal sister Churches", the *Note* actually echoes the language of Nicetas, who used the phrase "patriarchal sister Sees." Yet the *Note* diverges from his vision in a number of ways just as Garuti did. By describing the Byzantine position in terms of "this equalization of the sees" and "*only* a primacy of honour" to be accorded the see of Rome, the *Note* reflects the perspective of Camateros reasonably well but substantially coarsens that of Nicetas, for whom, as was seen above, honorary primacy and effective primacy went hand in hand. Additionally, whereas Nicetas ascribed ecclesial headship to the church of Rome, the *Note* puts forward an unspecific idea of the Pentarchy wherein the five Patriarchs are said to stand "at the head of the Church". By stripping patriarchal conciliarity of the element of a genuine *taxis* that Nicetas was careful not to remove from it, the *Note* makes such conciliarity a great deal less plausible than it actually was, and is.[134]

---

133 *Note*, n. 3.
134 In the *Note*, n. 3, there is reference to Rome as occupying "first place" among the five patriarchs, but the *Note* evidently fears that this place of Rome as the first see is not then one of "headship." For Nicetas it was. Cf. also the recent Ravenna Statement of

The acceptance in Rome today of the compatibility of Roman primacy and patriarchal conciliarity is further cast in doubt by the fact that in 2006, the title "Patriarch of the West" was removed from the list of titles given to the pope in the Vatican's official yearbook, the *Annuario Pontificio*.[135] This action can be seen as the logical consequence of what was expressed six years earlier in the *Note* in the assertion in the above quotation that the "patriarchal structure typical of the East never developed in the West."[136]

The local church and the universal church

One sentence in the CDF's *Note* declares that the universal church is "not sister but *mother* of all the particular Churches."[137] Some Catholic theologians have expressed concerns that this claim might represent a recrudescence of the medieval claim of the Church of Rome to be the mother of all other churches, a claim that was in conflict with an ecclesiology of sister churches then, and might be in conflict with it again today.

The *Note* was not the first text of the Catholic magisterium to propose the thesis that the universal church is mother of the particular churches. An earlier document of the CDF – its 1992 *Communionis notio*[138]– contained language expressing the idea that the particular churches are born of the universal church. This same document spoke in terms of the "priority" of the universal church over the local church.

---

the Joint International Commission for the Dialogue between the Roman Catholic Church and the Orthodox Church, n. 20 and n. 24, where a parallel understanding of headship is applied directly to the *protos* on the regional level and, by inference, to the *protos* on the universal level.

135 For an Orthodox response to this development, cf. Bishop (now Metropolitan) Hilarion Alfeyev, "Pope's Title 'Patriarch of the West' Removed," op. cit. See also Demacopoulos, "Gregory the Great and the Sixth-Century Dispute Over the Ecumenical Title," 1, n. 1, quoting an official response posted on the Web site of the Ecumenical Patriarchate, dated June 8, 2006 (and removed prior to October 2008): "by retaining these titles ["Vicar of Christ" and "Supreme Pontiff of the Universal Church"] and discarding the 'Patriarch of the West' the term and concept of 'sister Churches' between the Roman-Catholic and Orthodox Church becomes hard to use."

136 *Note*, n. 3. In 1990, Garuti had published a book questioning both the historical and doctrinal basis of the title of patriarch for the pope. A. Garuti, *Il Papa Patriarca d'Occidente? Studio storico dottrinale* (Bologna: Edizioni Francescane, 1990).

137 *Note*, n. 10 (original emphasis).

138 See above, p. 147-148, n. 118.

The Church universal ... is, in its essential mystery, a reality ontologically and chronologically prior to every single particular Church. From her origin, she has given birth to all the diverse local Churches ... In being born in and of the Church universal, it is of her and in her that they have their ecclesiality. In consequence, the formula of the Vatican Council: the Church in and from the Churches *(ecclesia in et ex ecclesiis)* (LG 23) is inseparable from this other formula: the Churches in and from the Church.[139]

In a *Festschrift* published in 1999 honoring Bishop Josef Homeyer, Cardinal Walter Kasper, then Bishop of Rottenburg-Stuttgart, and currently the President of the Vatican's Pontifical Council for the Promotion of Christian Unity, responded critically to *Communionis notio* on this point.[140] "The formula (of the universal Church's priority) would be completely problematic if, on an unspoken assumption, the universal Church were identified with the Roman church, *de facto* with the pope and the curia. If this happens, then one can say that the document of the CDF is not a help in clarifying communion ecclesiology (of Vatican II), but must be understood as the dismissal of that ecclesiology and an attempt to restore Roman centralism."[141] Over the course of the next two years as he engaged in a high-profile debate with then Cardinal Ratzinger, prefect of the CDF, Kasper espoused the view that, as Kilian McDonnell summarizes it, "[p]articular church and universal Church are in a relation of mutuality; they are perichoretically in one another."[142] In a response to Kasper published in November of 2001, Cardinal Ratzinger wrote that he could accept Kasper's formula of the simultaneity of the universal church and the particular churches;[143] at the same time, Ratzinger defended the CDF's formulation and asserted that, contrary to Kasper's fears, "the inner precedence of God's idea of

---

139 *Communionis Notio*, 9.
140 W. Kasper, "Zur Theologie und Praxis des bischöflichen Amtes," in W. Schreer and G. Steins, eds., *Auf neue Art Kirche Sein: Wirklichkeiten – Herausforderungen – Wandlungen* (Munich 1999), 32-48.
141 Ibid. 44, as quoted by J. Ratzinger, "The Local Church and the Universal Church," America (November 19, 2001), 8, and paraphrased by K. McDonnell, "The Ratzinger/Kasper Debate: the Universal Church and Local Churches," *Theological Studies* 63 (2002) 231.
142 McDonnell, "The Ratzinger/Kasper Debate," 230. Expressing Kasper's viewpoint in another way, McDonnell writes, 231, "What cannot be granted is that the formula *una, sancta, catholica, et apostolica ecclesia* refers exclusively to the universal Church, apart from the concrete historical reality of the local churches."
143 Ratzinger, "A Response to Walter Kasper," 10.

the one Church, the one bride, over all its empirical realizations in particular churches, has nothing whatsoever to do with the problem of centralism."[144]

Whether or not the CDF's thesis is, in theory, separable from the issue of Roman centralism, the two have actually been connected by Vatican officials themselves since the council. In the Draft Statement on Episcopal Conferences (1988), the following statement appears: "The Church is first of all a single and universal-catholic reality (right from its beginning, so visibly modest), the single 'communio,' people of God, and Body of Christ. The petrine primacy itself, understood as *'plenitudo potestatis,'* has no meaning and theological coherence except within the primacy of the one and universal Church over the particular and local churches."[145] This Draft Statement was widely criticized after its release.[146] It shows, in any case, that there were officials in Rome for whom the priority of the universal church was associated with matters of papal authority indeed.[147]

Discussion of precisely how the CDF's thesis of the priority of the universal church over the particular churches figures into its positions on the proper use of the expression "sister churches" shall be offered in the section below devoted to the contribution of Hervé Legrand, since this is a question Legrand specifically takes up.[148] For now, it may be observed that in Kasper's notion that between the universal church and the local church there is a relationship of

---

144 Ibid.
145 "Draft Statement on Episcopal Conferences," *Origins* 17/43 (April 7, 1988) 735. The Draft Statement was prepared by the Vatican Congregation for Bishops, in collaboration with other Vatican Congregations, including that of the Doctrine of the Faith.
146 See discussion of the Draft Statement in Thomas Reese, ed., *Episcopal Conferences: Historical, Canonical, and Theological Studies* (Washington, DC: Georgetown University Press, 1989), for example the comments on p. IX: "The Vatican *instrumentum laboris* was a great disappointment ... the theological reasoning was one-sided, inconsistent, and lacked any historical sense." In 1990, the Vatican reported its willingness to revise the Draft Statement according to some, if not all, of the criticisms it had received. (See, "Vatican Accepts Woodstock Recommendations," in *Woodstock Report*, March 1991, no. 25). A second draft of the Statement on Episcopal Conferences was completed in 1990 and the final text in 1998. See Kilian McDonnell, "Walter Kasper on the Theology and the Praxis of the Bishop's Office," *Theological Studies* 63 (2002) 725.
147 Cf. also Paul McPartlan, "The Local Church and the Universal Church: Zizioulas and the Ratzinger/Kasper Debate," *International Journal for the Study of the Christian Church* 4:1 (March 2004) 27.
148 See below, pp. 165-169.

mutual indwelling, one may see a certain correspondence with the notion suggested at various points in this study that the principles of primacy and conciliarity ought to be seen as mutually necessary and complementary. A one-sided emphasis on the priority of the universal church would then correspond with a one-sided emphasis on primacy, of the kind which tends to pit itself against the conciliarity of sister churches. At this point, these perceptions can be only suggested; more will be said to flesh them out in the section below on Legrand and in Chapter 6.

What also requires further elucidation, if we are to clarify how the CDF's position on "sister churches" might be conditioned by its thesis of the priority of the universal church over the particular churches, is what the CDF and others participating in the Catholic discourse mean by the term "universal church". One way of framing the question is to ask how the universal church relates to the Catholic Church. This question has indeed been broached already at certain points in this chapter, but must now be addressed more squarely, by direct consideration of another major subject of debate within post-conciliar Catholic ecclesiology: the significance of the phrase "subsists in" in *Lumen Gentium* 8.

Subsists in

Prior to Vatican II, the self-understanding of the Catholic Church as the one true Church was expressed in terms of a direct equivalency. Pius XII in his encyclical letter, *Mystici corporis* (1943), described the "true Church of Christ" as "holy, catholic, apostolic, and Roman"[149] and in his later encyclical, *Humani generis* (1950), he declared: "The mystical body of Christ and the Roman Catholic Church are one and the same thing *(unum idemque esse)*".[150] When the document that would become *Lumen Gentium* was being drafted at Vatican II, Article 7 of the original schema on the Church had stated, in line with Pius XII's ecclesiological teaching, that "The Roman Catholic Church is the mystical Body of Christ ... only that which is Roman Catholic has the right to be called Church."[151] However, among the bishops at the council there was considerable dissatisfaction with this language, which they voted to amend. Thus the final version of the Dogmatic Constitution on the Church used the phrase *subsistit in* rather than *est* to characterize the relationship between the Church of God

---

149 *Mystici corporis*, 13.
150 *Humani generis*, 27.
151 *Acta synodalia sacrosancti concilii Vaticani secundi*, 5 vols. (Vatican City: Typis polyglottis Vaticanis, 1970-1978) I/4, 15.

professed in the Nicene Creed and the Catholic Church in its visible administrative unity. The relevant passage, *Lumen Gentium* n. 8, reads as follows:

> This is the sole Church of Christ which in the Creed we profess to be one, holy, catholic and apostolic, which our Saviour, after his resurrection, entrusted to Peter's pastoral care (Jn. 21:17), commissioning him and the other apostles to extend and rule it (cf. Mt. 28:18, etc.), and which he raised up for all ages as 'the pillar and mainstay of the truth' (1 Tim. 3:15). This Church, constituted and organized as a society in the present world, subsists in the Catholic Church, which is governed by the successor of Peter and by the bishops in communion with him. Nevertheless, many elements of sanctification and of truth are found outside its visible confines. Since these are gifts belonging to the Church of Christ, they are forces impelling towards Catholic unity.[152]

In the years since the council, Catholic ecclesiologists have engaged in an ongoing debate about the proper interpretation of the phrase "subsists in" as it is used in the passage above. Some have argued that it expresses nothing essentially different from what Pius XII held about the Catholic Church as the unique and even the exclusive locus of true ecclesial reality on earth.[153] Others have seen in it a marked shift from previous Catholic ecclesiology.[154] Among the latter group, not all have agreed as to whether *Lumen Gentium* 8 implies that the one holy, catholic, and apostolic church professed in the creed might *subsist in* any other communion besides the Catholic communion. It was noted

---

152 This translation of LG 8 is that of A. Flannery, ed., *Vatican Council II: the Conciliar and post-Conciliar Documents* (Northport, NY: Costello Publishing, 1992).

153 See, for example, Karl J. Becker, "The Church and Vatican II's 'Subsistit in' Terminology," *L'Osservatore Romano* (weekly English edition), December 14, 2005 and reprinted in *Origins* 35.31 (January 19, 2006) 514-522. "The Catholic Church has always defended her total identity with the church of Christ, and she has continued to do so since the council" (519). Becker questions Vatican II's application of the term "church" to non-Catholic communities. "That these communities have a collective identity is certain[;] that this merits the name *church* is open to question" (520).

154 See, for example, F. Sullivan, "'Subsist In': The Significance of Vatican II's Decision to say of the Church of Christ not that it 'is' but that it 'subsists in' the Roman Catholic Church," *One in Christ* 22 (1986), 115-123. See also R. Gaillardetz, *The Church in the Making: Lumen Gentium, Christus Dominus, Orientalium Ecclesiarum* (New York: Paulist, 2006), 26, where the author states that the transformation of the text of *Lumen Gentium* from original schema to final draft "represents one of the most remarkable shifts in ecclesiology ever found in an ecclesiastical document," and 22, where he specifies that the change from "*est*" to "*subsistit in*" in LG 8 "was perhaps the most significant single word change in the history of all the council documents."

above that Waclaw Hryniewicz does see such an implication; and it will be shown below that Hervé Legrand has held a similar (though more moderate) view, seeing in LG 8 a basis for affirming that the Church of God subsists at least in the Orthodox Church as well as in the Catholic Church.[155]

As early as 1985, however, the Congregation for the Doctrine of the Faith rejected the idea that LG 8 asserted or even left open the possibility of more than a single subsistence of the one Church professed in the Creed. In March of that year, in a notification on the book *Church: Charism and Power* by Leonardo Boff,[156] the CDF wrote the following:

> L. Boff appeals to the Vatican II Constitution *Lumen Gentium* (no. 8). From the Council's famous expression, *"Haec ecclesia (scl. unica Christi Ecclesia) ... subsistit in Ecclesia Catholica"* ["this church (that is, the sole church of Christ) ... subsists in the Catholic Church"] he extracts a thesis exactly contrary to the authentic meaning of the Council text, when he asserts "in fact it (the one Church of Christ) can also subsist in other Christian churches" (p. 131). The Council, on the contrary, chose the word *subsistit* precisely to make clear that there is only one "subsistence" of the true Church, while outside her visible framework there exist only *"elementa ecclesiae"* which – being elements of the same Church – tend and lead towards the Catholic Church (LG 8). The Decree on Ecumenism expresses the same doctrine (UR 3-4) which was made clear again in the Declaration *Mysterium Ecclesiae*, no. 1 (AAS LXV [1973], pp. 396-398). This turning upside down of the conciliar text on the subsistence of the Church lies at the bottom of L. Boff's ecclesiological relativism ... in which a profound misunderstanding of the Catholic faith about the church of God in the world is developed and made explicit.[157]

Fifteen years later, in a footnote in the document *Dominus Iesus* (hereafter, DI), the CDF reiterated the same point[158]: "The interpretation of those who would derive from the formula *subsistit in* the thesis that the one Church of Christ could subsist also in non-Catholic Churches and ecclesial communities is ... contrary to the authentic meaning of *Lumen gentium*." The CDF then quoted from its 1985 "Notification" on Boff's book.

---

155 See below, p. 171.
156 L. Boff, *Church: Charism and Power: Liberation Theology and the Institutional Church* (New York: Crossroad, 1985).
157 "Notification," *L'Osservatore Romano*, English Weekly Edition (April 9, 1985), 11.
158 The Congregation for the Doctrine of the Faith, "Declaration '*Dominus Iesus*' on the Unicity and Salvific Universality of Jesus Christ and the Church" (August 6, 2000), 16, n. 56.

Notwithstanding that the one document cites the other, Francis Sullivan has drawn attention to a difference between DI and the "Notification" in terms of what they respectively say, and do not say, about non-Catholic churches.[159] In both documents, the Church of Christ is said to subsist solely in the Catholic Church. In the "Notification," however, it is said to do so in such a way that outside it there are only ecclesial elements.[160] In DI, meanwhile, it is said to do so in such a way that outside it there are true churches.[161] (They are such by virtue of their maintaining apostolic succession and a valid eucharist.) Sullivan sees in DI the only proper way of maintaining that the Church of Christ subsists solely in the Catholic Church, and he explains the coherence of this teaching by observing that this doctrine should be understood to imply "that the church Christ founded continues to exist in the Catholic Church with a fullness of the means of grace and of unity that are not found in any other church."[162] Quoting DI 16, which indeed states precisely that the Church of Christ "continues to exist fully only in the Catholic Church," Sullivan comments, "Here the word 'fully' plays a key role; it is only if 'subsists' means 'continues to exist fully' that one can say that the church of Christ subsists only in the Catholic Church."[163] Sullivan grants, then, that there can be a proper teaching of the sole subsistence of the Church of Christ with the latter understanding.

In the same year DI was released – and the *Note on the Expression "Sister Churches"* was issued – Cardinal Ratzinger published a paper on "The Ecclesiology of the Constitution *Lumen Gentium*," in which he offered more detailed observations on the term *subsistit*.

> The term *subsistit* derives from classical philosophy, as it was further developed in Scholasticism. The Greek word corresponding to it is *hypostasis*, which plays a central role in Christology, for describing the unity between divine nature and human in the Person of Christ. *Subsistere* is a special variant of *esse*. It is "being" in the form of an independent agent. That is exactly what is concerned here. The Council is trying to tell us that the Church of Jesus Christ may be encountered in this world as a concrete agent in the Catholic Church. That can happen only once, and the view that *subsistit* should be multiplied fails to do justice to the particular point intended.[164]

---

159 Sullivan, "*Quaestio Disputata*: A Response to Karl Becker," 408.
160 Cf. "Notification," 11.
161 Cf. DI, 17.
162 F. Sullivan, "The Impact of *Dominus Iesus* on Ecumenism," *America* (October 28, 2000) 8.
163 Sullivan, "The Impact of *Dominus Iesus* on Ecumenism," 8.
164 J. Ratzinger, "The Ecclesiology of the Constitution *Lumen Gentium*," in *Pilgrim*

Chapter 4: Catholic Theological Reflection on "Sister Churches"

After explicating this dimension of *subsistit*, having to do with the embodiment and agency of a single concrete entity, Ratzinger goes on to note a more complex aspect of the term. He writes:

> The distinction between *subsistit* and *est* does, however, imply the drama of the schism of the Church: although the Church is only one, and does really exist, there is being that is derived from the being of the Church, an ecclesiastical entity, even outside the one Church. Because sin is a contradiction, this distinction between *subsistit* and *est* is, in the end, something that cannot be entirely explained logically. Reflected in the paradox of the distinction between the uniqueness and the concrete existence of the Church, on the one hand, and, on the other, the continuing existence of a concrete ecclesiastical entity outside of the one active agent is the contradictory element of human sin, the contradictory element of schism.[165]

Two points of particular significance stand out in the remarks above. First, Ratzinger alludes to the paradoxical nature of the ecclesiological teaching of Vatican II in its twofold affirmation of (1) the Catholic Church as the unique embodiment of the Church of Christ and (2) the ecclesial reality of particular churches outside the Catholic Church.[166] Second, there is a conceptual issue to be raised that relates to the notion of dependence or derivation. Ratzinger says that even outside the one Church, by which in this context it is clear he means the canonical Catholic Church, "there is being that is derived from the being of the Church." What must be asked is whether by the word "Church" at the end of this last reference he means the Church of Christ, or the canonical Catholic Church in which the latter *subsists*. In what follows, it will be important to remain alert to the different ramifications involved in saying, on the one hand, that true particular churches outside the Catholic Church derive their being from the Catholic Church (in which *subsists* the Church of Christ), or saying, on the other, that they derive their being from the Church of Christ (which

---

Fellowship of Faith: the Church as Communion (San Francisco: Ignatius, 2005), 147 (original emphasis).

165 Ratzinger, *Pilgrim Fellowship of Faith*, 148. He goes on, "Such schism is quite different from the relativistic dialectic ... in which the divisions between Christians are divested of their pain and are not really schisms at all but merely a representation of the multitudinous variations upon a theme, in which all the variations are in some sense right, and all in some sense wrong. There is not in that case actually any inner requirement to seek for unity, because even without it the Church is everywhere and nowhere."

166 Cf. UR, 14-17.

subsists in the Catholic Church).¹⁶⁷ The latter option is compatible with "sister churches" across the confessional division; the former option is not.

In general, the interpretation of LG 8 in its use of "subsists in" has significant bearing on how the concept of sister churches in Catholic-Orthodox relations may be used and understood. Perhaps most obviously, if "subsists in" is taken to imply that outside the Catholic Church there are no more than ecclesial elements – the apparent position of the CDF's "Notification," sharply criticized by Sullivan and others – then doubt is certainly cast on the status of Orthodox particular churches as sister churches of Catholic particular churches. On the other hand, if one unequivocally affirms their status as such, does this imply that LG 8 must be interpreted – according to the position of Hryniewicz (and, as will be seen, also Legrand) – to mean that the Church of Christ can subsist in non-Catholic churches? This would seem to be required if true churches, and hence sister churches, are necessarily those in which the Church of Christ subsists. Such is the view of Hervé Legrand, as will be seen, but there is also another way of defining "true churches," one which would not require that the Church of Christ "subsists" in them.

6. Hervé Legrand

The French Dominican theologian Hervé Legrand has written extensively on issues of the local church and catholicity and on Catholic-Orthodox relations, among other topics in ecclesiology. Some attention will be devoted to an article he published on uniatism in 1993.¹⁶⁸ More comprehensive treatment will be given to his remarks in an article of 2004 entitled "La théologie des Églises Sœurs: réflexions ecclésiologiques autour de la declaration de Balamand."¹⁶⁹ As the title indicates, Legrand offers in this article an examination of the 1993 Balamand statement, "Uniatism, Method of Union of the Past, and the Present Search for Full Communion,"¹⁷⁰ in which it is stated – according to the official

---

167 See below, pp. 177-179.
168 H. Legrand, "Le dialogue catholique-orthodoxe. Quelques enjeux ecclésiologiques de la crise actuelle autour des Églises unies," *Bulletin / Centro pro Unione* 43 (Spring, 1993) 3-16, published in abridged form in English translation as "Uniatism and Catholic-Orthodox Dialogue," *Theology Digest* 42:2 (Summer, 1995) 127-133. Translations from the French are nevertheless my own.
169 H. Legrand, "La théologie des Églises Sœurs: réflexions ecclésiologiques autour de la declaration de Balamand," *Revue des sciences philosophiques et théologiques* 88 (2004) 461-496. Translations mine.
170 See above, Chapter 3, pp. 94-96; 104-105.

Chapter 4: Catholic Theological Reflection on "Sister Churches"

version of the Joint International Commission itself, published originally in French – that "the Catholic Church and the Orthodox Church recognize each other as sister churches, responsible together for maintaining the Church of God in fidelity to the divine purpose, especially in what concerns unity."[171] Legrand says that "the doctrinal key of the Declaration of Balamand" is found here in this statement.[172]

Significantly, the original French version of the passage differs from the English translation that was prepared by Rome (according to a standard procedure by which, also, a Greek translation is prepared by Constantinople). The English version of the same statement reads: "The Catholic Churches and the Orthodox Churches recognize each other as sister churches and responsible together for the maintenance of the Church of God in fidelity to the divine purpose, most especially in what concerns unity."[173] In the original French from which Legrand was working, it is the singular Catholic Church and the singular Orthodox Church that recognize one another as sisters, whereas here in the standard English version the mutual recognition is between Catholic churches and Orthodox churches in the plural.

One of the subheadings in Legrand's article poses the question: "Has the fraternity between the two Churches been doctrinally put in question on the Catholic side since Balamand?"[174] In this connection he observes that the *Note* (in para. 11) "judges inadmissible the designation of the Orthodox Church as the sister of the Catholic Church," and from this Legrand concludes that "[t]his *Note* seems to delegitimize the central assertion of Balamand."[175] Such a conclusion obviously makes more sense if Balamand stated that the singular Catholic Church and the singular Orthodox Church are sisters, as the original French version has it, than if the Balamand text used plural forms (as in what we have called usage 4) in stating that the Catholic *churches* and the Orthodox *churches* are sisters, which is what is said in the English version issued by Rome. For the CDF's *Note* does endorse, as we have seen, the expression "sister churches"

---

171 Balamand, "Uniatism: Method of Union of the Past," n. 14.
172 Cf. Legrand, "La théologie des Églises Sœurs," 461.
173 Legrand, "La théologie des Églises Sœurs," 461. It may be recalled that it was shown that in this sentence *as rendered in the English translation*, the many Catholic churches are almost certainly Eastern Catholic churches corresponding to national or patriarchal Orthodox churches; in other words, they are not particular Catholic churches. See Chapter 3 above, pp. 104-105.
174 Legrand, "La théologie des Églises sœurs," 465.
175 Ibid. 466.

when it is used to speak of the relationship between Catholic and Orthodox churches on the most basic level where ecclesial plurality is to be embraced – on the level of particular churches.

The discrepancy between the original French version of the Balamand text issued by the Joint International Commission and the English translation prepared by Rome seems to have garnered little notice. Legrand himself does not make any mention of it. Neither does the U.S. Orthodox-Catholic Consultation, whose own official response to the Balamand text clearly takes as its point of reference the English version in which the "sisters" in para. 14 are named not as the "Catholic Church" and the "Orthodox Church," but as the "Catholic Churches" and the "Orthodox Churches". In any case, the modification itself from the singular (in the French) to the plural (in the English prepared by Rome) would seem to support Legrand's general perception of a significant tension between Balamand's ecclesiological formulations and those of Rome issued subsequently.

Throughout Legrand's work, as has already been sufficiently indicated, he does not hesitate to speak of the Catholic Church and the Orthodox Church in their totalities as sister churches.[176] In this respect, he is similar to Lanne, Congar and Hryniewicz. Also in line with the approaches of Lanne and Congar[177] (but not Hryniewicz) is Legrand's exposition of the theological basis of the expression "sister churches" which he sees indicated in UR 14-17. "In light of our common past ... it can be demonstrated [from UR 14-17] that it is at once legitimate and necessary that the Catholic Church consider as sister churches the whole assemblage of the Eastern Churches, Chalcedonian or pre-Chalcedonian. The middle term of this demonstration is the fact that these Churches are true local or particular Churches. Why? Precisely because we have in common with them: (1) the same apostolic faith ... (2) The same Eucharist and the same ministry."[178] Additionally, Legrand follows Lanne – as well as Hryniewicz – in drawing a sharp contrast between the concept of sister churches and the phenomenon of uniatism.[179] Indeed, Legrand is emphatic in asserting the incompatibility of the two ecclesiological approaches. "*Either* the Orthodox Church cannot be considered as a sister church, in which case uniatism is permissible," he writes. "*Or* the Orthodox Church *can* legitimately be considered

---

176 An example may be found in Legrand's emphatic *either-or* formulation quoted just below, p. 164-165.
177 See above, pp. 114-116 and 124.
178 Legrand, "Le dialogue catholique-orthodoxe," 10.
179 See above, pp. 119-122 and 128-132.

as a sister Church," in which case "one cannot justify uniatism, neither as method nor as goal".[180] In the Balamand Statement, which for Legrand is a watershed, the latter option was unequivocally chosen. "The formulation of Balamand n. 14 [stating that Catholic and Orthodox churches are sister churches] is of great historical significance. In an immediate way, on the level of principle, it makes it possible to put an end to uniatism."[181] Yet Legrand contends that a number of documents issued by the CDF not only before but also after Balamand contain statements that are at odds with Balamand's ecclesiological perspective.

Legrand's critique of the idea of the priority of the universal church

Like Kasper,[182] Legrand is critical of the CDF's notion that the universal church gives birth to the particular churches, and thus has priority over them.[183] Legrand finds no basis for this idea in early Christian sources.

> The maternity of the Church in regard to *the faith of the faithful* is well attested in Tradition. One can discover there as well a real validation of the relation existing between *a founding church and a new church* founded by her; but the daughter church becomes ecclesiologically the equal of her mother insofar as she baptizes, celebrates the eucharist, and calls and ordains to the ministry. Such is the double ground of the validity of the idea of the mother church. However, *the idea of the maternity of the universal church in regard to all of the local churches seems never to have been formulated.*[184]

He thus calls this idea of the CDF a "new formulation."[185]

Theologically, Legrand's critique corresponds closely to that which was leveled by Kasper,[186] whom he cites. Legrand, too, is concerned lest "the maternity of the Church universal becomes covertly the maternity of the Church of Rome, according to the terms of Cardinal Walter Kasper." Moreover, Legrand says that "[t]his understanding of the maternity of the universal church induces finally a series of imbalances in the articulation between the diocesan churches and the whole church, [imbalances] which distance all of us [Catholics] imme-

---

180 Legrand, ""La théologie des Églises Sœurs," 486 (original emphasis).
181 Ibid. 462.
182 See above, pp. 154-156.
183 *Communionis Notio*, 9; *Note*, n. 3. See above, p. 155.
184 Legrand, "La théologie des Églises Sœurs," 476 (emphasis added). See also Chapter 1 above, pp. 13-21.
185 Legrand, "La théologie des Églises Sœurs," 469.
186 See above, pp. 154-156.

diately and without necessity, from the Orthodox Church".[187] He specifically mentions two effects, both negative, in his view, of this "innovative doctrine" of the maternity / priority of the universal church in relation to local churches. One effect is that "the episcopate and its unity with the pope has attributed to itself a sort of anteriority and exteriority to the body of the Church."[188] Legrand complains that this encourages and legitimates the high number of bishops who are not heads of local dioceses and whose office is thus not attached to any local eucharistic community.[189] A second effect noted by Legrand is that "one deprives groupings of dioceses of a real status of sister churches and renders them mere emanations of the primacy."[190]

By "groupings of dioceses" Legrand is referring to regional churches. In his 1993 article, he wrote of their importance in ecclesiology. First, he stated that "to adopt an ecclesiology of communion is to affirm and put into practice a mutual inclusion among local churches."[191] He then contrasted such a communion ecclesiology with "the juridical conception of collegiality in which the universal church is an immediate reality."[192] Collegiality in its proper sense, within the framework of communion ecclesiology, can and must, according to Legrand, be conceived instead

> as a coming together of bishops, each presiding over the communion of his local church, and thereby presiding (as a group) over the communion of the churches of their area or of the whole church. One thus encounters the grouping of regional churches as the unquestionable framework of activity for

---

187 Legrand, "La théologie des Églises Sœurs," 477.
188 Ibid. Legrand's language here echoes that of Henri de Lubac. In his 1993 article, Legrand wrote, "As Cardinal de Lubac asserted, 'a universal Church anterior to, or supposedly existing outside all the particular Churches, is nothing but a mental construct.'" Legrand, "Le dialogue catholique-orthodoxe," 8, with reference to de Lubac, *Les églises particulières dans l'Église universelle* (Paris: Aubier-Montaigne, 1971), 54.
189 Legrand, "La théologie des Églises Sœurs," 477-478.
190 Ibid. 478.
191 Legrand, "Le dialogue catholique-orthodoxe," 8. On the notion of "mutual inclusion" as a potential key for resolving the debate about the relationship between the local church and the universal church, see J. Komonchak, "The Local Church and the Church Catholic: the Contemporary Theological Problematic," *The Jurist* 52:1 (1992) 441-446. This paper was originally delivered at a special colloquium on "The Local Church and Catholicity" at the Universidad Pontificia in Salamanca, Spain, in April of 1991.
192 Legrand, "Le dialogue catholique-orthodoxe," 8.

bishops. The return to this traditional view signals our reconciliation with the Orthodox Church.[193]

In a remarkable statement, Legrand says of "the thesis of the ontological and chronological priority of the universal Church over the particular Churches" that it is the "principal element in the refusal to see in the Orthodox Church a sister Church".[194] Almost as striking as the statement itself is the fact that Legrand does not go on to explain why he makes this claim, so we are left to seek the explanation in his preceding comments. The critique we find there of the "anteriority and exteriority" of the episcopal college to the body of the Church would seem to provide an important clue.[195] If the universal church is given priority over the local church, then membership in the episcopal college would depend less on a bishop's presidency within any local diocese or participation in any regional synod of bishops, and more on his being in communion with the head of the universal college, namely the pope. Within this perspective, Orthodox bishops do not belong to the college.[196] The ecclesial status of the communion in which they do have membership – the Orthodox Church –

---

193 Ibid. (cf. "Uniatism," 128-129). Komonchak as well, in his paper cited in n. 191 above, touches on whether regional churches are to be considered as having a truly ecclesial status in their own right. "The question also arises as to whether ecclesial groups larger than the diocese may appropriately be called churches" (426). He observes that there is "an impressive tradition in favor of this view," a tradition in which Vatican II squarely stands insofar as it "had no hesitation in employing both 'local church' and 'particular church' for various groupings of diocesan churches." But he points out that not all theologians are in agreement on this point. "There is still a tendency among some authors ... to regard such groupings as churches in only an analogous sense." Komonchak cites Wolfgang Beinert in this connection (W. Beinert, "Dogmenhistorische Anmerkungen zum Begriff 'Partikularkirche,'" *Theologie und Philosophie* 50 (1975) 66). As was seen earlier (cf. above, pp. 117-118), Emmanuel Lanne is another author who has taken the view that supra-diocesan churches are churches in only an analogous sense. Komonchak, for his part, says that he is "not convinced" that the notion of analogy is appropriate to describe churches at any level, including the regional level, since this notion of analogy "is not adequate to the identity through mutual inclusion that characterizes the one Church in the many churches" (Komonchak, "The Local Church and the Church Catholic," 426).
194 Legrand, "La théologie des Églises Sœurs," 480.
195 See above, p. 166.
196 Cf. the observation made by Lanne that precisely this way of conceptualizing the episcopal college in the third chapter of LG and in the *Nota Praevia* cast doubt on the ecclesial status of the Orthodox churches (see above, pp. 121-122).

would then be in question, and the Orthodox Church would thus not be seen as a sister of the Catholic Church. Such appears to be the underlying logic in Legrand's claim that the CDF's thesis of the priority of the universal church over the particular churches is "the principal element in the refusal to see in the Orthodox Church a sister Church."

Legrand's analysis still does not account for why the CDF, while refusing to recognize the Orthodox Church as a whole as a sister church, does grant this status to particular Orthodox churches. Even if recognition on this level may be seen as inadequate, it would be helpful if Legrand addressed its significance, such as it is.

Another point in need of clarification is the meaning of "universal church". It may now be useful to look more closely into this question. That there is a need to distinguish between two possible meanings of "universal church" has been brought to light by Paul McPartlan in his article on local and universal church in the thought of Ratzinger, Kasper, and the Eastern Orthodox theologian John Zizioulas, who was not a participant in the debate between the two cardinals but whose perspective, McPartlan suggests,[197] can help to clarify certain issues they discussed. On the one hand, the universal church can be understood as the heavenly Jerusalem, the eschatological (and in some sense pre-existent) mystery of the Church of all times and places; on the other hand, the universal church can be understood as the present worldwide Church of today.[198] McPartlan argues that if it is the one Church in its eschatological fullness that is understood as having priority over the particular churches, then the thesis advocated by Ratzinger should be unobjectionable from Kasper's point of view. But if the universal church that has priority over the particular churches is, instead, understood as the worldwide church of today, then the thesis becomes problematic, for the reasons Kasper articulates. As McPartlan puts it, "If the worldwide Church has priority, then Rome and the curia naturally have a higher profile than they do if the worldwide Church and the local church are interpenetrating and simultaneous."[199] McPartlan argues that

---

197 See Paul McPartlan, "The Local Church and the Universal Church: Zizioulas and the Ratzinger/Kasper Debate," *International Journal for the Study of the Christian Church* 4:1 (March 2004) 21-33.

198 Ibid. 22. While these two conceptions are not separate from one another, a distinction between them does exist; it is, we might observe, the distinction between the Church of Christ and the Catholic Church when it is said that the one subsists in the other.

199 Ibid. 31-32.

Ratzinger and the CDF tend to blur the distinction between the heavenly Jerusalem (described in Gal 4:26 as "our mother") and the worldwide Church, because they identify "the transcendent Church-mystery" primarily with the pre-existent church which was manifested in history on the day of Pentecost.[200] Zizioulas' emphasis on the eschatological nature of the heavenly Jerusalem can therefore serve as a corrective, according to McPartlan. "There is no danger of confusing the transcendent Church-mystery and the current worldwide Church if the transcendent Church-mystery is a reality *still to come*, as Zizioulas believes."[201]

With regard to Legrand's critique, it would seem that only if the same distinction is blurred, i.e. only if "universal church" is collapsed into "current worldwide Church," will the thesis of the priority of the universal church be what Legrand judges it to be, namely: "the principal element in the refusal to see in the Orthodox Church a sister church." In other words, such a refusal is not a necessary consequence of the thesis in question. If the universal church that has priority over all the particular churches is the transcendent Church-mystery as "a reality still to come", then it might be possible to hold the thesis and still see in the Orthodox Church a sister of the Catholic Church. However, more must now be said about how the relationship between the mystery of the one transcendent Church of Christ and the worldwide Catholic Church is properly conceived, according to Legrand.

Legrand's interpretation of 'subsistit in'

Legrand argues that the expression "subsists in" at Vatican II "was chosen, in reality, in order to *avoid* the exclusive identification between the Catholic Church and the Church of Christ."[202] He also states that DI, issued some thirty five years after the council, tried to suggest the opposite – namely, that "Vatican II chose the expression 'subsists in' in order to *teach* the exclusive identification of the Catholic Church with the Church of Christ."[203]

---

200 Ibid. 32.
201 Ibid. As McPartlan points out, Zizioulas would also concur that this same Church-mystery is indeed pre-existent, but "only in the sense that, by the power of the Holy Spirit, its reality, which is truly *eschatological*, because history must run its course to the end and be respected, was already mysteriously operative from the beginning of time."
202 Legrand, "La théologie des Églises Sœurs," 481 (original emphasis).
203 Ibid. (emphasis added).

With respect to the first of these two points Legrand is on firm ground and offers ample support from the *Acta Synodalia* of Vatican II to show that the original language of article 7 of the schema, in which the word "is" was used to identify the Church of Christ with the Catholic Church exclusively, was considered unsatisfactory by a great many bishops at the council. Legrand quotes Cardinal Liénart, one of the ten cardinals on the council's Board of Presidency, as saying in 1962, "I demand, expressly, that the article 7 be done away with which equates in an absolute manner the Catholic Church and the mystical Body and that this schema be entirely revised."[204] Cardinal Liénart also said:

> It is absolutely necessary to avoid formulas prone to weaken the mystery of the Church. Therefore it is imperative not to affirm the identity of the Roman Church and the mystical Body, as if the mystical Body were totally included within the limits of the Roman Church. The Roman Church is the true Body of Christ but she does not exhaust it.[205]

In accordance with this perspective of Liénart, which was shared by the vast majority of conciliar fathers, the word "is" was changed in the final draft to "subsists in."[206] So much seems reasonably clear.[207]

However, Legrand's claim about DI that it teaches the exclusive identification of the Catholic Church with the Church of Christ, and so distorts the teaching of LG 8 about the meaning of "subsists in," must be challenged. What DI teaches (and claims that Vatican II taught) is not, in fact, the exclusive identification of the Church of Christ with the Catholic Church, but, more precisely, the exclusive subsistence of the Church of Christ in the Catholic

---

204   4, 127, as quoted ibid. 482, n. 91.
205   I, 4, 126, as quoted ibid. Legrand mentions (482, n. 92), that two years after the CDF's notification against Boff (see below), Cardinal Willebrands cited almost verbatim this same intervention of Cardinal Liénart, during a conference whose title was, Legrand observes, chosen purposefully by Willebrands: "The signification of 'subsistit in' in the ecclesiology of communion."
206   Sullivan explains that "est" was still there in the 2nd draft (1963) but was then changed in the 3rd draft (1964) to harmonize with the 2nd draft's acknowledgment of "elements" of the Church outside the visible bounds of the Catholic Church. Cf. Sullivan, "'Subsistit in'," *One in Christ* 22 (1986) 116.
207   As noted above, p. 158, n. 153, Karl Becker has called even this interpretation into question. See Francis Sullivan, "*Quaestio Disputata*: A Response to Karl Becker," op. cit. For another recent interpretation of "subsists in" similar to Becker's but even less adequate to the council's actual history and ecclesiology, see Thomas Storck, "What is the Church of Jesus Christ?", *Homiletic and Pastoral Review* (March, 2008) 24-45.

Church.²⁰⁸ These two ideas – exclusive identification and exclusive subsistence – are distinct and separable. Legrand treats them as though they were one and the same. Immediately after he makes the assertion about DI that it attributes to Vatican II a teaching of "exclusive identification," he quotes a statement in DI about exclusive subsistence.²⁰⁹

Legrand's actual concern is to maintain without compromise the teaching of Vatican II that the Orthodox churches are true churches in spite of their being outside the canonical Catholic Church. Like Sullivan, he insists that it is inadequate to say that outside the Catholic Church there are only ecclesial elements. Legrand takes issue, too, with the CDF's "Notification" condemning Boff's book insofar as the "Notification" used the language of "only elements" outside the Catholic Church.²¹⁰ Against this idea Legrand points appropriately enough to "the affirmation of LG 15, according to which Churches (and not just elements of the Church, as [the Notification] says), exist outside of the visible unity of the true Church".²¹¹ But he then goes a questionable step further in saying, "Without explicitly teaching that the Church of Christ subsists also in the Orthodox Church, Vatican II showed itself favorable to this perspective."²¹²

Legrand apparently does not see how the Church of Christ can be present and operative in particular churches outside the Catholic Church (such that these non-Catholic churches are recognized as true churches), yet subsist only in the Catholic Church. McPartlan, however, has suggested a way of harmonizing or reconciling these two teachings. In an unpublished paper²¹³ he refers

---

208 Cf. *Dominus Iesus*, n. 16 and n. 17.
209 Cf. Legrand, "La théologie des Églises Sœurs," 481, with reference to DI, footnote 56. That Legrand has conflated exclusive identification and exclusive subsistence can be seen also in the following passage: "Nothing in the discussions [recorded in the *Acta Synodalia* relative to LG 8] indicates that the choice of this expression [*subsistit in*] had for its purpose, or for its effect, the denial that the Church of Christ might subsist outside the body of the visible boundaries of the actual Catholic Church. On the contrary, the texts [of the *Acta*] permit us to establish, with a certitude almost absolute, that the phrase was invoked precisely in order to deny the exclusive identification of the Church of Christ and the Catholic Church." (Legrand, "La théologie des Églises Sœurs," 482).
210 Legrand, "La théologie des Églises Sœurs," 481. See above, pp. 159-160.
211 Ibid. 481-482.
212 Ibid. 483.
213 Paul McPartlan, "The Importance of Visible Unity: Some initial notes on Catholic texts and terminology," a 9-page typescript I am indebted to the author for having made available to me.

to the apparent difficulty raised by footnote 56 of *Dominus Iesus,* with its assertion: "The interpretation of those who would derive from the formula *subsistit in* the thesis that the one Church of Christ could subsist also in non-Catholic Churches and ecclesial communities is therefore contrary to the authentic meaning of *Lumen gentium*". McPartlan comments as follows:

> At first sight, these words seem particularly harsh and rather illogical with regard to the situation of the Orthodox Churches, because it seems reasonable to presume that, since *Dominus Iesus* says [elsewhere] that the Orthodox Churches are 'true particular Churches' in which 'the Church of Christ is present and operative', that the Church of Christ *subsists in* the Orthodox Churches. What else, we might well ask, can the words mean? The question arises: is there a coherence between the teaching of *Dominus Iesus* and that, overall, of the Council?[214]

In what McPartlan goes on to say, a solution is proposed to the dilemma of how the Church of Christ may be present and operative in Orthodox particular churches without subsisting in them. McPartlan writes:

> In fact, there is a possible logic here ... *Lumen Gentium* 8 itself does not say that the Church of Christ subsists in Catholic particular Churches, i.e. Catholic *dioceses,* but rather that it subsists in the Catholic Church itself, which is the communion of these dioceses with the Bishop of Rome. That particular structure of unity was bestowed by Christ (UR4), but is not operative in the Orthodox Churches. It seems to be precisely because that *unity* subsists in the Catholic Church (UR4), and obviously *only* there in its fullness, that the Church of Christ itself is being said to subsist in the Catholic Church *and only* there.[215]

McPartlan argues here that there is no equivalence between being a true particular church and being a church in which the Church of Christ subsists; indeed, according to McPartlan's analysis, the Church of Christ "subsists" not even in any true particular Catholic Church, nor in any grouping of true particular Catholic churches, but only in the Catholic Church as an entire communion, whose "structure of visible unity" – from the Catholic point of view, a gift of God that can never be lost – is decisive.[216]

---

214 McPartlan, "The Importance of Visible Unity," para. 14.
215 Ibid. para. 15.
216 McPartlan makes the point with clarity: "In other words, contrary perhaps to a common-sense presumption, 'subsists' is not equivalent to 'is really present and operative'. The Church of Christ is indeed really present and operative in particular Churches, both Catholic and Orthodox, but is not said to 'subsist' in them because the existence of particular Churches does not itself exhaust the Lord's purpose for

With regard to Legrand's analysis of LG 8, it may be said that Legrand believes that the fact that the Church of Christ is present and operative in particular churches outside the Catholic Church means that the Church of Christ subsists there. In fact, as McPartlan and Sullivan both suggest, though in different ways, there can be recognition of true particular Orthodox churches in which the Church of Christ is present and operative, without saying that the Church of Christ subsists anywhere but in the Catholic Church alone.

From this it would also follow that, contrary to what Legrand says, the Catholic recognition of Orthodox churches as sister churches can indeed be held together with the CDF's position that the Church of Christ does not subsist in them. It has thus been shown that the positions of the CDF, both on this question of "subsists in" and on the question of the relationship between the local church and the universal church, turn out not to be in direct conflict with the Balamand statement, as Legrand suggested they are – or at least, they turn out not to have to be. On both issues, the CDF's positions still leave room for the recognition of Orthodox churches as sisters of Catholic churches. This does not mean, however, that Legrand's perspectives have been somehow refuted, for there are elements in them – especially in what he says about regional churches – that have a valuable and even an indispensable role to play if Catholic ecclesiology, while remaining true to its principles, is to find common ground with Orthodox ecclesiology. More will be said on this in Chapter 6.

II. Concluding Observations

Important commonalities and divergences among the Catholic authors examined here may now be summarized, and certain under-treated or unresolved issues in their theological reflections pointed out.

Not all of the authors actually apply the expression sister churches to Catholic and Orthodox churches on the level of the particular, diocesan church. Lanne seems to do so, as Garuti and the CDF certainly do, but Congar and Hryniewicz do not. Hryniewicz and Legrand also readily apply the expression to Catholic and Orthodox churches on the regional level,[217] that is, on the level

---

his Church. It is the belief of the Catholic Church that Christ has willed and bestowed a structure of visible unity among the particular Churches and that that structure is so much part of his purpose that where it itself is not operative the Church of Christ cannot properly be said to subsist" (ibid. para. 16).

217 See above, pp. 132-134 and 166-167. Congar also seems open to this usage. See above, p. 126.

of the metropolitan or patriarchal church, with Legrand offering substantive reasons why it is ecclesiologically important to do so. Garuti and Lanne share, though for apparently different reasons, a strong hesitation to employ the expression on the regional level.[218] Finally, Lanne, Congar, Hryniewicz and Legrand all find it natural to speak of the whole Orthodox Church and the whole Catholic Church as sisters,[219] though none of them offers an explicit defense of this usage, unless it is to say that the two are sisters because the Church of Christ subsists in both of them. This, it was seen, is the basis of the argument made by Legrand. Garuti – along with the CDF – sharply opposes applying the expression sister churches to the Catholic Church and the Orthodox Church as such,[220] and the reason is again tied to the doctrine of "subsists in", except now interpreted differently: the two cannot be sister churches because the Church of Christ subsists only in the Catholic Church. A question arising with regard to Catholic ecclesiology is whether if there is only a sole subsistence, this really precludes recognizing the Orthodox Church as a sister of the Catholic Church, as both Garuti and Legrand assume it must.[221]

As to the theological foundations of the expression sister churches, there is widespread agreement that particular churches in which there is valid priesthood and eucharist may be recognized as sister churches from the Catholic point of view. Also typically mentioned in this connection is a shared past and a common apostolic faith. Garuti, however, asks whether Orthodox and Catholics do in fact share the same faith, and suggests that the Orthodox particular churches should really only be considered "true churches" in an "imperfect and analogous manner".[222] This is also because, Garuti says, they lack the "bonds of ecclesial government and communion" that Catholic churches share with one another.[223] Apart from Garuti, there is no evidence in the other authors or in Catholic magisterial documents that the Orthodox do not share with Catholics the same apostolic faith. Other writers do take account of the fact that Orthodox churches exist outside the "bonds of ecclesial government and communion" that Catholic churches share, but they speak of the Orthodox churches as

---

218 See above, pp. 117-118 and 143-144, 149-151. See also pp. 151-154 for the CDF's view, which resembles that of Garuti on this point.
219 For examples in each of these authors, respectively, see above, pp. 114; 124-125; 127-128; and 164-165.
220 See above, pp. 141-142; also, for the similar position of the CDF, p. 151-152.
221 This question will be taken up in Chapter 6 below, pp. 253-259.
222 See above, p. 149.
223 See above, p. 147.

"wounded" as a consequence of this circumstance, without suggesting that they are any the less deserving of the designation of true churches as a result.[224] The CDF, in this connection, distinguishes between "true" and "full" churches, the latter term being applicable only to Catholic churches.[225] Sullivan approves of this distinction.[226]

In addition to those already mentioned, three additional factors have been indicated, by one author or another, as essential in order for churches to recognize one another as sister churches. Lanne makes reference to the importance of an ongoing tradition of holiness in the sister churches of both East and West.[227] Congar considers independent apostolicity of origin to be a crucial characteristic.[228] Finally, in a more oblique way, another factor has been indicated which allows churches to recognize one another as sister churches, namely their expectation of reestablishing full communion with one another in the future.[229]

As to the consequences, or obligations, to be accepted when churches recognize each other as sisters, Lanne, Hryniewicz and Legrand have been clearest in identifying the most decisive of these consequences to be the renunciation of an ecclesiology of absorption or "return". In accord with a central principle of the Balamand Statement, these authors have emphasized that there must be no more seeking of converts from the other church into one's own. What sense would this make, if, as Congar has said, *"it is the same church"*[230] to which the members of both already belong?

Underlying their appreciation of this dimension of the concept of sister churches is an historical consciousness, demonstrated by the three authors mentioned above, of periods when the Catholic Church engaged in efforts to convert members and segments of Orthodox churches. Lanne, Hryniewicz, and

---

224 See, for example, McPartlan, "The Importance of Visible Unity," para. 11.
225 See above, p. 147-148; 160.
226 See above, p. 160.
227 See above, pp. 116-117.
228 See above, p. 125.
229 The words of the Catholic Patriarch Maximos IV Saigh quoted earlier give indirect expression to the idea that sister churches, in addition to being those that share a valid ministry and eucharist, the same apostolic faith, and a common past, are those that recognize each other as sharing a common future: "It would be possible to maintain that the relations between Rome and the various eastern churches were not definitively broken till the day when Rome became impatient of waiting for a general reunion of the churches or lost hope in its possibility". See above, p. 131.
230 See above, p. 124.

Legrand all discuss uniatism at length and with manifest regret about what they perceive to be the historical excesses and missteps of their own Church in its relations with the Christian East.[231] Congar does not refer nearly as much to uniatism, but in his historical treatments of ecclesiological developments in the West and their effects on relations with the Orthodox, he offers much the same kind of account in which an essential element of the drama involves a Catholic turn (or set of turns) for the worse in the 11th and 12th centuries (and again in the late 16th) and for the better in the 20th.[232]

Garuti scarcely speaks of uniatism at all.[233] For him the imbalances out of which (according to the other theologians mentioned) uniatism developed, are at most a marginal or incidental aspect of the historical account of relations between West and East, the essential drama instead having to do, in his perspective, with the rise in the East of an anti-Roman and anti-primatial mindset which expressed itself in an antagonistic way in the 12th century by means of the idea of sister churches.[234] Garuti ascribes to the concept of sister churches little or none of the positive value it has for Lanne, Hryniewicz, Congar and Legrand.

In the work of Hryniewicz especially, there is a concern not to forget how negative the Catholic evaluation of Orthodox ecclesiality actually was, and for

---

231 See above, pp. 119-122; 128-132; 164-165.
232 See above, Chapter 1, p. 26; also cf. Y. Congar, "De la communion des Églises à une ecclésiologie de l'Église universelle," in *L'Episcopat et l'Eglise universelle*, Unam Sanctam, no. 39, ed. Yves Congar and B.D. Dupuy (Paris: Cerf, 1962), 227-260; and Y. Congar, *After Nine Hundred Years*, 25ff. Some observations, largely inconclusive, on uniatism are offered by Congar in *After Nine Hundred Years*, 37-38.
233 Where he does mention it, it is without the concern that an author such as Lanne has expressed. Regarding the negative reaction that the Balamand Document received from a number of Orthodox, Garuti writes: "To use the analogy of a choral symphony, while the Catholic circles are singing the praises of the 'sister Churches', this is met by a series of discordant notes from the Orthodox side: reproaches against the Catholic Church, ultimatums, and open protestations against mutual recognition between the 'sister Churches'." He goes on in the immediately ensuing paragraph: "On the other hand, it makes no sense any more to bring up the so-called phenomenon of *uniatism / proselytism* and related implications and to ask the respective Churches to clarify their own positions and to put them into practice [here in a lengthy footnote Garuti quotes Lanne, doing precisely all of these things]. The Catholic Church has already recognized the ecclesial status – although imperfect – of the Orthodox Churches, with the soteriological consequences that follow therefrom: now it is the turn of the Orthodox Churches to take an analogous step" (Garuti, "Sister Churches," 308-309).
234 See above, p. 150.

how long, prior to the affirmation of the Orthodox churches as sister churches in the modern period. We saw that this focus makes it possible to appreciate a significance of the expression "sister churches" that it did not bear when it was used in previous epochs, but came to bear only in its use in 20th century Catholic-Orthodox relations, namely the significance of surprised discovery or rediscovery. Garuti himself speaks of this element when he writes of the "recognition, on the Catholic side, of the ecclesial status – though imperfect – of the Orthodox Churches and the euphoria over having rediscovered them as sisters",[235] though he does not give the same attention that other Catholic authors do to the rather more painful aspects of the concrete adjustments, the changes of attitude and approach, which the rediscovery may require of the Catholic Church. Instead he limits himself to observing that the feelings of euphoria "are not reciprocated on the Orthodox side."[236]

Drawing together the major strands of the analysis of this chapter, we may say that in Catholic reflection on the concept of sister churches there are essentially two poles, with a third position occupying a middle space between them. At one end of the spectrum, there is the approach that speaks of the Orthodox and Catholic churches as sister churches in such a way that suggests that they stand in symmetrical relationship and together comprise the Church of Christ (cf. Congar, Legrand). Sometimes accompanying this perspective is the notion that the Church of Christ subsists in the Catholic Church and in the Orthodox Church alike (cf. Legrand). At the other extreme, there is the approach that identifies the Catholic Church and the Church of Christ to such an extent that no room remains for any use of "sister churches" to refer to the Catholic Church and the Orthodox Church in their totalities, nor to refer to the Roman Catholic Church (as a patriarchate) in relation to one or more of the major sees of the East, nor even to describe Orthodox particular churches as sisters of Catholic particular churches except in an "imperfect and analogous manner" (cf. Garuti). Typically accompanying *this* view is an idea of the direct dependency of Orthodox particular churches on a universal church effectively identified as the Catholic Church.

The respective pitfalls of these two approaches are, in the first case, the idea that there is an exactly *symmetrical* relationship between Orthodox and Catholic churches, and in the second case, the idea that there is a relationship of direct *dependency* (of the Orthodox on the Catholic). In each case, a paradoxical dimension of the relationship is lost.

---

235 Garuti, "Sister Churches," 305.
236 Ibid.

But in between these two positions is a third interpretation, held by the CDF in many of its documents as these have been interpreted, in varying ways, by McPartlan, Sullivan, and Cardinal Ratzinger himself (i.e., in his personal writings reflecting on the work of the Congregation of which he was the prefect).[237] In this approach, Catholic-Orthodox relations are regarded as ecclesiologically asymmetrical. This is expressed in the teaching that the Church of Christ subsists in the Catholic Church alone. Just as important in this approach is the clear recognition that the asymmetrical relationship is not a relationship of dependence, certainly not in any direct way. For Orthodox particular churches are true churches that stand in relation to Catholic ones as "sister churches" not merely in an "imperfect sense" – as they would if the relation was one of dependency – but *in a proper sense*.[238]

The question of the "dependency" of non-Catholic churches is surely among the most important questions to be clarified in order to bring increased theological precision to the discussion of sister churches. What was once the standard teaching of the Roman Catholic Church is summarized in the following description by Garuti: "One of the most common formulae used to convey the growing awareness of the primacy of the Church of Rome and of her Bishop was '*Ecclesia Romana mater et caput omnium ecclesiarium*', with its consequent claim that all Churches 'receive their being, their origin, and their continuity from the Roman Church' and for this reason 'should follow their mother if they want to live at all'."[239] It may be asked whether this same medieval Catholic view of the dependency of the Eastern churches on the church of Rome is carried over into Garuti's analysis of present-day relations between the Orthodox churches and the Catholic Church. At the end of his section on the ambiguous ecclesial status of the Orthodox churches, he writes, as we have seen, that the Orthodox Churches "are Churches, but in an imperfect and analogous manner with respect to the Church, from which they derive their existence and salvific efficacy."[240]

---

237 Concerning the CDF: notwithstanding its quotation of its own 1985 "Notification" in footnote 56 as mentioned above (see p. 159), *Dominus Iesus* as a whole unequivocally affirmed the status of the Orthodox Churches as true particular churches. Concerning Cardinal Ratzinger, see above, pp. 160-162.
238 Cf. the CDF's *Note*, n. 11. See also Sullivan, "'Subsistit In'," 123: "the council did not hesitate to speak of the separated eastern Churches as 'particular Churches' without qualification".
239 Garuti, "Sister Churches," 263. See above, p. 150.
240 Ibid. See above, p. 149.

A pivotal question raised earlier[241] may be asked again here in reference to the use of the word "Church" in the above quotation. Is the Church that is spoken of here the Church of Christ (which subsists in the Catholic Church)? Or is it the Catholic Church (in which the Church of Christ subsists)? As observed earlier, Garuti does not always carefully distinguish between the two. The result is that the Orthodox churches as true particular churches are presented as deriving their being and their efficacy from the Catholic Church itself, rather than from the Church of Christ which subsists in the Catholic Church.

The following words from Congar, also quoted earlier, make clear the ecclesiological and historical inadequacy of this way of conceiving of the relationship, and the importance of the expression "sister churches" precisely as a corrective to it:

> The substance of faith and sacramental reality which is common to the Orthodox Church and the Roman Catholic Church does not come from the Roman church, as is the case with the Protestant communions of the Reformation. *Unitatis redintegratio* links it with apostolicity. So it is that the churches are sisters, not daughters. Paul VI went so far as to speak of a "universal and holy church of Christ" embracing the two sister churches.[242]

It must be noted, however, that there is no mention in this passage of the asymmetricality that must *also* be affirmed about the relationship of the Catholic and Orthodox churches in order to respect the unique subsistence that seems to be taught by Vatican II. Here the value of Garuti's contribution can be seen, even if his way of thinking cannot stand as the resting point for the discussion. For in any future usage of the language of sister churches in Catholic-Orthodox relations, this way of speaking would need to be purified of any of the sense of complete symmetricality that has often been attached to it; the CDF's chastising critique of the usage will then have served its proper purpose.

Finally, as a closing observation in regard to much of the foregoing analysis of this chapter, a word of caution is in order, drawn from convergent insights of Hryniewicz and Ratzinger – two thinkers otherwise often far apart in their theological reflection on the concept of sister churches. Both authors, in their own way, have called attention to the need to perceive the paradoxical nature of Christian division. Hryniewicz laid stress on this element of paradox when he spoke of "ecumenical aporetics".[243] Ratzinger wrote of "the contradictory element of schism" as reflected "in the paradox of the distinction between the

---

241 See above, p. 161-162, where the same question was posed in another context.
242 Congar, *Diversity and Communion*, 90. See above, p. 124-125.
243 See above, pp. 136-138.

uniqueness and the concrete existence of the Church, on the one hand, and, on the other, the continuing existence of a concrete ecclesiastical entity outside of the one active agent."[244] Of this distinction, which Ratzinger sees as bound up with the distinction "between *subsistit* and *est*" – and which can therefore also be seen as bound up with the question as to whether the Catholic and Orthodox churches are sister churches in spite of their visible separation – Ratzinger writes that it is, "in the end, something that cannot be entirely explained logically."[245] By no means is this acknowledgment of the reality of paradox to be mistaken as a dispensation from the responsibility to think through the issues related to the concept of sister churches as clearly and carefully as possible. It serves as a salutary warning, however, that in thinking them through, it is necessary to be alert to the points at which an internally consistent logic may be simply inadequate to a circumstance that is itself illogical. Cognizance must be taken of the fact that the whole complex of issues in Catholic ecclesiology involving sister churches in regard to the Orthodox, the relationship between the local church and the universal church, and the interpretation of "subsists in", can be argued either in one direction along logical lines, or in another. For example, we have seen Lanne maintain that the unicity of the Church *requires* Catholics to recognize Orthodox churches as sisters of their own,[246] while we have seen Garuti maintain that precisely this unicity of the Church *prevents* such a recognition.[247] Both approaches have their own internal logical consistency.

But it may be said that, as Ratzinger suggests, Catholic-Orthodox relations cannot fully make sense – and all attempts to render them entirely transparent to reason must fail – until such time as the visible unity of the two separated traditions is actually achieved. Prior to that time, there will necessarily be a paradoxical way in which each tradition alternately expresses and denies its need for communion with the other. Something of this is seen on the Catholic side in the tension between saying, on the one hand, that the Church of Christ subsists in the Catholic Church alone, and, on the other, that the Catholic Church itself is "wounded" by the division with the Eastern churches insofar as its universality in history is impaired by the division.[248] Whatever may be the

---

244 See above, p. 161.
245 See above, p. 161.
246 See above, p. 116, n. 17.
247 That is, except in an "imperfect and analogous manner". See above, p. 149.
248 Cf. UR, 4; *Communionis notio*, 17; and DI, 17. The notion that the Church of the West has a certain need for the Church of the East has also been expressed by Yves

consequences of this woundedness on the Catholic side, there is no question of its being fatal. For according to Catholic ecclesiology – and here Garuti does justice to the Catholic position – the continuity and unity and the visible presence in history of the one Church of Christ, in which all the means of grace are available, cannot be said to depend on reunification with the Orthodox Churches, a reunification which may or may not come about. Until it does, "maximalist" claims, however attired they may be in language meant not to offend, cannot be relinquished.

As will be seen in the next chapter, the Orthodox have an analogous view of the relationship between the two traditions, only with the center of gravity reversed. The fact that this similarity between the Orthodox and Catholic churches only adds to, rather than diminishes, the difficulty of their reconciliation, offers yet further testimony to the profoundly paradoxical significance of "sister churches" in modern Catholic-Orthodox relations, a dimension to which Hryniewicz and Ratzinger in their distinct ways have helped call attention.

Congar, e.g. in his remarks on "complementarity" in *Diversity and Communion*, 70-76, and by some of the Catholic bishops at Vatican II according to the recollections of one of the Orthodox delegate-observers at the council: "How many times one heard these simple and moving words: 'Help us,' for, without an agreement from the Orient, without its complementary contribution, no purely Occidental solution would ever attain its desired fullness." P. Evdokimov, "An Orthodox Look at Vatican II," *Diakonia* 1:3 (July 1966) 169.

Chapter 5
ORTHODOX THEOLOGICAL REFLECTION ON THE CONCEPT OF SISTER CHURCHES

If the concept of churches as sisters has been the subject of considerably less scholarly analysis among Orthodox theologians than among Catholic ones over the past forty years, one reason is that in Orthodox tradition the concept has long been taken more or less for granted. Many of the perceptions about the Church at which Lanne and Legrand arrive by a careful, painstaking reinterpretation of Catholic ecclesiology through the lens of Vatican II and the subsequent comments of Paul VI in *Anno Ineunte* are simply presupposed by most Orthodox: the idea of each local church as the full expression or instantiation of the one church catholic, the emphasis on communion among local churches, the awareness that uniatism as a method of union is opposed to an ecclesiology of communion. Of all this, the Orthodox have needed little or no convincing.

This surely accounts for why a number of Orthodox have viewed the use of the expression "sister churches" in modern Catholic-Orthodox relations favorably. Four such Orthodox thinkers, favorably disposed to the phrase, whose writings this chapter will consider are John Meyendorff, Metropolitan Maximos Aghiorgoussis, John Erickson, and Metropolitan Damaskinos Papandreou. None of these four, however, has offered such thoroughgoing analysis of the concept as was seen from Catholic writers. The reason, again, is that within the Orthodox world the expression's basic ecclesiological significance has never been seen as something in need of being established or proved in the first place. At another level, however, what opposition there has been among the Orthodox to the expression's modern use by Orthodox participants in Orthodox-Catholic dialogue has been far more vocal and entrenched than any of the criticism generated by the expression on the Catholic side. This opposition has been directed not against the concept per se but against its ecumenical use, i.e. in reference to relations between Orthodox and non-Orthodox churches. To be considered in this chapter among the sources of Orthodox opposition are a letter of the monastic community of Mount Athos addressed to Ecumenical Patriarch Bartholomew after the release of the Balamand Statement, writings of two professors of theology in Greece – John Romanides and George Metallinos – and a letter critical of the Balamand Statement written by a diocesan bishop of the Orthodox Church of America to the presiding bishop at the time, Metropolitan Theodosius.

Because the question of sacramental reality outside the Orthodox Church has such a crucial bearing on Orthodox attitudes toward the expression "sister churches" in Orthodox-Catholic relations, there will be some need in this chapter to examine this issue in its own right, by looking at the longstanding debate that has surrounded it in Orthodox ecclesiology.

I. Orthodox advocates of the idea of "sister churches" in Catholic-Orthodox relations

1. John Meyendorff

At the 1974 Vienna symposium at which Emmanuel Lanne presented a paper on the ecclesiological significance of the concept of "sister churches" from a Catholic point of view,[1] the Orthodox theologian John Meyendorff presented a corresponding paper from an Orthodox perspective. In Meyendorff's entire paper the expression "sister churches" appears only four times (three if one leaves out an occurrence in a quoted passage of Paul VI) and receives little direct analysis. Yet as the paper's title makes plain, the concept of "sister churches" is the topic throughout.

Meyendorff approaches the subject by noting three remarkable developments of his own time: the lifting in 1965 of the mutual anathemas of 1054 issued by representatives of the sees of Rome and Constantinople; the image of Pope Paul VI appearing publicly as the brother of another bishop; and Rome's official acceptance, reflected in Paul VI's Brief *Anno ineunte*, of the language of sister churches to describe relations between the two sees. In order to be able to appreciate and assess the true significance of these turns of events, Meyendorff considers it necessary to set them against the broad background of the history of the schism between East and West. Much of his article consists of an historical excursus meant to explore the schism's origins and nature.

"Everyone admits today that the East and the West separated from one another by a progressive 'estrangement' which was clearly apparent already in the fourth century,"[2] Meyendorff writes, adding that it would not become "a definitive schism" for another thousand years and more.[3] He maintains that the events of the year 1054 cannot be counted as decisive in themselves. Even after

---

1 See above, Chapter 4, p. 112-113.
2 J. Meyendorff, "Eglises-sœurs: Implications ecclésiologiques du Tomos Agapis," *Istina* 20 (1975), 36, with reference to Congar, *After Nine Hundred Years*, 4. Translations of Meyendorff's article are mine.
3 Meyendorff, "Eglises-sœurs," 38.

the fourth crusade (1204) the Byzantines were, in Meyendorff's words, "almost unanimous ... in considering the Latins as comprising still a part of the Christian *oecumene*."[4] This was true not only of "Latinophiles" among the Orthodox but also of theological conservatives who, in order to debate dogmatic divergences, advocated convening an ecumenical council. "Such was notably the position of the Palamite patriarchs after 1351. Until the start of the 15th century, however, the popes refused the idea of a 'union council' without preliminary penitence on the part of the Orthodox."[5] When the popes finally agreed to hold such a council (Ferrara-Florence), largely as a defensive move against Western conciliarists meeting elsewhere (Basel), the effort to reestablish unity between Rome and the Byzantine churches notoriously failed. It was only then, after the failure of Florence to achieve unity, that the schism took on an aspect of permanence. As Meyendorff puts it, it was only then that "the separation reached a stable state."[6]

Reaching back to the period before the separation, Meyendorff identifies a moment when the two churches reached a different kind of equilibrium, not in separation but in unity. This was at the council of 879-880 in Constantinople. "Until recently it was believed that the pope [John VIII] disavowed his legates upon their return to Rome and excommunicated [patriarch] Photius another time, when he learned of the decisions of the council. We know now that he did no such thing and that the two hierarchs, as well as their successors, remained faithful to the conciliar decrees."[7] In the East there have been theologians "as eminent and representative as Nicholas Cabasilas and Symeon of Thessalonica" who have referred to this assembly as the "eighth ecumenical council".[8] In the West, the same council was sanctioned by Rome for more than two hundred years and seen as having reestablished the unity of the Church.[9]

---

4   Ibid. At greater length Meyendorff elaborates the same point in his book *Rome, Constantinople, Moscow*, 89. See above, Chapter 1, p. 40-41.

5   Meyendorff, "Eglises-sœurs," 38. It was seen in Chapter 1, p. 29, that this was indeed the stance of Pope Innocent III in his correspondence with Patriarch John X Camateros.

6   Meyendorff, "Eglises-sœurs," 38.

7   Ibid. 39.

8   Ibid.

9   Only in the time of the 11th-century reforms was the slightly prior council of 869-870, known as the Ignatian council, which had been effectively nullified by the Photian council of 879-880, rehabilitated in the West and deemed the 8th ecumenical council. See above, Chapter 1, pp. 26-27.

Meyendorff wishes especially to draw out two important features of the council of 879-880. Both say something about how the relationship between Christian East and West might inform a vision of sister churches. First, there is what Meyendorff regards as the reciprocal nature of the council of 879-880. "On the canonical and disciplinary level, the two Churches recognize each other as superior instances in their respective territories; thus there is no papal 'jurisdiction' in the Orient (Canon I). The primacy of honor of Rome is, certainly, maintained, as well as the traditional limits of the Roman patriarchate, which included Illyricum."[10] Special notice should be given to the fact that in these comments, Meyendorff sees the church universal in terms of two churches, one of which is identified with "the Orient" and the other with the "Roman patriarchate". There is not an absolute symmetry between them, since the primacy of Rome is still maintained – thus there is no duality on the universal level – yet neither is there any notion that the Eastern church depends on the Western church directly, as is the case in the relationship between the church of Rome and the other churches within its own jurisdiction.

The second feature of the council of 879-880 highlighted by Meyendorff is more controversial. "On the dogmatic level, the council affirms the unity of faith, expressed by the maintenance by all the churches of the original text of the Symbol of Nicaea-Constantinople; any 'addition' to the text is formally condemned."[11] Meyendorff is quick to observe that this condemnation of the *filioque* "did not touch the authority of Rome, since the addition was not yet in usage in Rome,"[12] yet one wonders how, all these centuries later, the council's decrees could realistically be adopted – as Meyendorff recommends they should be – without Rome's authority being now undermined by the decree condemning the *filioque*. Elsewhere, Meyendorff seems to remain agnostic about whether the *filioque* is actually a dogmatically divisive issue,[13] but his emphasis on unity of faith as a prerequisite before full communion can be reestablished is very strong and bears noting. He expresses especially grave concerns about the dogmas of the Roman Catholic Church proclaimed in the 19th century. "In the case of [these] recent Latin dogmas, there was not simply pluralism [between Catholic and Orthodox positions], but there was conflict. Can we achieve unity without resolving this?"[14]

---

10 Meyendorff, "Eglises-sœurs," 39.
11 Ibid.
12 Ibid.
13 Ibid. 43.
14 Ibid. 43. He evidently has in mind the mariological and papal dogmas of 1854 and 1870, respectively.

Meyendorff might seem here to be substantiating the conviction held by Adriano Garuti that between the Catholic and Orthodox churches there is not unity of faith. But in fact he is far from settled in his view of this question. Meyendorff observes that "our two traditions are in agreement in considering unity of faith as a unique and necessary condition for reestablishing sacramental and canonical relations," and he asks, "Does this unity already exist? What is the real situation, in this regard, from the Orthodox point of view?"[15]

The question is not answered in Meyendorff's ensuing remarks. These develop on two related but distinct planes. The first has to do with what Meyendorff describes as a lack of consensus in Orthodoxy about the ecclesial status of non-Orthodox Christians, including Catholics.[16] Here he enters briefly into the contentious question of how Orthodoxy understands non-Orthodox sacraments, and concludes that the status of sacraments outside the canonical boundaries of the Orthodox Church can be established only by means of discernment. "This essential task of 'discernment' is obviously not only a question of information, intelligence or simple good sense: it is accomplished with the cooperation of the Holy Spirit who gives it its authenticity and its true spiritual signification."[17] The question of ecclesial reality outside the Orthodox Church is one that Meyendorff leaves carefully open here, and indeed answers affirmatively elsewhere.[18]

At this point, Meyendorff's discussion shifts onto another plane as he offers remarks of a more impressionistic nature on trends in the Roman Catholic Church as of 1975, and how these were perceived by the Orthodox. "I believe that a certain discernment is already operating, in the bosom of the Orthodox Church, in regard to the remarkable events of these last fifteen years [since the preparatory phase of Vatican II]. The results are not uniquely positive."[19] Meyendorff goes as far as to speak of a postconciliar "crisis" in Catholic thought and life which he believed had only further distanced Catholics and Orthodox from one another.[20] He does not offer details here, but in an editorial column of the previous decade, he spoke of what he regarded then as an excessive

---

15 Ibid. 44.
16 Ibid.
17 Ibid.
18 For example, in an editorial column of April, 1967 in the newspaper *The Orthodox Church* (of which he was editor from 1965-1984), entitled "Orthodoxy and Ecumenism – II", reprinted in J. Meyendorff, *Witness to the World* (Crestwood, NY: St. Vladimir's Seminary Press, 1987), 17.
19 Meyendorff, "Eglises-sœurs," 44.
20 Ibid.

latitude in spirituality and theology within the rank and file of the Catholic Church in the climate created by Vatican II's (proper, he believed) rejection of an earlier authoritarian Catholic ecclesiology. He also decried what he perceived to be a new reactionary movement in which the Vatican was reverting to former authoritarian tendencies. Despite these criticisms, Meyendorff's column may be viewed as a product of his understanding of the Orthodox and Catholic churches as siblings:

> It is difficult, and often improper, to comment on the affairs of others. The fact is, however, that Roman Catholics cannot be totally the 'others' for us: they have too much in common with Orthodoxy and there is too much solidarity between all Christians in today's secular world. What happens in American Roman Catholicism is not only in the public eye through the channels of the mass communications media, but it reflects on the image of Christianity as a whole. Our comments, therefore, are not inspired by Orthodox self-righteousness – a disease we have often condemned in these pages – but by the desire to spur among both Orthodox and Roman Catholics a constructive and truly Christian attitude towards the crisis.[21]

Altogether, Meyendorff stops well short of pronouncing a definitive judgment either on Vatican II, whose true meaning, he wrote in another context, would take years to evaluate,[22] or on the Catholic Church in the council's aftermath. What is clear is that he felt it was imperative to follow Roman Catholic developments very closely and saw the possibility that they might move either in a negative or in a positive direction.

Moreover, Meyendorff hastens to add that the Orthodox themselves were responsible in part for the difficulties being experienced within the Catholic Church. He suggests that if the witness of the Orthodox had been "more explicit and more coherent and, obviously, if the schism did not exist," then the recent ravages of secularism in the Christian West might have been more limited.[23] In Meyendorff's idea of the responsibility shared by *both* traditions for the perceived maladies from which one is suffering, one can see something of what he may envisage by regarding the Orthodox and Catholic churches as sisters, though he does not speak of the concept explicitly just here.

---

21 J. Meyendorff, "Crisis in Roman Catholicism" (December, 1968), in *Witness to the World*, 62.
22 Cf. J. Meyendorff, "Vatican II: A Preliminary Reaction," *St. Vladimir's Seminary Quarterly* 9 (1965), 32: "the real significance of the decrees adopted will be fully revealed only through the manner in which they are put into effect."
23 Meyendorff, "Eglises-sœurs," 44. Note that Meyendorff's comment contains an implicit acknowledgment that blame for the schism does not lie all on the Catholic side.

Elsewhere, he does speak of it explicitly, and makes clear that he is very much in support of applying it to the relationship between Catholic and Orthodox churches. "I certainly believe that the theology of 'sister Churches' is the right method for the dialogue between Catholics and Orthodox."[24] In his summary analysis of *Anno Ineunte,* he observes that Paul VI was invoking "a classic notion of Orthodox ecclesiology" when he used the expression "sister churches."[25]

Meyendorff notes that according to the pope's Brief, the theological basis of the expression, now applied not only to Orthodox churches among themselves (as it was in Vatican II's *Decree on Ecumenism*[26] but to the relationship *between* Catholic and Orthodox churches, rests "in the mystery of the sacramental presence of Christ," a mystery operating in every local church, whether Catholic or Orthodox. It may be asked whether Meyendorff endorses this viewpoint himself or is only describing what is set forth in the Brief of Paul VI. The answer emerges in the next paragraph when Meyendorff states what he believes are the implications of Paul VI's text. "The rapprochement between the East and the West must be understood as a progressive mutual recognition between local Churches," Meyendorff writes, "and not as a 'return' to *canonical obedience* to Rome." He goes on: "It is certain that this point of view is indeed that of the Orthodox Church since she participates in the ecumenical movement, bearing in mind that the rapprochement with Rome has an ecclesiological foundation much more solid than the contacts with the Protestants."[27] In distinguishing between the Roman Catholic and Protestant communions in their relation to the Orthodox, Meyendorff does seem to be endorsing Paul VI's idea that the same sacramental mystery of Christ is present in Catholic and Orthodox churches.

Indeed, Meyendorff sees in the pope's text "the foundations of an ecumenical method based on the theology of the local church, which was always that of the Orthodox and which, now, seems to be officially adopted by Rome."[28] Earlier Meyendorff spoke of a "theology of 'sister Churches'";[29] here of "the theology of the local church". By these two formulations he seems to intend the same meaning, though he does not spell out what it is in detail.

---

24 Meyendorff, "Eglises-sœurs," 44.
25 Meyendorff, "Eglises-sœurs," 42.
26 Cf. UR, 14.
27 Meyendorff, "Eglises-sœurs," 42.
28 Ibid.
29 See above, p. 188.

Almost two decades later, in his introduction to the 1992 edition of *The Primacy of Peter*,[30] Meyendorff again invoked the expression "sister churches" with approval, and again in reference to Orthodox-Catholic relations. In one of two relevant passages,[31] he wrote:

> Rome and Orthodoxy ... unavoidably define their ecclesiological positions – and even their internal problems – within the framework of the same scriptures and the same history of the first Christian millennium. This is the true meaning of the assertion that they are indeed 'sister-churches'. But, between quarrelling 'sisters,' reconciliation involves many intimate feelings and long-established perceptions. Union can be realized only through ultimate and reciprocal honesty, and readiness to engage in constructive self-criticism.[32]

In this passage Meyendorff offers a somewhat different view of what constitutes the basis of the expression "sister churches" than he did in his article of 1975. There, he spoke of "the mystery of the sacramental presence of Christ" residing in each local church celebrating the eucharist;[33] here the focus is on the fact that the Catholic and Orthodox communions understand themselves "within the framework of the same scriptures and the same history of the first Christian millennium." While not incompatible, the two formulations emphasize different factors. In the later formulation, the focus is on why there is hope ("union can be realized") for resolving the differences that separate Catholics from Orthodox. It is not simply that they share a common past, but that this common past remains alive in both traditions as they attempt to move forward.

Two additional points about the passage are worthy of notice. The first is Meyendorff's willingness to apply the expression "sister churches" across the confessional division between Orthodox and Catholics. The second is that the particular ecclesial subjects that Meyendorff describes as 'sister churches' in the passage above are "Rome and Orthodoxy". Meyendorff has no objection to using the expression to speak of the two communions as a whole.

---

30 J. Meyendorff, ed., *The Primacy of Peter: Essays in Ecclesiology and the Early Church* (Crestwood, NY: St. Vladimir's Seminary Press, 1992); first published in English by The Faith Press, Ltd. in 1963.
31 In the other one of the two, he expressed the opinion that the official Catholic texts of the 1960s that spoke of Catholic and Orthodox churches as "sister churches" were of greater importance than the 1965 lifting of the anathemas of 1054. (Meyendorff, *The Primacy of Peter*, 8.)
32 Meyendorff, *The Primacy of Peter*, 10.
33 See above, p. 188.

Finally, mention may be made of the issue with which Meyendorff ended his reflections in 1975: the role of Constantinople within the communion of Orthodox churches. His article's closing paragraph reads as follows:

> Orthodox ecclesiology excludes the idea that a local church can possess a universal jurisdiction, but it does not at all exclude that of a center, where the conciliarity of the church would manifest itself in a permanent way ... Within the Orthodox episcopacy, the see of Constantinople possesses a "Petrine" primacy (which is clearly not attached, by divine right, to a particular locality). I say indeed "Petrine" – even if, in case of union, this character may be restored anew to the bishop of Rome – because Peter alone is the "first" apostle, and there is thus no other primacy than that of Peter. But this primacy, in order to be useful to the Church, must be at the service of all and possess the means to exercise itself fruitfully, reflecting the thought and the opinions of all the churches, channeling the different opinions toward their common solutions. A permanent consultative organ can provide the church with these means ... It is thus the avenue to pursue in order to attain an authentic renewal of historic Orthodoxy, but also to make possible a truly representative dialogue with Rome.[34]

Here Meyendorff expresses his view that an increasingly central role for Constantinople in exercising a ministry of unity among the Orthodox churches is a requirement if the dialogue between the entire Orthodox Church and the Roman Catholic Church is to be able to proceed effectively. Based on what he says here, it would seem that the very possibility of calling the Orthodox Church as a whole the sister of the Catholic Church depends on a certain primacy of Constantinople within Orthodoxy.

2. Metropolitan Maximos Aghiorgoussis of Ainou

Metropolitan Maximos of Ainou, the presiding bishop of the Greek Orthodox Diocese of Pittsburgh, has been a member of the North American Orthodox-Roman Catholic Consultation without interruption since its inception in 1965 and Co-Chairman since 1987. He wrote an article on the subject of sister churches in 1994,[35] reviewing the research of Lanne into the antecedents and early uses of the expression and summarizing the relevant ecclesiological positions of Lanne, Congar and Meyendorff. Although covering little new ground,

---

34 Meyendorff, "Eglises-sœurs," 46.
35 Originally in Greek, translated into English as "'Sister Churches:' Ecclesiological Implications," in M. Aghiorgoussis, *In the Image of God* (Brookline, MA: Holy Cross Orthodox Press, 1999), 153-195.

the article by Aghiorgoussis deserves to be treated both because it represents the views of a prominent Orthodox hierarch and because it is a relatively rare instance of an Orthodox presentation devoted *entirely* to the meaning of the expression sister churches.

Aghiorgoussis regularly applies the term to the relationship between the two communions as a whole. For him this seems to be the paradigmatic use of the expression. Near the start of his article, he writes of his intention to explore "the profound ecclesiological meaning of the expression as applied to the two major Christian Churches, Eastern Orthodox and Roman Catholic, which are established by history and called today to be 'sister churches,' in full communion with one another."[36]

Aghioroussis sees little divergence among the ecclesiological perspectives of Congar, Lanne, and Meyendorff.[37] Of their viewpoints that he discusses, nearly all with approval, three may be singled out. First, Aghiorgoussis heartily agrees with Congar's idea of the independent apostolicity of origin of the Eastern churches, an idea which Aghiorgoussis summarizes simply: "In other words, Rome is not the 'mother Church' of the East."[38] Second, he concurs with Meyendorff's observation that in Paul VI's *Anno ineunte,* the Catholic Church effectively took the step of saying that union with the Orthodox is no longer envisioned in terms of a return to canonical obedience to Rome but in terms of a "mutual progressive recognition between local churches."[39] Third, Aghior-

---

36 Aghiorgoussis, *In the Image of God*, 153; cf. also 163, 164, for further examples of his applying the expression to the two churches as a whole.

37 One difference he notes is Meyendorff's emphasis on the need for a clear resolution of apparent doctrinal differences prior to any reestablishment of full communion, whereas Lanne seemed to advocate acceptance of a certain pluralism perhaps even on the dogmatic level between East and West. On this point, Aghiorgoussis sides with Meyendorff (cf. Aghiorgoussis, *In the Image of God*, 185-186).

38 Aghiorgoussis, *In the Image of God*, 170. Aghiorgoussis quotes at length from Congar's *Diversity and Communion,* 90-91, where Congar in various ways substantiates his basic point that the "substance of faith and sacramental reality which is common to the Orthodox Church and the Roman Catholic Church does not come from the Roman Church, as is the case with the Protestant communions of the Reformation. *Unitatis Redintegratio* links it with apostolicity. So it is that the churches are sisters, not daughters." At the end of an extended quotation from Congar, Aghiorgoussis writes, 172, "We cannot express ourselves better than Fr. Congar, with whom we fully share his feelings."

39 Aghiorgoussis, *In the Image of God*, 185, alluding to the comments of Meyendorff, "Eglises-sœurs," 42. See also above, p. 188.

goussis quotes and endorses Congar's statement that at Florence, it was not as though there was thought to be on one side the church and on the other something that was not the church.[40] Rather, there was an understanding that the differences to be resolved were internal to one and the same church to which both East and West belonged. Aghiorgoussis writes: "To corroborate this argument, let us not forget that the bishops on both sides had no problem recognizing one another as bishops of the church. They could not agree on many issues because of their *estrangement* (Fr. Congar's own word ...); but they were in agreement that on both sides there was real episcopacy representing the One Church of Christ."[41] In this same connection, Aghiorgoussis speaks of what at Florence was widely understood as "the still existing unity between the two sister churches".[42]

Aghiorgoussis encapsulates his position with respect to "the theology of 'sister churches,'" which he sees as applying properly to "the Eastern Orthodox and the Roman Catholic Churches," by writing: "There is no doubt that the two churches are not yet in 'full communion.' But to say that there is no communion at all is also inaccurate."[43] He then states with particular clarity: "In spite of the division, the separate ways of the two churches, and the dogmatic formulations in the West following the separation, the one Eucharist of the church is always celebrated on both sides, and in the same ecclesial context. Can we say that this does not keep our churches profoundly united?"[44]

For Aghiorgoussis, the Orthodox and Catholic churches clearly relate to one another as sister churches already in the present. They do so in spite of their canonical separation and dogmatic divergences, which Aghiorgoussis describes as "following" the schism, rather than precipitating it. Also in the passage above, Aghiorgoussis affirms very strongly the reality of Roman Catholic sacraments. Aghiorgoussis says once again in his conclusion that he agrees with Meyendorff that "full agreement in the faith should be restored, before we share our communion," but he affirms that in the meantime it is possible for Orthodox and Catholics alike to "enjoy the abundance of God's gifts, offered to both of our sister churches by our one heavenly Father through Christ the Lord, in the communion of God's Holy Spirit."[45]

---

40 Aghiorgoussis, *In the Image of God*, pp. 168-169, with reference to Congar, *Diversity and Communion*, 89. See also Chapter 4, p. 124.
41 Aghiorgoussis, *In the Image of God*, 169.
42 Ibid.
43 Ibid. 189.
44 Ibid.
45 Ibid. 190.

Finally, it may be noted that in Aghiorghoussis' paper there is no direct attention given to the sharp criticisms that by the time of its publication in 1994 had been leveled by some Orthodox against use of the term "sister church" to refer to any non-Orthodox church.

3. John Erickson

It is chiefly in the writings of John Erickson, a longstanding member of the North American Orthodox-Roman Catholic Consultation, that one finds direct engagement with the negative responses within Orthodoxy to the use of the expression "sister churches" in Orthodox-Catholic relations. Many of these negative responses came in the wake of the Balamand Statement (1993), in which the expression "sister churches" had a significant place.[46] In his 1997 article, "Concerning the Balamand Statement," Erickson describes and responds to several of the most salient points of criticism.[47] He discusses issues directly or tangentially related to the concept of sister churches in several other articles also.[48] In general, Erickson's writings on the topic of sister churches are more expository than analytical. He describes the work done by the Joint International Commission for Theological Dialogue between the Roman Catholic Church and the Orthodox Church, some of the political circumstances surrounding this work, and the reactions it has generated in the Orthodox world. Athough Erickson does not undertake a comprehensive theological analysis of the issues, the theological dimensions of a number of the positions expressed by the Joint Commission or by its critics do emerge in his account and receive some evaluation.

Prior to the meeting in Balamand in 1993, a plenary meeting of the Joint International Commission took place in Freising in 1990, and a meeting of the Commission's joint coordinating committee in Ariccia in 1991, at both of which the subject of uniatism was addressed, contrary to the scheduled agenda

---

46 Cf. "Uniatism, Method of Union of the Past ..." n. 12, 14, 27.

47 J. Erickson, "Concerning the Balamand Statement," *Greek Orthodox Theological Review* 42:1-2 (1997) 25-43.

48 Cf. "A Retreat from Ecumenism in Post-Communist Russia and Eastern Europe?", speech delivered at the Harriman Institute at Columbia University, New York, April 7, 2000; "On the Cusp of Modernity: the Canonical Hermeneutics of St. Nikodemos the Haghiorite (1748-1809)," *St. Vladimir's Theological Quarterly* 42:1 (1998) 45-66; "The Reception of Non-Orthodox into the Orthodox Church: Contemporary Practice," *St. Vladimir's Theological Quarterly* 41 (1997) 1-17; and "Divergencies in Pastoral Practice in the Reception of Converts," *Orthodox Perspectives on Pastoral Practice* (Brookline, MA: Holy Cross, 1988) 149-177.

of the Commission.⁴⁹ The departure from the original plan was due to new developments sparked by the fall of the Berlin Wall and the subsequent resurgence of Eastern Catholic churches in the former Soviet bloc. The change in plan was itself according to Orthodox wishes, and, as Erickson observes, "The resulting Freising Statement, developed 'on the spot' without the usual preliminary drafts, was issued at the request of the Orthodox, who considered it highly favorable to Orthodox interests and therefore have invoked it repeatedly since then in an effort to pressure the Vatican into restraining the uniates more effectively."⁵⁰ In language that would be largely incorporated into the draft text of Ariccia, and then into the Balamand Statement, the Freising Statement already invoked the expression "sister churches" to signify an ecclesiology in sharp contrast to uniatism. The latter it defined precisely as "the effort which aims to bring about the unity of the Church by separating from the Orthodox Church communities or Orthodox faithful without taking into account that, according to ecclesiology, the Orthodox Church is a sister-Church which itself offers the means of grace and salvation."⁵¹

Erickson provides this background information in order to highlight what he regards as the irony of the fact that the Balamand Declaration, upon its release, was denounced by many Orthodox, a number of whom even accused the Joint International Commission of having produced it hastily and in secrecy, under pressure from the Vatican. A central aim of Erickson's presentation is to make abundantly clear that the Balamand Declaration was largely a product of *Orthodox* pressure and was, in fact, found satisfactory by those Orthodox most directly affected by the situation it sought to address. The two largest Orthodox churches of Eastern Europe, the Russian Orthodox Church and the Romanian Orthodox Church, both issued official statements expressing approval of the document.⁵² Meanwhile the Orthodox Church most vocal in its opposition to

---

49 The Commission had prepared a draft statement on "Ecclesiological and Canonical Consequences of the Sacramental Structure of the Church" for deliberation at Freising.

50 Erickson, "Concerning the Balamand Statement," 29. Erickson points out, 30, that the Ariccia draft, like the Freising text before it (cf. Chapter 3 above, p. 94, for discussion of the Freising text), was considered by most observers to be highly sensitive to Orthodox concerns and was regarded by many Eastern Catholics as something of a "sell-out" of their interests.

51 Freising Statement, para. 6b, as quoted by Erickson, "Concerning the Balamand Statement," 29. The text of the Freising Statement is available in *Information Service* 73 (1990/II) 52-53 and in *Sourozh* 43 (February 1991) 24-27.

52 Cf. Erickson, "Concerning the Balamand Statement," 34, citing a formal acceptance

Balamand, namely the Church of Greece – whose Holy Synod declared it "unacceptable to the Orthodox,"[53] and from among whose theologians and monastic communities came several sharp denunciations of Balamand[54] – faced few of the practical problems associated with uniatism that existed in Romania and Russia.[55] Overall, according to Erickson,[56] Balamand was broadly supported

---

of Balamand by the Holy Synod of the Romanian Orthodox Church at its meeting of July 6-7, 1993 and a joint communiqué of the Russian Orthodox Church and the Vatican in March 1994.

53 The official reaction of the Permanent Holy Synod of the Church of Greece was issued on December 8, 1994 and published in Ἐκκλησιαστικὴ Ἀλήθεια (January 16, 1995). See Erickson, "Concerning the Balamand Statement," 26, n. 2.

54 See below, pp. 205-231, for treatment of the critical responses of the Monastic Community of Mount Athos and two theologians of the Orthodox Church of Greece, John Romanides and George Metallinos. See also the article by another prominent theologian of the same church, Theodore Zissis, "The Recent Statement of Balamand Concerning the Uniate" ("Τὸ Νέο Κείμενο περὶ Οὐνίας τοῦ Μπαλαμάντ,") serialized in Ἐκκλησιαστικὴ Ἀλήθεια (March 16, 1994; April 1, 1994; April 16, 1994; May 16, 1994; and July-August, 1994). Also by Zissis, see (in English) "Uniatism: A Problem in the Dialogue Between the Orthodox and Roman Catholics," *Greek Orthodox Theological Review* 35:1 (1990) 21-31, a paper originally read at the meeting of the Joint Sub-Commission on Uniatism (Vienna, January 26-31, 1990) of the International Joint Commission for the Theological Dialogue between the Orthodox Church and the Roman Catholic Church, of which sub-commission Zissis was a member.

55 As Erickson reports, "Greece has only a very negligible uniate population. Out of approximately 60,000 Catholics, only about 2300 belong to the 'Byzantine Apostolic Exarchate.'" Erickson goes on to offer some explanation for the apparent contradiction. "But that exarchate," he continues, speaking of the Byzantine (Catholic) Apostolic Exarchate in Greece, "does represent some of the worst aspects of uniatism. It was created by proselytization precisely as a token of Rome's opposition to the ecclesial claims of the established Orthodox Church, without even pretending to be a real union of churches. Its continued maintenance by Rome today is understandably taken as a deliberate affront by the Orthodox Church of Greece." Erickson, "Concerning the Balamand Statement," 35. For similar concerns expressed by E. Lanne and W. Hryniewicz, see Chapter 4 above, p. 119-120; 132-133.

56 Erickson cites here as well the positive statements issued by the U.S. Orthodox-Catholic Consultation (the relevant text is available in Borelli and Erickson, *Quest for Unity*, 184-190, and is quoted and discussed in Chapter 3 above, pp. 96-97) and the Catholic-Orthodox Mixed Commission of France (English translation available in *Eastern Churches Journal* 1:2 [Summer, 1994] 57-62).

by canonical Orthodoxy, whereas it was much more poorly received among many Eastern Catholics.[57]

Beyond the illuminating chronicle that he provides of the reception of the Balamand Declaration in Orthodox circles, Erickson offers two paragraphs that contain a more directly theological discussion of the concept of sister churches. In the first of the two, he writes:

> In employing the language of "sister churches," the Orthodox have in mind the ecclesiology which was characteristic of the first millennium of the Church's life and is still characteristic of Orthodoxy, according to which the Church is conceived as a κοινωνία of local sister churches. As church history shows, full communion between these churches, expressed preeminently in eucharistic fellowship, sometimes has been broken by disputes of various sorts, including disputes over doctrinal issues ... Yet even then, certain other aspects of κοινωνία (veneration of holy places, charitable assistance, etc.) continued, allowing hope for future reconciliation, and the same basic understanding of ecclesiology remained in place. From the eleventh century, this began to change in the West. Popes began to claim Rome as the "universal mother Church." Against such claims the East reasserted its ancient understanding. For example, at the beginning of the thirteenth century Patriarch John X Camateros writing to Innocent III insisted that "Rome is the first among equal sisters of the same dignity."[58]

For Erickson as for Meyendorff and Aghiorgoussis the language of sister churches essentially signifies an ecclesiology of communion among local churches.[59] Erickson emphasizes that, historically, such a communion ecclesiology of sister churches often persisted, in an impaired but still very significant way, in circumstances when churches were divided by disputes over disciplinary or doctrinal matters, and he suggests that this ongoing mutual sense of being still sister churches was always closely tied to a shared "hope for future reconciliation". Erickson offers evidence in the following paragraph that this hope endured on the Orthodox side through the many centuries of division between East and West, and that although it was dimmed on the Catholic side for a long period of time, it was rekindled in the latter part of the 20th century.

---

57 See Erickson, "Concerning the Balamand Statement, 30, 34, 36. As evidence that at least some Eastern Catholics took a favorable view of Balamand from quite early on, Erickson (34) mentions the Ukrainian Catholic Cardinal Myroslav Ivan Lubachivsky who, in his pastoral letter "On Christian Unity" (English translation in *Eastern Churches Journal* 1:2 [Summer, 1994] 7-47), expressed approval of the Balamand statement and a resolve to see its recommendations implemented.

58 Erickson, "Concerning the Balamand Statement," p. 37-38.

59 See above, p. 188, 191.

Chapter 5: Orthodox Theological Reflecion on "Sister Churches"

> The expression "sister church" did not cease to be used for the Western Church after full communion ended ... In the nineteenth century, for example, N.A. Muraviev, Assistant Ober-Procurator, and Metropolitan Platon of Kiev both referred to the Western Church as the "sister" of the Eastern Church; in 1948 Patriarch Alexis I – certainly no friend of Roman Catholicism – nevertheless called the Roman Church a "sister church." What is remarkable about the use of the term since 1963, when Patriarch Athenagoras I and Pope Paul VI reintroduced it into modern Orthodox/Roman Catholic dialogue, is not that the Orthodox should use it with reference to the Roman Church but that Rome should use it with reference to the Orthodox Churches. While the precise significance and practical implications of the expression have not been fully explored – it is not, after all, a technical term in canon law – virtually everyone has acknowledged that its use by modern popes represents a breakthrough in relations.[60]

In the context of Erickson's earlier remarks, it can be inferred that this breakthrough points to Rome's now having renewed its hope in a general reunion of Catholic and Orthodox churches, which would further logically imply an end to Rome's earlier attempts to bring about unity merely by means of a "return" of Orthodox churches to obedience to Roman authority. This change cannot be understood apart from the increasing openness on Rome's part to an ecclesiology of communion among local churches, such as Erickson and the other Orthodox authors examined thus far associate with the concept of sister churches.

In the remainder of his article, Erickson discusses Orthodox reactions to Balamand's recommendation that there should be no (re)baptism of members of either church entering the other. The positions of Orthodox writers who favor (re)baptizing Catholic converts to Orthodoxy – and who therefore particularly object to Balamand's assertion, "it is clear that any rebaptism must be avoided"[61] – will receive extensive treatment below.[62] Erickson has written extensively on the shortcomings of their canonical hermeneutics, and some of his positions on how Orthodox tradition has actually approached the question of non-Orthodox sacraments will be noted in the analysis of their outlook later in this chapter. For now, it is sufficient to observe that Erickson affirms the reality of Roman Catholic sacraments, and that the 1755 decree of Patriarch

---

60 Erickson, "Concerning the Balamand Statement," 38.
61 Cf. para. 13 of the Balamand Statement, cited by Erickson, "Concerning the Balamand Statement," 41.
62 See below, especially pp. 216-231.

Cyril V of Constantinople, condemning all non-Orthodox baptism, was, according to Erickson, a departure from what until then had been the prevailing Orthodox approach to the issue of schismatic and heretical baptism. Erickson has made clear his own view that the decree of 1755, theoretically still in effect even though seldom followed in practice, should be formally revoked, and he has made this plea in the context of discussing contemporary relations between Orthodox and Catholic churches and their mutual recognition as sister churches.[63]

As to Erickson's more general ecclesiological perspective, it should be noted that in recognizing Catholic sacraments as authentic, Erickson does not actually imply – as many Orthodox critics assume must be implied by such recognition – that the unity of the Church somehow straddles the two divided communions as though they were two coequal centers. He identifies one, and not both, as the privileged locus of the unity and continuity of the Church. "Certainly the Orthodox Church has always had the self-awareness of being the One, Holy, Catholic and Apostolic Church of Christ."[64] It is just that it is not an absolutely exclusive identification. "The question is, when and how did the Orthodox Church develop the awareness that the Roman Catholic Church was altogether outside this reality?"[65] The word "altogether" in this sentence is significant, for it suggests that for Erickson, the Roman Catholic Church, since the schism, would at any rate not be considered to be located precisely inside this reality, at least not in the same way that the Orthodox Church is. His point is that the Roman Catholic Church should not be regarded as being outside this reality *altogether*. His understanding that separated communities stand in varying degrees of proximity to the visibly united church derives from St. Basil, who maintained that not all schismatic communities were entirely cut off from the

---

63 Erickson, "Reception of Non-Orthodox into the Orthodox Church," 16. "It would be helpful ... if the Patriarchate of Constantinople at long last would rescind its 1755 decree on heretic baptism." This remark, coming in the penultimate paragraph of the article, is shortly followed by the following comment with which Erickson concludes (17): "Many Orthodox as well as Catholics have a sincere desire for rapprochement and unity, but all too often their desire has been frustrated because of misinformation and the distrust of the few. Theologians can help to establish an atmosphere of trust by exposing falsehood and dispelling error. This is their vocation, and for this they have been trained. Without patient labor at this arduous and often thankless task, talk of mutual recognition as sister churches may well remain an empty formula."
64 Erickson, "Concerning the Balamand Statement," 40.
65 Ibid.

Church; certain of them still, in some sense, belonged to it.⁶⁶ Here an implicit idea of the *ecclesia extra ecclesiam* is present, such as will be expressly articulated by another Orthodox author to be considered below.⁶⁷

4. Metropolitan Damaskinos Papandreou of Switzerland

Damaskinos Papandreou was co-chairman of the unofficial symposium of Orthodox and Catholic theologians held in Vienna in 1974,⁶⁸ and he has written a number of articles on Orthodox-Catholic relations and on issues of Roman Catholic ecclesiology in their ecumenical implications.⁶⁹ In the months of late 2000 and early 2001, Papandreou exchanged letters with Cardinal Joseph Ratzinger, then prefect of the Congregation for the Doctrine of the Faith, which, only a few months earlier, in the summer of 2000, had issued the two documents *Dominus Iesus* (August, 2000) and the *Note on the Expression "Sister Churches"* (June, 2000). In his letter to Cardinal Ratzinger, Papandreou offered some specific comments on these documents, as relatively few Orthodox have done.⁷⁰

---

66 Basil of Caesarea, *Ep. CLXXXVIII*, I, in Philip Schaff and Henry Wace (eds.), *Nicene and Post-Nicene Fathers* vol. 8 (Peabody, MA: Hendrickson, 1994), 223-224.
67 See below, p. 203.
68 It was at this symposium, it will be recalled, that both Emmanuel Lanne and John Meyendorff presented papers on the topic of sister churches. See above, Chapter 4, pp. 112-113, and Chapter 5, p. 183.
69 See, e.g., Met. Damaskinos, "Une évaluation de l'encyclique du pape Jean-Paul II 'Ut unum sint,'" *Episkepsis*, 519 (June 30, 1995) 27-31; Met. Damaskinos, "Conscience conciliare et experience sacramentelle dans l'œuvre du concile de Trente," *Episkepsis* 524 (November 30, 1995) 11-25. From 1969 to 2001, Papandreou was director of the Orthodox Center of the Ecumenical Patriarchate at Chambèsy, Switzerland. The Center was founded in 1966 with the aim of fostering inter-Orthodox contacts and theological exchange, as well as ecumenical relations between Orthodox and other Christian communions.
70 Another Orthodox commentary on the same two texts of the Catholic magisterium is that of Demetri Kantzavelos, "The Declaration 'Dominus Iesus': On the Unicity and Salvific Universality of Jesus Christ and the Church and Note on the Expression 'Sister Churches': A Greek Orthodox Response," in *Ecumenical Trends* (March 2002) 8-10, originally presented at the annual retreat of the Council of Religious leaders of Metropolitan Chicago on November 28, 2000. However, Kantzavelos' paper, while offering occasional references to the expression "sister churches," does not enter into a substantive discussion of the concept either in its treatment by the CDF or as it is understood by the Orthodox.

Like the other Orthodox authors considered thus far, Papandreou finds it natural and fitting to describe the Catholic and Orthodox communions in their totalities as sister churches. Recounting the relationship he developed with the young professor Ratzinger as his teacher and friend during his years as a student in Germany, Papandreou observes in his letter of October 30, 2000: "We discovered together what it means to belong to the Roman Catholic Church and to the Orthodox Church: two Churches that have rediscovered each other as sister Churches."[71] Further reflecting on the period when he and Ratzinger developed their friendship in the 1960s, Papandreou states, "We experienced the fact that we shared the same apostolic faith".[72] Perhaps in the sheer forthrightness of this affirmation, a difference may be discerned between Papandreou and the other Orthodox writers previously examined, above all Meyendorff, whose emphasis on the need to resolve outstanding doctrinal differences was quite pronounced. Papandreou offers a vision of theological pluralism without any hint of the idea, which Meyendorff raised, of dogmatic conflict between East and West.

> We have experienced the way in which the revealed truth was differently received, lived out, and understood in East and West and that the variance in theologies can be understood as compatible within one and the same faith; and all the more, when a keen awareness for the transcendence of the mystery and for the mainly apophatic character that its human expression has to assume can leave free play for a legitimate pluralism of theologies within the bosom of the same traditional faith; and that one ought not to be a priori inclined to identify faith, and its expression, with particular theologies.[73]

Insofar as he recognizes that the theological dialogue is of real importance,[74] it may be assumed that Papandreou acknowledges the need for the Orthodox and Catholic churches to come to a common mind about the nature of their differences, but in Papandreou's presentation it seems presupposed that this common mind will emerge almost inevitably; whereas Meyendorff left the question more uncomfortably open.

In other respects, however, the positions of Papandreou correspond with those of Meyendorff. Echoing Meyendorff's association of the language of

---

71 Met. Damaskinos, "Exchange of Letters between Metropolitan Damaskinos and Cardinal Joseph Ratzinger," in J. Ratzinger, *Pilgrim Fellowship of Faith: the Church as Communion*, trans. Henry Taylor (San Francisco: Ignatius, 2005), 217-241, at 218.
72 Met. Damaskinos, "Exchange of Letters," 218.
73 Met. Damaskinos, "Exchange of Letters," 220-221.
74 Cf. ibid. 218.

"sister churches" with the "theology of the local church,"[75] Papandreou states: "the local Church ... can in the view of Orthodox theology lay claim to being the one, holy, catholic, and apostolic Church – on condition, of course, that she is living in *communion* with the other local Churches."[76] This characteristically Orthodox vision of catholicity as a more qualitative than quantitative reality also informs Papandreou's critique of how the local church is often designated in official Catholic parlance: "the term 'particular Church' as a concept interchangeable with 'local Church' is liable to be moving toward a universalistically structured ecclesiology, which conceives of the local Churches as subordinate parts of the *Una Sancta*."[77] Again the preference for seeing each local church as the catholic church in its wholeness is strongly indicated. Also in another way, Papandreou says something similar to Meyendorff when he discusses the way in which ecclesial East and West must be understood as belonging together in spite of the separation – an idea Meyendorff often expressed in terms of the Byzantine vision of the single *oecumene*.[78] Papandreou puts it this way: "And we arrived together at the realization that East and West can meet and recognize one another again only if together they remember their original affinity and common past. As a first step, they would have to become aware of how East and West, despite all their differences, belong organically to one single Christendom."[79]

Because he is responding directly to Catholic magisterial texts, Papandreou addresses two of the issues that were prevalent in the previous chapter of this study – the question of applying "sister churches" to the Orthodox and Catholic churches in their totalities, and the controversy over "subsists in". Papandreou states that he disagrees with the position of the CDF that it is illegitimate to describe the entire Catholic Church as the sister of the entire Orthodox Church.[80] He interprets Paul VI as having, in fact, used the language of sister churches in just this way when he stated (in the same passage quoted by the CDF in its *Note*), "God is now granting us the grace, after long differences of opinion and disputes, of our Churches once more recognizing each other as sister Churches, despite the difficulties that have arisen between us in earlier

---

75 See above, p. 188.
76 Met. Damaskinos, "Exchange of Letters," 225.
77 Ibid.
78 See above, p. 184, and Chapter 1, pp. 40–41.
79 Met. Damaskinos, "Exchange of Letters," 220.
80 Cf. Met. Damaskinos, "Exchange of Letters," 226. "I deny that the concept 'sister Church', as it occurs in the Brief *Anno ineunte* of Pope Paul VI to Patriarch Athenagoras I, may be restricted in the way that occurred in the *Note* on sister Churches."

ages."[81] In Papandreou's interpretation, "This form of words may not only be applied as from the 'particular Church' of Rome to the 'particular Church' of Constantinople, but it also applies to the mutual recognition of the Roman Catholic Church and the Orthodox Church as sister Churches."[82] This is one of the rare instances where a writer is explicitly defending what in Chapter 3 was presented as usage 2: the specific application of "sister churches" to the two churches in their totalities. We have seen that a number of writers, Catholic as well as Orthodox, have used the expression that way, but not very self-consciously, nor with evident awareness of the distinction between this usage and the usage on the level of particular churches. Meanwhile the writers who *have* called attention to the distinction (e.g., Garuti) have done so in order to urge that the expression's application be restricted to the level of particular churches. Papandreou stands out in making a deliberate case that it should be considered acceptable to speak of the Catholic Church and the Orthodox Church as sisters. As a first step in making his case, Papandreou argues for the legitimacy of speaking of these two of them as, indeed, two churches, something of which the *Note* disapproved.

> The assertion that the use of the term "our two Churches" should be avoided on the grounds that this would "imply a plurality not merely on the level of particular Churches, but also on the level of the one, holy, catholic, and apostolic Church confessed in the Creed, whose real existence is thus obscured"[83] appears among other things to contradict even the joint declaration of Pope Paul VI and Patriarch Athenagoras I, at the end of the Patriarch's visit to Rome on October 28, 1967.[84]

The text to which Papandreou refers contains a passage which reads, as he renders it: "In their prayers, their public declarations and their private conversations, the Pope and the Patriarch wished to emphasize that a substantial contribution is made toward the restoration of full communion between the Roman Catholic Church, on one hand, and the Orthodox Church, on the other, by the renewal of the Church and of individual Christians, in faithfulness to the

---

81 Here Papandreou is quoting the *Note*'s quotation of *Anno ineunte*. For the relevant passage in *Anno ineunte*, see Stormon, *Towards the Healing of Schism*, 162, n. 176. There the wording differs slightly, since Papandreou, as he indicates on 226, bases his own rendering on the official German translation of the *Tomos Agapis*.
82 Met. Damaskinos, "Exchange of Letters," 226.
83 *Note*, n. 11.
84 Met. Damaskinos, "Exchange of Letters," 226.

traditions of the Fathers and to the inspirations of the Holy Spirit, who is always present with the Church."[85]

Thus far, Papandreou has based his case on empirical criteria: concrete instances, to which he can point, when the highest officials of the Catholic and Orthodox churches have indeed applied the expression sister churches to the two entire communions and have indeed spoken of "our two churches". But in the concluding paragraph of his letter, he goes a step further, reflecting theologically on how the relationship of the two churches of East and West may be understood. Papandreou does not explicitly bring in the idea of "subsists in" in Catholic ecclesiology, but what he says is of direct and obvious relevance to that issue.

> The use of the term "our two Churches" in no way relativizes the Roman Catholic Church's claim to be the Church in a complete and absolute sense, on one hand, or that of the Orthodox Church, on the other, in their claim to be, and to continue as, the one, holy, catholic, and apostolic Church ... Can we apply a "both–and" here, or does the canonical character of the Church oblige us to take "either–or" as our starting point? Both Churches take the view that they are continuations of the one, holy, catholic, and apostolic Church, without thereby being necessarily exclusive. In any case, one can in my view recognize the continuing existence even of the *ecclesia extra ecclesiam*, in the full sense of the word *ecclesia*, wherever there is unity in the essentials of the *pistis* (that is, of the great conciliar creeds) and wherever the fundamental ordering of the *ecclesia*, that is, the *successio apostolica*, has been preserved unbroken.[86]

According to Papandreou, it should be possible for a communion that identifies itself as the continuation of the one, holy, catholic and apostolic church to rec-

---

85 Quoted by Met. Damaskinos, "Exchange of Letters," 227. The version of the same text in Stormon, *Towards the Healing of Schism*, 181, n. 195, again reads somewhat differently: "In the prayers which they offered, in their public declarations, and in their private discussion, the Pope and the Patriarchh wished to emphasize their conviction that an essential contribution for the restoration of full communion between the Roman Catholic Church and *the Orthodox Churches* [emphasis added] is to be found within the framework of a renewal of the Church and of Christians, in fidelity to the traditions of the Fathers and to the inspirations of the Holy Spirit, who remains always with his Church." Papandreou's rendering – with the singular "Orthodox Church" rather than the plural "Orthodox Churches" – certainly better serves his argument. But the discrepancy is of minor significance when one considers how many other texts he might have cited that would have served his argument equally well. Cf. above, Chapter 3, pp. 82-98.
86 Met. Damaskinos, "Exchange of Letters," 227-228.

ognize outside itself the existence of ecclesial reality that is ecclesial in the full sense.[87] Such a recognition depends, according to Papandreou, on two principal factors: that there is unity in the essentials of the faith (in conformity with the ancient creeds), and that there is unbroken apostolic succession.

Papandreou should not be understood as suggesting that so long as these basic criteria are met, then in either of any two communions divided from one another, the one, holy, catholic and apostolic church continues on in just the same way. It is significant that he speaks of the *ecclesia extra ecclesiam* when he refers to the situation of schism. For in such a formulation, there still remains a distinct difference between the realm inside the visibly united Church and the realm outside; the boundaries of the Church are not so much blurred as they are paradoxically traversed. It is not that the Church simply and in the same way exists everywhere regardless of the schism. Rather, with the phrase *ecclesia extra ecclesiam*, the Church is understood as being anchored in only one communion, though also paradoxically present elsewhere. There is thus a strong resemblance between this understanding and that which is expressed in Catholic ecclesiology by the notion of "subsists in".[88]

It may be observed that although Papandreou attends to the distinction between describing particular Catholic and Orthodox churches as sisters and describing the two whole churches as such, he has little to say about the concept of sister churches on the level in between – that is, on the level of regional, or patriarchal, churches. It is also to be noted that while Papandreou engages in discussion of some of the most salient points raised in recent Catholic critiques of the expression "sister churches" as it is sometimes used, he does not engage, as Erickson does, in discussion of the most salient points raised by Orthodox critics. It is to these points of criticism leveled by Orthodox authors, who oppose

---

87 Here it may be observed that where Papandreou uses the adjective "full" to describe the ecclesiality recognized outside the visible unity of the church, the CDF uses the adjective "true," in a manner meant to suggest something less than "full" (see Chapter 4 above, p. 148, 160). Papandreou, rather than following the CDF's pattern of contrasting the two terms, seems to mean by "full" roughly what is meant by "true" in the CDF's usage. In other words, he seems to want to say that outside the visible unity of the church there may be recognized *authentic* ecclesiality even though its form may in certain respects be imperfect compared to that which is maintained within.

88 More will be said about this resemblance in Chapter 6. Here I have in mind not the interpretations of "subsists in" that were put forward by Garuti and Becker on one side, and by Hryniewicz and Legrand on the other, but the more careful (and paradoxical) interpretation as one finds it variously articulated by Sullivan, McPartlan, Ratzinger, and the CDF's *Communionis notio* and *Dominus Iesus*.

any use of the expression "sister churches" in Orthodox-Catholic relations, that we now turn.

II. Orthodox critics of "sister churches" in Catholic-Orthodox relations

1. Letter to the Ecumenical Patriarch from the Sacred Community of Mount Athos

On December 8, 1993, a letter signed by all the representatives and presidents of the twenty monasteries of Mount Athos was sent to Ecumenical Patriarch Bartholomew on the subject of the Balamand Declaration issued in June of that year at the end of the seventh plenary meeting of the Joint International Commission for Theological Dialogue between the Roman Catholic Church and the Orthodox Church.[89] The tone of the letter is not always measured and the overall assessment of Orthodox ecumenical activity is largely negative, though in the early part of the letter one finds an avowed openness to ecumenical engagement. "We note that at times the word of Truth is rightly divided," the authors write, referring to Orthodox participants in bilateral dialogues, "and, at times, compromises and concessions are made regarding fundamental matters of the Faith."[90] The letter proceeds with an itemization of alleged compromises and highlights its primary subject of concern. "The gravest matter ... is the unacceptable change in the position of the Orthodox that arises from the joint statement at the June, 1993, Balamand Conference of the mixed commission for the dialogue between Roman Catholics and Orthodox. It adopted anti-Orthodox positions, and it is mainly to this that we call the attention of Your All Holiness."[91]

The first, though not yet the central, complaint about Balamand expressed by the authors of the letter from Mount Athos has to do with the statement's handling of the issue of uniatism. As they see it, the fact that Balamand unequivocally condemns uniatism as a method of union does not go far enough in addressing the issue. Until all the members of churches born of such a method have actually been reaffiliated as Latin Catholics, the authors of the letter do not see how the dialogue between Orthodox and Roman Catholics can continue.

---

89 *Letter to the Patriarch of Constantinople from the Sacred Community of Mount Athos*, Dec. 8, 1993, originally published in Ὀρθόδοξος Τύπος (March 18, 1994) and available in English translation in *Orthodox Life* 44:4 (1994) 27-39. Quotations below are taken from the English translation in *Orthodox Life*, to which all page numbers refer.
90 *Letter to the Patriarch of Constantinople*, 28.
91 Ibid. 29.

The letter's authors refer approvingly to strong statements they recall the Ecumenical Patriarch having made in the past, describing "the Uniate movement [as] an insurmountable obstacle" to Orthodox-Catholic dialogue, and they express bewilderment that now, in the Balamand Statement, with its acknowledgment of the right of Eastern Catholic churches to exist[92] and, moreover, with its invitation to them to be participants in Catholic ecumenical relations with the Orthodox[93], "Unia is receiving amnesty and is invited to the table of theological dialogue".[94]

The letter from Mount Athos turns next to what is said to be the cause of "the greatest scandal" of the Balamand Declaration, namely "the ecclesiological positions of the document."[95] Among these, the first to which the letter calls attention is the notion in the Balamand statement that a vision of ecclesiological and soteriological exclusivism developed within Orthodoxy as a reaction to the claim of the Catholic Church to be the sole locus of salvation.[96] The letter from Mount Athos states:

> As Orthodox, we cannot accept this view. It was not as a reaction against Unia that our Holy Orthodox Church began to believe that she exclusively possessed salvation, but She believed it before Unia existed, from the time of the Schism, which took place for reasons of dogma. The Orthodox Church did not await the coming of Unia in order to acquire the consciousness that she is the unadulterated continuation of the One, Holy, Catholic, and Apostolic Church of Christ, because she has always had this self-awareness just as she had the awareness that the Papacy was in heresy. If she did not use the term heresy frequently, it was because, according to Saint Mark of Ephesus, "The Latins are not only schismatics but heretics as well. However, the Church was silent on this because their race is large and more powerful than ours ... and we wished not to fall into triumphalism over the Latins as heretics but to be accepting of their return and to cultivate brotherliness." But when the Uniates and the agents of Rome were let loose on us in the East in order to proselytize the suffering Orthodox by mainly unlawful means, as they do even today, Orthodoxy was obliged to declare that truth, not for purposes of proselytism but in order to protect the flock.[97]

---

92 Cf. "Uniatism, Method of Union of the Past," para. 16.
93 Cf. ibid. paras. 16 and 34.
94 *Letter to the Patriarch of Constantinople*, 29.
95 Ibid.
96 Cf. "Uniatism, Method of Union of the Past," para. 10.
97 *Letter to the Patriarch of Constantinople*, 29-30.

A pervading theme in this passage is that ever since the schism at the start of the second millennium, Orthodox East and Catholic West have been divided by a difference of dogma so fundamental that the Catholic West must be understood as having been in heresy from that time to the present. According to the letter from Mount Athos, the positions of the Catholic West that are heretical include the *filioque,* papal primacy and infallibility, created grace, purgatory, the immaculate conception, and rejection of the doctrine of the uncreated energies of God.[98] Because of these errors, there can be no doubt that the Roman Catholic Church has ceased to be the continuation of the Church of Christ, with which the Orthodox Church alone may still be identified.

Later in the letter, the authors turn their attention to the question of Roman Catholic sacraments. These the authors regard as invalid, and the reason is tied to the characterization of Roman Catholicism as heretical. "Do these serious theological deviations [the filioque, papal primacy, purgatory, and the others mentioned above] of Rome amount to heresies or not? If they are, as they have been described by Orthodox Councils and fathers, do they not result in the invalidity of the Mysteries and the apostolic succession of heterodox and cacodox of this kind? ... Is it possible to distinguish Christ of the truth from Christ of the Mysteries and apostolic succession?"[99]

The letter takes particular exception to Balamand's insistence on refraining from (re)baptizing converts from one church to the other.[100]

> [A]re the signers of this document unaware that many Roman Catholics today groan under the foot of the Pope (and his scholastic, man-centered ecclesiological system) and desire to come into Orthodoxy? How can these people who are tormented spiritually and desire holy Baptism not be received into Orthodoxy because the same Grace is supposedly both here and there? Ought we not, at that point, to respect their religious freedom, as the Balamand declaration demands in another circumstance, and grant them Orthodox Baptism? What defense shall we present to the Lord if we withhold the fullness of Grace from them who, after years of agony and personal searching, desire the holy Baptism of our One, Holy, Catholic, and Apostolic Church?[101]

Closely linked with its position on Roman Catholic baptism is the letter's opposition to Balamand's use of the expression sister churches to describe the Catholic and Orthodox churches in relation to one another. "[H]ow is it possible for

---

98 *Letter to the Patriarch of Constantinople,* 30-31.
99 *Letter to the Patriarch of Constantinople,* 32.
100 Cf. "Uniatism, Method of Union of the Past," para. 13.
101 *Letter to the Patriarch of Constantinople,* 32.

two Churches to be considered 'Sister Churches' ... because of their so-called common confession, sanctifying Grace, and priesthood *despite their great differences in dogmas?*"[102] The letter similarly states: "From what we know about Church History, Churches were called Sister Churches when they held the same faith. Never was the Orthodox Church called a sister of any heterodox churches, regardless of the degree of heterodoxy or cacodoxy they held."[103]

It has been seen in the course of this study that it is possible to find instances, since the schism began, when Orthodox churches were, in fact, called sister churches of Rome, the patriarchate of the West: both Nicetas and Camateros used this language in spite of the confessional division. It is true, however, that the church of Rome seems to have been regarded in such instances as holding the same faith as the Orthodox; it was not regarded as heterodox. The words of Nicetas may be recalled: "but although we are not in disagreement with the Roman Church in the matter of the Catholic faith, how can we be expected to accept ... decisions ... taken without our advice and of which we know nothing ...?"[104]

Unlike Nicetas then, the authors of the letter from Mount Athos regard the schism as a result of a profound dogmatic divergence, indeed as its own proof of such a divergence. The letter contrasts what it calls the "totalitarian ecclesiology" of the Roman Catholic Church with Orthodoxy as a "theanthropic communion, or, in a phrase of Gregory Palamas, a "communion of theosis."[105] More generally, the letter seems to presuppose the categorical illegitimacy of one or the other side of the schism. To suggest that there could be legitimacy on both sides is to fall into relativism.

> It is apparent that the [Balamand] document adopts, perhaps for the first time by the Orthodox side, the position that two Churches, the Orthodox and the Roman Catholic, together constitute the One Holy Church or are two legitimate expressions of her. Unfortunately, it is the first time that Orthodox have officially accepted a form of the branch theory ... [T]his theory comes into screaming conflict with Orthodox Tradition and Consciousness until now. We have many witnesses to the Orthodox Consciousness that our Church alone constitutes the One Holy Church ...[106].

---

102 Ibid. (original emphasis).
103 Ibid. 33.
104 See above, Chapter 1, p. 34.
105 *Letter to the Patriarch of Constantinople*, 31.
106 Ibid. 33.

The letter goes on to cite a number of texts meant to support the letter's understanding that there is an absolute and exclusive identity between the Orthodox Church and the one Church of Christ professed in the creed. "It is self-evident," the letter's authors conclude, "that two complete bodies of Christ cannot exist."[107]

The similarity between what is said here by the authors of the letter from Mount Athos and what would be written only a few years later by Adriano Garuti about the impermissibility of speaking of the whole Orthodox and Catholic communions as sisters (or even as "our two churches") is striking. Both the Athonite letter and the reflections of Garuti maintain that the unicity of the Church would be compromised if, given their canonical separation, the Catholic Church and the Orthodox Church were to be considered as sisters. By contrast, Papandreou in his letter to Cardinal Ratzinger argued – invoking the notion of the *ecclesia extra ecclesiam* – that to recognize the other communion as church (and thus potentially as sister church) need not involve any relativizing of the claim of each communion to be the one Church of Christ, and therefore by implication any compromise regarding belief in one Church.

In the concluding section of the letter, the authors summarize their opposition to the Balamand statement:

> [B]y means of that joint declaration Roman Catholics have succeeded in gaining from certain Orthodox recognition as the legitimate continuation of the One Holy Church with the fullness of Truth, Grace, Priesthood, Mysteries, and Apostolic Succession. But ... the concessions by the Orthodox are not philanthropic. They are not for the good of either the Roman Catholics or the Orthodox. They jump from *the hope of the Gospel* (Col. 1:23) of Christ, the only God-Man, to the Pope, the man-god and idol of Western humanism. For the sake of the Roman Catholics and the whole world, whose only hope is unadulterated Orthodoxy, we are obliged never to accept union or the description of the Roman Catholic Church as a "Sister Church," or the Pope as the canonical bishop of Rome, or the "Church" of Rome as having canonical Apostolic Succession, Priesthood, and Mysteries without their expressly stated renunciation of the Filioque, the infallibility and primacy of the Pope, created grace, and the rest of their cacodoxies. For we shall never regard these as unimportant differences or mere theological opinions, but as differences that irrevocably debase the theanthropic character of the Church and introduce blasphemies. ... Remaining faithful to all that we have received from our Holy Fathers, we

---

107 Ibid. 36.

shall never accept the present Roman "Church" as co-representative with ours of the One, Holy, Catholic, and Apostolic Church of Christ.[108]

In the vision of the authors of the Athonite letter, theological dialogue can serve no purpose unless it is for the party in error to be brought to repentance by the party that knows the truth. This vision has a certain affinity with the medieval understanding of the Church of Rome as the *mater et magistra* of all other churches, a self-understanding which led Innocent III to refuse to convene an ecumenical council until the Orthodox East first acknowledged the supremacy of Rome, and which also led to the method of union known as uniatism. According to the definition of one scholar of the historical interactions between East and West since the schism, uniatism may be seen as "an act of drawing over to oneself, whereby the one side wish only to give and think it is only the others who are to receive, so that what is sought is not a mutual benefit, but quite simply the obedience of the other side".[109] In such an approach, there is a direct dependency of the separated community on the visibly one Church. This relationship of direct dependency is incompatible with a relationship of sister churches.

2. John S. Romanides

The letter from Mount Athos quotes approvingly and on more than one occasion from the writings of John Romanides (1928-2001), who represented the Greek Church to the World Council of Churches for many years and was involved in Orthodox international dialogues with the Lutheran church and the Oriental Orthodox churches. In 1993, in response to the release of the Balamand statement earlier that year, Romanides published an article entitled "Orthodox and Vatican Agreement,"[110] in which he says relatively little about the text of Balamand itself, but offers a number of observations that indicate his evaluation of its general approach to Catholic-Orthodox relations. Like Meyendorff, Romanides begins with a substantial historical excursus concerned with the causes and nature of the schism.

---

108 Ibid. 37-38. At another place in the letter, the authors underscore the same point on which the passage above concludes, when they make reference to "the One, Holy, Catholic, and Apostolic, in other words Orthodox, Church" (ibid. 28).

109 E. Suttner, *Church Unity: Union or Uniatism?* (Rome: Centre for Indian and Inter-Religious Studies and Bangalore: Dharmaram Publications, 1991), 29.

110 J. Romanides, "Orthodox and Vatican Agreement," originally published in Θεολογία (Athens, Greece), vol. 6, issue 4 (1993) 570-580. Available online at www.romanity.org/htm/rom.13.en.orthodox_and_vatican_agreement.htm (accessed March 17, 2009).

It is to be noted that Romanides does not use the term "Catholic" to refer to the western church.[111] Also conspicuous is Romanides' adamant rejection of the distinction between "Greek East" and "Latin West". According to his understanding of church history, the schism customarily thought to have come about between Greek East and Latin West, was actually between "the Franco-Latins," on the one hand, and the "West and East Romans," on the other.[112] Romanides contends that the modern papacy arose in the Middle Ages as a result of the enslavement of the West Romans by the Franks, who include the Normans and the Lombards and who throughout history are the real enemies of the East Romans. "The Franco-Latins began their final attack on the freedom and Romanity of the Papacy in 973-1003 and completed the subjugation of the Roman Papacy and the freedom of the Papal States between 1009 and 1046. Thereafter the Popes are all members of the Franco-Latin nobility who use the name Roman Pope and Roman Papacy in order that the West Romans may continue to believe that they still had a Roman Pope."[113] The takeover, however, had begun more than two centuries earlier, "from the time the Franks decided in 794 to provoke the schism with the so-called 'Greeks' for political reasons. The Church of Old Rome fought heroically to remain united to New Rome up to 1009."[114] It was a losing battle due to the relentless determination of the Franks to delegitimize the Christian East. "From 809 onward the Franks never deviated from their position that the East Romans, i.e. their Greeks, are heretics. Up to 1009 the Church of Old Rome vigorously resisted this deliberate Frankish policy which was finally imposed by force."[115]

From that time on, according to Romanides, there has been no Roman Catholic Church in the West, but only the Frankish papacy. One of the last attempts by the authentic West Roman papacy at maintaining unity with the East Romans occurred in 879-880 at what Romanides describes as "the 8th Ecumenical Council," which, with the full sanction of Pope John VIII, "condemned the Frankish heresies on icons and the Filioque, without however naming the heretics for fear of reprisals."[116]

---

111 Even the international theological dialogue between East and West is described by Romanides as the "Orthodox-Vatican Dialogue" (cf. Romanides, "Orthodox and Vatican Agreement," para. 1), and of course the very title of his paper designates the two parties in these same terms.
112 Romanides, "Orthodox and Vatican Agreement," para. 16.
113 Ibid. para. 15.
114 Ibid. para. 16.
115 Ibid. para. 17.
116 Ibid. para. 15.

In his idiosyncratic account of the division between Old Rome (under centuries of occupation by the heretical Franco-Latins) and New Rome, there are certain questionable aspects from an historical point of view. Romanides refers, for example, to the "Frankish" heresy on icons without giving due account of the fact that iconoclasm was a pervasive heresy precisely among "Roman Orthodox"[117] (i.e., Byzantine) churches, and was an important factor in why the church of Old Rome felt the need to distance itself from the "East Roman Empire"[118] in the late eighth and ninth centuries.

Nevertheless Romanides touches on several points that have been made previously in Orthodox presentations, including presentations by advocates of "sister churches" in Catholic-Orthodox relations. His attention to the rise of a separate imperial polity in the West beginning around the turn of the 9th century and its negative impact on ecclesial unity reflects a standard Orthodox view that goes back as far as Nicetas and is found in recent writers including Meyendorff. His notion that the council of 879-880 ought to be regarded as the eighth ecumenical council also coincides with a position held by Meyendorff and others.[119] In addition, Romanides' historical presentation lends support to the view advanced by Erickson (and disputed by the authors from Mount Athos) that the West's denial of the ecclesial reality of the East preceded the East's denial of the ecclesial reality of the West. Romanides dates the western move to delegitimize the East very early – to the 9th century. He also notes its continuation up to the eve of Vatican II.

> That this tradition [of considering the "Greeks" as heretics, which the Franks began to do in the early 9th century] continued into the middle of the 20th century was so evident during this writer's youth. In Latin books on Apologetics the Orthodox were vehemently described as heretics and without saints. Evidently this was due to the Filioque controversy which broke out in earnest prior to the Eighth Ecumenical Council of 879. So supposedly the Orthodox had no Fathers of the Church after St. John of Damascus (circa 675-749) and St. Theodore of Studium (759-826).[120]

---

117 For an example of his use of this term, cf. ibid. para. 3.
118 Cf. ibid. para. 12.
119 See above, pp. 184-185. Nicholas Lossky is another Orthodox theologian who has expressed support for Meyendorff's proposal with regard to the council of 879-880; cf. N. Lossky, "Conciliarity-Primacy in a Russian Orthodox perspective," in James Puglisi, ed., *Petrine Ministry and the Unity of the Church: Toward a Patient and Fraternal Dialogue* (Collegeville, MN: Liturgical Press, 1999), 127-136, at 135-136.
120 Romanides, "Orthodox and Vatican Agreement," para. 18. In light of this passage, it is of value to recall Emmanuel Lanne's suggestion that the recognition of the

Romanides is clear that on an official level, the stance of the Roman Catholic Church in its evaluation of Orthodoxy underwent a remarkable shift later in the 20th century, when "the Vatican made an about face and produced Vatican II's unilateral recognition of Orthodox sacraments."[121] But whereas such Orthodox advocates of "sister churches" in Catholic-Orthodox relations view this change positively, Romanides views it with profound suspicion, even cynicism.

> The question remains: Is this transformation from War to Love real? Or is it still the love of the wolf now dressed up in sheep's clothing out to catch its traditional prey? The Vatican's invasion of Orthodox countries with so many clerics hunting for prey seems to speak for itself.[122]

Romanides alludes at the end of this passage to uniatism as a still active form of aggressive imperialism on the part of the Latin West. It might be expected, then, that he would respond favorably to the Balamand Statement insofar as such activity is expressly repudiated in that document. Romanides does acknowledge that with Balamand, "[t]he raison d'être of Uniatism ceases to exist,"[123] and he actually goes rather far in envisioning what might eventually happen as a result of Rome's implementation of the ecclesiology espoused by Balamand (which he assumes has the full support of the Vatican): "It is also possible that the pope at some point may desist from appointing a successor to at least one of his current Uniate Archbishops or even Patriarchs and put his local Uniate faithful under the spiritual leadership of the local Orthodox Archbishop or Patriarch as a trial test."[124] But Romanides nevertheless does not look favorably upon the Balamand Statement, even given the prospect of such extraordinary developments that he thought might result from it.

The reasons for his critical stance emerge most discernibly in the section of his paper called "Ecclesiology". Here he expresses the same understanding of the Church as was articulated in the letter from Mount Athos with its notion, taken from Gregory Palamas, of the Church as the "communion of theosis."[125] According to Romanides, the glorification, or theosis, of the human being is the essence of Orthodox Christianity and is alien to the Christianity of the West in

---

Orthodox Church as a sister of the Catholic Church has involved, among other things, recognizing an ongoing presence of saintliness in Eastern Orthodoxy since the schism. See above, Chapter 4, pp. 116-117.
121 Romanides, "Orthodox and Vatican Agreement," para. 21.
122 Ibid.
123 Cf. ibid., subheading for section IV, following para. 30.
124 Ibid. para. 34.
125 See above, p. 208.

the predominant form it has taken ever since its captivity to the Franco-Latins more than a thousand years ago. "Neither from the 7th century till 1054, nor since, have the Franco-Latin bishops and popes had the slightest knowledge of, or interest in, the cure of the human personality via the purification and illumination of the heart and glorification (theosis)."[126]

It is because of the doctrine of *theosis* and its alleged rejection by the Vatican that Romanides opposes use of the expression "sister churches" to describe relations between contemporary Orthodox churches and those of the Latin tradition in communion with the church of Old Rome. "This agreement," he writes, speaking of the Balamand Statement, "takes advantage of those naïve Orthodox who have been insisting that they are a 'Sister' Church of a Vatican 'Sister' Church, as though glorification *(theosis)* can have a sister otherwise than herself."[127] The same paragraph raises the question of Orthodox recognition of Roman Catholic sacraments.

> The Orthodox at Balamand fell into their own trap since this presupposes the validity of Latin sacraments. This is a strange phenomenon indeed since the Latins never believed that glorification in this life is the foundation of apostolic succession and the mysteries (sacraments) of and within the Body of Christ. Even today the Latins and the Protestants translate 1 Cor 12:26 as 'honored' instead of 'glorified.'[128]

Romanides suggests that Orthodox recognition of Catholic sacraments was long sought by the Catholic Church and was only obtained by deceptive means.[129] However, he actually avoids making an outright statement that the sacraments of the Roman Catholic Church are invalid. His remarks on this subject are of interest since they distinguish him from the authors of the letter from Mount Athos with whom, in other respects, he is substantially in agreement. About the question of sacramental reality inside and outside the Orthodox Church, Romanides writes:

> More important than the validity of mysteries is the question of who participates in them. Glorification is God's will for all, both in this life and in

---

126 Romanides, "Orthodox and Vatican Agreement," para. 23; cf. also para. 25.
127 Ibid. para. 26.
128 Ibid.
129 He writes, "But Vatican II had also set its trap of unilaterally recognizing Orthodox mysteries (sacraments) into which the Balamand Orthodox fell according to plan" (ibid. para. 27). Clearly, Romanides does not believe that Orthodox recognition of Catholic sacraments had any basis in Orthodox tradition itself, going back to the early Church.

Chapter 5: Orthodox Theological Reflecion on "Sister Churches"

the next life. But God's glory in Christ is eternal life for those who are properly cured and prepared. But this same uncreated glory of Christ is eternal fire for those who refuse to be cured. In other words mysteries can be valid and not participated in at the same time. As important as valid mysteries is purification and illumination of the heart and glorification in this life which are the central reality of the mysteries and in the participation in them. This holds true for non Orthodox and Orthodox equally.[130]

As will be seen later on, the idea that "mysteries can be valid and not participated in at the same time" has much in common with the sacramental theology of Georges Florovsky, who in turn drew upon Augustine.[131] Romanides' paper singles out Augustine for criticism at many points,[132] yet without ever mentioning the insights of Augustine related to the controversy with the Donatists and the question of baptism outside the visible unity of the Church. In his denial, at the beginning of the passage below, that there are sacraments outside the Body of Christ, it might seem that Romanides is denying non-Orthodox sacraments, but as the rest of the passage indicates, membership and non-membership in the Body of Christ do not fall neatly along Orthodox and non-Orthodox lines, in his view.

> Neither of these two means of entry into the Church [by "akribeia" or by "oikonomia"] is in itself a judgment on the validity or non-validity of the sacraments of the Church of origin, since there are no mysteries outside the Body of Christ. One is either a member of the Body of Christ by his baptism of the Spirit, i.e. illumination and/or glorification in Christ or one is still in the state of purification by his baptism by water unto forgiveness of sins and in the process of becoming a member of the Body of Christ and a temple of the Holy Spirit. One may be a believer in Christ without belonging to either of these categories. This holds true for nominal Orthodox also. It is up to each Synod of Orthodox bishops to decide the status of each group of those who are seeking communion within the Body of Christ.[133]

Although a number of issues are left unresolved in this passage, it conveys quite clearly the idea that Orthodox Christians themselves are potentially outside the Body of Christ, depending on their degree of real participation in the mysteries offered. At the same time, it is not taken for granted, either, that non-Orthodox Christians *must* be outside the Body of Christ. Rather, "the status of each

---

130 Romanides, "Orthodox and Vatican Agreement," para. 28.
131 See below, p. 230 and in Chapter 6, pp. 267-272.
132 Cf. Romanides, "Orthodox and Vatican Agreement," paras. 43-46.
133 Ibid. para. 39.

group" of non-Orthodox is to be discerned by the Orthodox bishops faced with the decision of how to receive them. The notion that there is a need for discernment in assessing the ecclesial status of those outside of canonical Orthodoxy recalls an insight of Meyendorff emphasized earlier.[134] Romanides' possible openness to the idea that *theosis* might occur in a non-Orthodox context is expressed again, if indirectly, when he writes: "[i]n regard to the cure of purification, illumination and glorification there is no difference between Latins and most Protestants since, or if, they are not engaged in this cure ... This holds true for nominal Orthodox also."[135] Rather than simply writing "since" they are not engaged in being deified, Romanides here writes "since, or if" they are not, thus leaving open the possibility that some in fact are engaged in it.

Romanides' possible openness to a reality of *theosis* among non-Orthodox Christians stands in marked contrast to his previously quoted comment summarily dismissing the idea held by some "naïve Orthodox," that "they are a 'Sister' Church of a Vatican 'Sister' Church, as though glorification *(theosis)* can have a sister otherwise than herself."[136] In that earlier comment, Romanides clearly identified the Orthodox Church as the one and only communion of *theosis*.

3. George D. Metallinos, and the Orthodox debate concerning non-Orthodox baptism

In 1983, George Metallinos, a priest in the Orthodox Church of Greece, published a book in Greek entitled Ὁμολογῶ ἓν βάπτισμα ("I profess one baptism"), which was translated into English and published in an expanded and slightly revised form in 1994 by St. Paul's Monastery on Mount Athos.[137] The book does not engage directly with the significance or legitimacy of the concept of sister churches. Its concern, as the parenthetical portion of the book's subtitle indicates, is with the question of the status of non-Orthodox sacraments, in particular the sacrament of baptism, from an Orthodox standpoint. The link between the evaluation of non-Orthodox sacraments and the recognition of a

---

134 See above, p. 186.
135 Romanides, "Orthodox and Vatican Agreement," para. 40.
136 See above, p. 214.
137 G. Metallinos, *I Confess One Baptism ...: Interpretation and Application of Canon VII of the Second Ecumenical Council by the Kollyvades and Constantine Oikonomos (A contribution to the historico-canonical evaluation of the problem of the validity of Western baptism)*, trans. Priestmonk Seraphim (Holy Mountain: St. Paul's Monastery, 1994).

non-Orthodox church as a sister church has been suggested at various points in this chapter,[138] and it is further confirmed by the fact that Metallinos himself makes extensive reference to the Balamand Statement in the Preface to the English Edition of his book published in 1994.

He contends that the Orthodox delegates to Balamand, by agreeing to Balamand's proposal of "mutual recognition of sacraments" between Orthodox and Catholics, were "seeking a de facto union with the Papacy."[139] The practice of (re)baptizing Roman Catholic converts to the Orthodox Church is one that Metallinos firmly supports, and his opposition to Balamand, centered as it is on Balamand's stance against such (re)baptism,[140] also entails an implicit opposition to Balamand's promotion of the idea that the Catholic and Orthodox churches are sister churches.

Metallinos describes his own understanding of the relationship between the objectives of his book and those of Balamand in the following way.

> I believe that this study ... offers a solution to the problem [of how to view non-Orthodox sacraments], a solution defended by our patristic tradition and faith. Especially today, it is necessary that we be well acquainted with this tradition, living as we do in the aftermath of the obscuration brought on by the unforgivable haste of certain ecclesiastical personalities on the subject of Ecumenism, and mainly in the area of relations with the Latin Church (which is identical with the "Vatican State"), due to the interference, once again, of purely secular criteria in the so-called "Ecumenical Dialogue." This trend led to the recent decision of the Seventh Plenary Session of the Joint International Commission for the official Theological Dialogue between Catholics and Orthodox (Balamand, Lebanon, 17-24 July 1993). In no uncertain terms, the delegates from the nine Orthodox Churches represented at this meeting ... propose to their Churches the mutual recognition of sacraments, ignoring Ecumenical Councils, dogma, and history, and thus seeking a de facto union with the Papacy.
>
> It is nothing unusual, then, that the Greek-language Uniate newspaper *Katholike* emphasizes paragraph 13 of the Balamand [Declaration] which ends as follows: "It is clear that within this framework, *any re-baptism is excluded* ...". Of course, the theologically correct response to this is that the Orthodox Church, on the basis of her self-understanding, does not *re*-baptize non-Orthodox converts, but canonically *baptizes* them as having never received the one and canonical baptism of the Church. This, anyway, is the response of the [18th century] writers whose testimony we invoke in the present study. Aside from

---

138 See above, pp. 186, 188, 192, 197-198, 209.
139 Metallinos, *I Confess One Baptism* ..., 12.
140 Cf. "Uniatism, Method of Union of the Past," paras. 13-14.

all this, any chance recognition of Latin sacraments (and primarily of Holy Orders) on our part notwithstanding leads to the rejection of our whole ecclesiology, of the Ecumenical Councils, and, in a word, of patristic theology (on the basis of which there exist no sacraments amongst the Latins who still, in fact, speak about *"gratia creata"*).[141]

From this passage several points might be singled out for notice, including the assumption (which was that of Romanides as well) that Balamand was warmly welcomed by Eastern Catholics,[142] and – on a more theological plane – the implication that the Western doctrine of "created grace" is of such central importance and stands in such direct opposition to the authentic apostolic faith as to render the Roman Catholic Church (which still "speaks of" the doctrine) altogether devoid of sacramental reality.[143] However, the main point in the passage that calls for close examination is Metallinos' view that the Orthodox tradition in its entirety ("our whole ecclesiology") is opposed to recognizing Roman Catholic sacraments.

The debate within Orthodoxy over the status of non-Orthodox sacraments occupies a place in this chapter analogous to the place occupied in the previous chapter by the Catholic debates over the relationship between the local church and the universal church and over "subsists in". The stance of Orthodox writers on non-Orthodox sacraments relates no less closely to their understanding of "sister churches" than does the stance of Catholic writers on those other two issues. Indeed it seems that the correlation in this case is even clearer and more direct. No Orthodox author who denies that there is sacramental reality in the Roman Catholic Church accepts the language of sister churches to describe relations between the Orthodox and Catholic churches. Metallinos, as has been said, does not actually say anything about the language of sister churches, but his stance on non-Orthodox baptism is the stance of virtually all Orthodox authors who do speak out against the language of sister churches, and he

---

141 Metallinos, *I Confess One Baptism* ..., 11-13.

142 In fact, as Erickson has indicated, it was generally received much more positively by Orthodox than by Eastern Catholics in the regions where friction between the two groups was greatest. See above, pp. 195-196.

143 Interestingly, in the section of his book that comes under the heading, "Latins are 'heretics' and 'unbaptized'" (66-70), there is nothing about the doctrine of created grace. One of the writers of the period on whom Metallinos focuses, Neophytos Kafsokalyvitis (1713-1784), rector from 1749 of the Athonias School on Mount Athos, is quoted as having said, "The Latins differ from Orthodoxy on five points. As regards the other [four] differences, they are schismatics. Only as regards the Spirit's procession also from the Son are they heretics" (Metallinos, *I Confess One Baptism* ..., 67).

explicates this position on non-Orthodox baptism in a far more thorough way than the others do; hence the inclusion of his work in this study.

An overview of the history of the problem of non-Orthodox baptism may be given as follows: The ancient canons did not all seem to say the same thing on the subject. Some, such as Canon 7 of Laodicea (360 AD), Canon 1 of St. Basil (378 AD) and Canon 7 of Constantinople I (381 AD), drew distinctions among various types of groups separated from the visible unity of the Church. (Re)baptism was required of converts from some groups, but not from others. According to St. Basil, schismatics as a general rule were not to be (re)baptized, while heretics were;[144] but this terminological distinction was sometimes blurred in the canons, which came increasingly to describe all separated groups as heretical and to draw a distinction between more and less severe forms of heresies. Converts from the less severely heretical groups – and even Arians and Apollinarians were among the "less severe" heretics, e.g. according to Canon 7 of Constantinople I[145] – were to be received by anointing with chrism, rather than by (re)baptism.

However, another set of canons made no distinction between more and less severe types of heresies, and simply called for the (re)baptism of all heretics. Canon 46 of the so-called Apostolic Canons states: "We order that a bishop or presbyter that recognized the baptism or sacrifice of heretics be defrocked."[146] Canon 1 of St. Cyprian (the Council of Carthage, 258 AD) went even farther in what it laid down: "Decreeing now also by vote what we firmly and securely hold for all time, we declare that no one can possibly be baptized outside the catholic Church, there being but one baptism, and this existing only in the catholic Church." In the Byzantine period, medieval canonists like Zonaras and

---

144 See the relevant portion of the presentation of Erickson above, 198-199.
145 Canon 7 of Constantinople I begins, "As for heretics who convert to Orthodoxy ...", and proceeds to offer an initial list, comprised of those to be received not by baptism but merely "when they submit written statements, and anathematize every heresy that does not believe as the holy, catholic, and Apostolic Church of God believes, and are first sealed with holy Myron." It includes on this list Arians and Apollinarists. A second list follows, of those to be received "as pagans" and to be baptized; here are included Eunomians ("who are baptized with one immersion") and Montanists (who also did not baptize in the name of the Trinity).
146 In the 9th century, Theodore Studite would interpret even this Apostolic Canon as making a distinction implicitly among varying types of separated groups and as calling "heretics" only those who are either not baptized at all or not baptized in the name of the Trinity. Cf. Erickson, "Divergencies in Pastoral Practice in the Reception of Converts," 161.

Balsamon saw a canon such as this, in spite of its inclusion among the canons sanctioned by an ecumenical council retroactively,[147] as having less weight than canons which were actually *issued* by ecumenical councils themselves: thus for Zonaras and Balsamon, the stipulation to (re)baptize all converts was not binding.[148] Theirs was indeed the predominant view. Even so stalwart a defender of the Orthodox faith as Mark of Ephesus, who opposed ratification of the union between East and West at the council of Florence, and was unabashed in calling the Latins heretics, testified to reception by chrismation as the "universal practice" of the East in receiving western converts. The same practice was stipulated by the 1484 council of Constantinople. Nonetheless, indications of a different approach at various points in the Eastern tradition can also be found – for example, in complaints from the West, e.g. from Humbert in the 11th century and later at the Lateran Council (1215), that the Orthodox were (re)baptizing Latin converts (though that was not official policy)[149] in the decision of 1620 of the Moscow Patriarchate insisting on (re)baptism of Roman Catholic converts (though this was overturned in 1667)[150] and most notably of all – especially since it has yet to be revoked – in the 1755 decree of Cyril V of Constantinople, entitled *A Definition of the Holy Church of Christ defending the Holy Baptism given from God, and spitting upon the baptisms of the heretics which are otherwise administered.*

This 1755 *Definition*, together with its vigorous defense in the 18th and 19th centuries, forms the subject of the book by Metallinos, himself a supporter of the decree. He focuses on the work of a half dozen writers from the period, the earliest being Eustratios Argenti, who may have had a hand in writing the actual *Definition*[151] and who was, in any case, the author of a treatise published in the heat of the controversy, called *Manual on Baptism* (1754 or 1755).[152] Four other 18th century writers of somewhat later vintage who drew on Argenti's work to a considerable degree were part of a monastic movement known at the time as the *Kollyvades*. The most renowned of the *Kollyvades* was St. Nikodemos of the Holy Mountain (1749-1809), the principal compositor of the *Philo-*

---

147 Cf. Trullo canon 2.
148 Cf. Erickson, "On the Cusp of Modernity," 55, citing PG 137, 1096-1097, 1104.
149 See Timothy (now Metropolitan Kallistos) Ware, *Eustratios Argenti* (Oxford: Clarendon, 1964), 66.
150 See Ware, *Eustratios Argenti*, 83.
151 Cf. ibid. 61.
152 For the question of the date, see Ware, *Eustratios Argenti*, 60-61; for extensive bibliographical information, see ibid. 76.

kalia and the author of, among numerous other works, the massive *Pedalion (The Rudder)*, a compilation of the canons of the Eastern Church, accompanied by his own commentaries.[153] Besides Nikodemos, the other three *Kollyvades* who wrote in support of Cyril's 1755 *Definition* on baptism were Neophytos Kafsokalyvitis (1713-1784), Saint Makarios (1731-1805), and Athanasios Parios (1722-1813). In addition, Metallinos quotes extensively from the work of a writer from the following century, Constantine Oikonomos (1780-1857), who also wrote on the subject of Latin baptism and whose views closely correspond to those of the *Kollyvades* and Argenti.

What follows is a summary of the main lines of argument set forth by these authors in their defense of the 1755 *Definition* with its condemnation of all non-Orthodox baptism. They were well aware of the apparent inconsistency between the *Definition* and much of the earlier canonical witness of the Orthodox East in how converts had been received from the Latin West since the schism and, prior to that, from groups deemed heretical like the Arians and Appolinarians. How they explained the apparent inconsistency was by means of three interwoven lines of argument, one hermeneutical, another pastoral and ecclesiastical, the third historical. Underlying and conditioning all of them was a deeper set of ecclesiological presuppositions, as I shall show.

Their hermeneutical move had to do with their interpretation of canons at variance with one another. Instead of giving priority, as Zonaras and Balsamon and others had done, to texts like canon 7 of Constantinople I and canon 95 of the Quinisext Council (Trullo) which ruled that certain converts be received by anointing with chrism, over texts like canon 46 of the Apostolic Canons or Canon 1 of St. Cyprian which called for (re)baptism of all converts,[154] the *Kollyvades* and those of like mind with them reversed this priority. They spoke of the Apostolic Canons – which in fact were a fourth-century compilation – as being literally set down by the apostles themselves, and they gave precedence also to Cyprian's council, though it was a local council, over ecumenical councils that came later.[155]

---

153 For a bibliography of St Nikodemos' works see C. Cavarnos, *St Nicodemos the Hagiorite* (Belmont, MA: Institute for Byzantine and Modern Greek Studies, 1974).

154 Metallinos, *I Confess One Baptism* ..., 51. The quotation from Zonaras is found in PG 137, 1103.

155 John Erickson observes that Nikodemos' reading of the canonical corpus was at odds with how it had otherwise been interpreted in the East. "In the early and Byzantine periods, texts that insist on rebaptizing all heretics (Cyprian's council of 256 AD or the Apostolic Canons) either were ignored or were interpreted in the light of St Basil

It was still necessary, however, to explain why the Church had ever promulgated canons that prescribed a different rule for receiving non-Orthodox converts than the allegedly earliest and most authoritative canons had laid down – that is, the "strict" ones with which the 1755 *Definition* was in conformity. The anomaly of Canon VII, for example, of the second ecumenical council (Constantinople I, 381 AD), which gave a positive evaluation of schismatic and even heretical baptism so long as it was performed in a Trinitarian manner,[156] was one that the *Kollyvades* were keen to account for.[157]

Their explanation, which had a pastoral and ecclesiastical character, came in the form of the famous theory of sacramental economy articulated, first, by Argenti, and in a more elaborate way, by Nikodemos. According to this theory, the Church acts sometimes by enforcing the strict rule *(akribeia)* and at other times by exercising leniency *(economia)*. Why at any particular moment it acts according to one mode or the other has to do with what it discerns to be best for the Church in the given circumstances. The dogmatic vision remains the same in either case, even where pastoral discipline may be relaxed.

As to the irregularity of Canon 7 of Constantinople I, specifically, and all the canonical decisions of the second millennium that were similar to it – such as the ruling of Constantinople in 1484 – accepting Latin converts by mere anointing with chrism, these were to be explained by the fact that the Church had been in too weak a position to risk inflaming the heretical group in question by openly denying the validity of its baptism. Nikodemos, for example, operating with the assumption that early on in the second millennium the Orthodox did (re)baptize the Latins, argued that "later they [the Orthodox of the 15th century and thereafter] used the chrism method, for it was not good, given the utter weakness of our nation, to further excite the fury of the Papacy."[158]

---

canon 1, I Constantinople 'canon 7,' Trullo canon 95, and the many other texts that make a distinction between heretics properly so-called and those 'whose separation admits of a remedy.' The *Pedalion* systematically reverses this perspective. According to St Nikodemos, the position represented by the Apostolic Canons and Cyprian was that of the universal ancient church and of the fathers generally ... [I]t was to be regarded as normative for all ages" (Erickson, "On the Cusp of Modernity," 59-60).

156 Cf. P. Schaff and H. Wace, *NPNF* (2nd ser.), vol. 14, 185. Canon XCV of the sixth ecumenical council is very similar.

157 Cf. Nicodemos, *Pedalion*, 53.

158 Nikodemos, *Pedalion*, 57, as quoted by Metallinos, *I Confess One Baptism* ..., 90-91. Cf. also the similar explanation of Athanasios Parios, Ὅτι οἱ ἀπὸ Λατινῶν ἐπιστρέφοντες ἀναντιρρήτως, ἀπαραιτήτως καὶ ἀναγχαίως πρέπει νὰ βαπτίζωνται, καὶ Ἐπιτομὴ ... τῶν θείων τῆς πίστεως δογμάτων ... *(That Latin converts must indisput-*

Of course with the 1755 *Definition*, the exercise of *economia* (the "chrism method") was set aside again in favor of *akribeia* (strictly applying the requirement to be (re)baptized).[159] What had changed? Here the historical line of argument enters in. The writers on whom Metallinos draws suggest that during the period when *economia* was exercised by the Church, the Latin West had still been administering the sacrament of baptism in a manner that was formally correct, but that a defective form had since become widespread. The historical view of the *Kollyvades* was, as Metallinos summarizes it, that "up until the Council of Trent (16th cen.) – and even up until the eighteenth century – 'the Apostolic form' of baptism also survived in the West."[160] By the middle of the 18th century, they said, this was no longer the case.[161]

How Latin baptism had come to be, as they believed, formally defective, was that it had ceased to be administered by immersion. In the 12th and 13th centuries in the West, baptism by immersion (whether total or partial) increasingly gave way to baptism by affusion or infusion (with water poured over the forehead), or aspersion (sprinkling).

As well as on this historical argument, the *Kollyvades* based their stance on defective form on yet another hermeneutical move related to the ancient canons. They interpreted one of these canons in particular, namely Apostolic Canon 50, in such a way that its definition of formally defective baptism might be seen as applying to Latin baptism by affusion or aspersion. This is indeed the assumption of the 1755 *Definition* itself, which states: "we follow the sacred and divine Apostles who order us to baptize aspirants with three immersions ... and in each immersion to say one name of the Holy Trinity." The allusion is to

---

ably, indispensably and necessarily be baptized, and Digest ... of the Divine Dogmas of the Faith) (Leipzig 1806), quoted by Metallinos, *I Confess One Baptism* ..., 91, and of Neophytos Kafsokalyvitis, Ἐπιτομὴ τῶν Ἱερῶν Κανόνων (Digest of the Sacred Canons) (unpublished), quoted by Metallinos, *I Confess One Baptism* ..., 90.

159 The *Kollyvades* argued that the Orthodox Church was now protected from the West by its Ottoman overlords, but Ware convincingly shows how vulnerable the Orthodox East remained to Latin expansionism. See below, pp. 228-229.
160 Metallinos, *I Confess One Baptism* ..., 87.
161 In its essential form, this line of argument also goes back to Argenti. The entire purpose of his *Manual on Baptism* had been to expose what Argenti called "the false baptism (ψευδοβάπτισμα) used by the westerners of the present time" (E. Argenti, *Manual on Baptism*, 6-7, quoted by Ware, *Eustratios Argenti*, 90) and to show, as Ware puts it, "that the defects and corruptions of Latin Baptism are such as to place it outside the scope of any lawful application of economy" (Ware, *Eustratios Argenti*, 90) – just as the *Kollyvades* were keen to demonstrate.

Canon 50 of the Apostolic Canons, according to which, "If any bishop or presbyter does not perform the one initation with three immersions, but with giving one immersion only, into the death of the Lord, let him by deposed."[162] Of course, this canon could not be applied very naturally to the case of Latin baptism, which was faulted by the Orthodox not for immersing the initiate only once, but for carrying out a threefold *affusion* or *aspersion* instead of a threefold *immersion*. Nevertheless the *Definition* seeks to include Latin baptism under the condemnation given by this canon, as also under the condemnations found in canon 7 of Constantinople I and canon 95 of the Quinisext Council (Trullo), "which order us to receive as unbaptized those aspirants to Orthodoxy who were not baptized with three immersions ... and in each immersion did not loudly invoke one of the divine hypostases, but were baptized in some other fashion."[163] The *Kollyvades* read these canons as if they were really concerned with the distinction between immersion and affusion more than – or at least as much as – the distinction between one and three.

To summarize what has been presented thus far of the position of the 1755 *Definition*'s defenders: (1) the ancient canons requiring (re)baptism of converts from *all* schismatic and heretical groups take precedence over those canons that allowed converts from some such groups to be received by mere chrismation; (2a) the fact that there were any canons at all of the latter type is attributable to the pastoral nature of the Church and its legitimate authority to exercise leniency, or *economia*, in certain circumstances; (2b) the specific circumstances that occasioned its exercise in the case of reception of Latin heretics in the centuries when they were received without (re)baptism was the political weakness of the Church vis-à-vis the Latin West; (3a) why this leniency was even possible at all was that well into the 16th century, at least baptism was widely administered correctly in the West, by the criteria laid down in the "lenient" ancient canons; (3b) but Latin baptism is no longer even formally correct, according to those same criteria: for the ancient canons judged that baptism administered otherwise than by three immersions was formally defective (never mind that the actual target of those canons was clearly single-immersion baptism, not triple-aspersion baptism); thus it is necessary to (re)baptize Latin converts.[164]

---

162 Cf. P. Schaff and H. Wace, eds., *NPNF* (2nd ser.), vol. 14, *The Seven Ecumenical Councils* (Peabody, MA: Hendrickson, 1999), 597.

163 Metallinos, *I Confess One Baptism* ..., 135.

164 Florovsky would criticize this entire approach as dishonest and evasive of the real question of sacramental validity. Cf. Florovsky, "The Limits of the Church," *Church Quarterly Review* 11 (Oct. 1933), 117-133.

It remains now to consider what seems to have been the specific set of ecclesiological presuppositions which lay underneath all of the criss-crossing lines of argument indicated above. In a sense, the particulars of the arguments about *economia* and its limits, the reasons why it was exercised, and the formal defects of Latin baptism, turn out to be less decisive for the writers in question than do the deeper convictions they hold about the nature of the unity of the Church and the nature of the schism between Orthodox East and Catholic West.

In the 1755 *Definition*, rejection of non-Orthodox baptism is based not only on the issue of defective form. It is based as well on an ecclesiology in which there is a complete identification of the Orthodox Church with the one Church of Christ. In the following passage, this ecclesiological exclusivism is expressed in the clearest terms: "We, who by divine mercy were raised in the Orthodox Church, and who adhere to the canons of the sacred Apostles and divine Fathers, recognize only one Church, our holy, catholic, and Apostolic Church. It is her Mysteries, and consequently her baptism, that we accept."[165]

In North Africa around the turn of the 5th century the same line of argument was put forward by the Donatists, whose position Augustine sought to refute in his work *De Baptismo*.[166] The Donatists, for their part, relied on the ecclesiology of St. Cyprian as inscribed in the local council over which he had presided in Carthage in 256 AD. There, the problem with sacraments outside the visible unity of the Church had had nothing to do with how they were administered, but only with where or by whom: "we declare that no one can possibly be baptized outside the catholic Church, there being but one baptism, and this existing only in the catholic Church."[167]

The Cyprianic-Donatist position, and the 1755 *Definition*'s wholesale appropriation of it, is what Argenti, the *Kollyvades*, Oikonomos, and finally Metallinos himself seek to present as reflective of the normative ecclesiology of the Eastern tradition. The comment of Metallinos quoted earlier may be recalled: "Aside from all this, any chance recognition of Latin sacraments (and

---

165 Metallinos, *I Confess One Baptism* ..., 134.
166 Augustine of Hippo, *De baptismo contra Donatistas*. PL 43, 107-244. Translated by J.R. King, in P. Schaff, ed., *NPNF* (1st ser.), vol. 4 (Peabody, MA: Hendrickson, 1994), 411-514.
167 Canon I of St. Cyprian, as rendered in Appendix I of Metallinos, *I Confess One Baptism* ..., 122. For a slightly different translation, cf. "The Council of Carthage Held Under Cyprian, AD 257," in P. Schaff and H. Wace, eds., *NPNF* (2nd ser.), vol. 14, *The Seven Ecumenical Councils* (Peabody, MA: Hendrickson, 1999), 516-519, at 518.

primarily of Holy Orders) on our part notwithstanding leads to the rejection of our whole ecclesiology".[168] In the perception of Metallinos, "our whole ecclesiology" is precisely the ecclesiology of Cyprian, which was so clearly espoused by Cyril V, Argenti and the *Kollyvades* and "which, moreover, the entire Orthodox East followed as a rule," according to Metallinos. The effort to square this ecclesiology with the facts of the Eastern canonical tradition accounts for all of the elaborate argumentation put forward in defense of the 1755 *Definition*.

This argumentation finally begins to sink under its own weight. In addition to attributing the Church's leniency of previous centuries to political expediency, the *Kollyvades* occasionally mention another factor: namely, the notion that more Latins would be drawn to the Orthodox Church if (re)baptism was not required of them. According to Oikonomos again, Mark of Ephesus held that *economia* in the reception of Latin converts was exercised (while it was) not only to appease the brutal and aggressive West but also to "attract them to Orthodoxy."[169] Oikonomos presents *economia* in this light:

> If the Council deems it necessary for the Church in certain places (such as a large country comprised of many and diverse heretical ethnic groups),[170] for the sake of evangelical *economia*, to consent for a short time to something that ought not to be (as Evlogios once said), and opportunely exercises a certain concession towards those who come over from heresies when any of them sincerely desire to enter life, but become less willing because of the *acrivia* of the Canon; in any case, the Church of Christ shall do what is deemed best, inasmuch as her Bridegroom remains with her inseparably until the end of time. He it is who preserves the *acrivia* of the divine dogmas and sacraments blameless and unadulterated in her, and Who enlightens her and guides her in the exercise of *economia*, in the proper place and time, towards those who join from without.[171]

---

168 See above, p. 218.
169 Metallinos, I Confess One Baptism..., 92, quoting Oikonomos, Τὰ σωζόμενα ἐκκλησιαστικὰ συγγράμματα Κωνσταντίνου Πρεσβυτέρου καὶ Οἰκονόμου τοῦ ἐξ Οἰκονόμων (*The extant ecclesiastical writings of Constantine Presbyter and Oikonomos of the Okonomoi*, published by Soph. C. of the Oikonomoi), vol. I (Athens, 1862), 475.
170 The "Council" mentioned here is a theoretical one that was widely seen as necessary at the time in order to resolve the controversy over non-Orthodox baptism. (Cf. Metallinos, *I Confess One Baptism* ..., 111-113.) Oikonomos himself, like the *Kollyvades* before him, considered the issue effectively settled by the alleged rigor of the Fathers and the early canons and did not agree that it awaited synodal resolution. Yet for the sake of argument he did consider the scenario proposed by advocates of a Council to address the issue.
171 Oikonomos, 480, as quoted by Metallinos, *I Confess One Baptism* ..., 114.

The curious idea set forth here is that although, in reality, Latins have not been baptized, they may be more apt to convert to Orthodoxy if this unfortunate fact of their prior life as Latin Christians is not insisted upon. As may be expected, this particular justification of *economia* has received some of the sharpest criticism from those Orthodox who have serious reservations to begin with about the theory of sacramental economy.[172] Oikonomos was not alone, in any case, in advancing the idea that the strict requirement of (re)baptism might impede some conversions to the Church of Christ from heretical groups. According to Nikodemos, one of the reasons why the Fathers of the Second Ecumenical Council used leniency to admit some kinds of heretics into the Church without (re)baptizing them was "in order to attract them to Orthodoxy and to correct them more easily".[173]

Interestingly, the matter is put entirely the other way around by one of the other *Kollyvades*, Neophytos, who insists that the salvation of heretics and their incentive for entering the Orthodox Church would be undermined if the requirement that they be (re)baptized were relaxed. Neophytos writes that the baptism of heretical groups "is not capable of providing remission of sins," and that converts from such groups must therefore be baptized without exception. He goes on: "For if it does provide [remission of sins], then they join the Church for no reason, and the heretics who do not join hear this."[174]

In this brief remark – which is, according to Metallinos, one that Neophytos "correctly adds" – two points are made: (1) heretical baptism cannot effect remission of sins; (2) if it could there would be nothing pulling those outside the Church back into its fold. The grammatical transition ("for if ... then") suggests that for Neophytos the second of the two points was paramount. In other words, because it is unthinkable that those outside the Church should have the pressure on them to return to it removed, it cannot be allowed that their baptism *extra ecclesiam* is capable of remitting sins.

Instead of the usual argument of the *Kollyvades* marked by what Oikonomos called "evangelical *economia*," with *economia* (anointing with chrism) seen as easing the way for heretics to rejoin the Church and thus be saved, exactly the opposite argument, marked by what might be called "evangelical *akreibia*," is advanced, suggesting that only the strict application of the alleged canonical

---

172 See especially Florovsky, "The Limits of the Church," op. cit.
173 Nikodemos, *Pedalian*, 53, as quoted by Metallinos, *I Confess One Baptism* ..., 54. The other reason was the standard one (political *economia*) usually given: "so that it might not happen that they further infuriate them against the Church".
174 Neophytos, 147, as quoted by Metallinos, *I Confess One Baptism* ..., 39, n. 41.

requirement ([re]baptism) would bring heretics back in. Nor is it that the two different arguments simply have their proper applications in different times and places. It is rather that with respect to one and the same situation, diametrically opposed views of whether *economia* or *akreibia* will better contribute to the "salvation of souls" are offered. If nothing else, this suggests at least a certain improbability about the theory of sacramental economy altogether.

The basis of the theory is further undermined when its use by the *Kollyvades* is compared to an idea put forward by Ware, which directly conflicts with what the 18th century writers typically said. Ware suggests that the open and rigid denial by Cyril V of the sacramental reality of Latin baptism had to do, not so much with any particular zeal to bring Roman Catholics into Orthodoxy, as with the desire to keep Orthodox people from going over to Rome.[175] He mentions the inroads made not many years earlier by Latin missionaries in the once exclusively Orthodox sees of Antioch and Alexandria, and the fears of a crypto-Roman party establishing itself in Constantinople.

> Cyril was therefore anxious at all costs to curtail Roman Catholic influence in his Patriarchate and to prevent further infiltration by the Latins. Such must have been the end which he had in view when he declared Latin Baptism entirely invalid. He wanted ... to make it absolutely clear to his flock that the Orthodox Church, and it alone, was the true Church of Christ. Surely prospective converts would reflect more carefully before seceding to Rome, if it were forcibly emphasized that the Orthodox Catholic Church was the sole treasury of valid sacraments ... Faced by Latin encroachments and infiltration, Cyril answered by setting up a wall of partition between Orthodoxy and the west. Aware of his weakness on the temporal level, he took refuge in an inflexible and uncompromising assertion of the spiritual claim of the Orthodox Church to be the exclusive possessor of Baptism.[176]

Nowhere in the study by Metallinos is it suggested that the strict stance of rejecting Latin baptism as no baptism might itself have been conditioned by the political *weakness* of the Orthodox East relative to the Latin West. Always, in Metallinos' presentation, weakness on the temporal plane is associated with *economia*, strength with *akribeia*. Ware, however, introduces the idea of what may be called "political *akribeia*". According to this conception, the Orthodox

---

175 The same view is expressed, in fact, by the authors of the letter from Mount Athos. "Orthodoxy was obliged to declare that truth [viz., that Latins were heretics and their sacraments void], not for purposes of proselytism but in order to protect the flock" (see above, p. 206).

176 Ware, *Eustratios Argenti*, 79-80.

East rejects Latin baptism (or appears to reject it), not from genuine theological conviction, or at least not purely so,[177] but as a means of self-protection against western imperialism and uniatism.

On the whole, the theory of sacramental economy represents a boldly creative but ultimately unsuccessful attempt to reconcile or harmonize the historical and canonical data, unsuccessful because riddled with too many internal inconsistencies. It cannot be said to tie together in a satisfactory way the loose ends contained in the Eastern tradition of receiving converts from outside the visible unity of the Church. The alternative certainly cannot be to conclude – simply because there are such loose ends – that the issue must be somehow irresolvable. Rather, the attempt must be made anew to arrive at a satisfactory resolution of this topic of ongoing ambiguity in Orthodox ecclesiology.

One possible path toward that end, to be explored in Chapter 6, is an approach that is effectively a *via media* between, on the one hand, the exclusivist ecclesiology of the critics of "sister churches" and, on the other, the ecclesiological relativism that they decry, and that they associate with the so-called Branch Theory.[178] Such an approach that manages to steer clear of both

---

177 Ware goes out of his way to say that the position of Cyril V on Latin baptism was and can be supported by meaningful theological argument, but even when he makes that point, he does not entirely clarify whether, in his own view, the politics might not still have driven the theology to an excessive degree. He writes: "[T]o treat the whole incident simply as a matter of ecclesiastical politics would be a grave injustice to Cyril V and Eustratios Argenti. Certainly Cyril had practical motives for condemning Latin Baptism, but his action was *not merely* a piece of religious opportunism, for he *could also* defend it on serious theological grounds" (Ware, *Eustratios Argenti*, 80; emphasis added).

178 In its classical form, the Branch Theory, chiefly conceived by the Oxford theologian William Palmer (1803-1885) in his two-volume *Treatise on the Church of Christ* (London and New York, 1841), holds, in the summary definition given by F.L. Cross & E.A. Livingstone, eds., *The Oxford Dictionary of the Christian Church*, 3rd edition (Peabody, MA: Hendrickson, 1997), 232, that "though the Church may have fallen into schism within itself and its several provinces or groups of provinces be out of communion with each other, each may yet be a branch of the one Church of Christ, provided that it continues to hold the faith of the original undivided Church, and to maintain the apostolic succession of its bishops. Such, it is contended by many Anglican theologians, is the condition of the Church at the present time, there being now three main branches, the Roman, the Eastern, and the Anglican Communions." The principal shortcoming of the Branch Theory is that it does not insist on the restoration of full communion among the separated branches or account for the possi-

exclusivism and relativism may be discerned in the reflections of the 20th century Orthodox theologian Georges Florovsky (1893-1979). Florovsky holds an unusual place as an authority in matters relating to Orthodox ecclesiology in that he is one of the few modern writers to whose work appeal is regularly made by both hard-line "traditionalists" and broad-minded "ecumenists". Erickson touches on the paradoxical place of Florovsky in recent Orthodox thought on schismatic or heretical baptism when he observes that anti-Balamand authors, including those from Mount Athos, cite Florovsky with approval, yet "without noting ... that he was an outspoken opponent of the economic approach to sacramental theology and the exclusivist ecclesiology which they present as true Orthodoxy."[179] Florovsky unequivocally identified the Orthodox Church as the one true Church of Christ, but did so in such a way that did not exclude the possibility that ecclesial and sacramental reality might also be found outside its canonical boundaries. Like Papandreou, he espoused a version of the idea of the *ecclesia extra ecclesiam*, and, while acknowledging the power and clarity of Cyprian's thought, and the evidence of some Cyprianic inclinations in Orthodox ecclesiology, he nevertheless insisted that contemporary Orthodoxy must articulate its understanding of non-Orthodox sacraments on the basis of the thought of Augustine, whose distinction between "validity" and "efficacy" he regarded as essentially compatible with Orthodox theology. In Chapter 6, Florovsky's reflections on the topic of non-Orthodox baptism will be shown to provide a theologically cogent basis for describing the Orthodox and Catholic churches as sister churches, without compromising the doctrine of the unicity of the Church.

4. Archbishop Dmitri Royster of Dallas

Archbishop Dmitri Royster, only the second convert consecrated to the Orthodox episcopate in America, is the author of several books on the teachings, parables, and miracles of Christ.[180] In September, 1994, Royster sent a four-page, single-spaced letter to Metropolitan Theodosius, then the primate of the Orthodox Church in America, responding to a synodal request of his fellow OCA bishops asking him to provide an evaluation of the theological implications of the Balamand Statement.

---

bility that full communion might never be restored. See below, Chapter 6, pp. 267, 273-275.
179 Erickson, "Concerning the Balamand Statement," 43.
180 Archbishop Dmitri (Royster), *The Miracles of Christ* (Crestwood, NY: St. Vladimir's Seminary Press, 1999).

After more than a page of factual description of the Balamand document and the conflicting accounts of why six Orthodox churches did not participate in the plenary session that produced it, Royster offers a number of comments critical of the text's ecclesiology as he understands it. First, he objects to the idea expressed in Balamand's paragraph 10 that it was in reaction to the soteriological exclusivism of the post-Tridentine Catholic Church that Orthodoxy came to hold that salvation could be obtained only in the Orthodox Church. "The fact is that the Orthodox Church's consciousness of being the one true Holy Catholic and Apostolic Church to which salvation was entrusted did not develop as a reaction to the Unia, but was always the position of the Orthodox Church."[181] Royster's observation here echoes that of the authors of the letter from Mount Athos made public in December of the preceding year.[182]

Royster sees the most problematic aspect of the Balamand Statement to be its use of the language of sister churches to characterize relations between Orthodox and Catholic churches.

> It is when we come to paragraph #12 that the major objectionable portions of the document begin. Even though uniatism ... is declared to be "no longer accepted either as a method to be followed nor as a model of unity our Churches are seeking," it is on the basis of a consideration by both Catholics and Orthodox of each other "in relationship to the mystery of the Church," and "the discovery of each other 'once again' as Sister Churches," that this uniatism is now outmoded. It is inconceivable that the Orthodox, especially the bishops, priests and teachers, should agree to describe a Church that is not in total doctrinal agreement with her as a "Sister Church." The only Sister Churches for an Orthodox Church are the other Orthodox Churches. To promote such

---

181 Archbishop Dmitri of Dallas and the South, *Letter of September 23, 1994 to His Beatitude, Theodosius, Archbishop of Washington and Metropolitan of All America and Canada* (obtained through the archives of the Chancery of the Orthodox Church in America, Syosset, NY), 2. Mention of Archbishop Dmitri's letter and a substantial quotation from it appear in the monthly publication (issued by the Saint Edward Brotherhood of Surrey, England), *The Shepherd: An Orthodox Christian Pastoral Magazine* (vol. 16, issue 4 [Jan. 1996], 22), in which the statement is made that the letter "has recently been published in 'Orthodox Christian Witness'," the reference here being to a periodical published by an Old Calendarist Greek Orthodox community in Washington state. My efforts to obtain (or even identify) the back issue of *Orthodox Christian Witness* in which Archbishop Dmitri's letter would have appeared were unsuccessful. The item from *The Shepherd* was subsequently printed in *Sourozh: A Journal of Orthodox Life and Thought* 63 (Feb. 1996), 52.

182 See above, p. 206.

an understanding of the Roman Catholic Church, without its correcting itself, is to contradict and to betray the Fathers who have defended Orthodoxy against Papism, the Filioque, the immaculate conception, their doctrine of grace, and other crucial distortions.[183]

It is especially instructive to compare this passage with the views of Meyendorff, who also insisted that there could be no union of the Orthodox and Catholic churches without first resolving their dogmatic differences which, he suggested, involved not just a healthy pluralism of theological perspectives but actual contradiction.[184] In this sense, he shared with Royster a firm commitment to unity of faith as a prerequisite for full communion. At the same time, he, unlike Royster, saw positive value in the language of sister churches in the bilateral dialogue. Meyendorff was keenly aware of and encouraged by the shift that the expression "sister churches" represented *for Catholic ecclesiology*, a shift from a universalist ecclesiology very much at odds with Orthodox tradition to a communion ecclesiology far more compatible with it. Royster makes no mention of that shift. It is, of course, possible that he was simply ignorant of such details in the internal life of the Catholic Church, but a likelier explanation is that he saw too many impediments to the authentic union of the Orthodox Church and the Roman Catholic Church to consider improvement in this one area as reason for hope. Meyendorff, it may be recalled, did not count the *filioque* among the western doctrines necessarily in essential conflict with Orthodox theology; and he said nothing of the western doctrine of grace. Altogether, his list of truly fundamental doctrinal issues in need of resolution is considerably shorter than Royster's, which indeed extends to unspecified "other crucial distortions". Royster's list also extends back farther in time than does Meyendorff's list, which mainly concerns issues that hardened into dogma from the 19th century on. Royster shares the presupposition of the Athonite monks and of Metallinos that there has been a profound theological chasm between Orthodox East and Catholic West ever since the schism.[185] The relative widening or narrowing of the chasm can make little difference if its immensity is such as to make it effectively unbridgeable in any case.

---

183 Archbishop Dmitri, *Letter of September 23, 1994 to His Beatitude, Theodosius*, 2.
184 See above, pp. 185-186.
185 Metallinos commends that segment of Orthodoxy which, represented by Cyril V and the *Kollyvades* (and "standing its ground even today" among those Orthodox who reject Latin baptism), "sees the differences between Roman Catholicism and Orthodoxy in their real dimensions, i.e. not as mere ritual and administrative differentiations, but as buoys indicating the deep alteration which the Christian truth has sustained in the regions of the papal West." (Metallinos, *I Confess One Baptism* ..., 106.)

Royster's assertion in the passage above that the only sister churches for an Orthodox church are the other Orthodox churches overlooks – as the Athonite monks also did in their letter – the fact that the 12th century Byzantines Nicetas and Camateros invoked the phrase in spite of the division between East and West. Their identification of their own church as the one Church of Christ professed in the creed did not prevent their recognizing the Latin church as still truly church as well, whereas for Royster, it is an exclusive identification indeed. After quoting Balamand's paragraph 13 in which the rediscovery of the Church as communion is connected with the recognition on both sides "that what Christ has entrusted to His Church ... cannot be considered the exclusive property of [either] one of our Churches," Royster offers the following comment:

> One is led to ask if by "the Church as communion," Orthodox and Roman Catholics mean the same thing. What are we to do[186] with the Fathers and the councils which indeed considered the things that Christ entrusted to His Church the exclusive property of the One Holy Catholic Apostolic Orthodox Church? Will we simply ignore them, declare that they were mistaken, or boast that we at the end of the 20th century have some better understanding of the issues involved? Do we indeed have the same concepts as the Roman Catholics of the Mysteries, the celebration of the one sacrifice of Christ and the apostolic succession of bishops? There is a glaring difference in the last mentioned matter ...[187].

Notable is Royster's addition of the name "Orthodox" into the creedal expression for the one Church of God, much as Pius XII in *Mystici corporis* described this same Church of God as "holy, catholic, apostolic, and Roman".[188] Also striking is an apparent disregard for the fact that communion ecclesiology was hardly something foisted on the Orthodox by Catholic members of the dialogue but something generally understood as characteristic of the East in its approach

---

186 The coincidence of language between Royster's rhetorical question, "What are we to do ...?" and the description given by Waclaw Hryniewicz of "ecumenical aporetics" (see Chapter 4 above, pp. 136-138), "We do not know what to do ...", seems to be worth pondering. Of course in Royster's case there is no true "aporia" associated with the idea of "sister churches" in Orthodox-Catholic relations, precisely because for him there is no real uncertainty about what to do.

187 Archbishop Dmitri, *Letter of September 23, 1994 to His Beatitude, Theodosius*, 3.

188 *Mystici corporis* 13. See Chapter 4 above, p. 157. The authors of the letter from Mount Athos also, like Royster, make the terminological move of conjoining the name of the one Church professed in the Creed to the name of the Orthodox Church when they write of "the One, Holy, Catholic, and Apostolic, in other words Orthodox, Church" (*Letter to the Patriarch of Constantinople*, 28). See above, p. 210, n. 108.

to the nature and structure of the Church. The impression is given once again that Royster is incognizant of, or at least unimpressed by, the considerable challenges that had to be overcome on the Catholic side in order for *them* to resolve "what *they* were to do" about a formidable tradition of their own of considering the things that Christ entrusted to His Church *their* exclusive property.

With respect to paragraphs 12 to 14 in the Balamand Statement, Royster writes:

> If the principles stated in the above three paragraphs were to be accepted by the Orthodox, there would be no obstacle to entering into communion with the Roman Catholics. On the other hand, the primary goal of the theological dialogue must be what is stated in the following paragraph (#15): "a full accord on the content of the faith and its implications." There is only one way to achieve this accord: the return of the Roman Catholic Church to the faith of the Apostolic Church, that is, the faith of the Orthodox Church. To enter into communion before this is accomplished is unthinkable.[189]

With apostolicity preserved on just one side of the division, the dialogue can serve no constructive purpose but to bring about the return of the Roman Catholic Church to the true faith of the Orthodox Church. The exchange of gifts is not merely disproportionate, with one side capable of contributing much more and the other much less; it is exclusively in one direction. Royster takes a similar approach in his response to the idea in Balamand's paragraph 30 that future priests of both traditions should be educated in such a way that will "lead to an awareness that faults leading to separation belong to both sides"[190]. He complains, "Thus, the Orthodox priests of the future would be obliged to recognize that the Orthodox Church was as much to blame for the schism as the Roman Catholics, without any reference to the doctrinal distortions of Rome."[191] Balamand itself did not say that blame was to be apportioned equally, only that there was some measure of responsibility on both sides. But in order for even that to be acknowledged, it would seem that one would have to concur with the basic premise of Congar, with which Meyendorff and Aghiorgoussis both express agreement, that the schism was the result of a gradual estrangement. Royster is of the rather different view that full-blown doctrinal distortions in the Latin church were what precipitated the schism. Thus, whereas Meyendorff

---

189 Archbishop Dmitri, *Letter of September 23, 1994 to His Beatitude, Theodosius*, 3.
190 "Uniatism, Method of Union of the Past," para. 30.
191 Archbishop Dmitri, *Letter of September 23, 1994 to His Beatitude, Theodosius*, 3.

indicated that the East shouldered at least some responsibility for the schism,[192] and that between the "quarreling sisters" there was not merely right all on one side and wrong all on the other but a need for reciprocal honesty and healthy self-criticism,[193] Royster maintains the attitude that Rome alone stands in need of repenting for a long list of errors.

In the concluding sentence of his letter, Royster states: "It is my conviction that it is impossible for the Orthodox Church, if it is to be true to itself, to accept the ecclesiological principles along with the practical rules that derive from these principles, that are enunciated by the Balamand Statement."[194] One can assume that among the practical rules Royster finds unacceptable is Balamand's guideline against (re)baptism of converts from one tradition to the other. In the letter's penultimate paragraph, Royster writes in reference to the Orthodox participants at Balamand: "They seem to have been enticed, by accepting Rome's formula for ending Uniatism, into recognizing the Roman Catholic Church as a Sister Church, with the same apostolic succession, sacraments and priesthood."[195] Royster evidently shares with Metallinos and the Athonite authors the belief that such recognition is at odds with traditional Orthodoxy.

III. Concluding Observations

In Orthodox reflection on the concept of sister churches in relations between Orthodox and Catholic churches there appear to be three more or less interlocking pieces that make up the respective arguments of all the various authors considered. One is the doctrinal piece: to what extent is the faith of the Catholic Church different from that of the Orthodox Church? Another is the sacramental piece: is the baptism received in the Catholic Church the same baptism as that which is received in the Orthodox Church? A third piece has to do with how the schism is understood historically and ecclesiologically: is it something that *happened*, like a clean cut, in such a way that made the Orthodox and Catholic churches altogether disconnected and different from one another (or revealed them to be so) once and for all? Or is it something that began gradually to be in the *process of happening*, and which has never become so complete that one can say even today that it is an absolute *fait accompli*, no longer in process and able to be reversed?

---

192 See above, p. 187.
193 See above, p. 189.
194 Archbishop Dmitri, *Letter of September 23, 1994 to His Beatitude, Theodosius*, 4.
195 Ibid.

In examining the positions of Orthodox authors, especially those who deny that the Catholic Church is a sister church in relation to their own, it is often difficult, if not impossible, to view any one of these three interlocking pieces in separation from the other two. For example, the authors of the letter from Mount Athos take the view that Roman Catholics are heretics, in the full sense of the word – i.e., their faith is essentially at odds with the faith of the Orthodox – and that this nullifies Roman Catholic sacramental reality. "Do these serious theological deviations of Rome amount to heresies or not? If they are, as they have been described by Orthodox Councils and fathers, do they not result in the invalidity of the Mysteries ...?"[196] Furthermore, the heresy and sacramental invalidity are said to date back *to the very start of the schism,* since which time, saving grace is conferred within the Orthodox communion alone. "[O]ur Holy Orthodox Church began to believe that she exclusively possessed salvation ... from the time of the Schism, which took place for reasons of dogma."[197]

The same correspondences among the three interrelated issues – schism, dogma, sacraments – can be found also in the writings of Metallinos and Royster in a similarly straightforward way. Metallinos' entire study is grounded in the conviction of the writers on whom he draws that the Catholic West has been in heresy and its sacraments devoid of sanctifying grace ever since the schism. As for Royster, he too clearly ties the schism to issues of what he regards as fundamental dogmatic divergence,[198] and although not as explicit about non-Orthodox sacramental validity, he effectively conveys a negative judgment on the latter when he presents as normative the view that considers "the things that Christ entrusted to His Church the exclusive property of the One Holy Catholic Apostolic Orthodox Church".[199] Romanides, who is somewhat more complex than other Orthodox critics of "sister churches" in how he understands non-Orthodox sacraments and how he accounts for the schism, still does not actually affirm (as Orthodox advocates of "sister churches" do), either that Roman Catholic sacraments are valid sacraments or that the schism was still unfolding gradually even after the 11th century. Moreover, Romanides is quite as adamant as other Orthodox critics of "sister churches" in Orthodox-Catholic relations in his claim that there is an irreconcilable difference between Western theology and the Orthodox understanding of *theosis.*

---

196 See above, p. 207.
197 See above, p. 206.
198 See above, pp. 231-232.
199 See above, p. 233.

From Orthodox advocates of the language of "sister churches" in the bilateral dialogue with the Catholic Church, a different understanding has emerged of the three issues of dogmatic divergence, the schism, and non-Orthodox sacramental validity. Even more than their agreement (substantial though it is) on each of the three issues taken singly, what stands out in comparing their positions is their overall agreement on the proper ordering of the three, chronologically and conceptually. Their ordering may be represented as follows: (1) the schism; (2) sacramental reality; and (3) dogma. (The schism unfolded gradually, such that sacramental reality was preserved on both sides, and with dogmatic divergences – whether substantial or largely superficial – increasingly entering in as a result of the separation.) This ordering stands in sharp contrast to that of Orthodox critics, for whom the order would be rendered: (1) dogma; (2) the schism; and (3) sacramental reality. (Dogmatic divergences – definitely substantial – produced the schism which rendered Latin sacraments invalid.)

The question of the gravity of the doctrinal differences between East and West is, as has been seen, a serious one especially for Meyendorff. He insists that some of these differences amount to conflicts and must be resolved.[200] However, he shows an inclination to see them more as a consequence of the schism than as its cause, and therefore as susceptible to possible resolution through dialogue.[201] Aghiorgoussis, who concurs with Meyendorff that "full agreement in the faith should be restored, before we share our communion,"[202] inclines also toward Meyendorff's view that dogmatic divergences did not precede or precipitate the schism but came about as a result of it.[203] He strongly affirms the reality of Roman Catholic sacraments.[204] Both authors actually invoke Congar's description of the schism as a "gradual estrangement" rather than a clean break. Erickson is clearly of the same view about the schism,[205] and

---

200 See above, pp. 185-186.
201 Meyendorff mentioned the existence of the schism as itself a contributing factor to later western distortions (see above, p. 187), thus implying that dogmatic deviations in the West resulted more from the separation – and the consequent lack of any balancing, complementary input from the East over the course of centuries – than the other way around.
202 See above, p. 192.
203 See above, p. 192: "the dogmatic formulations in the West *following* the separation ..." (emphasis added).
204 See above, p. 192.
205 See above, p. 196.

from his recommendation that the 1755 *Definition* on baptism be rescinded,[206] it is evident that he affirms the reality of Roman Catholic sacraments. Erickson says less about dogmatic differences, directly. Papandreou, for his part, stands out in the clarity with which he affirms that Catholics and Orthodox share the same apostolic faith.[207] He does not address the issue of Roman Catholic baptism but leaves little doubt that he fully affirms the integrity and reality of apostolic succession in the Roman Catholic Church,[208] implying thereby a recognition of Roman Catholic priesthood and sacraments more generally. Papandreou also says nothing directly about the causes and character of the schism. However, his use of the notion of the *ecclesia extra ecclesiam* indicates that for him as for Meyendorff, Aghiorgoussis and Erickson, the formal disruption of full communion between Orthodox East and Catholic West did not mean that ecclesial reality existed from that point forward in only one of the two churches, and not at all in the other.

From the foregoing summary, it may be seen that among Orthodox advocates of "sister churches" in the bilateral dialogue, there is particular clarity on *two of the three* inter-connected issues that have been itemized as the schism, the sacraments, and dogmatic differences. All of these authors are clear that the schism did not represent a clean break (and incline also toward the view that it did not come about as a result of doctrinal matters), and all in one way or another affirm the ongoing validity of the sacraments of the Catholic Church. However, about the issue of dogmatic differences *today* (as opposed to at the outbreak of the schism), these authors are not as clear. Of the four of them, only Papandreou makes the unqualified statement that Orthodox and Catholics share the same apostolic faith. Erickson and Aghiorghoussis are reserved on this point, and Meyendorff, who characterizes certain of the West's more recent dogmatic turns as being in outright conflict with the Orthodox faith, does not stop short of using the term "heresy" himself for at least one of them, namely papal infallibility.[209]

It may be said, then, that for Orthodox advocates of the language of sister churches vis-à-vis the Catholic Church, there remains work to be done before it would be possible to speak of a complete reconciliation between Orthodox East and Catholic West. There is more to be done, in other words, than simply

---

206 See above, p. 198, n. 63.
207 See above, p. 200.
208 See above, p. 203.
209 See J. Meyendorff, "Crisis in Roman Catholicism," in *Witness to the World*, op. cit., 62.

the act of reconciliation itself, which is sometimes all that seems to be outstanding from the perspective of certain Catholic authors.

In the Balamand statement itself there is evident awareness of the need to work out remaining issues of doctrinal disagreement – as one would fully expect from a commission whose express purpose is to undertake theological dialogue.[210] But these issues of disagreement are, again, seen as not having altogether severed one party or the other from the mystery of the Church. How Balamand expresses its view that neither tradition has ceased to participate in this mystery is primarily by means of statements on, precisely, sacraments and the nature of the schism. Balamand has somewhat more to say about the first subject than about the second. Its stipulation that neither Church should (re)baptize converts from the other comes into view at several points and, together with related affirmations of the sacramental reality in both communions, is a central motif of the document.[211] Balamand's discussion of the nature of the schism is more limited.[212]

However, it may be suggested that what distinguishes critics from advocates of Balamand and its language of "sister churches" is, more than anything else, the way in which the phenomenon of schism is understood by each group – both schism in general, and schism in the particular case of the division between Orthodox East and Catholic West. The critics' view of non-Orthodox sacraments seems to depend on their distinct understanding of schism, rather than the other way around. This was the point made earlier in the present chapter in the discussion of the baptismal controversy of the 18th century: namely, that a particular set of ecclesiological presuppositions underlay and conditioned how the authors supportive of Cyril V's 1755 *Definition* interpreted the canons, how they read history and what they came up with in their theory of sacramental economy. All of it derived from their understanding of Orthodox ecclesiology as essentially "Cyprianic". This ecclesiology, more than anything else, is what leaves no room for the expression "sister churches" in ecumenical relations – i.e., in reference to any church outside one's own communion. But it has been seen that it is impossible to make the argument that this "Cyprianic" ecclesiology has indeed been predominant or normative in the Orthodox East, except by means of the theory of sacramental economy, which itself has been

---

210 Cf. "Uniatism, Method of Union of the Past," para. 15, 20.
211 Cf. ibid. para. 13, 28, 29, 30.
212 Cf. ibid. para. 30. Certainly in the objections to Balamand that have been raised, attention has been focused more heavily on the document's call for mutual recognition of sacraments than on what it says about the schism per se.

shown here to be seriously deficient as a means of accounting for why the Orthodox East so often received converts from the West as already baptized. Without the theory of sacramental economy, there is no case for saying that Orthodoxy has traditionally understood schism always as a clean break, such that ecclesial reality ceases to exist in the separated group at once.

What remains, then, is to arrive at a clearer understanding of how, if the Orthodox East has traditionally viewed separations in a more complex way, this more complex view of schism still does not undermine the doctrine of the unicity of the Church. The notion of the *ecclesia extra ecclesiam* has an important function in this task. For the anti-Balamand writers, the only alternative to the absolute and exclusive identification of the canonical Orthodox Church with the Church of Christ is a type of ecclesiological relativism. These writers present an either–or between Cyprian's exclusivist ecclesiology and the Branch Theory.[213] In between these two possibilities, however, there is an ecclesiological approach that indeed privileges only one party to every schism, yet still acknowledges that in both parties there may well continue to be true sacraments and other ecclesial gifts by which sanctification and even salvation may be obtained. Such an approach is reflected in the idea of the *ecclesia extra ecclesiam*, whose capacity to make sense of the canonical tradition of the Orthodox East, and whose compatibility with Vatican II's ecclesiology and with the concept of sister churches in Orthodox-Catholic relations, will be further explored in the next chapter.

---

213 See above, p. 208.

Chapter 6
THE ADEQUACY AND VALUE OF THE CONCEPT OF SISTER CHURCHES FOR CATHOLIC AND ORTHODOX ECCLESIOLOGY

This chapter is comprised of three principal sections (and a concluding section). The first compares Catholic and Orthodox advocates of the concept of sister churches, advocates being defined as those who support the expression's use in Catholic-Orthodox relations without significant restrictions. Points where it is possible to discern an overlapping or parallel perspective between Catholic and Orthodox advocates will be noted as well as other points where their perspectives diverge. The second section follows a similar plan in comparing Catholic and Orthodox critics of the concept in its use in relations between the two traditions. The third section, divided into two parts, responds to the central claims put forward by Catholic and Orthodox critics, respectively, as to why the expression in its use across the confessional division is ecclesiologically problematic, whether altogether (as Orthodox critics say), or in some of its usages (as Catholic critics say). Section IIIA consists of a theological response to the argument of Catholic critics that the expression's use on the level of the two churches as a whole is illegitimate. Here the aim is twofold: first, to offer reassurance to such critics that the term can indeed be used in this manner while respecting their concerns; and second, to offer positive reasons why the usage in question is not only permissible but valuable, in ways its critics often overlook and even its advocates seem to under-appreciate. Section IIIB sets forth a response to the claim of Orthodox critics that there can be no sister church or churches outside the canonical limits of the Orthodox Church. Finally, a concluding section rounds out the chapter.

I. Comparison of Catholic and Orthodox advocates of "sister churches"

Between Catholic authors who support the expression's use (not just on the level of Catholic and Orthodox particular churches, but unrestrictedly) and Orthodox authors who fully endorse it, there are several commonalities and certain differences, some of which were noted at various points in Chapter 5. Since there also exist, as was seen in Chapters 4 and 5, differences among Catholic advocates themselves, and among Orthodox advocates themselves, the points of comparison to be highlighted in this section between Catholic and

Orthodox advocates will be those that seem most clearly to reflect the *general tendencies* of either group as a whole.

What Catholic and Orthodox advocates have most obviously in common is a basic interest in seeing an ecclesiology of communion increasingly flourish in the contemporary Catholic Church. They share the view that the adoption of the language of sister churches by the Catholic magisterium since Vatican II has signaled an openness to a "theology of the local church"[1] that they perceive as having been all too absent from Rome's universalist ecclesiology of previous centuries. For these authors, the concept is valuable as an antidote to an exaggerated form of Roman centralism. They believe that Catholic use of the expression in the post-Vatican II era reflects a recovery of a more sacramental and less purely juridical understanding of what makes a church a church.

It thus entails, from the point of view of these authors, an auspicious shift in the ecumenical perspective of the Catholic Church vis-à-vis Orthodoxy, from regarding the Orthodox as schismatics simply outside the Church to regarding them as being in substantial, if still imperfect, communion with the Catholic Church, possessing the same sacraments and apostolic priesthood. These authors especially appreciate as one of the consequences of this shift the fact that the Catholic Church no longer envisions unity between East and West strictly as a matter of the "return" of the former to the latter, and no longer espouses uniatism as a method of overcoming the schism. What the concept of sister churches specifically means, according to its advocates, in direct contrast with the ecclesiology underlying uniatism is that it is possible for members of either church, even in the anomalous situation of the schism, to be in communion with God through the gifts of God entrusted to his Church, that is, to have access to the means of salvation. This access and communion may be, in the view of those of one tradition, *threatened* by what they perceive as absent or distorted in the other, and thus there is no lack of urgency in healing the wound of the schism, but these authors all share the conviction that the schism has never reached the point of severing either tradition from the means of grace.

In a closely related way, Catholic and Orthodox advocates of the concept of sister churches are fundamentally in agreement about how the East-West schism unfolded – namely, *gradually,* and, in large measure, as a result of a certain Roman imperialism that went along with the ecclesiological reforms of the 11th century and that expressed itself at that time in an idea of Rome as the mother of all other churches, including those of the East. We may recall here

---

1   The expression is Meyendorff's. See above, Chapter 5, p. 188.

Chapter 6: The Adequacy and Value of the Concept of Sister Churches 243

that it was possible for Aghiorgoussis to quote Congar at length on the subject of the schism and to say that he could not have expressed his own perspective better than Congar had done.[2] Neither the Catholic nor the Orthodox advocates of the concept of sister churches are of the view that the schism occurred as a result of such doctrinal divergences between East and West as the *filioque*, or the western teachings on created grace and purgatory.

At the same time, the question of doctrinal difference is one that Catholic and Orthodox advocates do not necessarily approach in just the same way. Between Lanne and Meyendorff this was especially evident, and the distinction between them is one that seems to be archetypal of Catholic and Orthodox advocates generally, in spite of some variation that may be discerned especially among Orthodox advocates. Lanne lays more emphasis on the need for theological pluralism; Meyendorff, more on the need for unity in faith.[3] Still, although it may be that Lanne would be more satisfied than Meyendorff with the current level of doctrinal agreement between the two traditions and more apt to see it as sufficient for restoring full communion, Lanne nevertheless is in agreement with Meyendorff on the need to revisit and reinterpret, together with the East, the understanding of the authority of the papacy that was dogmatized by the Catholic West in the late 19th century.[4]

Catholic and Orthodox advocates of "sister churches" apply the expression to the two entire communions.[5] This is as true of Legrand and Papandreou, writing after the CDF issued its *Note* in 2000, as it was of those writing before. Legrand and Papandreou do supplement their usage, as the earlier authors did not, with some deliberate discussion of why it is theologically defensible. Legrand, however, argues the case on what has been shown to be an unsound basis[6] while Papandreou proceeds on a more solid footing but without developing his argument very far or showing directly how it might be correlated with the terms of the Catholic debate.[7] Thus in the writings of Catholic and Orthodox advocates, one finds no adequate response to the CDF's position against applying "sister churches" to the two communions in their totalities.

---

2 See above, Chapter 5, p. 191, n. 38.
3 See above, Chapter 4, p. 122, n. 37 and Chapter 5, p. 186.
4 See above, Chapter 4, pp. 122-123.
5 On the Catholic side, it is this that I am saying distinguishes advocates from critics, for there are no Catholic authors who explicitly reject the expression's ecumenical use out of hand. See below, pp. 245-246.
6 See above, Chapter 4, pp. 169-173.
7 See above, Chapter, 5, p. 203.

With some exceptions, it is difficult to tell the extent to which advocates of "sister churches" distinguish between its application on the level of what Catholic ecclesiology terms particular churches, on the one hand, and groupings of particular churches on the other. Lanne, it was seen, does make such a distinction at least at one point, suggesting that the application of the term to particular churches is the one that reflects the most essential meaning of the concept; he expresses doubt, meanwhile, about the significance of the concept when applied to groupings of particular churches such as metropolitan provinces or patriarchates.[8] Hryniewicz clearly ascribes a certain importance to "sister churches" on the level of patriarchates and other types of regional groupings, yet still without fleshing out the actual *reasons* why the concept on this level should be considered important in its own right.[9]

The author who begins to offer substantive theological support for this regional usage is Hervé Legrand. Legrand maintains that with the thesis of the priority of the universal church (over the local church) put forward by the CDF, "one deprives groupings of dioceses of a real status of sister churches and renders them mere emanations of the primacy,"[10] and he argues that an authentic ecclesiology of communion involves "a mutual inclusion among local churches,"[11] the idea of "mutual inclusion" here being presented as a corrective to the faulty notion that "the universal church is an immediate reality". As a reality that is, instead, mediated by each local church in its place, the universal church – which *is* the "mutual inclusion" of all the particular churches[12] – is a reality, so Legrand's analysis implies, that *happens*.[13] The universal church as the mutual inclusion of all the particular churches happens by means of "a coming together of bishops, each presiding over the communion of his local church, and thereby presiding (as a group) over the communion of the churches of their area or of the whole church. One thus encounters the grouping of regional

---

8 See above, Chapter 4, pp. 199-200.
9 See above, Chapter 4, pp. 132-134.
10 Legrand, "La théologie des Églises Sœurs," 478. See above, Chapter 4, p. 166.
11 Legrand, "Le dialogue catholique-orthodoxe," 8. See above, Chapter 4, p. 166.
12 Cf. Komonchak, "The Local Church and the Church Catholic," 442: "the communion that constitutes the universal Church is precisely the mutual inclusion of all the local churches."
13 Komonchak writes that "the Church's catholicity is always something that must be achieved." He observes that it is guaranteed, on the one hand, by the promise and gifts of God to his Church, but that on the other hand, it does not become a reality except within and among the local churches in the concreteness and freedom of their unfolding relations (Komonchak, "The Local Church and the Church Catholic," 446).

churches as the unquestionable framework of activity for bishops."[14] Legrand is the only one of the authors writing on sister churches to have made such an explicit theological commitment to the concept's essential applicability on the level of regional churches.

It may be that Orthodox authors simply take the legitimacy and value of this application for granted – in fact, they probably always intend its application primarily on this level rather than on the level of the "particular" church – but in any case they do not enter very far into the reasons *why* regional sister churches are of essential ecclesiological importance in the life of the Church.[15] Legrand endeavors to do so, one might say, for them, as well as for Catholics. Would the Orthodox advocates of sister churches recognize his perspective on regional churches as their own? Legrand himself believes that what he is describing is an ecclesiology convergent with that of Orthodoxy. "The return to this traditional view," he writes, in the continuation of the passage quoted above, "signals our reconciliation with the Orthodox Church."[16]

II. Comparison of Catholic and Orthodox critics of "sister churches"

Between Catholic and Orthodox critics of the concept of sister churches in modern Catholic-Orthodox relations, there are more differences and – especially at first glance – fewer similarities than have been observed in the comparison of Catholic and Orthodox advocates. Even in the degree of their criticism, Catholic critics and Orthodox critics are dissimilar. Catholic critics, as has been seen, wish to restrict in certain ways how the language of sister churches may be used across the division, but they do not suggest that the language ought to be prohibited altogether, as do Orthodox critics, for whom it is inconceivable that a non-Orthodox church could be construed as the sister either of an Orthodox local church or of the Orthodox Church as a whole.

It could be argued that where those being categorized as "Catholic critics" are concerned, the line between what constitutes advocacy and what constitutes criticism is somewhat blurry. As a matter of fact some of the concerns expressed by Catholic "critics" of the concept of sister churches have been shown

---

14 Legrand, "Le dialogue catholique-orthodoxe," 8. See above, Chapter 4, p. 166.
15 John Erickson has written in this connection that Orthodox theologians have given relatively little attention to "the basis for intermediary ecclesial entities. The issue of primacy on any level but the universal ... has not been addressed from a theological perspective." J. Erickson, "First Among Equals: Papal Primacy in an Orthodox Perspective," *Ecumenical Trends* 27:2 (February, 1998) 7/23.
16 Legrand, "Le dialogue catholique-orthodoxe," 8. See above, Chapter 4, p. 166.

to be able to provide a necessary corrective, or purification, of the concept as it sometimes has been used incorrectly.[17] However, if those being categorized here as Catholic "critics" are actively interested in the concept's preservation even in purified form, this is not as apparent from the evidence of their writings as it might be. The CDF, which, on the basis of its *Note,* is included among "Catholic critics" for the purposes of this section, does affirm, as has been seen,[18] at least one usage of the expression unequivocally, and in this respect perhaps deserves less to be separated off from "Catholic advocates" than does Garuti, who wishes to ban some usages and seriously qualify the rest.[19] And yet even the CDF's *Note* itself does not accompany its statement of *approval* of the usage on the level of particular churches with any points of theological substance, as it does its statements of *disapproval* of other usages. It does not specify what might be lost if the expression in its proper usage were to fall out of currency, as it specifies the harm that it believes might be done if the expression in its improper usage were to be allowed to continue. Thus one is left with the impression that even the endorsed usage, though permitted, is not urgently recommended.

Here already, then, in what presents itself as one of the most obvious differences between Catholic critics of "sister churches" and Orthodox critics – namely, the fact that the Catholic critics all approve of the expression's use in Catholic-Orthodox relations in some form, while the Orthodox critics do not – there may be discerned a certain concealed similarity. In the writings of both groups, there is an almost complete lack of emphasis or attention given to what the concept is or ever has been a corrective *of.* We have seen that in the writings of the concept's *advocates* there is a great deal of attention given to just that. Orthodox and Catholic advocates alike frequently emphasize how the use of "sister churches" by the official Catholic Church after Vatican II represented an important and welcome shift from an overly centralized, "universalist" ecclesiology toward an ecclesiology of communion.

Another difference between the Catholic and Orthodox critics is that for Catholic critics, reservations about "sister churches" closely relate to a commitment to safeguard the primacy of the bishop of Rome, whereas this of course is not a concern of Orthodox critics. In the writings of the Catholic critics one finds the concept of sister churches often described in terms that suggest that it is a direct threat to the principle of primacy. It will be recalled that something

---

17 See above, Chapter 4, p. 179.
18 See above, Chapter 4, p. 153.
19 See above, Chapter 4, pp. 141-143 and 148-149.

of this either–or approach was seen in the CDF's complaint about the theory of the Pentarchy that "no Roman Pontiff ever recognized this equalization of the sees".[20] It was seen as well in Garuti's charge against Nicetas and Cameteros alike that they invoked the expression "sister churches" in their 12th century exchanges with the West in a spirit that was "decidedly anti-Roman and opposed to the primacy of the Bishop of Rome."[21]

However, here too, the difference between Catholic critics and Orthodox critics may only conceal an underlying similarity. Despite their different views of primacy, it may be suggested that Catholic critics and Orthodox critics alike understand the relationship between conciliarity and primacy as an either–or. That this is the case with the Orthodox critics is not immediately as apparent since they do not explicitly pit "sister churches" against Roman primacy as the Catholic critics do. One might have expected Orthodox critics to *favor* the concept precisely to the extent that it makes Catholic champions of papal primacy uneasy, but the Orthodox critics we have examined actually do not come out and say that the Roman primacy (to which they object) may be effectively countered by the ecclesiology of "sister churches". Nonetheless, a close examination of their reflections suggests that they too regard "sister churches" and Roman primacy as incompatible realities.

Orthodox critics of "sister churches" have no objection to the concept in itself. As a term to describe relations between or among Orthodox churches in full communion, they see it as perfectly appropriate. For them the problem is not with "sister churches" per se but with including the Roman Catholic Church under this designation. Metallinos identifies the entirety of the latter church with "the Papacy," and insists that the Orthodox signatories to Balamand were seeking a "de facto union" with this "Papacy" when they went along with Balamand's idea of the mutual recognition of sacraments.[22] In effect, since such mutual recognition of sacraments constitutes the primary basis for mutual recognition as "sister churches" (even though Metallinos does not invoke that phrase), Metallinos can be understood as saying here that "Papacy" and "sister churches" are mutually exclusive. The same is true of the authors of the letter from Mount Athos. According to their presentation, the world's "only hope" is "unadulterated Orthodoxy," which they identify with "the *hope of the Gospel* (Col. 1:23) of Christ, the only God-Man," in direct contrast with "the Pope, the man-god and idol of Western humanism," which they suggest lies at the heart

---

20 *Note*, n. 3. See above, Chapter 4, p. 153.
21 Garuti, "Sister Churches," 263. See above, Chapter 4, p. 150.
22 See above, Chapter 5, p. 217.

of Roman Catholicism. Seeing the two traditions in these starkly polarized terms leads them to declare, "we are obliged never to accept union or the description of the Roman Catholic Church as a 'Sister Church'", and they go on to list among the doctrines that must be renounced by Rome "the infallibility and primacy of the Pope".[23] Thus, an essential reason why Rome cannot be "sister church" is precisely Roman primacy (the primacy of Rome among churches and, correlatively, of the pope among bishops).

Archbishop Dmitri Royster offers a similar view: "The only Sister Churches for an Orthodox Church are the other Orthodox Churches. To promote such an understanding of the Roman Catholic Church, without its correcting itself, is to contradict and to betray the Fathers who have defended Orthodoxy against Papism, the Filioque, the immaculate conception, their doctrine of grace, and other crucial distortions."[24] If Royster would be prepared to distinguish what he condemns as "Papism" (the very first item on his list) from a form of Roman primacy that he might regard as acceptable he does not indicate this. The impression is given once again that Orthodoxy has an ecclesiology of sister churches, Roman Catholicism an ecclesiology of "primacy," and that the two ecclesiologies are incompatible.

In an article of the mid-1990s condemning uniatism, an official of the Moscow Patriarchate's Department of External Church Relations expressed this point of view in particularly clear terms, when he suggested that in *Ut unum sint* John Paul II tried to have it both ways by speaking on the one hand of unity structured around St. Peter's successor, and on the other hand of unity based on the notion of sister churches.

> For an Orthodox theologian a fundamental question arises here: What is it that the search for unity should be built upon? Is it the idea of primacy or the idea of 'sister Churches', since these two ideas are mutually exclusive in the Orthodox understanding? We cannot use sophistry to make it appear that these two ideas do not essentially contradict each other, otherwise the whole of the Orthodox tradition will arise against us.[25]

What is given expression in this passage, suggesting a stark opposition between "the idea of primacy" and "the idea of 'sister Churches'," is the characteristic

---

23 See above, Chapter 5, p. 209.
24 Archbishop Dmitri, *Letter of September 23, 1994 to His Beatitude, Theodosius*, 2. See above, Chapter 5, p. 231.
25 Georgi Zyablitsev, "Uniatism as an Ecclesiological Problem Today," in B. Groen and W. van den Bercken, eds., *Four Hundred Years Union of Brest (1596-1996): A Critical Reevaluation* (Nijmegen, the Netherlands: Peeters, 1998), 193-199, at 196.

viewpoint not only of Catholic critics of "sister churches" but, equally, of Orthodox critics. Both groups adhere to the notion that primacy and sister churches are "mutually exclusive," with Catholic critics wishing to keep a supposedly Eastern ecclesiology of sister churches from encroaching on (Roman) primacy, and Orthodox critics wishing to keep a supposedly Western ecclesiology of primacy from contaminating (Orthodox) sister churches.

Meanwhile, critics of "sister churches," Catholic and Orthodox alike, have little to say about the value of the concept specifically on the level of regional churches. It has been noted that the approach of Catholic critics allows for Rome's being considered as a particular church, but not as a patriarchate. Were Orthodox critics to recognize Rome as having ecclesial reality, they would surely want above all to affirm Rome's status as patriarchate of the West, but their incentive for making the case for this is suppressed by their larger commitment to the position that the church of Rome is no church on any level at all. The result, ironically, is that Orthodox critics are in a kind of agreement with the Catholic magisterium's denigration of "sister churches" as applied to Catholic and Orthodox churches on the regional level. (For the same reason, they concur with the official Catholic line that between Orthodox East and Catholic West there is no reality of sister churches on the level of the two entire communions). They disagree only with the official Catholic line that between Orthodox East and Catholic West there is a reality of sister churches on the level of particular churches. Catholic "restrictions" on the concept of sister churches, in other words, do not bother Orthodox critics – except insofar as they stop short of being a complete repudiation of the concept in relations between the two separated communions.

Finally, in terms of what was described in Chapter 5 as a set of three more or less interlocking pieces involving perspectives on sacraments, doctrine, and the schism, Catholic critics differ from Orthodox critics very noticeably. In regard to how each group views the sacraments of the other church, Catholic critics affirm the validity of Orthodox sacraments, while Orthodox critics deny the reality of Roman Catholic sacraments. This difference is then tied together with two other differences. The different evaluation of the sacraments of the other tradition is closely connected, first, to a different evaluation of doctrinal discrepancies. Orthodox critics regard a number of Roman Catholic doctrines as heretical; Catholic critics generally view the two traditions as sharing the same apostolic faith.[26] And this difference connects, in turn, with yet another,

---

26 Garuti does, however, raise the question as to whether there really is an identity of faith from the Catholic point of view. See above, Chapter 4, p. 147, n. 115.

concerning the nature and cause of the schism. For Orthodox critics, the schism came about as a result of the heresy of the Catholic West. For Catholic critics, its cause lay in the rejection of the proper authority of the pope by the Orthodox East. It should be pointed out here that while the difference of approach in regard to the others' sacraments and doctrinal positions is genuinely that – a difference – the dissimilarity of approach in regard to the cause of the schism is yet another of those dissimilarities which seem to conceal a profound resemblance. In each approach, the other side is seen as having left the Church, the East by its departure from the bond of unity whose ultimate criterion is communion with the bishop of the leading see, and the West by its departure from the bond of unity whose ultimate criterion is love in the truth. In neither case did misunderstanding or "gradual estrangement" play a significant role.

To encapsulate the approaches of Catholic critics and Orthodox critics: (1) the former generally approve of at least some limited usage of "sister churches" in relations between the two traditions while the latter do not. Yet even Catholic critics say little if anything, positively, about why it is actually important to maintain the specific usage of which they say they approve. (2) Roman primacy (or rather a certain perception of it) turns out to be a chief reason why "sister churches" in bilateral relations is opposed – opposed by Catholic critics in order that the primacy may be fully safeguarded, and opposed by Orthodox critics in order that authentic "sister churches" may not be adulterated by primacy ("the papacy"). (3) Neither Catholic nor Orthodox critics recommend that the concept of sister churches in Catholic-Orthodox relations be applied on the level of regional churches. Orthodox critics see no place for the concept of sister churches in Catholic-Orthodox relations on any level; Catholic critics more specifically have reservations about the concept's applicability on the regional level lest Rome be mistakenly perceived as one of several patriarchal sees and lest its primacy on the universal level be thereby, as it were, cramped. For the same set of distinct reasons, neither Orthodox critics nor Catholic critics favor applying the concept to the two traditions as a whole. (4) Catholic critics are able to accept the faith and sacraments of the Orthodox, in part because the cause of the schism is, in their view, Orthodox rebellion against the authority of Rome; Orthodox critics, by contrast, attribute the schism to distortions in the very faith of Catholics leading also to the invalidation of their sacraments. A commonality here is that both groups regard the other tradition as having departed from the unity of the Church, a unity primarily conceived by Orthodox critics as a unity on the level of faith and sacraments, and by Catholic critics as a unity on the level of administration and authority.

In light of the last point of comparison, yet a further underlying resemblance may be identified between Catholic critics and Orthodox critics. There is a sense in which the question in Orthodoxy of non-Orthodox sacramental reality and the question in Roman Catholicism of the meaning of "subsists in" are really the same question. It is the question of how the doctrine that the Church is one may be maintained in the face of the fact of the schism, and Catholic and Orthodox critics may be said to answer it similarly. To say that "subsists in" is exactly the same as "est,"[27] and to say that outside of Orthodoxy there are no authentic sacraments,[28] are parallel ways of meeting the challenge of upholding the doctrine of the unicity of the Church.[29] In both instances, this is accomplished in a manner that is conceptually crisp and simple to understand – the Church is here, not there – but that does not seem adequate either to history or to present reality as many people perceive and experience it in the circumstance of the schism. Hence a great many Orthodox today do not share the view of the so-called rigorists that there are no true sacraments outside the Orthodox Church, and a great many Catholics do not follow the corresponding position of their own hard-liners about the meaning of "subsists in." Indeed, on the level of the official churches, these ecclesiologically exclusivist positions have generally not been adopted over the past half century. And yet they remain theologically powerful positions, each exerting a strong pull within its respective communion, above all because there remains no fully articulated alternative to them that would be more adequate than they are to the complex realities of history and present experience and, at the same time, just as capable as they are of preserving the doctrine of the unicity of the church.

III. Proposals in response to critics of "sister churches"

The quantity of theological writing in favor of the concept of sister churches in Catholic-Orthodox relations has somewhat dwindled over the decades while the literature opposed has grown. It seems that advocacy of the concept has spurred criticism, more than the other way around. This pattern has its exceptions, to be sure. Erickson is an Orthodox advocate of "sister churches" who does re-

---

27 See above, Chapter 4, p. 158, especially n. 153.
28 See above, Chapter 5, pp. 207, 217-218, 235-236.
29 It is perhaps fitting that Orthodox ecclesiology would work out its response in terms of the sacramental dimension of the life of the Church and Catholic ecclesiology in terms of the administrative dimension. In the course of the schism, each side has played to what may be considered its "strength".

spond to Orthodox critics. Legrand is a Catholic advocate who responds to Catholic critics. Papandreou, though himself Orthodox, also responds to certain objections raised on the Catholic side. Nevertheless, one still has the overall sense of an unfinished conversation in which, in an initial phase, proponents expressed themselves, rather more freely than fully, not yet having the advantage of knowing what resistance they would meet by members of a mounting opposition, who, in a subsequent phase, let loose a barrage of heavy artillery, in the wake of which little has been heard. Very much in retreat, advocates of the concept of sister churches have offered only sporadic and not especially forceful responses, hardly amounting to anything that could be described as a counter-offensive.

The aim of this section is to rekindle the conversation, specifically by looking at how the major broadsides of Catholic and Orthodox critics might yet be met by Catholic and Orthodox advocates, based on what advocates have said thus far. The attempt will be to take what advocates have said and redeploy it to more forceful effect, and at times to acknowledge certain gaps or holes in their presentations and fill them in.

Specifically, the aim in this section will be to respond to the two most powerful blows that have been dealt to the concept of sister churches in the context of modern Catholic-Orthodox relations: first (A), the claim of Catholic critics that the Orthodox Church and the Catholic Church cannot be sisters (even while particular Orthodox churches and particular Catholic churches can be); second (B), the claim of Orthodox critics that no church outside the Orthodox Church can be a sister church.

A. Response to Catholic concerns

1. Why the Orthodox Church may be called the sister of the Catholic Church

In what follows, I argue that it should be possible for the Catholic Church to recognize the Orthodox Church as a sister church. This is the conclusion also of Hervé Legrand, as has been seen,[30] but my argument proceeds along lines different from those laid down by Legrand. Legrand based his position on an interpretation of LG 8 as meaning that the Church of Christ subsists in the Catholic Church and the Orthodox Church alike, a position which has been rejected by the CDF and which indeed seems difficult to defend. My argument

---

30 See above, Chapter 4, p. 171.

has more affinity with the approach of Metropolitan Damaskinos Papandreou, who, in his correspondence with then Cardinal Ratzinger, likewise took the position that the Catholic Church ought to be able to recognize the Orthodox Church as a sister church, but who gave more consideration than Legrand did to the danger of ecclesiological relativism. Papandreou, in order to explain how an affirmation of the two entire communions as sister churches may avoid that danger, invoked the paradoxical idea of the *ecclesia extra ecclesiam*.[31] Relevant and potentially illuminating as it is, however, even this concept and the use to which it was put by Papandreou still could not penetrate very far inside the Catholic debate, for which purpose it would be necessary to take more carefully into account certain key points in that debate that have been made about "subsists in" and about the relation between particular church and universal church. In the following analysis, the basic position is the same as that of Papandreou – the Orthodox Church should be able to be called the sister of the Catholic Church, without undermining the claim of the Catholic Church to embody in a uniquely definitive way the one, holy, catholic and apostolic Church[32] – but here the attempt is made to support this position through an appeal to specific ecclesiological principles expressed by Catholic theologians and by the CDF itself, using as much as possible their language and their categories.

The doctrine of "subsists in" is usually associated in postconciliar Catholic ecclesiology with the Catholic Church as a whole. It is not as much associated with particular Catholic churches. This was certainly true of the language of LG 8 and UR 4, both of which speak of the Church of Christ as subsisting in the singular Catholic Church. In view of this pattern, Paul McPartlan was led to the conclusion that the doctrine actually cannot be applied to particular Catholic churches. He argued that the Church of Christ no more "subsists in" any particular Catholic Church than it does in any particular Orthodox church.[33]

Such an approach *could* be said to dispel any confusion as to why the CDF's *Note* would have endorsed the concept of sister churches for Catholic and Orthodox particular churches but not for the two churches as a whole. This approach, whereby any two churches might be sister churches even though the Church of Christ subsists in neither of them, has a certain resemblance to the inverse idea, put forward by Legrand, that two churches may be sister churches

---

31 See above, Chapter 5, p. 203.
32 Nor the corresponding claim made by the Orthodox Church, a matter to be taken up in the next section.
33 See above, Chapter 4, p. 172.

only if the Church of Christ subsists in both of them. But instead of following either of these approaches, the intention here is to suggest that churches may be sister churches, in fact, when the Church of Christ subsists in one of them and not in the other.

In order to make this claim it will be necessary to show that according to Catholic ecclesiology, it is indeed possible to speak of the Church of Christ subsisting in particular Catholic churches. These already are acknowledged, in official Catholic teaching, as sister churches of particular Orthodox churches, and the CDF seems to have moved in the direction of saying, or at least making it possible to say, that in Catholic particular churches the Church of Christ does subsist.

My argument that "subsists in" applies to particular Catholic churches is based on two main supports. One is Sullivan's way of understanding what "subsists in" means. The other is certain evidence in recent magisterial documents on ecclesiology that the relationship between the Catholic Church as a whole and each particular Catholic church is best understood as a relationship of mutual indwelling. Here emphasis should be given to the word "mutual". Vatican II made clear in LG 23 that the universal church – by which it seemed to mean the Catholic Church – is constituted by the particular churches "in and out of which it is formed". The CDF, as will be seen shortly, has wished to emphasize that it is no less true that the bond of communion that characterizes the universal church is constitutive of each particular church. Not only is it necessary to say that the many dwell in the one, but just as much, to say that the one dwells in the many. From out of this notion of the reciprocal inseparability of particular church and whole church, together with Sullivan's view of what "subsists in" really means, I intend to fashion my argument that "subsists in" applies as much to particular Catholic churches as to the Catholic Church as a whole.

Let us begin with Sullivan's interpretation of "subsists in". Explication of his interpretation will be illuminated in part by comparing Sullivan's approach with McPartlan's. Sullivan, it will be recalled, drew attention to what he regarded as the very important statement of *Dominus Iesus* 16 that the Church of Christ "continues to exist fully only in the Catholic Church."[34] Sullivan saw in this statement the basis for a proper understanding of what "subsists in" actually means. According to his thinking, "it is only if 'subsists' means 'continues to exist fully' that one can say that the church of Christ subsists only in the Catholic Church."[35]

---

34 See above, Chapter 4, p. 160.
35 Sullivan, "The Impact of *Dominus Iesus* on Ecumenism," 8. See above, p. 160.

Chapter 6: The Adequacy and Value of the Concept of Sister Churches 255

Sullivan's understanding turns out to be the same as that which has been officially sanctioned by the CDF in its most recent document on the subject. In a text issued in 2007, the CDF wrote that "subsists in" should be understood precisely to signify "the perduring, historical continuity and the permanence of all the elements instituted by Christ in the Catholic Church, in which the Church of Christ is concretely found on this earth."[36] It is important to observe that the CDF text does not say here that the Church of Christ is not concretely to be found anywhere else on this earth than in the Catholic Church, but that it is to be found nowhere else with the same continuity and permanence of "all the elements" with which Christ endowed the Church. This is simply another way of saying that the Church of Christ "continues to exist fully" only in the Catholic Church.

Neither in Sullivan's remarks, nor in the text of *Dominus Iesus* that he quotes, nor in the more recent CDF text, which seems once again to corroborate his basic point, do we find any explicit idea that the Church of Christ could be said to "subsist in" a particular Catholic church. It is always the singular and whole Catholic Church that is mentioned as the entity in which the Church of Christ is said to continue to exist fully with all the elements Christ bestowed on his Church – i.e., to "subsist". At the same time, neither is there anything in either the CDF texts or in Sullivan's writings that *rules out* the possibility that the Church of Christ could be said also to subsist in all the particular Catholic churches which constitute the Catholic Church in its entirety.

In this respect at least, Sullivan's manner of interpreting what "subsists in" means differs from that of McPartlan. It will be recalled that as McPartlan understands the concept it is not applicable to particular churches, not even to Catholic particular churches.[37] A clear demarcation is laid down between the Catholic Church as a whole in which the Church of Christ subsists, and the particular Catholic churches in which it does not.

But if Sullivan's definition of "subsists in" as "continues to exist fully" is accepted, a different conclusion seems warranted. Sullivan himself does not address what McPartlan proposes and it is only by extrapolation that his position is being presented here as representing a dissimilar approach. (In fact we cannot be sure he would object to the conclusion at which McPartlan arrives.) Conversely, given that there are points in McPartlan's own presentation where, as will be seen, his perspective agrees with Sullivan's, it is uncertain whether he

---

36 "Responses to Some Questions Regarding Certain Aspects of the Doctrine on the Church" (June 29, 2007), Response to Second Question, para. 2.
37 See above, Chapter 4, pp. 171-172.

himself would object to Sullivan's definition of "subsists in" or even, perhaps, to the conclusion that I suggest flows from it – which differs, so it would seem, from McPartlan's own. Very much like Sullivan, McPartlan sees the doctrine of the sole subsistence of the Church of Christ in the Catholic Church as expressive of an idea that there are certain ecclesial gifts preserved nowhere else but in the Catholic Church. To speak of this idea McPartlan also uses the language of "fullness," much in the way that Sullivan does. Having quoted *Communionis notio* 13, where Orthodox churches are described as wounded because they lack "communion with the universal Church, represented by Peter's successor," McPartlan observes: "So, these Churches are indeed 'Churches', but they lack the fullness of communional unity."[38] That same fullness does belong to Catholic particular churches. Hence even on the level of the particular church, there is an asymmetry between Catholic and Orthodox churches; it is important to note that McPartlan does grant this in spite of his suggestion elsewhere that it is only at the level of the *whole* Catholic Church that "subsists in" can be said to differentiate Catholic from Orthodox ecclesial reality. The question I am raising is whether the asymmetry at the level of particular churches can be properly represented by the notion of "subsists in," as it is at the level of the two churches as a whole.

One finds in McPartlan's analysis another observation that lends itself to the view that perhaps it can be. "It is the belief of the Catholic Church," he writes, "that Christ has willed and bestowed a structure of visible unity among the particular Churches and that that structure is so much part of his purpose that where it itself is not operative the Church of Christ cannot properly be said to subsist."[39] McPartlan clearly wishes to emphasize here that the structure of visible unity of which he speaks is something that transcends any one particular Catholic church; hence he uses the preposition "among" in attempting to describe where Christ has bestowed the gift of this structure of unity: it is "among" the particular Catholic churches rather than "in" them. But it is doubtful that McPartlan's emphasis here should be taken in such a way as to suggest that the gift of "communional unity" (as he describes it at another point) is something merely outside of, extrinsic to, each particular Catholic church that participates in it. When McPartlan says that the Church of Christ does not subsist *in* particular churches, it seems that what he really means is that it does not subsist in them individualistically, atomistically. This is because, as he puts it, "the existence of particular Churches does not itself exhaust the

---

38 McPartlan, "The Importance of Visible Unity," para. 11.
39 Ibid. para. 16.

Lord's purpose for his Church."⁴⁰ But so long as "in" is used in a sense that is held together with "among", that is, so long as it does not connote the self-enclosure or self-sufficiency of each particular church, then might it not be possible to affirm, after all, that the gift of communional unity is a gift that Christ has bestowed not just *among* but also precisely *in* each of the particular churches? If so, it would mean that the Church of Christ subsists both in the whole Catholic communion and in the particular Catholic churches in and out of which it is formed.

Such a perspective seems to be not only possible but strongly called for by certain statements made by the CDF. In the following passage from *Communionis notio*, we read: "... for each particular Church to be fully Church, that is, the particular presence of the universal Church with all its essential elements, and hence constituted *after the model of [in the image of] the universal Church*, there must be present in it, as a proper element, the supreme authority of the Church: the Episcopal college *'together with their head, the Supreme Pontiff, and never apart from him.'*"⁴¹

Of exceptional interest in this passage is the phrase "the particular presence of the universal Church". What is expressed here is the idea that it should be possible for every characteristic of the universal church to be manifested in each particular church.⁴² The language of "fullness," which Sullivan applied to the whole Catholic Church, is applied – in a way that was never ruled out by Sullivan – to each particular Catholic church as the presence of the whole Catholic Church in a given place. The particular Catholic church is said to be that presence of the whole Catholic Church "with all its essential elements," including, precisely, the element of what McPartlan calls the "structure of visible unity," and which the CDF in the passage above calls "the supreme authority of the Church".

It seems that from this we may be able to conclude that the asymmetry at the level of the two communions as a whole, the Catholic and the Orthodox, in only one of which the Church of Christ subsists, exists also at the level of the particular Catholic and Orthodox churches. For if it is possible, as the text of *Communionis notio* says it is, "for each particular Church to be fully Church,

---

40 Ibid. para. 16.
41 *Communionis notio* 13 (original emphasis). See above, Chapter 4, pp. 147-148, n. 118.
42 Cf. also the remark of Dom Gréa, "the particular church is in substance all that the universal Church is," quoted by H. de Lubac, "Les Églises particulières," 42, and in turn by McPartlan, *The Eucharist Makes the Church* (Edinburgh: T & T Clark, 1993; Fairfax, VA: Eastern Christian Publications, 2006), 111.

that is, the particular presence of the universal Church with all its essential elements," then it would necessarily follow that in each particular Church that *is* fully Church, i.e. in each particular Catholic church, the Church of Christ must subsist just as it subsists in the Catholic Church as a whole.[43] Then, since the CDF certainly *does* favor the idea that particular Catholic and Orthodox churches are sisters, it follows that two churches may be sisters even if the Church of Christ subsists in one of them and not in the other. This is the conclusion to which we have come, contrary to the suggestion of McPartlan that Catholic and Orthodox particular churches are sisters even though the Church of Christ subsists in neither of them, and the thesis of Legrand that if two churches are to be sisters the Church of Christ must subsist in them both. Instead, the asymmetrical relationship between one church in which the Church of Christ subsists and another in which it does not should not be seen as inconsistent with mutual recognition as sister churches. From the fact that such mutual recognition is already extended, with the approval of the Catholic magisterium, on the level of any two particular Catholic and Orthodox churches, it should be possible from the standpoint of Catholic ecclesiology also to affirm the Orthodox Church as a whole as the sister church of the Catholic Church as a whole, while adhering still to the position that the Church of Christ subsists only in the Catholic Church.

2. What is valuable about the supra-diocesan usage

There would be little point in going to the trouble of demonstrating that it should be permissible to speak of the two communions as a whole as sister churches unless there were some reason why there is an actual advantage in doing so. What is there that is gained by this usage that is not equally well secured by using the expression "sister churches" to refer to Catholic and Orthodox particular churches?

---

43 The CDF here seems to use "universal Church" and "Catholic Church" interchangeably. Although this is problematic as has often been noted in this study, I am following the CDF's terminology as a provisional method here, since there would be one too many moving pieces to keep track of, it seems, were there alternate senses of "universal Church" at play in this analysis. A fuller synthesis of the ideas of this section would require that the distinction be observed more carefully between the worldwide Catholic Church of today and the Church of Christ in its transcendent, eschatological mystery. Clearly, the Church of Christ does not "subsist in" the universal Church understood as the transcendent Church-mystery in its eschatological fullness – it *is* that Church-mystery – as it subsists in the canonical Catholic Church.

Chapter 6: The Adequacy and Value of the Concept of Sister Churches

I will address this question in two related steps. In the first, the focus will be on the limitations of the use of the expression "sister churches" exclusively on the level of particular churches. The analysis at this stage will have to do with the importance of supra-diocesan usage in general, with much of the discussion being about sister churches on the regional level. Then, as a next step, I will address in a more specific way the importance of the usage that describes the two entire communions as sisters.

As far as I am aware, Orthodox ecclesiologists have yet to concern themselves with the question of the inadequacy of the concept of sister churches if it is confined to the level of what Catholic ecclesiology calls particular churches. The question seems not to be raised in any of their writings. Papandreou must have it somehow in mind when he expresses his misgivings about the term "particular church" as used in Catholic ecclesiology and, again, when he takes issue with the CDF's prohibition on the application of "sister churches" to the two entire Catholic and Orthodox churches. But he still does not formulate, let alone answer, the question of what might be the actual ecclesiological *problem* with restricting the usage to the level of particular churches.

I shall attempt now to outline an answer to this question. The answer has both an ecclesiastical-historical and a dogmatic-theological component. In terms of ecclesiastical history, what has always concretely *mattered* about the concept of sister churches for the Orthodox in their dealings with the West has been the concept's significance on the supra-diocesan level.[44] Orthodox have applied it either to churches on the regional level – especially patriarchal sister churches – or to the two communions as a whole. It was seen in Chapter 1 that apart from its New Testament occurrences the language of sister churches was, in fact, always used historically to speak of churches on the level of metropolitan provinces or patriarchates; from the start of the Constantinian period onward it was never used to speak of diocesan churches.[45] It might perhaps be thought that the CDF, in reviving the application of the concept to churches at the most local level, i.e., that of the diocese, is somehow going back to a purer, pre-Constantinian meaning such as Lanne considered to be the most elemental, rooted in the basic fraternity of all Christians and of each and every Christian community, in contrast to the association that the language of sister churches later came to have with various canonical developments granting special status and prerogatives to this or that see over and above others.[46] But far from being

---

44 See above, Chapter 2, especially pp. 53-56, and Chapter 3, pp. 103-105.
45 See above, Chapter 1, pp. 11-13, 28-37.
46 See the discussion of Lanne's observations on this point in Chapter 4, pp. 115-116

a mere accomodation to the Roman empire, the phenomenon of sister churches at the supra-diocesan level, involving a canonically specified network of pre-eminent, metropolitan or patriarchal "mother churches," may be seen to have inherent theological value. This becomes apparent when the alternative – the absence of such a network of regional sees – is considered from the standpoint of an ecclesiology of communion.[47]

If "sister churches" applies only on the level of particular churches, then the conciliarity that would presumably characterize the relations among the sister churches has the least possible capability of coming into concrete contact with the only primacy that is affirmed beyond this level, namely, the universal primacy of the particular church of Rome. This lack of concrete contact between conciliarity (confined to the level of the particular churches) and primacy (reserved for the universal level) is to the detriment of both. There is a sense in which the conciliarity of all particular churches with all others throughout the entire world will have great difficulty in ever being anything more than an abstraction. In order to function realistically, the conciliarity of particular churches requires the activity and authority of primates at a level nearer to itself than the primacy of the universal *protos* can carry out or provide.

This line of thought has a certain affinity with the concept of "mutual inclusion" that was put forward by Hervé Legrand.[48] The phrase "mutual inclu-

---

and p. 118. Among Orthodox theologians, John Zizioulas, at least in his seminal book *Being as Communion* (Crestwood, NY: St. Vladimir's, 1985), 252, came out against the idea that there are truly churches on any level but the diocesan level. "[I]n spite of efforts made by some modern Orthodox to give to the patriarchates the name of 'local Church,' the principle of the equality of all bishops from the point of view of ecclesiological status has made it again impossible to create a special *ecclesial* entity out of the patriarchate." See Zizioulas' further remarks in the attendant footnote, n. 7. Here Zizioulas sounds much like Lanne. However, it may be said that in this respect Zizioulas supports a view not typical within Orthodoxy.

47 The fact that the 2007 Ravenna Document of the Joint International Commission for Theological Dialogue between the Roman Catholic Church and the Orthodox Church manifests an interest in reviving an appreciation for regional churches as being intrinsically important, makes all the more clear how pressing this issue is in current ecumenical and ecclesiological reflection. See the Ravenna Statement of October 13, 2007, "Ecclesiological and Canonical Consequences of the Sacramental Nature of the Church: Ecclesial Communion, Conciliarity and Authority," 10, 23-31. Available at www.vatican.va/roman_curia/pontifical_councils/chrstuni/ch_orthodox_docs/rc_pc_chrstuni_doc_20071013_documento-ravenna_en.html

48 See above, Chapter 4, p. 166.

sion" in its ecclesiological use goes back at least to Henri de Lubac, who said that "[w]henever there is mutual presence and inclusion, there is a perfect relationship."[49] It was used by Pope John Paul II in an address to the Roman curia in 1984 in which he was commenting on *Lumen Gentium* 13, where the subject of particular churches with their own traditions is addressed. The pope wished first to emphasize the distinctive Christian experiences of particular churches in their own socio-cultural contexts, and second, the requirement that these distinctive experiences, in order to be fruitful, "must not be lived in isolation or independently of, not to say in contradiction to, the lives of the churches in other parts of the world." The pope went on to invoke the phrase "mutual inclusion" in an important passage for our topic.

> In fact among the individual particular churches there is an ontological relationship of mutual inclusion: every particular church, as a realization of the one Church of Christ, is in some way present in all the particular churches 'in which and out of which the one and unique catholic Church has its existence.' This ontological relation must be translated on the dynamic level of concrete life, if the Christian community does not wish to be in contradiction with itself: the basic ecclesial choices of believers in one community must be able to be harmonized with those of the faithful in the other communities, in order to allow the communion of minds and hearts for which Christ prayed at the Last Supper.[50]

In the context of the intra-Catholic debate of the 1980s about the status of episcopal conferences, Joseph Komonchak derives from this passage several insights that may be seen as pertinent to the discussion of sister churches on the regional level in the bilateral dialogue between Catholics and Orthodox. Komonchak observes that in the passage above, a conceptual schema is offered that differs subtly yet significantly from standard presentations of the relation between the one church universal and the many particular churches. Rather than a relation between one (the universal church) and many (the particular churches) as though the one were *other* than the many historical local churches, a relation is posited between each (of the particular churches) and all (of the other particular churches). In this approach, it can still be said that the universal is included in each of the particular churches, but now it is not some prior

---

49 Cf. W. Kasper, "On the Church: A Friendly Reply to Cardinal Ratzinger," *America* (April 23-30, 2001), 12. Kasper attributes the quotation to de Lubac but without citing a specific text. Cf. H. de Lubac, *Les Eglises particulieries dons l'Eglise universelle*, Paris, Aubier Montaigne, 1971.
50 John Paul II, address to the Roman Curia, December 21, 1984: AAS 77 (1985), 503-514, as quoted by Komonchak, "The Local Church and the Church Catholic," 441.

or ideal universal church that is included, but precisely the church universal *as the communion of all*. By figuring the universal church in this way as the communion of all the particular churches rather than as something "out there" beyond the particular churches, Pope John Paul II has avoided de Lubac's well known criticism: "A universal church which would have a separate existence, or which someone imagined as existing outside the particular churches, is a mere abstraction."[51]

The connection between the idea of mutual inclusion and the role of regional churches can be seen by following the logic of John Paul II's thought. If this mutual inclusion is to be "translated on the dynamic level of concrete life," it cannot be that all are in relation to all in the same degree of immediacy. There are family relations. It is indeed a comparatively disembodied conception of the communion of the particular churches that would suggest that there is only an essential and universal likeness of all to all, on the one hand, and an individual distinction of each from each, on the other – without noting that in between universality and particularity, there are, as well, intermediary spheres of mutual inclusion, where some number of individual particular churches are characterized by something beyond their individual distinctions, but short of their universal characteristics.[52] What makes this intermediary sphere definitive as an ecclesial reality in its own right is the existence of a *protos* who makes possible, as the ordinary bishop does on the diocesan level and the pope does on the universal level, the reconciled diversity that is the mark of ecclesiality at any level.

---

51 Quoted by Kasper, "On the Church," 13, with reference to H. de Lubac, *Les églises particulières dans l'Église universelle*, 54.

52 The document of the Joint International Commission for Theological Dialogue between the Roman Catholic Church and the Orthodox Church, "The Mystery of the Church and of the Eucharist in the Light of the Mystery of the Holy Trinity, issued in Munich in 1982, says something similar: "This recognition [between one local church and others] is achieved first of all at the regional level. Communion in the same patriarchate or in some other form of regional unity is first of all a manifestation of the life of the Spirit in the same culture or in the same historical conditions. It equally implies unity of witness and calls for the exercise of fraternal correction in humility. This communion within the same region should extend itself further in the communion between sister churches" ("Mystery of the Church," III,3 [b]). See also above, Chapter 3, pp. 88-89. Although ambiguous, the reference to "sister churches" could be interpreted as speaking of a further extending of recognition between one entire grouping of local churches and another entire grouping. If so, this would be consistent with the argument I am making here.

Just as the Church as a whole can be addressed as "thou", and the church as a diocese can be addressed as "thou", so too the church as a province or patriarchate can be as well. This takes nothing away from the unity of the whole but contributes to it. It means, however, that the process of mutual indwelling, or mutual inclusion, must be understood in such a way that the universal church is formed in and out of the particular churches not just as so many freely floating interchangeable portions, but as they exist in their integrated context as members of one another in regional groupings, and thus more closely related to some than to others, as is the case in any real organism.[53]

3. How "sister churches" may apply to the two overarching churches of East and West

According to the canonical tradition accepted in the East unequivocally and, with some ambivalence, also in the West, there has always been a tiered structure among the patriarchal sees, a *taxis,* such that it is not Rome alone that stands above all the other patriarchates at the same distance, but differentiated relationships existing among the others as well. Here the *secondness* of Constantinople – a secondness that entails its own primacy in relation to the other major sees of the Byzantine East – has had a significance canonically and his-

---

53 Although the foregoing analysis has argued that "sister churches" at the level of particular churches is not enough, and that there must be comparable structures of conciliarity among regional churches as well, it should be said that "sister churches" at the regional level is not in itself sufficient, either, without the reality of "sister churches" at the level of the particular churches. This may seem self-evident, but the need to mention it arises in light of recent developments in one Orthodox jurisdiction in North America whose metropolitan abruptly announced a decision, apparently initiated by the jurisdiction's patriarch overseas, to change the status of those who until then had been diocesan bishops, such that from now on they would be auxiliary bishops (cf. Article 77 of "The Decision Regarding the Amending of Articles Concerning Bishops According to the By-laws of the Patriarchate," February 24, 2009; published in *The Word* (Englewood, NJ) 53:4 (April 2009) 15-17). With this decision – should it hold – it may be said that the ordinary bishops of the jurisdiction in question are rendered, in effect, "mere emanations of the [regional] primacy" (the expression is Legrand's; see above, Chapter 4, p. 166) and the entire Metropolitan province a virtual "single diocese" much in the way Congar described the ecclesiology resulting from the reforms of the 11th century Latin West. In this sense, in point of fact the CDF's embrace of "sister churches" on the level of particular churches might well be taken to heart, as offering, if not an all-sufficient, certainly an indispensable principle for both Orthodox and Catholic ecclesiology.

torically that cannot be overlooked. This secondness of Constantinople, which precedes the schism and was reflected very strongly in the Photian council of 879-880,[54] in later history was to be reinforced by the place of the patriarch of Constantinople as the ethnarch of the Rûm millet in the Ottoman Empire, and it was also in some sense expressed at the time of the fall of the Ottoman Empire in the encyclical of 1920[55] issued by the patriarchate of Constantinople with the self-understanding of having a role at the forefront of the ecumenical movement (in which at that time Rome still declined to participate).

In the *Tomos Agapis,* as has been seen, there are many indications that 20th century popes and ecumenical patriarchs alike have understood Constantinople as the leading see of the East, and therefore as being uniquely in a position to represent the other churches of the East, while Rome represented all the churches of the West.[56] While this put the two sees of Old Rome and New Rome on an equal footing in one respect, since it differentiated the two of them from all others, it did not make them mere coequals of one another, for the primacy of Old Rome continued to be assumed.[57] Thus the *secondness* of Constantinople is distinct from – one might even say, the antidote to – any duality on the level of the universal church.

This widely recognized secondness of the Ecumenical Patriarchate – as a canonically sanctioned form of primacy in itself which gained increasing importance in history, especially with the severely diminished influence of the other three Eastern patriarchal sees after the Muslim conquests – should make us pause before dismissing as an illegitimate innovation the use of "sister churches" to refer to the Roman Catholic Church in relation to the entire grouping of all the Eastern churches among which Constantinople has the first place. Today, Constantinople is by no means the only vibrant Eastern patriarchal see; there are again numerous others besides the ecumenical patriarchate, which itself in terms of sheer size is indeed dwarfed by several of them – above all, by the Russian Orthodox Church – and there is considerable reason once more for invoking the concept, roughly on the model of the ancient pentarchy,

---

54 See above, Chapter 5, pp. 184-185.
55 "Unto the Churches of Christ Everywhere," *Encyclical of the Ecumenical Patriarchate, 1920,* in Michael Kinnamon and Brian E. Cope, eds, *The Ecumenical Movement: An Anthology of Key Texts and Voices* (Grand Rapids and Geneva: Eerdmans and WCC Publications, 1997), 11-14.
56 See above, Chapter 3, pp. 109-110.
57 Cf. above, Chapter 2, p. 63, n. 55, Athenagoras' use of the phrase "younger sister" to refer to Constantinople in its relationship to Rome.

of *numerous* sister patriarchal churches in Catholic-Orthodox relations, all the more so to the extent that there might be an augmentation of the role and status of regional or national episcopal conferences within the Roman Catholic Church, as has been recommended by some Catholic ecclesiologists.[58]

Still, whatever may be the future of such regional ecclesial units in the West, and notwithstanding the relative proliferation of patriarchal churches in the East in modern times, the fact remains that the leading roles played by the two sees of Old Rome and New Rome in seeking to bring an end to the division between Orthodox churches and Catholic churches is no accident. It is reflective of a reality of the headship of the church of Rome in the West and the headship – however differently exercised – that has continued to be recognized as proper to the church of Constantinople in the East in spite of what must appear in purely temporal terms to be its exceeding insignificance. This reality of a Western church able to be represented by Rome and an Eastern church able, through somewhat different means, to be represented by Constantinople was very frequently expressed in the latter decades of the twentieth century by the phrase "sister churches" used intuitively, and without hesitation, to describe the relationship between the two communions as a whole. This need not, as has been said repeatedly, entail a simple parity between the two sisters, nor mean that in the event that full communion between them is restored, the universal church would then be a two-headed organism. It simply means that the *secondness* of Constantinople as a structural reality in the Church would continue to operate, as a primacy of its own, inlaid, as it were, within Rome's universal primacy, in such a way that the latter would not have the same immediate jurisdiction in the East as it does in the West.

B. Response to Orthodox concerns

Orthodox critics of "sister churches" in relations between Orthodox and Catholic churches maintain that there can be no authentic church outside the canonical boundaries of the Orthodox Church. From their point of view, the Catholic West is heretical in what it teaches, and its sacraments are inauthentic. But it has been seen that the positions of Orthodox critics of "sister churches" rejecting the faith and sacraments of the Catholic West are inseparable from their ecclesiological understanding of the unity of the Church and the nature of schism. For them, the notion that the Catholic West even conceivably could

---

58 See, for example, Thomas J. Reese, ed., *Episcopal Conferences: Historical, Canonical and Theological Studies* (Washington, DC: Georgetown, 1989).

turn out to hold the same faith as that of the Orthodox East, or that the sacraments of the Catholic West could turn out to be the very sacraments of the Church of Christ, seems to be excluded *a priori* by the fact that communion between the two traditions has been broken. The schism is its own disclosure of an ontological difference – a chasm that cannot be crossed, least of all by "reinterpretation" of disputed points of doctrine or of the condemnations of the past which, for Orthodox critics of "sister churches," have the status of infallible dogmas.

This is, as has been said, to adhere to a Cyprianic approach that Orthodox critics of "sister churches" have put forward as traditional, but that in fact does not reflect the complexity of the canonical tradition in the East, and cannot resolve that complexity. Nevertheless, the claim of Orthodox critics that there is no acceptable alternative to Cyprian's understanding of Church unity and the nature of schism – no alternative that does not amount to a form of ecclesiological relativism – remains a formidable challenge to contemporary Orthodox ecclesiology and, in particular, to advocates of the concept of "sister churches" in relations between Orthodox and Catholics.

The aim of the following pages is to demonstrate that it is possible from an Orthodox point of view to affirm the Roman Catholic Church as a sister church without falling into the ecclesiological relativism of the Branch Theory or approaches like it. My argument primarily builds on the groundwork laid, in rather different ways, by two Orthodox theologians, Georges Florovsky and John Zizioulas. Florovsky, as has been said, saw the sacramental theology of Augustine as providing the basic terms with which contemporary Orthodox ecclesiology can and even must articulate its own understanding of the question of the sacraments of those outside the visible unity of the Church.[59] Florovsky found Augustine's distinction between the validity and efficacy of sacraments to be profoundly consonant with Orthodox Christianity's understanding of the synergy, or cooperation, that must occur between the initiative of God's grace and the response of human love if human beings are to participate in the life of God, which is salvation. Florovsky also offered, though without expressly indicating as much, an important modification of Augustine's approach to the question of sacramental grace outside the unity of the Church. Zizioulas contributes, by means of his explication of eucharistic ecclesiology, a vision of the Church as an eschatological reality whose continuity in history must be understood as being rooted as much in the future as in the past. His perspective provides a way of coming to see that both the relativism of proponents of the

---

59 See above, Chapter 5, p. 230.

Branch theory and the exclusivism of its most ardent critics are ecclesiologically deficient in the same basic way: both claim to know more already about the true nature of the relationship between separated churches than can be known without reference to the future of that relationship.

Florovsky's appropriation of Augustine will be considered first. Florovsky rejected the theory of sacramental economy used by Nicodemos the Hagiorite and other 18th century defenders of Cyril V's *Definition* on baptism in their argument that the Orthodox tradition has always been fundamentally Cyprianic. According to Florovsky, "The 'economical' interpretation is not the teaching of the Church. It is only a private 'theological opinion,' very recent and very controversial, having arisen in a period of theological confusion and decadence in a hasty endeavor to dissociate oneself as sharply as possible from Roman theology."[60] Florovsky insisted that if it were really true that Roman Catholic baptism is no baptism at all, then a convert from the Roman Catholic Church *must* be baptized. To allow the sacrament to be dispensed with, for reasons of pastoral accommodation, was, for Florovsky, both theologically incoherent and pastorally reckless. This was because Florovsky, like Augustine, maintained that the sacraments themselves have an irreducible reality. "They have their own subsistence."[61] His approach thus differs from that of Cyprian who held that sacramental reality is determined by ecclesial context entirely. Florovsky believed that the thought of Augustine rather than Cyprian was capable of offering the proper foundation on which Orthodox sacramental theology could rest solidly and, after all, in conformity to its own ancient tradition, despite its having developed independently of Augustine.

> The sacramental theology of St. Augustine was generally not well known by the Eastern Church in antiquity. It also was not received by Byzantine theology, but not because they saw or suspected something alien or superfluous in it. In general, St. Augustine was not very well known in the East. In modern times the doctrine of the sacraments has been not infrequently expounded in the Orthodox East and in Russia on a Roman model and there is still no creative appropriation of St. Augustine's conception.[62]

---

60 G. Florovsky, "The Boundaries of the Church" (frequently translated elsewhere as "The Limits of the Church"), in *Ecumenism I: A Doctrinal Approach* (vol. XIII of *The Collected Works of Georges Florovsky*, ed. Richard S. Haugh [Belmont, MA: Nordland, 1989]), 41.

61 G. Florovsky, "The Doctrine of the Church and the Ecumenical Problem," *The Ecumenical Review* 2:2 (1950), 152-161, at 155.

62 Florovsky, "The Boundaries of the Church," 43.

Florovsky wrote these words in 1933. His characteristic dissatisfaction with the sort of treatment of the sacraments typical of the 'Roman model' of the manual theology of the 1930s is well known.[63] But whatever the limitations of some of these articulations, Florovsky saw in Augustine's thought on the sacraments an essential resource for the East no less than for the West. "Contemporary Orthodox theology," he wrote, "must express and explain the traditional canonical practice of the Church in relation to heretics and schismatics on the basis of those general premises which have been established by St. Augustine."[64]

Specifically, in the distinction which Augustine had drawn between the "validity" and "efficacy" of the sacraments Florovsky recognized the same intuition that lies at the heart of the Orthodox understanding of human participation in the salvation offered by God. Far from being mere juridical categories, these two terms signified "the two inseparable factors of sacramental existence, Divine grace and human love," which Florovsky regarded as "characteristic of the whole sacramental theology of St. Augustine". On the one hand, as Florovsky put it: "the sacrament is accomplished by [divine] grace and not by [human] love". And on the other hand: "man is saved in freedom and not in compulsion, and for that reason grace somehow does not burn with a life-giving flame outside Catholicity and love".[65]

For Augustine, it was precisely this love that could be neither present nor operative among those who were in schism. The gift of the sacraments was as freely offered by God to them as to those in the unity of the Church, but the gift could not be fruitfully received by those outside, because of the absence of charity among them. Augustine, then, considered that between Catholics and schismatics there was something in common as well as a decisive difference. There was, as he put it, "something which is Catholic outside the Catholic Church,"[66] namely the gift of the sacraments themselves, so long as their administration was formally correct, but outside the Catholic Church there was not that love by which sacramental grace is able to be received fruitfully for salvation.

---

63 The penetration of Latin scholasticism into Russia in the 17th century is what led Florovsky to speak critically of a "pseudomorphosis", or "Babylonian captivity", of Orthodox theology beginning at that time. See "Patristic Theology and the Ethos of the Orthodox Church," in *The Collected Works of Georges Florovsky*, vol. IV, part II (Belmont, MA: Nordland, 1987), 15-22.
64 Florovsky, "The Boundaries of the Church," 43.
65 Ibid.
66 Augustine, *De Baptismo*, Book VII, ch. 39.77, in P. Schaff, ed., *NPNF* (1st ser.), vol. IV (Peabody, MA: Hendrickson, 1994), 508.

On this point, Florovsky actually modifies Augustine's approach in an important way, though without explicit acknowledgment of doing so. Augustine identified the moment when schismatic baptism becomes fruitful for salvation with the moment when an individual who was baptized in schism returns to the catholic fold. Florovsky speaks somewhat differently of a dynamic process that begins already to unfold prior to the moment of reunification and that is characterized by a welling up of love in those who have been in schism. This upsurge of love is associated with the sacraments as a mysterious presence and activity of the Church beyond its visible unity.

> In the sects themselves and even among heretics the Church continues to perform her saving and sanctifying work. It may not follow, perhaps, that we should say, the schismatics are *still in the Church;* at all events this would not be very precise. It would be more accurate to say that the Church continues to work in the schisms in expectation of the mysterious hour when the stubborn heart will be melted in the warmth of "preparatory grace", when the will and thirst for communality and unity will burst into flame and burn. The "validity" of the sacraments among schismatics is the mysterious guarantee of their return to Catholic plenitude and unity.[67]

It will be recalled that Basil the Great was the one to have spoken of schismatics as being "still of the Church."[68] Florovsky prefers to put it the other way around and say that the Church is still at work in *them*. The entire passage is permeated by an idea of the *ecclesia extra ecclesiam*. In this regard it should be further noted that Florovsky refers not exclusively to schismatics as individuals, as Augustine tended to do, but, at more than one point in the passage above, to schismatic communities: "In the sects themselves ...", "the Church continues to work in the schisms". Florovsky's idea of "preparatory grace" seems to envision a corporate movement toward catholic unity on the part of a schismatic community as a whole.

Florovsky does not address the question of how much time might elapse between the moment when "preparatory grace" begins to be active within a schismatic community and the moment when such a community actually enters, formally, into communion again with the catholic church in its unity. The impression may be that there would be very little time in between, but it would be reasonable to suppose that there might be a more extended interval from the moment when the "will and thirst for communality and unity" first flares up in the hearts of those separated to the moment when this burning desire for catho-

---

67 Florovsky, "The Boundaries of the Church," 43 (original emphasis).
68 See above, Chapter 5, pp. 198-199.

lic unity is fulfilled in formal, visible reconciliation with the Church in its canonical integrity.

The profound ecumenical importance of Florovsky's notion of "preparatory grace" is that it allows for, and renders theologically coherent, the possibility that out in the very realm of those formally in schism, the drama of the battle between the schismatic and the catholic spirit might not have ceased to take place; the sacraments, according to Florovsky's understanding, are the essential and mysterious guarantee that this drama might still meaningfully take place there too. This is possible because of the "something Catholic" that the sacraments perfectly and indestructibly embody.[69]

Of course if there is such a possibility, then it will be impossible for those *within* the inner sanctum of the Church to be anything but passionately interested in the unfolding of this dramatic battle taking place among those outside the unity of the Church but still "within" the *ecclesia extra ecclesiam*, and in doing everything they possibly can to encourage the eventual victory of the catholic, rather than the schismatic, spirit in such formally schismatic communities. This may be said to be the basis of the ecumenical movement from the Orthodox point of view – and, indeed, from the Roman Catholic point of view as well. A separated community may or may not be essentially schismatic in spirit; one can no longer simply assume this, as though it were axiomatic. Yves Congar's studies of Christian division led him to a similar conclusion,[70] and Vatican II's Decree on Ecumenism unequivocally attributes the longing for unity *among separated Christians* to nothing less than the grace of the Holy Spirit. When, in the same vein, the author to whom we shall shortly turn, Metropolitan John Zizioulas, is able to speak of an historical "lack of love" between separated Christians "which is now, thank God, disappearing," he too refers to the same reality that Florovsky describes as being mysteriously present

---

69 Although Florovsky speaks of the sacraments among schismatics as "the mysterious guarantee of their return to Catholic plenitude and unity", it seems preferable to think of them more precisely as the mysterious guarantee of the ongoing possibility of their return, that is, the guarantee of the reality among them of an authentically ecclesial drama such as I have described. This indeed is more in keeping with the overall logic of Florovsky's own thought. As he wrote himself in a passage previously quoted, "Man is saved in freedom and not in compulsion" (see above, p. 268). So it is not the hoped-for outcome but its real possibility that is secured by the gift of the sacraments among schismatics.

70 Cf. Congar, *After Nine Hundred Years*, 4-5: "... when one passes from the sin of schism personally and formally committed, to Christian communities in a state of schism, the thing becomes rather more complicated."

even where division visibly remains.⁷¹ The centrifugal forces that once led certain communities to separate from the unity of the Church are not *guaranteed* to go on prevailing over the centripetal forces also capable of shaping those same communities, indeed shaping them from within, impelling them in the direction of catholic unity.

We have here a paradox at a level even deeper than the one that lay at the center of Augustine's treatise on baptism. That was the paradox, unimaginable to the Donatists, of a unity of sacraments between the visibly one Church and those separated. Here there is the further, paradoxical possibility of an actual unity of love between the visibly one Church and those separated. Was it not the surprised rediscovery of this reciprocal love by Catholic and Orthodox Christians in the 20th century that led them to invoke the language of sister churches in spite of their having been so long separated?⁷²

The ecclesiological vision of Zizioulas provides a further lens through which to see how *even in the realm of formal schism* there might be the presence of a love already mysteriously uniting schismatics and catholics. By the way in which it understands sacramental grace as an inbreaking of the *future* into the present in the life of the Church, eucharistic ecclesiology⁷³ offers a framework in which it is possible to conceive of the paradoxical growth, not without dramatic tension, of a life-giving catholic love from out of the very ground where a death-dealing spirit of division may have once threatened a given community. This again is possible because the Holy Spirit who hallows that ground does so by coming to it not exclusively, or even primarily, from the *past* but from the *future*.

---

71 J. Zizioulas, "Orthodox Ecclesiology and the Ecumenical Movement," *Sourozh* 21 (1985) 16-27, at 23.
72 This love is not susceptible to categorization in the same way as the sacraments are according to formal criteria of validity, and so on; it is as subjective and spontaneous as the sacraments are objective and given. But it is no less real, and no less capable of being visibly realized and discerned. The significance of the language of "sister churches" in 20th century Catholic-Orthodox relations cannot be understood fully apart from this subjective dimension. In fact, the words "sister churches" not only refer to the love between the two traditions but embody it, and actively communicate it.
73 It should be noted that in some presentations of eucharistic ecclesiology, the eschatological dimension is less pronounced, whereas it is brought out very strongly in the works of Zizioulas and McPartlan, whose respective presentations I have most in mind here. On the comparative neglect of an eschatological focus in the eucharistic ecclesiology of de Lubac, see McPartlan, *The Eucharist Makes the Church*, 105-113.

Zizioulas has written that the "body of Christ, which is the body of the Eucharist and of the Church at the same time, is the body of the *Risen*, the eschatological Christ."[74] In this understanding, one community separated from another by walls of visible division in the present, but whose destiny is to be united with the other in the near future by a love that is already at work in it mysteriously, is able to be nourished in that love and drawn forward, one may aptly say *quickened*, by the eucharist, in which the fullness of the eschatological Christ is made present. Each community is indeed offered the chance to experience in the eucharist mysteriously – even though still celebrated in separation – the joyous hope of its coming unity with the other.[75] This must not be taken to mean that each separated community *will* be nourished in this hope and be drawn forward by it to the point of actually reuniting with the Church in its visible unity. (Such ongoing forward movement toward unity is not guaranteed, either by the sacrament's validity or by whatever signs may be discerned, presently, of the formally schismatic community's desire to be moving in such a direction.) But it *may* be: this much is guaranteed, so long as there is the combination of sacramental validity and some discernible sign of "preparatory grace" active in the separated community in question.

The Branch theory inverted

How all of this reflects a very different ecclesiology from the Branch Theory can be easily seen from a brief comparison of the two approaches. With the Branch Theory, the unity of the various branches with one another is considered to be an already established fact; it is rooted in their unity in the past, along with certain verifiable constants (e.g., apostolic succession). The Branch Theory crowns the branches as Church already now and without reference at all to the direction in which they may grow in the future in relation to each other. Should

---

74 Zizioulas, "The Ecclesiological Presuppositions of the Holy Eucharist," *Nicolaus* 10 (1982) 333-349, at 342 (original emphasis).
75 Zizioulas has written as follows about the mysterious presence of the future in the eucharist: "the Church's *anamnesis* acquires the eucharistic paradox which no historical consciousness can ever comprehend, i.e. the *memory of the future*, as we find it in the anaphora of the Liturgy of St. John Chrysostom: 'Remembering the cross, the resurrection, the ascension *and the second coming*, Thine own of Thine own we offer Thee'" (J. Zizioulas, *Being As Communion*, op. cit., 180 [emphasis in original].) I am suggesting here that this meta-memory of the eschatological fulfillment may contain within itself, also, more particular memories of what has yet to be realized in time and will be realized *before* the second coming.

they continue to grow farther and farther apart, this would not alter the fundamental continuity which marks, so the theory assumes, the relation of each with the past common to all. But in the eschatological framework of the eucharistic ecclesiology of Zizioulas, as this has been shown to cast light on Florovsky's understanding of present schism and future unity, it is as though the Branch Theory were turned on its head. Here, the foundation of the unity of the presently separated branches is located in a future in which they will have converged – or not.

Indeed, the inverted branch theory I am proposing would be no better than a dangerously "realized eschatology" were it to pretend that it can know that the future convergence it envisions will come to pass. It must somehow simultaneously hold open the possibilities that it will and that it will not. Light on the issue may be shed by looking at how the unity of the Church in the first millennium was rendered, for periods of time, ambiguous by certain schisms (e.g., the Acacian schism [484-518], the so-called Photian schism [863-867], etc.) which proved to be impermanent. In retrospect one *can* say that the Church continued to be present and operative on both sides of those divisions while they lasted – much as the Branch Theory proponents are inclined to say, in general. But in contrast to the Branch Theory, the basis for this affirmation of the true and ongoing ecclesiality of both branches, or streams, which divided from one another temporarily in the first millennium, lies in the fact that they eventually reunited. Prior to the moment when the divided streams were reintegrated, there would necessarily have been, from the internal standpoint of each, *uncertainty* about the status of the other. The both–and possibility (both branches are indeed the Church) would have been held open, but so too an either–or possibility (only one or the other is the Church), since there was no absolute assurance of a happy ending to the schism.

The present schism, between Orthodox East and Catholic West, may be seen in the pattern of earlier ones such as these, for like them, and in spite of its much longer duration, which has had to do with many factors including political ones, this division too may end happily but is not assured of ending happily. As was necessary then, so too in the present circumstances it is necessary to hold open both the either–or *possibility* and the both–and *possibility* – as a paradoxical "both-and" in itself.

In view of these observations, it may be possible to offer a certain clarification about the significance of "open" and "closed" communion, such a clarification being able to shed light on how two churches barred from one another's communion may still be sister churches. Contrary to a common understanding, the shut door of "closed communion" is not a final act, signifying an end of relations between those inside and those without. It is rather a sign of the urgent need for relations to be restored. By and large, advocates of an ecumenical approach patterned on the Branch Theory believe that there ought to be "open communion" among all Christians baptized in the name of the Trinity. But this misses the point of the essential difference between baptism and eucharist, which is that the sacrament of baptism, as an unrepeatable act of initiation, is capable of signifying and effecting unity, and only unity. One cannot be cut off from the sacramental reality of baptism once it is given. Yet as early as in the Corinthian community overseen by Paul we find a possibility of being cut off from the eucharist – and then also of being readmitted.[76] Were it not for the possibility of removal from the unity of the gathering, this unity would quickly lose all content and meaning.

What applies in the case of individuals in a local gathering also may be said to apply in the case of individual communities in the larger scope of the Church as a whole. If the unity among all the local churches with one another is to be dynamic rather than static, there will need to be this possibility of putting some outside, but still not without hope of their being readmitted. Of course in the case of some schisms in the history of the Church there is the further complexity that both parties put one another outside, as was so between the sees of Rome and Constantinople in 1054 and remains so for the whole Catholic and Orthodox churches to this day. But regardless of which of the two is properly to be counted as maintaining itself within the unity of the Church and which of the two is regarded as being outside, the discipline of "closed communion" signifies, in any case – as baptism cannot do – that brokenness has arisen among those baptized, that there is an inside and an outside in need of being reintegrated. And it makes present the threat that this brokenness might be final, though it does so, to say it again, without removing the hope of its being only temporary. In other words, a break in eucharistic communion between two or more local churches is not a final statement. To designate a schismatic or a "heretical" community as being outside the unity of the Church is not to *answer* the question of that community's ultimate identity (as being of the Church or not of the Church); it is rather to raise it, in the most serious possible way.

It may be asked, with regard to the baptized individual whose very identity as a Christian has been conspicuously put in question by his being kept from receiving the eucharist: is he still a brother in Christ to those whose identities as Christians has *not* been conspicuously put in such dreadful question?

---

76 Cf. 1 Cor 5:3-5 and 2 Cor 2:5-11.

Throughout *De Baptismo*, Augustine relates the sin of schism to other forms of sin, specifically those that occur *within* the formal limits of the Church in its visible unity and that also create a rupture which, if not healed, will eternally separate the person in question from the true body of "the chaste dove," the Church.[77] He maintains that formally correct baptism is valid *everywhere* it is administered and, at the same time, is of no avail to *anyone* who receives it unworthily, that is, in sins for which he refuses to repent. It makes no difference whether a person enclosed in sin is "openly severed from us, or secretly severed whilst within our body"[78] – in other words, whether outside the canonical limits of the Church or inside.

> For ... neither the one nor the other of these men is found in the body of the one uncorrupt, holy, chaste dove, which has neither spot nor wrinkle. And just as baptism is of no profit to the man [inside the visible limits of the Church] who renounces the world in words and not in deeds, so it is of no profit to him who is baptized in heresy or schism; but each of them, when he amends his ways, begins to receive profit from that which before was not profitable, but was yet already in him.[79]

According to Augustine, a question mark hangs over the identity of the secretly unrepentant sinner *within* the Church in its visible unity just as it does, only in a more conspicuous way, over the identity of the openly separated schismatic. The possibility is there for both alike to remain severed. If it were on no more than this basis, the solidarity between the one and the other would be of rather little interest, for it would be only solidarity in sin; but in addition, the possibility is there as well for both alike to amend their ways and be healed. The Christian brotherhood of the two is a function of their both having these twin possibilities, either of being drawn into full participation in the pure body of the Church by the gift that is already in them, or of resisting being drawn into such participation. And in fact these twin possibilities are characteristic of the circumstance of every individual Christian. For although not all who remain in the visible unity of the Church are, like the example of Augustine's hypocrite, secretly severed from it, all have the potential to be.

---

77 He does so in the process of making the argument for his famous principle *ex opere operato*, which says that sacraments are gifts of God that cannot be polluted by the failures of those who administer them, and thus that even schismatic sacraments are still valid.
78 Augustine, *De Baptismo*, Book IV, ch. 4.6, in P. Schaff, ed., *NPNF* (1st ser.), vol. IV, 448.
79 Ibid.

We may now ask, similarly, with respect to whole separated *communities* of the baptized: do they, even while a dreadful question mark conspicuously hangs over their identity as Christian communities (insofar as they are denied full participation in the eucharist of the Church in its visible unity), nevertheless remain sister churches to those communities over which there is no such conspicuous question mark?

Florovsky's observation that "the Church continues to work in the schisms", and does so precisely through the sacraments which remain valid there, indicates a positive answer to the question. To say that the "Church continues to work" in a separated Christian community is much the same as saying that it is "present and operative" there (as the Catholic magisterium puts it in describing the ecclesial reality it recognizes outside the Catholic Church).[80]

Thus it becomes possible to see how two local communities, one within the canonical limits of the Church and the other outside, may be sister churches of one another. They are so paradoxically. There is a paradoxical *asymmetry* to their relationship as sister churches, an asymmetry that is directly tied to the need for keeping open the either–or possibility (that just one "branch" *or* the other will turn out to be the Church). There is a sturdier branch and a weaker. One is in no danger of falling fatally away as the other is. What makes this asymmetrical aspect of the relationship all the more paradoxical is that both traditions, Catholic and Orthodox alike, insist upon it in just the same way, though they reverse their respective positions, as was mentioned above.[81] But each has its ecclesiologically indispensable language for expressing the possibility that it may turn out to be the Church alone.

This either–or *possibility* is accounted for in Catholic ecclesiology by "subsists in" (in its moderate interpretation, e.g. by the CDF and Sullivan) and in Orthodox ecclesiology by the notion of the *ecclesia extra ecclesiam*. In each approach, the either–or possibility is allowed to remain just that – a possibility – and no more; it is not hardened into a certainty. The both–and possibility is accounted for, meanwhile, in Catholic and Orthodox ecclesiology alike, by the expression "sister churches". If understood properly, "sister churches" between Catholics and Orthodox does not exclude the understanding expressed by the principle of "subsists in" or *ecclesia extra ecclesiam*. It may be said that a proper understanding of each doctrine is conditioned by a proper understanding of the other.[82] Interpretations of "subsists in" become distorted when they cease to

---

80 See *Dominus Iesus*, 17.
81 See above, Chapter 4, pp. 178-179.
82 It may be recalled here that John Paul II used the term "doctrine" in reference to

account for the both–and possibility held open by "sister churches" (cf. Garuti, Becker) as well as when they brighten that possibility virtually to the point of rendering it an already certain reality (cf. Hryniewicz, Legrand). As has been mentioned, the paradoxical grammar of the phrase *ecclesia extra ecclesiam* seems to hold both the either–or and the both–and possibilities together precisely as possibilities.

The ecumenical significance of "sister churches" in Catholic-Orthodox relations is, then, that it leaves *dogmatically open* the possibility of convergence. Although this is a possibility and not a certainty, it is a possibility guaranteed – certainly guaranteed – by a variety of concrete realities, some already given in the past (e.g., baptism, apostolic succession), others discerned as alive in the present (e.g., "preparatory grace").

It should be observed that one could envision a circumstance in which over the course of time the both–and possibility might reach a point of ceasing to be applicable. If, another thousand years from now (or two thousand or three), there were to have been no movement in the canonical status of the churches concerned, Orthodox churches would still then be said to be sister churches of one another, but it is doubtful that Orthodox and Catholic churches could still then be described meaningfully as sister churches as they can be today. Perhaps it is too much to suggest that the expression in its ecumenical use between Catholics and Orthodox has an expiration date attached to it – who could fix such a date, in any case? – yet the expression's meaning should certainly be understood in connection with the very particular *kairos* in which it has arisen.

IV. Concluding Observations

A constant presupposition of the preceding two parts of section III has been that the only way in which the Catholic Church and the Orthodox Church may regard themselves as sister churches of one another is if the relationship between them is understood to be asymmetrical. Indeed throughout this study as a whole there has been an effort to dislodge the idea of the sameness of sister churches.

"sister churches" in *Ut unum sint*, n. 60 (see above, Introduction, p. 1). Just as "sister churches" does not conflict with "subsists in" properly understood, so too it does not conflict with the Orthodox notion of the *ecclesia extra ecclesiam*. Indeed it may be said about the latter that it, even more than "subsists in," by the very nature of its paradoxical grammar, seems to contain *both* the both–and significance of "sister churches" *and* the either–or significance required by the doctrine of the unicity of the Church.

In general, and even quite apart from the circumstance of the schism, sister churches cannot properly relate to one another unless there is, at each level, one among them that is the first, and there is something paradoxical even here[83]; but the requirement that relations between or among sister churches be asymmetrical takes on an added paradoxical significance when the churches in question are formally divided. For then it is not only that just one among them must be recognized as first (in view of the normal workings of their common life together), but that just one among them must be identified as the very locus of the enduring unity of the Church (in view of the possibly ongoing circumstance of their separation). If they should persist in their division *in perpetuam*, both cannot be the Church.

Till now the question has been left conspicuously unaddressed whether, if full communion is to be restored between the Catholic Church and the Orthodox Church, there must first be agreement between them as to which of the two is correct in its claim to be the privileged ecclesial locus that the other is not. In other words, in order for there to be unity, must not the Orthodox first agree that the Church of Christ subsists in the Catholic Church alone? Or, conversely, must not Catholics first agree with respect to the phrase and concept of the *ecclesia extra ecclesiam* that the *"ecclesiam"* – that is, the visibly one church – is the Orthodox Church, and that it is the Catholic Church that has existed outside of this since the schism?

A few observations may be offered in regard to this issue. To be the one and only church in which subsists the Church of Christ that also, however, is paradoxically present and operative in another church – indeed, is *discerned and proclaimed* to be present and operative there, thus qualifying the other church as a sister church – implies an asymmetry with regard to which great care is required in order not to draw incorrect conclusions. It would be a mistake, for example, to suppose that this asymmetry pertains to the present life of the sister churches in such a way that would prejudge the contributions of the separated church as being in every circumstance less valuable than, or somehow merely reduplicative of, what is already apprehended by the visibly one church. In

---

83 As may be seen in the congratulatory message sent by Ecumenical Patriarch Bartholomew to Patriarch Kirill of Moscow and All-Russia on January 27, 2009: "On the occasion of your well-deserved election today as the new Head of the *most holy sister and chosen daughter Church of Russia*, we convey to you our heartfelt brotherly salutation, both of the Church of Constantinople, the Ecumenical Patriarchate, and of our Modesty personally" (*SEIA Newsletter on the Eastern Churches and Ecumenism*, n. 160 [January 31, 2009], 4.)

every tension between the church in which the Church of Christ subsists and the church in which the Church of Christ is "only" present and operative, it cannot be assumed that the former has the more comprehensive and balanced view.[84]

So long as there are two churches, in one of which the Church of Christ subsists, and in the other of which the Church of Christ is truly present and operative, it must be said that *either of them without the other* may be capable of going egregiously wrong. The self-sufficiency of either one is unknowable based on the current situation of still real, if imperfect, communion between them.[85] Their ongoing, though less than full, communion establishes the conditions of a certain interdependence. It is not such as to mean that the visibly one church *could* not do without the sister church outside, *if* the latter were to cease to be, in fact, a sister church, that is, a true church in which the grace of God is given and discernibly received. The principle of asymmetry that is expressed by "subsists in" signifies precisely that the visibly one church *could* do very well without the other *in that event*. But short of that event, the visibly one church meanwhile perceives that here and now it cannot do without what there is of the discernible reality of the Church of Christ outside itself; at least, it would neither dare nor wish to try.

It *could* do without the other – this is what "subsists in" means. It *cannot* do without the other – this is what "sister churches" means. So long as the separated community survives and continues to be fruit-bearing, the visibly one church by its very nature will identify itself with it, seek to unite itself with it, be open at once to receiving from it all the gifts it already is producing. These the visibly one church will recognize as gifts "from above", even before the unity it seeks with the separated community is fully or formally fulfilled.

---

84 Cf. *Unitatis Redintegratio*, 17, whose observations are consistent with this point.
85 The proof of either one's self-sufficiency could not be established except by means of a test which only a madman would wish to see performed: namely, the ongoing separation – indeed, the increased isolation – of the two communions in order to see which of the two might survive "on its own," and which would be the first to collapse. Paradoxically, the church which would be quickest to refuse any such experiment, and to prefer even to admit its need for the other church instead of undertaking such a mad venture, would perhaps prove, precisely by renouncing its claim to be the *sine qua non* of Christian reality in the world, to be after all the genuine locus of the *mater ecclesia* on earth. Here the obvious parallel suggests itself with the story of the two rival claimants to being the true mother of the child whom Solomon proposes to cut in half in 1 Kings 3:16-28. It is the one who would prefer to have the child live than to be recognized as its mother who is revealed as the true mother.

In light of these observations, it may be suggested that a mutual acknowledgment of interdependence on the part of Catholics and Orthodox might be a sufficient basis for the two churches to move forward with the reestablishment of full communion – were other outstanding issues adequately resolved – without first, or ever, having to reach an agreement about each other's exclusive claim to be the visibly one church. It may also be said that the recognition of one another as sister churches is tantamount to such a mutual acknowledgment of interdependence. If there is any dogmatic content to the concept of sister churches, it is certainly to be found here: sister churches are those that realize they cannot know they have no need of one another. At the same time, we have seen that together with the principle of interdependence expressed in "sister churches", the principle of asymmetricality expressed in *subsistit in* and *ecclesia extra ecclesiam* must be seen as an equally important dogmatic marker in the paradoxical context of the division.

The challenge is to hold the twin principles of interdependence and asymmetricality in the proper tension required by the *actual situation* in which the two churches find themselves – always an evolving situation. Neither principle can be entirely dispensed with so long as the two churches remain divided and remain truly churches in one another's eyes. One principle or the other, however, will and should become a more accentuated point of reference as circumstances warrant. Were nothing in the manner of authentic ecclesial gifts to pass between them any longer, only the one and not the other would be the embodiment of the Church, and it can be said, in faith, already now that this would be the case. But the extent to which this needs to be said recedes as communion between the two in the present continues to be more and more unmistakably real and vital, in other words as the day when restoration of full communion between them draws nearer. With so much circulation of ecclesial lifeblood passing now between the two, even to speak of either of them as that church in which "alone" the Church of Christ subsists has less and less pertinence to the actual situation; it becomes more and more hypothetical. The "visibly one church" becomes ever more difficult for either church to identify as itself apart from the other, with which it is ever more manifestly in real communion.

Chapter 7
CONCLUSION

In their mutual relations since the start of Vatican II, Catholics and Orthodox have used the language of sister churches to convey a variety of meanings. Broadly speaking, these have related either to questions about the structure of the Church as a communion of many churches or to questions about the nature of schism. In the first sense, the expression has served as a kind of shorthand for the communion ecclesiology that was a hallmark of so much thinking about the Church especially in the latter half of the 20th century. This ecclesiology entails a renewed appreciation for the catholicity of the local church as the full presence of the Church universal in each place, for the sacramental rather than only the juridical dimension of episcopal office, for the importance of "inculturation" for the mission of the Church, and for the value of legitimate diversity in liturgical forms, canonical discipline, and even theological expression. When intended to call to mind these fundamental tenets of ecclesiology, the expression "sister churches" has conveyed a relatively stable set of meanings.

However, it has also been used to convey something not as susceptible to being articulated in constant terms, something about the nature of the schism between Catholic West and Orthodox East that is remarkably different from what either tradition would have said about their separation a century or two earlier and that does not lend itself, either, to being considered as a fixed description applicable to the two traditions into the indefinite future, without reference to the possible directions in which they go in relation to each other from now on. Because of this more open-ended significance of the expression, and in order to affirm the self-sufficiency of the Catholic Church whether its unity with the Orthodox is ever restored or not, Garuti has seen fit to say of particular Orthodox Churches that they should be considered, from a Catholic standpoint, as sister churches only in an "imperfect" sense.[1] However, the more precise conclusion to which this study's analysis has pointed is that Catholic and Orthodox Churches are sister churches of one another not in an imperfect sense but in what might be called a future perfect sense. They are sister churches now on the basis of the hope that they will turn out to have been sister churches – a hope not at all "optimistic" but sober, indeed dogmatic in character, rooted as it is in given realities, together with corroborative present

---

1 See above, Chapter 4, p. 149.

experience that is also real. The fulfillment of this hope is not guaranteed, but that should not prevent the expression's being used across the confessional divide. For in fact even when we speak of a configuration of Catholic churches among themselves, or Orthodox churches among themselves, it is still always only by means of a certain borrowing from the future that we ever speak in the present tense of being related as sister churches. We say – even in this case – that churches are so only in the sense that we have the basis in the present for hoping that they will continue to be so. Particular Catholic churches can go in this or that direction over time and cease to be Catholic. So too particular Orthodox churches may find themselves non-Orthodox at a later point in time. With concrete communities – sister churches – this has always been and will always be the way.

The two broad sets of meanings outlined here may be described as the ecclesiological and the ecumenical dimensions of the concept of sister churches, with the ecclesiological having in some sense the more well-defined content, and the ecumenical being more paradoxical and, one might even say, apophatic (i.e., one must say that the other is a sister church because one cannot say that it is not). Ironically perhaps, and apart from the discomfort of Garuti with the expression's ecumenical significance, the Catholic side has been the one since Vatican II that has been more firm in its commitment to the expression "sister churches" in its paradoxical ecumenical implications. Here the monumental idea of "subsists in" – as properly interpreted so that its paradoxical character is preserved – has played a key role. Among the Orthodox, the notion of the *ecclesia extra ecclesiam* has just as much potential, if not even more, for doing justice to the paradoxical reality of formally divided "sister churches" while also upholding the doctrine of the Church as one, but its promise has yet to be effectively mined. In consequence, Orthodox discomfort with the ecumenical dimension of the concept of sister churches remains widespread. Meanwhile on the Catholic side there has been an increasing uneasiness about the *ecclesiological* dimension of the concept of sister churches, about which the Orthodox have never had any doubt. Here again, however, the lack of a more comprehensive and cogent articulation of the authentic Orthodox position seems to have contributed to the difficulty all around.

In particular, by propounding and advocating "sister churches" as though it were the self-sufficient alternative to or bulwark against the supposed evil of primacy, instead of what it truly is, a reality complementary to and inextricable from primacy, the Orthodox have done much to encourage a correspondingly one-sided Catholic view that would suggest that primacy is the all-important principle to be safeguarded from the threat allegedly posed by "sister churches".

Chapter 7: Conclusion

One manifestation of this unfortunate separation of primacy from conciliarity (and vice versa) has been the CDF's restriction of "sister churches" in Catholic-Orthodox relations to the level of ecclesial life farthest removed from the universal primacy of Rome – namely, to the level of the particular churches. Orthodox advocates of the concept have voiced surprisingly little protest over this restriction, given that it devalues, if not actually denies, the significance of the concept on the regional level where the expression is most commonly and characteristically applied in their own usage (and indeed in that of the Christian tradition generally). Perhaps the reason for their lack of protest is that next to the stance of Orthodox critics rejecting the concept's ecumenical use at all levels, the stance of Catholic critics restricting usage to just the level of particular churches looks ecumenically favorable by comparison. But the ecclesiological limitations of this stance have been shown, and its alternative, which emphasizes regional sister churches as structurally important in the life of the Church, has been suggested. According to this alternative vision, there are sister churches at three levels at least (the level of the diocese, the level of the autocephalous or patriarchal church, and the level of the two whole churches of East and West), and corresponding primacies at each level. Always there must be a primacy *within* each sister church, by virtue of which each is a corporate personality, and there must be a primacy *among* or *between* the sister churches, in other words a proper *taxis*, by virtue of which at each level there is assured the means of a unified diversity of the sisters.

In the circumstance of schism, and in particular, of the schism between Orthodox East and Catholic West, it has been seen that the relationship of sister churches is bound up not only with the matter of primacy (as is the case even where there is no schism), but also with questions about the unicity and continuity of the Church. It has been argued that in this context, the two churches as a whole, insofar as they have recognized one another in recent decades as sister churches, have effectively acknowledged their interdependence, yet in such a way that involves a paradox – namely, that of an ongoing asymmetry. The meaning of this asymmetry can perhaps be best expressed by saying that if the anomaly of their division were to become complete and permanent, one of the two alone would be the Church. But it has also been shown that it is a mistake to derive from this principle of asymmetry any notion (so long as there continues to be communion between the two churches, even if imperfect) of the self-sufficiency of the visibly one church apart from the separated church, or – what amounts to the same thing – any notion of a direct dependency of the separated church on the visibly one church. This again is Garuti's mistake. By claiming that Orthodox particular churches derive their ecclesial being, not from the Church of Christ but from the Catholic Church, Garuti effectively excludes the possibility of an interdependence of any kind between the Catholic Church in which subsists the Church of Christ and the Orthodox Church in which is present and operative that same Church of Christ. In this respect his outlook mirrors that of Orthodox critics of "sister churches" who similarly identify the Orthodox Church with the Church of Christ, with nothing vital of the latter remaining outside the canonical boundaries of Orthodoxy. Against both views, it has been argued here that so long as there *is* the reality of the *ecclesia extra ecclesiam*, a reality that the visibly one church itself perceives, then this visibly one church cannot be sure of needing nothing from the separated church in which God still communicates himself.

When it comes to recognizing or not recognizing the sacramental and ecclesial reality of a separated community – and thus identifying, or not identifying it, as a sister church – there can be no question of playing it safe. There is only what Meyendorff once called "the risk of faith".[2] For if the choice is made not to baptize converts who, in reality, have not yet been baptized, the gift of God is withheld from those who stand in need of it. But if the choice is made to proceed with baptizing those who in fact have been baptized, or otherwise to bring into the Church of Christ those who have been in it, then we deny Christ himself in them.[3] This is nothing short of saying that "my Christ" is other than "your Christ" and thus is, precisely, to divide Christ. It is in order to avoid this division in the body of the Lord that Catholic and Orthodox Christians must continue to take the greatest care in using and understanding the expression "sister churches".

---

2   J. Meyendorff, *Living Tradition* (Crestwood: St. Vladimir's Seminary Press, 1978), 37.
3   "When it is said to a Christian, 'Be a Christian,' what other lesson is taught, save a denial that he is a Christian? Was it not the same lesson which those persecutors of the Christians wished to teach, by resisting whom the crown of martyrdom was gained?" (Augustine, *De Baptismo*, Book II, ch. 7.10.)

BIBLIOGRAPHY

1. Patristic, medieval and early modern works

Anastasius, Librarian of the Roman Church. *Praefatio Anastasii in Synodum Octavam.* Mansi, *Sacrorum Conciliorum nova et amplissima collectio* (Florence and Venice, 1758-1798), 16:7.

Anselm of Havelberg. *Dialogi.* First published by Dom Lucas d'Achery in Spicilegium sive collection veterum aliquot scriptorium, vol. 1, 161-207 (2nd ed. 1723), and reprinted in J.P. Migne, *Patrologia Latina* (PL), 217 vols. (Paris 1844-1855), 188: 1139-1248. Book I, with introduction, translation and notes by Gaston Salet, has been issued in Sources chrétiennes No. 118 (1966). A French translation of Book II (without introduction or notes) by P. Harang, entitled "Dialogue entre Anselme de Havelberg et Néchitès de Nicomedie sur la procession du Saint Esprit", has appeared in *Istina* 17 (1972) 375-424.

Anthony, Patriarch. *Letter to Basil I.* In F. Miklosich and I. Müller, Acta patriarchatus Constantinopolitani, vol. 1 (Vienna, 1862), 188-192. Translation in J.W. Barker, *Manuel II Palaeologus, 1391-1425.* New Brunswick, NJ, 1909.

Augustine of Hippo. *De baptismo contra Donatistas.* PL 43, 107-244. Translated by J.R. King, in P. Schaff, ed., *Nicene and Post-Nicene Fathers of the Christian Church (NPNF),* 1st ser., vol. 4. Buffalo, NY: Christian Literature, 1887. Reprint Peabody, MA: Hendrickson, 1994.

Basil of Caesarea. *Epistles.* Migne, *Patrologia Graeca* (PG), 161 vols. (Paris 1857-1866), 32, 743-756. Translated by Blomfield Jackson, in P. Schaff and H. Wace, eds., *NPNF,* 2nd ser., vol. 8. Buffalo, NY: Christian Literature, 1895. Reprint Peabody, MA: Hendrickson, 1999.

Camateros, John X, Patriarch. *Letters 1 and 2 to Innocent III.* Full Greek text, with translated excerpts, in A. Papadakis and Alice Mary Talbot, "John X Camaterus Confronts Innocent III: An Unpublished Correspondence," *Byzantinoslavica* 33 (1972) 22-41.

Clement of Rome. *First Letter to the Corinthians.* Migne, PG 1, 199-328. Translation in A. Menzies, ed., *Ante-Nicene Fathers,* vol. 9. Buffalo, NY: Christian Literature, 1896/97. 4th ed. Reprint, Peabody, MA: Hendrickson, 1999.

Cyprian of Carthage. *Ad Fortunatum.* PL 4, 651-676. Translation by Ernest Wallis, in A. Roberts and J. Donaldson, eds., *Ante-Nicene Fathers (ANF),* vol. 5:496-507. Edinburgh: T & T Clark, 1868-1873. Buffalo, NY: Christian Literature, 1886. Reprint Peabody, MA: Hendrickson, 1994.

–, *The Council of Carthage Held Under Cyprian, AD 257.* In Labbe and Cossart, *Sacrosancta concilia ad regiam editionem exacta,* vol. 1:786. Translation by Henry Percival, in P. Schaff and H. Wace, eds., *NPNF,* 2nd ser., vol. 14, The Seven Ecumenical Councils. Reprint Peabody, MA: Hendrickson, 1999.

Gregory the Great. *Registrum Epistolarum.* PL 77. Translation by James Barmby, in P. Schaff and H. Wace, eds., *NPNF,* 2nd ser., vols. 12 and 13. Reprint Peabody, MA: Hendrickson, 1999.

Gregory Nazianzen. *Epistles.* PG 37, 21-386. Translation of selected letters by Charles Browne and James Swallow, in P. Schaff and H. Wace, eds., *NPNF,* 2nd ser., vol. 7. Reprint Peabody, MA: Hendrickson, 1999.

Ignatius of Antioch. *Epistles.* PG 5, 643-728. Translation by Cyril Richardson, *Early Christian Fathers.* New York: Touchstone, 1996. Also translated by Michael Holmes, *The Apostolic Fathers,* rev. ed. Grand Rapids: Baker, 1999.

Innocent I. *Epistolae.* PL 20. Mansi, *Sacrorum Conciliorum nova et amplissima collectio,* vol. 3.

Innocent III. *Epistolae.* PL 214. Ep. 211 (liber secundus) and ep. 354 (liber primus). Translation by S. Runciman, *The Eastern Schism,* op. cit., 142-143.

Irenaeus. *Contra Haereses.* PG 7, 433-1226. Translation in A. Roberts and J. Donaldson, eds., *ANF,* vol. 1, 314-578. Reprint Peabody, MA: Hendrickson, 1994.

Kafsokalyvitis, Neophytos. Ἐπιτομὴ τῶν Ἱερῶν Κανόνων (Digest of the Sacred Canons) (unpublished).

Leo the Great. *Ep. 119.* PL 54, 1040D-1046A. Translation in P. Schaff and H. Wace, eds., *NPNF,* vol. 12. Reprint Peabody, MA: Hendrickson, 1999.

Leo IX. *Epistle to Michael Archbishop of Constantinople.* Cornelius Will, *Acta et scripta quae de controversiis ecclesiae graecae et latinae saeculo undecimo composita extant.* Leipzig and Marburg, 1861. Reprint, Frankfort: Minerva, 1963, 89-92.

Maximos the Confessor. *Ep. 13.* PG 91, 509B-534A. Mansi, *Sacrorum Conciliorum nova et amplissima collectio,* vol. 10:692. Translation in F. Dvornik, *Byzantium,* op. cit., 98.

Methodius of Olympus. *The Symposium: a Treatise on Chastity.* Greek text in G.N. Bonwetsch, ed., *Methodius,* vol. 27 of *Die griechischen christlichen Schriftsteller der ersten drei Jahrhunderte* (Leipzig; Berlin, 1901-). Translation in *St. Methodius: The Symposium, a Treatise on Chastity,* translated and annotated by Herbert Musurillo, *Ancient Christian Writers,* vol. 27 (Westmister, MD: The Newman Press, 1958).

Nicetas of Nicomedia. *Addresses in debate with Anselm of Havelberg, 1136 AD* (see Anselm). PL 188, 1217D-1218A; 1219AD. Excerpts translated in F. Dvornik, *Byzantium,* op. cit., 145-146.

Nicephoras, "Apology for the pure, unadulterated Faith of Christians against those who accuse us of idolatry," PG 100, 533-834.

Nikodemos the Haghiorite. *The rudder (Pedalion) of the metaphorical ship of the one holy Catholic and apostolic church of Orthodox Christians.* Translated by D. Cummings from the fifth edition published in Athens, Greece, 1908. Chicago: Orthodox Christian Educational Society, 1957.

Oikonomos, Τὰ σωζόμενα ἐκκλησιαστικὰ συγγράμματα Κωνσταντίνου Πρεσβυτέρου καὶ Οἰκονόμου τοῦ ἐξ Οἰκονόμων *(The extant ecclesiastical writings of Constantine Pres-*

byter and Oikonomos of the Okonomoi, published by Soph. C. of the Oikonomoi), vol. I (Athens, 1862).

Palmer, William. *Treatise on the Church of Christ.* London and New York: D. Appleton, 1841.

Parios, Athanasios, Ὅτι οἱ ἀπὸ Λατινῶν ἐπιστρέφοντες ἀναντιρρήτως, ἀπαραιτήτως καὶ ἀναγχαίως πρέπει νὰ βαπτίζωνται, καὶ Ἐπιτομὴ ... τῶν θείων τῆς πίστεως δογμάτων ... *(That Latin converts must indisputably, indispensably and necessarily be baptized, and Digest ... of the Divine Dogmas of the Faith)* (Leipzig, 1806).

Peter the Venerable, abbot of Cluny. *Ep. 39, to Emperor John II.* PL 189, 260C-262A.

Polycarp. *Letter to the Philippians.* PG 5, 1005-1016. Translation by Cyril Richardson, *Early Christian Fathers.* New York: Touchstone, 1996.

Syropoulos, Silvestros. *Les mémoires du grand ecclésiarque de l'Église de Constantinople Sylvestre Syropoulos sur le Concile de Florence (1438-1439).* Paris: Éditions du Centre national de la recherche scientifique, 1971.

Tertullian. *Liber de Praescriptionibus Adversus Haereticos.* PL 2. Translation in A. Roberts and J. Donaldson, eds., *ANF,* vol. 3 (reprint Peabody, MA: Hendrickson, 1999), 243-265.

Theodoret, Bishop of Cyrrhus. *Ecclesiastical History.* Translation in *The ecclesiasticall history, 1612 / Theodoret. Translated from Greek into English.* Ilkley, UK: Scolar Press, 1976.

Theodosius. *De Situ Terrae sanctae* (circa 550). In P. Geyer, ed., *Corpus Scriptorum Ecclesiasticorum Latinorum* 39 (Vienna, 1898), 135-150.

2. Modern works concerned wholly or in part with the subject of "sister churches"

Aghiorgoussis, Maximos. "'Sister Churches:' Ecclesiological Implications." In idem, *In the Image of God,* 153-195. Brookline, MA: Holy Cross Orthodox Press, 1999. Originally published as "'Sister Churches:' Ecclesiological Implications," in Ἐπιστημονιχὴ Παρουσία Ἑστίας Θεολόγων Χάλχης Τόμος Γ: Ἑχατονπεντηκονταεθρὶς Ἱερᾶς Θεολογιχῆς Σχολῆς Χάλχης 1844-1994, 349-399. Athens, 1994.

Chirovsky, Andriy. "'Sister Churches': Ecumenical Terminology in Search of Content." *Logos: A Journal of Eastern Christian Studies* 34 (1993) 396-421.

Congar, Yves. "De la communion des églises à une ecclésiologie de l'Eglise universelle." In *L'Episcopat et l'Eglise Universelle,* Unam Sanctam 39, ed. by Y. Congar and B.D. Dupuy, 227-260. Paris: Cerf, 1962.

–, *Diversity and Communion.* Mystic, CT: Twenty-Third Publications, 1985.

Congregation for the Doctrine of the Faith. *Note on the Expression "Sister Churches".* June 30, 2000. In *L'Osservatore Romano* (October 28, 2000): 6; also in *L'Osservatore Romano* (English Weekly Edition) (November 1, 2000) 9.

Erickson, John. "Concerning the Balamand Statement." *Greek Orthodox Theological Review* 42 (1997) nos. 1-2, 25-43.

Fahey, Michael A. "Ecclesiae Sorores ac Fratres: Sibling Communion in the Pre-Nicene Christian Era." *Proceedings of the Catholic Theological Society of America* 36 (1981) 15-38.

–, *Orthodox and Catholic Sister Churches: East is West and West is East*. Milwaukee, WI: Marquette University Press, 1996.

Freeman, Anthony. "Sister Churches and Sisters in the Church: How do we Think about such Things?" *Modern Believing* 43 (Jan. 2002) no. 1, 11-21.

Garuti, Adriano. "Sister Churches: Reality and Questions." In idem, *The Primacy of the Bishop of Rome and Ecumenical Dialogue*, translated and ed. by Michael Miller, 261-327. San Francisco: Ignatius Press, 2004. Originally published as "'Chiese sorelle': Realtà e interrogative," *Antonianum* 71 (1996) no. 4, 631-686.

Hallensleben, Barbara. "Églises sœurs. Principe herméneutique dans les relations entre Églises ad intra et ad extra." *Comprendre les enjeux du prochain Concile de l'Église orthodoxe*. Colloque organisé par l'Institut de théologie orthodoxe Saint-Serge et le Centre œcuménique de l'Université catholique de Leuven en partenariat avec le Collège des Bernardins et la revue Contacts. Paris, 18-20 octobre 2012 (= Contacts 65 [Juillet-Septembre 2013] no. 243), 534-548.

Hryniewicz, Waclaw. "Between Trust and Mistrust: Ecumenical Relations and Theological Dialogue between the Catholic Church and the Orthodox Church." *The Challenge of Our Hope: Christian Faith in Dialogue*, op. cit., 167-184. Originally published in *Exchange. Journal of Missiological and Ecumenical Studies* (Utrecht) 32 (2003) no. 2, 168-187.

–, *The Challenge of Our Hope: Christian Faith in Dialogue*. Washington, DC: Council for Research in Values and Philosophy, 2007.

–, "Der Dialog der Schwesterkirchen. Nach dem wiederholten Treffen der Katholisch-Orthodoxen Kommission in Bari." *Ostkirchliche Studien* 36 (1987) 311-326.

–, "Reconciliation and Ecclesiology of Sister Churches." *Eastern Churches Journal* 2 (1995) no. 3, 55-72.

–, "The 'Union' of Brest and the Ecclesiology of Sister Churches." *Eastern Churches Journal* 4:1 (1997) 107-124.

–, "Vertrauen oder misstrauen? Die Krise des Begriffs 'Schwesterkirchen'." *Ostkirchliche Studien* 52 (2003) no. 1, 21-36.

Joint International Commission for Theological Dialogue between the Roman Catholic Church and the Orthodox Church. "Uniatism, Method of Union of the Past, and the Current Search for Full Communion." Balamand, Lebanon, June 23, 1993. Full text in *Eastern Churches Journal* 1 (Winter 1993/94) no. 1, 17-25. Also available at www.vatican.va/roman_curia/pontifical_councils/chrstuni/ch_orthodox_docs/rc_pc_chrstuni_doc_19930624_lebanon_en.html (accessed October 24, 2009).

Kallarangatt, Joseph. "Theology of Sister Churches or Uniate Churches?" *Christian Orient* (Kottayam, India) 12 (March, 1991) no. 1, 7-19.

Kantzavelos, Demetri. "The Declaration 'Dominus Iesus': On the Unicity and Salvific Universality of Jesus Christ and the Church and Note on the Expression 'Sister Churches': A Greek Orthodox Response." *Ecumenical Trends* (March 2002) 8-10. Paper originally presented at the annual retreat of the Council of Religious leaders of Metropolitan Chicago, November 28, 2000.

Krawchenko, Oleh. "Response to Fr. Andriy Chirovsky: 'Sister Churches: Ecumenical Terminology in Search of Content'." *Logos: A Journal of Eastern Christian Studies* 34 (1993) 422-426.

Lanne, Emmanuel. "Églises sœurs: implications ecclésiologiques du Tomos Agapis." *Istina* 20 (1975) 47-74. Reprinted in E. Lanne, *Tradition et Communion des Églises*, op. cit., 501-535.

–, "Églises unies ou Églises sœurs: un choix ineluctable." *Irénikon* 48 (1975) no. 3, 322-342. Translated as "United Churches or Sister Churches: A Choice to be Faced," *One in Christ* 12 (1976) 106-123. Original French text reprinted in E. Lanne, *Tradition et Communion des Églises*, op. cit., 485-500.

–, *Tradition et Communion des Églises: recueil d'études*. Louvaine: Leuven University Press, 1997.

Legrand, Hervé. "Le dialogue catholique-orthodoxe. Quelques enjeux ecclésiologiques de la crise actuelle autour des Églises unies." *Bulletin / Centro pro Unione* 43 (Spring, 1993) 3-16. Translated in abridged form as "Uniatism and Catholic-Orthodox Dialogue," *Theology Digest* 42:2 (Summer, 1995) 127-133.

–, "La théologie des Églises Sœurs: réflexions ecclésiologiques autour de la declaration de Balamand." *Revue des sciences philosophiques et théologiques* 88 (2004) 461-496.

Mattiussi, Richard. "The Roman Primacy & Reunion as a Communion of Sister Churches." *Eastern Churches Journal* 9 (2002) no. 3, 51-92.

Meyendorff, John. "Eglises-sœurs: Implications ecclésiologiques du Tomos Agapis." *Istina* 20 (1975) 35-46.

Papandreou, Metropolitan Damaskinos and Ratzinger, Cardinal Joseph. "Exchange of Letters between Metropolitan Damaskinos and Cardinal Joseph Ratzinger." In J. Ratzinger, *Pilgrim Fellowship of Faith: the Church as Communion*, translated by Henry Taylor, 217-241. San Francisco: Ignatius Press, 2005.

Paris, Matthew. *Chronica Majora*, in 7 vols. Ed. by H.R. Luard. London: Longman, 1872-1883.

Romanides, John. "Orthodox and Vatican Agreement." In Θεολογία (Athens, Greece) 6 (1993) no. 4, 570-580: www.romanity.org/htm/rom.13.en.orthodox_and_vatican_agreement.htm (accessed March 17, 2009).

Royster, Archbishop Dmitri. *Letter of September 23, 1994 to His Beatitude, Theodosius, Archbishop of Washington and Metropolitan of All America and Canada*. Obtained through the archives of the Chancery of the Orthodox Church in America, Syosset, NY.

Sacred Community of Mount Athos. *Letter to the Patriarch of Constantinople from the Sacred Community of Mount Athos, Dec. 8, 1993.* Translation in *Orthodox Life* 44 (1994) no. 4, 27-39. Originally published in Ὀρθόδοξος Τύπος (March 18, 1994).

Zissis, Theodore. "Το Νέο Κείμενο περί Ούνιας του Μπαλαμάντ." Ἐκκλησιαστική Ἀλήθεια (Athens) March 16, 1994; April 1, 1994; April 16, 1994; May 16, 1994; and July-August, 1994.

–, "Uniatism: A Problem in the Dialogue Between the Orthodox and Roman Catholics." *Greek Orthodox Theological Review* 35 (1990) no. 1, 21-31. Paper originally read at the meeting of the Joint Sub-Commission on Uniatism (Vienna, January 26-31, 1990) of the Joint International Commission for Theological Dialogue between the Roman Catholic Church and the Orthodox Church.

3. Official ecclesiastical texts, correspondence between hierarchs, and ecumenical documents

Antioch, Patriarchate of. "The Decision Regarding the Amending of Articles Concerning Bishops According to the By-laws of the Patriarchate," February 24, 2009. In *The Word* (Englewood, NJ) 53 (April 2009) no. 4, 15-17.

Bartholomew, Ecumenical Patriarch. *Message sent to Patriarch Kirill of Moscow and All-Russia, January 27, 2009.* In the *Secretariat for Ecumenical and Interreligious Affairs (SEIA) Newsletter on the Eastern Churches and Ecumenism* 160 (January 31, 2009) 4.

Borelli, J. and Erickson, J., eds., *The Quest for Unity: Orthodox and Catholics in Dialogue. Documents of the Joint International Commission and Official Dialogues in the United States 1965-1995* (Crestwood, NY and Washington, DC: St. Vladimir's Seminary Press and United States Catholic Conference, 1996).

Catholic-Orthodox Mixed Commission of France. "Response to Balamand from France: Declaration of the Catholic-Orthodox Mixed Commission of France on the Balamand Agreed Statement." Unofficial translation in *Eastern Churches Journal* 1:2 (Summer, 1994) 57-62. Original French text in *Service Orthodoxe de Presse*, Document 184.A, January 1994.

Congregation for Bishops. "Draft Statement on Episcopal Conferences." *Origins* 17/43 (April 7, 1988) 735.

Congregation for the Doctrine of the Faith. *Communionis notio.* May 28, 1992. AAS 85 (1993) 838-850. English translation in *L'Osservatore Romano*, English Weekly Edition (June 17, 1992) 8.

–, *Dominus Iesus.* August 6, 2000. AAS 92 (2000) 742-765. English translation in *L'Osservatore Romano*, English Weekly Edition (September 6, 2000), special insert.

–, *Notification on the Book "Church: Charism and Power. Essay on militant Ecclesiology" by Father Leonardo Boff, O.F.M.* March 11, 1985. AAS 77 (1985) 756-762. English translation in *L'Osservatore Romano*, English Weekly Edition (April 9, 1985) 11.

–, *Responses to Some Questions Regarding Certain Aspects of the Doctrine on the Church.* June 29, 2007. AAS 86 (1994) 820-821. English translation in *L'Osservatore Romano*, English Weekly Edition (August 3, 1994) 2.

"The Decision Regarding the Amending of Articles Concerning Bishops According to the By-laws of the Patriarchate, February 24, 2009." *The Word* (Englewood, NJ) 53:4 (April 2009) 15-17.

Florence, Council of. "Laetentur caeli." July 6, 1439. In Denzinger, *Enchiridion symbolorum definitionum et declarationum de rebus fidei et morum*, edition XL, 1300-1308. Vienna: Herder, 1999.

John Paul II. *Letter to Dimitrios I, November 23, 1988.* In French translation at www.vatican.va/holy_father/john_paul_ii/letters/1988/%20documents/hf_jp-ii_ let_19881123_dimitrios-i_fr.html (accessed April 18, 2009).

–, *Letter to Ecumenical Patriarch Bartholomew, November 26, 1995.* In French at www.vatican.va/holy_father/john_paul_ii/letters/1995/documents/hf_jp-ii_let_ 19951126_patriarca-costantinopoli_fr.html (accessed May 2, 2008).

–, *Slavorum Apostoli* (June 2, 1985), no. 27. The encyclical is available at www.vatican.va/holy_father/john_paul_ii/encyclicals/documents/hf_jp-ii_enc_ 19850602_slavorum-apostoli_en.html (accessed May 7, 2008).

Joint International Commission for Theological Dialogue between the Roman Catholic Church and the Orthodox Church. "Ecclesiological and Canonical Consequences of the Sacramental Nature of the Church: Ecclesial Communion, Conciliarity and Authority." Ravenna, October 13, 2007. Full text published in *The Ecumenical Review* 60 (July 2008) no. 3, 319-333. Also available at www.vatican.va/roman_curia/pontifical_ councils/chrstuni/ch_orthodox_docs/rc_pc_chrstuni_doc_20071013_documento-ravenna_en.html (accessed June 14, 2009).

–, "Faith, Sacraments, and the Unity of the Church." Bari, Italy, June 10, 1987. Full text in J. Erickson and J. Borelli, eds., *The Quest for Unity*, op. cit., 93-104.

–, Freising Communiqué. In *Information Service* 73 (1990/II) 52-53. Reprinted in *Sourozh* 43 (February 1991) 24-27.

–, "The Mystery of the Church and of the Eucharist in the Light of the Mystery of the Holy Trinity." Munich, June 30 – July 6, 1982. Full text in *St. Vladimir's Theological Quarterly* 26 (1982) no. 4, 251-258. Available at www. vatican.va/roman_curia/pontifical_ councils/chrstuni/ch_orthodox_docs/rc_pc_chrstuni_doc_19820706_munich_en. html (accessed June 14, 2009).

North American Orthodox-Catholic Consultation (formerly called the U.S. Orthodox-Catholic Consultation). "A Response of the Orthodox-Roman Catholic Consultation in the United States to the Joint International Commission for Theological Dialogue between the Orthodox Church and the Roman Catholic Church regarding the Balamand Document (Dated June 23, 1993): 'Uniatism, Method of Union of the Past, and the Present Search for Full Communion." Full text in J. Erickson and J. Borelli, eds., *The Quest for Unity*, op. cit., 184-190.

–, "Apostolicity as God's Gift in the Life of the Church." Brighton, MA, November 1, 1986. Full text in J. Erickson and J. Borelli, eds., *The Quest for Unity*, op. cit., 125-130.

–, "A Response of the Orthodox-Roman Catholic Consultation in the United States to the Joint International Commission for Theological Dialogue between the Orthodox Church and the Roman Catholic Church regarding the Document: 'The Mystery of the Church and of the Eucharist in the Light of the Mystery of the Holy Trinity." Full text in J. Erickson and J. Borelli, eds., *The Quest for Unity*, op. cit., 65-68.

Pius XI. *Ecclesiam Dei*. November 12, 1923. AAS 15 (1923) 573-582.

–, *Rerum Orientalium*. September 8, 1928. AAS 20 (1928) 277-288.

Pius XII. *Humani Generis*. August 12, 1950. AAS 42 (1950) 561-578.

–, *Mystici Corporis*. June 29, 1943. AAS 35 (1943) 193-248.

Second Vatican Council. *Lumen Gentium*. November 21, 1964. AAS 57 (1965) 5-71. English translation in Austin Flannery, ed., *Vatican II: The Conciliar and Post Conciliar Documents*. New Revised Edition. (Northport, NY: Costello, 1992).

–, *Nota explicativa praevia*. November 21, 1964. AAS 57 (1965) 72-75.

–, *Orientalium Ecclesiarum*. November 21, 1964. AAS 57 (1965) 76-89.

–, *Unitatis Redintegratio*. November 21, 1964. AAS 57 (1965) 90-112.

Stormon, E.J., ed., *Towards the Healing of Schism: the Sees of Rome and Constantinople. Public statements and correspondence between the Holy See and the Ecumenical Patriarchate, 1958-1984*. Mahwah, NY: Paulist Press, 1987.

Tanner, Norman, ed. *Decrees of the Ecumenical Council*, Vol. II. London and Washington, DC: Sheed & Ward and Georgetown University Press, 1990.

"Unto the Churches of Christ Everywhere." Encyclical of the Ecumenical Patriarchate, 1920. In Michael Kinnamon and Brian E. Cope, eds., *The Ecumenical Movement: An Anthology of Key Texts and Voices* (Grand Rapids and Geneva: Eerdmans and WCC Publications, 1997) 11-14.

"Visit of Vatican Delegation to the Ecumenical Patriarchate for the Feast of St. Andrew." November 30, 1988." *Information Service* 69 (1989/I) 13.

4. Other works

Afanasiev, Nicholas. *The Church of the Holy Spirit*. Translated by Vitaly Permiakov. Notre Dame, Indiana: University of Notre Dame Press, 2007.

Alfeyev, Hilarion. "Pope's Title 'Patriarch of the West' Removed." *OrthodoxyToday.org*, March 9, 2006. www.orthodoxytoday.org/articles6/HilarionPope.php (accessed January 26, 2009).

Battifol, Pierre. *Cathedra Petri: études d'histoire anciènne d'église* (Unam Sanctam 4). Paris: Cerf, 1938.

Becker, Karl J. "The Church and Vatican II's 'Subsistit in' Terminology." *L'Osservatore Romano* Weekly English Edition (December 14, 2005) 11. Reprinted in *Origins* 35.31 (January 19, 2006) 514-522.

Berschin, Walter. *Greek Letters and the Latin Middle Ages,* rev. ed. Translated by Jerold C. Frakes. Washington, DC: Catholic University of America Press, 1988.

Bobrinskoy, Boris. "Catholic-Orthodox relations: the need for love as well as knowledge." *Sobornost* (incorporating *Eastern Churches Review)* 15 (1993) no. 2, 28-38.

Boff, Leonardo. *Church: Charism and Power – Liberation Theology and the Institutional Church.* New York: Crossroad, 1985.

Cavarnos, C. *St Nicodemos the Hagiorite.* Belmont, MA: Institute for Byzantine and Modern Greek Studies, 1974.

Congar, Yves. *After Nine Hundred Years.* New York: Fordham University Press, 1955.

–, "Évaluation ecclésiologique des Églises non-catholiques." In *Unitatis Redintegratio 1964-1974: the Impact of the Decree on Ecumenism,* ed. by Gerard Békés and Vilmos Vajta, Studia Anselmiana, ed. by P. Giustiano Farnedi, vol. 71, 63-97. Rome: Pontificio Ateneo S. Anselmo, 1977.

Daley, Brian. "Position and Patronage in the Early Church: the Original Meaning of 'Primacy of Honour'." *Journal of Theological Studies* (New Series) 44 (1993) 529-553.

–, "Structures of Charity: Bishops' Gatherings and the See of Rome in the Early Church." In *Episcopal Conferences: Historical, Canonical and Theological Studies,* ed. by Thomas J. Reese. Washington, DC: Georgetown, 1989, 25-58.

Darrouzès, J. "Les documents byzantins du XIIe siècle sur la primauté romaine." *Revue des Études Byzantines* 23 (1965) 42-88.

De Lubac, Henri. Les églises particulières dans l'Église universelle, suivi de La maternité de l'église et d'une interview recueillie par G. Jarczyk. Paris: Aubier-Montaigne, 1971. Published in English translation as The Motherhood of the Church: followed by Particular Churches in the Universal Church and an interview conducted by Gwendoline Jarczyk, translated by Sergia Englund (San Francisco: Ignatius, 1982).

Delahaye, Karl. *Ecclesia Mater chez les Pères des Trois Premiers Siècles.* Traduit de l'allemand par P. Vergriete et É. Bouis. Paris: Cerf, 1964.

Demacopoulos, George. "Gregory the Great and the Sixth-Century Dispute Over the Ecumenical Title." *Theological Studies* 70 (2009) 1-22.

Dragas, George D. "The Manner of Reception of Roman Catholic Converts into the Orthodox Church with Special Reference to the Decisions of the Synods of 1484 (Constantinople), 1755 (Constantinople) and 1667 (Moscow)." *Greek Orthodox Theological Review* 44 (spring-winter 1999) no. 1-4, 235-271.

Dunn, Dennis J. *The Catholic Church and Russia.* Aldershot, Hants, England and Burlington, VT: Ashgate, 2004.

Dvornik, Francis. *Byzantium and the Roman Primacy.* New York: Fordham University Press, 1966.

–, *The Photian Schism: History and Legend.* London: Cambridge University Press, 1948 (reprint 1970).

Erickson, John. "Divergencies in Pastoral Practice in the Reception of Converts." In *Orthodox Perspectives on Pastoral Practice*, ed. by T. Stylianopoulos, 149-177. Brookline, MA: Holy Cross Orthodox Press, 1988.

–, "Leavened and Unleavened: Some Theological Implications of the Schism of 1054." *St. Vladimir's Theological Quarterly* 14 (1970) 155-176.

–, "On the Cusp of Modernity: the Canonical Hermeneutics of St. Nikodemos the Haghiorite (1748-1809)." *St. Vladimir's Theological Quarterly* 42 (1998) no. 1, 45-66.

–, "The Reception of Non-Orthodox into the Orthodox Church: Contemporary Practice." *St. Vladimir's Theological Quarterly* 41 (1997) 1-17.

–, "A Retreat from Ecumenism in Post-Communist Russia and Eastern Europe?" Speech delivered at the Harriman Institute at Columbia University, New York, April 7, 2000. www.orthodoxresearchinstitute.org/articles/ecumenical/erickson_ecumenism_russia. pdf (accessed May 4, 2009). A revised and expanded version of this speech, given at the 2001 National Workshop on Christian Unity, was published in *Ecumenical Trends* 30 (October 2001) no. 9, 1/129-10/138.

–, "First Among Equals: Papal Primacy in an Orthodox Perspective." *Ecumenical Trends* 27 (February, 1998) no. 2, 1/17-9/25.

Evdokimov, Paul. "An Orthodox Look at Vatican II." *Diakonia* 1:3 (July 1966) 166-174.

Florovsky, Georges. "The Doctrine of the Church and the Ecumenical Problem." *The Ecumenical Review* 2 (Winter, 1950) no. 2, 152-161.

–, "The Limits of the Church." *Church Quarterly Review* 11 (Oct. 1933) no. 233, 117-131. Reprinted as "The Boundaries of the Church," in *Ecumenism I: A Doctrinal Approach*, vol. XIII of *The Collected Works of Georges Florovsky*, ed. by Richard S. Haugh (Belmont, MA: Nordland, 1989).

–, "Patristic Theology and the Ethos of the Orthodox Church." In *The Collected Works of Georges Florovsky*, vol. IV, part II, ed. by Richard S. Haugh, 15-22. Belmont, MA: Nordland, 1975.

Frazee, Charles. "1054 Revisited." *Journal of Ecumenical Studies* 42:2 (Spring 2007) 263-279.

Gaillardetz, Richard. *The Church in the Making: Lumen Gentium, Christus Dominus, Orientalium Ecclesiarum*. New York: Paulist Press, 2006.

Garuti, Adriano. *Il Papa Patriarca d'Occidente? Studio storico dottrinale*. Bologna: Edizioni Francescane, 1990.

Geanakoplos, Deno John. *Byzantine East and Latin West*. New York: Harper Torchbooks, 1966.

Gudziak, Boris. *Crisis and Reform: The Kyivan Metropolitanate, the Patriarchate of Constantinople, and the Genesis of the Union of Brest*. Cambridge, MA: Harvard University Press, 1998.

Imkamp, Wilhelm. *Das Kirchenbild Innocenz' III (1198-1216)*. Stuttgart: Anton Hiersemann, 1983.

Iorga, N. *Byzantium after Byzantium*. Translated by Laura Treptow. Portland, OR: Center for Romanian Studies, in Cooperation with the Romanian Institute of International

Studies, 2000. Originally published as *Byzance après Byzance* (Bucharest: Editions de l'Institut d'études byzantines, 1935).

Kerame, O. "The Basis for Reunion of Christians: the Papacy Reconsidered." *Journal of Ecumenical Studies* 8 (Fall 1971) no. 4, 792-814.

Kasper, Walter. *Homily at the Mass in Honor of Our Lady of Kazan*, St. Peter's Basilica, August 26, 2004. www.vatican.va/roman_curia/pontifical_councils/chrstuni/card-kasper-docs/rc_pc_chrstuni_doc_20040826_homily-kazan_en.html (accessed April 18, 2009).

–, "On the Church: A Friendly Reply to Cardinal Ratzinger," *America* (April 23-30, 2001) 8-14.

–, "Zur Theologie und Praxis des bishöflichen Amtes." In *Auf neue Art Kirche Sein: Wirklichkeiten – Herausforderungen – Wandlungen*. Munich: Bernward bei Don Bosco, 1999, 32-48.

Kinnamon, M. and Cope, B., eds. *The Ecumenical Movement: An Anthology of Key Texts and Voices*. Geneva and Grand Rapids, MI: WCC Publications and Eerdmans, 1997.

Komonchak, Joseph. "The Local Church and the Church Catholic: the Contemporary Theological Problematic." *The Jurist* 52 (1992) no. 1, 416-447.

Lanne, Emmanuel. "The Connection between the Post-Tridentine Concept of Primacy and the Emerging Uniate Churches." *Wort und Wahrheit* Supplementary Issue Number 4 (December 1978), 99-108. Reprinted in *Selection of the Papers and Minutes of the Four Vienna Consultations between Theologians of the Oriental Orthodox Churches and the Roman Catholic Church: 1971, 1973, 1976 and 1978 in one volume* (Vienna: Ecumenical Foundation Pro Oriente, 1988).

Lees, Jay Terry. *Anselm of Havelberg: Deeds into Words in the Twelfth Century*. Leiden; New York: Brill, 1998.

Legrand, Hervé. "'One bishop per city': Tensions around the Expression of the Catholicity of the Local Church since Vatican II." *The Jurist* 52 (1992) 369-400.

L'Huiller, Peter. *The Church of the Ancient Councils*. Crestwood, NY: St. Vladimir's Seminary Press, 1996.

Lieu, Judith. *The Second and Third Epistles of John: History and Background*. Edinburgh: T & T Clark, 1986.

Lossky, Nicholas. "Conciliarity-Primacy in a Russian Orthodox perspective." In *Petrine Ministry and the Unity of the Church: Toward a Patient and Fraternal Dialogue*, ed. by James Puglisi, 127-136. Collegeville, MN: Liturgical Press, 1999.

–, "La présence orthodoxe dans la 'diaspora' et ses implications ecclésiologiques, de même que celles des Églises orientales catholiques." *Irénikon* 65 (1992) 352-362.

Louth, Andrew. *Greek East and Latin West: the Church AD 681-1071*, vol. III of the Church in History series. Crestwood, NY: St. Vladimir's Seminary Press, 2007.

Lubachivsky, Archbishop Myroslav Ivan. "On Christian Unity." In *Eastern Churches Journal* 1 (Summer 1994) no. 2, 7-47.

McDonnell, Kilian. "The Ratzinger/Kasper Debate: the Universal Church and Local Churches." *Theological Studies* 63 (2002) 227-250.

–, "Walter Kasper on the Theology and the Praxis of the Bishop's Office." *Theological Studies* 63 (2002) 711-729.

McPartlan, Paul. *The Eucharist Makes the Church : Henri de Lubac and John Zizioulas in Dialogue.* Edinburgh : T & T Clark, 1993 (2nd edition Fairfax, Va.: Eastern Christian Publications, 2006).

–, "The Importance of Visible Unity: Some initial notes on Catholic texts and terminology." 9-page typescript (unpublished).

–, "The Local Church and the Universal Church: Zizioulas and the Ratzinger/Kasper Debate." *International Journal for the Study of the Christian Church* 4 (March 2004) no. 1, 21-33.

Meyendorff, John. *Imperial Unity and Christian Divisions, 450-680 AD.* Crestwood, NY: St. Vladimir's Seminary Press, 1989.

–, ed. *The Primacy of Peter: Essays in Ecclesiology and the Early Church.* Crestwood, NY: St. Vladimir's Seminary Press, 1992. First published in English by The Faith Press, Ltd., 1963.

–, *Rome, Constantinople, Moscow: Historical and Theological Studies.* Crestwood, NY: St. Vladimir's Seminary Press, 1996.

–, "Vatican II: A Preliminary Reaction." *St. Vladimir's Seminary Quarterly* 9 (1965) 26-37.

–, *Witness to the World.* Crestwood, NY: St. Vladimir's Seminary Press, 1987.

Metallinos, George. *I Confess One Baptism ...: Interpretation and Application of Canon VII of the Second Ecumenical Council by the Kollyvades and Constantine Oikonomos (A contribution to the historico-canonical evaluation of the problem of the validity of Western baptism).* Translated by Priestmonk Seraphim. Mount Athos: St. Paul's Monastery, 1994.

Obolensky, Dimitri. *The Byzantine Commonwealth.* New York: Praeger, 1971.

Papandreou, Metropolitan Damaskinos. "Conscience conciliare et experience sacramentelle dans l'oeuvre du concile de Trente." *Episkepsis* 524 (November 30, 1995) 11-25.

–, "Une évaluation de l'encyclique du pape Jean-Paul II 'Ut unum sint'." *Episkepsis* 519 (June 30, 1995) 27-31.

Phidas, Vlassios. "Papal Primacy and Patriarchal Pentarchy in the Orthodox Tradition." In *The Petrine Ministry: Catholics and Orthodox in Dialogue*, ed. by Walter Kasper, 65-82. Mahwah, NJ: Newman Press, 2006.

Plumpe, Joseph. *Mater Ecclesia: An Inquiry into the Concept of the Church as Mother in Early Christianity.* Washington, DC: The Catholic University of America Press, 1943.

W.H. Principe. "Monastic, Episcopal, and Apologetic Theology of the Papacy, 1150-1250." In *The Religious Roles of the Papacy: Ideals and Realities, 1150-1300*, ed. by Christopher Ryan, 117-70 (Toronto: Pontifical Institute of Medieval Studies, 1989).

Ratzinger, Joseph. "The Ecclesiology of the Constitution Lumen Gentium." In idem, *Pilgrim Fellowship of Faith: the Church as Communion*. San Francisco: Ignatius, 2005: 123-152.

–, "The Local Church and the Universal Church." *America* (November 19, 2001) 7-11.

Reese, Thomas, ed. *Episcopal Conferences: Historical, Canonical, and Theological Studies*. Washington, DC: Georgetown University Press, 1989.

Roberson, Ronald. *The Eastern Christian Churches*, 6th edition. Rome: Edizioni Orientalia Christiana, 1999.

Romanides, John. *Franks, Romans, Feudalism, and Doctrine: An Interplay Between Theology and Society*. Brookline, MA: Holy Cross Orthodox Press, 1981.

Royster, Archbishop Dmitri. *The Kingdom of God: the Sermon on the Mount*. Crestwood, NY: St. Vladimir's Seminary Press, 1992.

–, *The Miracles of Christ*. Crestwood, NY: St. Vladimir's Seminary Press, 1999.

Runciman, Steven. The *Eastern Schism: A Study of the Papacy and the Eastern Churches during the XIth and XIIth Centuries*. Oxford: Clarendon, 1955.

Russell, Norman. "Anselm of Havelberg and the Union of the Churches." *Sobornost* 1 (1979) no. 2, 19-41 and *Sobornost* 2 (1980) no. 1, 29-41.

Saigh, Patriarch Maximos IV. "The Catholic East and Christian Unity: our Vocation as Unionists." Speech given in Düsseldorf, 1960. Excerpted in E.J. Barbara Fry, "Patriarch Maximos IV and the Vocation of the Catholic Eastern Churches," *The Eastern Churches Quarterly* 15 (1963) nos. 1-2, 81.

Schatz, Klaus. *Papal Primacy: From Its Origins to the Present*. Translated by John Otto and Linda Maloney. Collegeville, MN: Michael Glazier, 1996.

Smith, D. Moody. *First, Second, and Third John*. Louisville: John Knox Press, 1991.

Spiteris, Jannis. *La critica bizantina del primato romano nel secolo XII*. Rome: Edizioni Orientalia Christiana analecta, 1979.

–, "Attitudes fondamentales de la théologie byzantine, en face du rôle religieux de la papauté au XIIème siècle." In *The Religious Roles of the Papacy: Ideals and Realities, 1150-1300*, ed. by Christopher Ryan, 171-192 (Toronto: Pontifical Institute of Medieval Studies, 1989).

Storck, Thomas. "What is the Church of Jesus Christ?" *Homiletic and Pastoral Review* 108 (March, 2008) no. 6, 24-45.

Strecker, George. *The Johannine Letters: A Commentary on 1, 2, and 3 John*. Translated by Linda M. Maloney. Minneapolis: Augsburg Fortress, 1996.

Sullivan, Francis. "The Impact of Dominus Iesus on Ecumenism." *America* 183 (October 28, 2000) no. 13, 8-11.

–, "Quaestio Disputata: A Response to Karl Becker, S.J., on the Meaning of Subsitit in." *Theological Studies* 67 (2006) 395-409.

–, "'Subsist In': The Significance of Vatican II's Decision to say of the Church of Christ not that it 'is' but that it 'subsists in' the Roman Catholic Church." *One in Christ* 22 (1986) 115-123.

Suttner, Ernst. *Church Unity: Union or Uniatism?* Rome and Bangalore: Centre for Indian and Inter-Religious Studies and Dharmaram Publications, 1991.

Taft, Robert. "The Problem of 'Uniatism' and the 'Healing of Memories': Anamnesis, not Amnesia." Paper delivered on the occasion of the 21st Kelly Lecture, University of St. Michael's College, Toronto, Canada, Dec. 1, 2000. In *Logos: a Journal of Eastern Christian Studies* 41-42 (2000-2001) 155-196.

Ware, Timothy. *Eustratios Argenti.* Oxford: Clarendon, 1964.

–, *The Orthodox Church.* London: Penguin, 1963; repr. 1993.

Zizioulas, Metropolitan John. *Being as Communion.* Crestwood, NY: St. Vladimir's, 1985.

–, "The Ecclesiological Presuppositions of the Holy Eucharist." *Nicolaus* 10 (1982) 333-349.

–, "Orthodox Ecclesiology and the Ecumenical Movement." *Sourozh* 21 (1985) 16-27.

–, "Roman Primacy: An Orthodox Perspective." In *Petrine Ministry and the Unity of the Church: Toward a Patient and Fraternal Dialogue,* ed. by James Puglisi, 115-125. Collegeville, MN: Liturgical Press, 1999.

Zyablitsev, Georgi. "Uniatism as an Ecclesiological Problem Today." In *Four Hundred Years Union of Brest (1596-1996): A Critical Reevaluation,* ed. by B. Groen and W. van den Bercken, 193-199. Nijmegen, the Netherlands: Peeters, 1998.

Index of Names

A

Acacius 273
Adrian II, Pope 26
Afanasiev, Nicholas 59
Aghiorgoussis ↗ Maximus, Metropolitan
Alexander III, Pope 41
Alexis I, Patriarch 197
Alexis II, Patriarch 132
Alexius, Emperor 35
Anastasius, Librarian 38
Andrew, Apostle XI, 57, 68, 76, 78-80, 87, 91-2
Anselm of Havelberg 28-31, 33, 45, 149
Anthimus of Tyana, Bishop 18
Anthony, Patriarch 41, 46, 109
Argenti, Eustratios 220-3, 225-6, 228-9
Athenagoras, Ecumenical Patriarch VI, IX, XI, XIII, 1, 48, 50-70, 74-6, 79, 82-3, 85-6, 89, 98-9, 108, 113-4, 119, 122, 125-6, 197, 201-2, 264
Attridge, Harold 5
Augustine of Hippo 14, 215, 225, 230, 266-9, 271, 275, 284

B

Balsamon 220f
Barker, J.W. 41
Bartholomew, Ecumenical Patriarch X-XI, 79, 182, 205, 278
Basil I, Prince of Moscow 41, 46
Basil the Great I, 11-3, 17-9, 31-2, 198-9, 219, 221, 269
Battifol, Pierre 22
Bea, Augustin, Cardinal XIII, 53-4, 57, 59-60, 74, 82, 99
Becker, Karl J. 158, 160, 170, 204, 277
Beinert, Wolfgang 167

Békés, Gerard 123
Benedict XVI, Pope ↗ Ratzinger X
Berschin, Walter 28
Betti, U. 148
Boff, Leonardo 159, 170-1
Boniface III, Pope 33
Boniface, priest 12
Borelli, J. 90-7, 195

C

Cabasilas, Nicholas 184
Cavarnos, C. 221
Cerularius, Michael 24-5, 58-9
Chadwick, Henry 28-9, 37
Charlemagne 22-3, 34
Chrysostom, Metropolitan 61, 74
Clement of Rome I, 9
Clément, Olivier VI
Comnena, Anna 29, 46
Congar, Yves II, 2-3, 21-3, 26, 36, 41, 50, 111, 123-9, 142-5, 164, 173-83, 190-2, 234, 238, 243, 263, 270
Cope, Brian E. 49, 264
Coxe, Alexander Cleveland XV
Cross, F.L. 229
Cushing, Richard, Cardinal 50
Cyprian of Carthago 13, 17, 219, 221-2, 225-6, 230, 239-40, 266-7
Cyril of Jerusalem 14, 17
Cyril V, Patriarch 198, 220-1, 226, 228-9, 232, 239, 267

D

Daley, Brian 21, 32
Damaskinos (Papandreou), Metropolitan III, 3, 66, 182, 199-204, 209, 230, 238, 243, 252-3, 259
Damasus, Pope 20

Index of Names

David 35
Decentius of Gubbio 20
Demacopoulos, George 21, 154
Dewter, E.R.A. 46
Dimitrios I, Ecumenical Patriarch 48, 69, 72, 77-9, 87-91, 99-103, 107, 143
Dinkha IV, Patriarch 140
Diogenes 18
Długosz, Jan 128
Dmitri (Royster), Archbishop III, 3, 230-6, 248
Dominic of Grado, Patriarch 25
Donaldson, James XV
Duchesne, L. 33
Dunn, Dennis J. 132
Duprey, Pierre, Bishop 61, 66, 99
Dupuy, Bernard Dominique 26, 176
Dvornik, Francis 24, 26-7, 30-1, 34, 38-40, 45, 97

E

Erickson, John III, XIII-XIV, 3, 90-7, 182, 193-8, 204, 212, 218-22, 230, 238, 245, 251
Eugenios, Archbishop 63, 108
Eugenius III, Pope 29
Eugenius IV, Pope 42
Eustathius, Patriarch 58
Evdokimov, Paul 181
Evlogios 226

F

Farnedi, Giustiano 123
Flannery, Austin 65, 158
Florovsky, Georges 215, 224, 227, 230, 266-71, 273, 276
Frakes, Jerold, C. 28
Francis, Pope X-XI
Frazee, Charles 24
Fry, E.J. Barbara 131
Fustel de Coulanges, Numa Denis 23

G

Gaillardetz, R. 158
Galvin, John XIII
Garuti, Adriano II, V, 2-4, 111, 138-54, 173-81, 186, 202, 204, 209, 246-7, 249, 277, 281-4
Geanakoplos, Deno John 39, 42-3
Gelasius of Caesarea 14
Giakalis, Ambroios 42
Gréa, Marie-Etienne-Adrien 257
Gregory Nazianzen 11, 17-8
Gregory the Wonderworker 11
Gregory the Great, Pope 20-4, 106, 154
Gregory VII, Pope 26
Groen, B. 248
Gros, J. 30
Gudziak, Boris 129

H

Hallensleben, Barbara XIV
Haugh, Richard S. 267
Hierax 14
Hilarion (Alfeyev), Metropolitan 103, 154
Hilarius, Pope 20
Hildebrand 26
Hippolytus 20
Homeyer, Josef 155
Hovorun, Cyril 40
Hryniewicz, Waclaw II, XIII, 1-2, 111, 126-38, 159, 162, 164, 173-6, 179, 181, 195, 204, 233, 244, 277
Humbert of Silva Candida (of Moyenmoutier) 23-6, 220
Hussey, J.M. 30

I

Iakovos, Archbishop 52
Ignatios, Patriarch 26, 184
Ignatius of Antioch I, 9-10
Innocent I, Pope I, 11-3, 19-21, 31-2, 62, 80

Index of Names

Innocent III, Pope   22, 28, 35-7, 149-51, 184, 196, 210
Innocent IV, Pope   37
Iorga, N.   46
Irenaeus of Lyons   14-6

J

Jerome   14
Johannes of Cataadioce   33
John Chrysostom   14, 272
John II Comnenus   39
John of Antioch, Patriarch   XI
John of Trani, Bishop   24
John Palaeologus, Emperor   42
John Paul II, Pope   VIII, 1, 78-9, 88-9, 91, 95, 100-1, 124, 132, 140, 145-6, 248, 261-2, 276
John the Faster   21, 24
John VIII, Pope   26, 109, 184
John X Camateros, Patriarch   22, 28, 30-1, 35-7, 80, 125, 149-50, 153, 184, 196, 208, 233, 247
John XXIII, Pope   48-52, 55, 60, 85, 108
John, Evangelist   I, 5-8, 15-6
Joseph, Patriarch   42-4
Junius Rusticus   14
Justin Martyr   14
Justinian, Emperor   38, 45

K

Kafsokalyvitis, Neophytos   218, 221, 223, 227
Kantzavelos, Demetri   199
Kasper, Walter   16, 32, 109, 155-6, 165, 168, 261-2
Kerame, O.   22
King, J.R.   225
Kinnamon, Michael   49, 264
Kirill, Patriarch   278
Koch, H.   20
Koch, Kurt, Cardinal   I, VII-IX

Komonchak, Joseph   XIII-XIV, 12, 166-7, 244, 261

L

L'Huiller, Peter, Archbishop   46
Lanne, Emmanuel   II, 2, 5-12, 15-8, 31, 111-30, 142-5, 164, 167, 173-6, 180-3, 190-1, 195, 199, 212, 243-4, 259-60
Lees, Jay T.   29
Legrand, Hervé   III, 3-4, 111, 135, 156-77, 182, 204, 243-5, 252-3, 258, 260, 263, 277
Leo the Great, Pope   38-9, 75
Leo IX, Pope   24-6
Leo, Archbishop of Ochrida   24
Leo, Emperor   38
Leontius of Arles, Bishop   20
Lewis, C.S.   XIV
Liénart, Achille, Cardinal   170
Lieu, Judith   5
Livingstone, E.A.   229
Lossky, Nicholas   147, 212
Lothair III, Emperor   28
Louth, Andrew   27
Lubac, Henri de   166, 257, 261-2, 271

M

Makarios, Saint   221
Maloney, Linda M.   5, 28
Mansi, J.D.   XV, 38, 40, 132
Manuel II Palaeologus, Emperor   41-2
Marcion   15-6
Mark of Ephesus   206, 220, 226
Martin, Joseph Marie, Archbishop   61
Maximos (Aghiorgoussis), Metropolitan   III, 3, 17, 30, 55, 60, 74, 182, 190-3, 196, 234, 237-8, 243
Maximos IV Saigh   131, 175
Maximos the Confessor   40
May, Herbert   5
McDonnell, Killian   155-6

McPartlan, Paul XIII-XIV, 111, 156, 168-73, 175, 178, 204, 253-258, 271
Meliton, Metropolitan 47, 57, 61, 72, 74-5, 78, 83-4, 87, 98, 101
Mercier, B.-Charles 17
Metallinos, George III, 182, 195, 216-228, 232, 235-6, 247
Methodios, Metropolitan XI
Methodius of Olympus 14-5
Metzger, Bruce 5
Meyendorff, John III, 3, 40-1, 109, 112, 182-192, 196, 199-201, 210, 212, 216, 232, 234, 237-8, 242-3, 284
Migne, J.P. XV
Miklosich, F. 41
Miller, Michael 139
Moody Smith, D. 5
Morossini (Patriarch) 37
Müller, I. 41
Muraviev, N.A. 197

N

Nicephorus, Patriarch 39
Nicetas, Archbishop of Nicomedia 28-37, 45, 80, 125, 149-50, 153, 208, 212, 233, 247
Nicholas I, Pope 27
Nikodemos the Hagiorite (of the Holy Mountain 193, 220-2, 227

O

O'Malley, John 47
O'Malley, Sean, Cardinal XI
Obolensky, Dimitri 41
Oikonomos, Constantine 216, 221, 225-7
Origen 11, 14
Otto, John 28

P

Palamas 208, 213
Palmer, William 229
Pange, J. de 23

Parios, Athanasios 221-2
Paris, Matthew 37
Paul, Apostle XI-XII, 9, 13-4, 35, 76-78, 113, 136, 216, 274
Paul VI, Pope II, XI, 1, 47, 50, 55-70, 74-9, 82-89, 98-100, 108, 111, 113-115, 119, 122, 125, 128, 143, 145, 179, 182-3, 188, 191, 197, 201-2
Permiakov, Vitaly 59
Peter, Apostle XI-16, 20, 24, 26, 32-3, 40, 57, 66, 68, 76-78, 80, 86, 109, 113, 121-2, 126, 138, 145, 158, 189-90, 248, 256
Peter of Antioch 25
Peter the Venerable 39
Phidas, Vlassios 32
Phocas, Emperor 32-3
Photius, Patriarch 26-7, 109, 184, 264, 273
Pius IX, Pope 46
Pius XII, Pope 50-1, 157-8, 233
Platon of Kiev 197
Plumpe, Joseph 13-20
Polycarp 14
Principe, W.H. 29
Pseudo-Melito 14
Puglisi, James 212

R

Raes, A. 17
Ratzinger, Joseph (Benedict XVI) 155-6, 160-1, 168-9, 178-181, 199-200, 204, 209, 253, 261
Reese, Thomas J. 21, 156, 265
Richards Luard, Henry 37
Richardson, Cyril 10
Roberts, Alexander XV
Roger, King 29
Romanides, John S. III, 3, 117, 182, 195, 210-216, 218, 236
Roncalli, Angelo Giuseppe ↗ John XXIII, Pope 49-50

52   Ernst Christoph SUTTNER: Kirche und Theologie bei den Rumänen von der Christianisierung bis zum 20. Jahrhundert. 258 S., 2009.
51   Augustin SOKOLOVSKI: *Matrix omnium conclusionum*. Den *Augustinus* des Jansenius lesen. VIII + 322 S., 2013.
50   Cyril PASQUIER osb : Aux portes de la gloire. Analyse théologique du millénarisme de Saint Irénée de Lyon. 176 p., 2008.
49   Ernst Christoph SUTTNER: Staaten und Kirchen in der Völkerwelt des östlichen Europa. Entwicklungen der Neuzeit. 484 S., 2007.
48   Barbara HALLENSLEBEN / Guido VERGAUWEN (Hg.): Letzte Haltungen. Hans Urs von Balthasars „Apokalypse der deutschen Seele" – neu gelesen. 360 S., 2006.
47   Hilarion ALFEYEV : Le mystère sacré de l'Église. Introduction à l'histoire et à la problématique des débats athonites sur la vénération du nom de Dieu. 448 p., 2007.
46   Urs CORRADINI: Pastorale Dienste im Bistum Basel. Entwicklungen und Konzeptionen nach dem Zweiten Vatikanischen Konzil. 560 S., 2008.
45   Gottfried W. LOCHER: Sign of the Advent. A Study in Protestant Ecclesiology. 244 S., 2004.
44   Mariano DELGADO und Guido VERGAUWEN (Hg.): Glaube und Vernunft – Theologie und Philosophie. Aspekte ihrer Wechselwirkung in Geschichte und Gegenwart. 248 S., 2003.
43   Hilarion ALFEYEV: Geheimnis des Glaubens. Einführung in die orthodoxe dogmatische Theologie. 280 S., 2003; 2. Auflage 2005.
42   Jorge A. SCAMPINI o.p. : „La conversión de las Iglesias, una necesidad y una urgencia de la fe". La experiencia del *Groupe des Dombes* como desarrollo de un método ecuménico eclesial (1937–1997). 672 p., 2003.
41   Iso BAUMER: Von der Unio zur Communio. 75 Jahre Catholica Unio Internationalis. 536 S., 2002.
40   Adrian LÜCHINGER: Päpstliche Unfehlbarkeit bei Henry Edward Manning und John Henry Newman. 368 S., 2001.
39   Klauspeter BLASER : Signe et instrument. Approche protestante de l'Eglise. Avec la collaboration de Christian Badet. 216 p., 2000.
38   Kurt STALDER: Sprache und Erkenntnis der Wirklichkeit Gottes. Texte zu einigen wissenschaftstheoretischen und systematischen Voraussetzungen für die exegetische und homiletische Arbeit. Mit einem Geleitwort von Heinrich Stirnimann o.p., hg. von Urs von Arx, unter Mitarbeit von Kurt Schori und Rudolf Engler. 486 S., 2000.
37   Marie-Louise GUBLER: Im Haus der Pilgerschaft. Zugänge zu biblischen Texten. 300 S., 1999.
36   Iso BAUMER: Begegnungen. Gesammelte Aufsätze 1949–1999. 356 S., 1999.
35   Barbara HALLENSLEBEN / Guido VERGAUWEN o.p. (éd.) : *Praedicando et docendo*. Mélanges offerts à Liam Walsh o.p. 345 p., 1998.
34   Son-Tae KIM: Christliche Denkform: Theozentrik oder Anthropozentrik? Die Frage nach dem Subjekt der Geschichte bei Hans Urs von Balthasar und Johann Baptist Metz. 626 S., 1999.
33   Guido VERGAUWEN o.p. (éd.) : Le christianisme : Nuée de témoins – beauté du témoignage. 152 p., 1998.
32   Marcelo Horacio LABÈQUE : Liberación y modernidad. Una relectura de Gustavo Gutiérrez. 444 p., 1997.
31   Bernd RUHE: Dialektik der Erbsünde. Das Problem von Freiheit und Natur in der neueren Diskussion um die katholische Erbsündenlehre. 296 S., 1997.

www.ingramcontent.com/pod-product-compliance
Lightning Source LLC
Chambersburg PA
CBHW050620300426
44112CB00012B/1582